T0384082

Astrobiology and Christian Doctrine

In recent decades, powerful telescopes have enabled astrophysicists to uncover startling new worlds and solar systems. An epochal moment took place in 1995, when an exoplanet – 51 Pegasi b – was located orbiting another star like our own sun. This discovery profoundly changed perceptions of the universe. Since then, thousands of planets have followed. These astounding findings have transformed understandings of the cosmos and have renewed speculation about the potential for extraterrestrial life.

Drawing particularly on Thomas Aquinas, Andrew Davison considers a succession of fascinating questions that challenge Christianity's traditional focus on earth and human beings. Does the possibility of life elsewhere compromise human value? Would other creatures be subject to the same story of sin and redemption? Might God be incarnate elsewhere? Thinking about these topics helps Christians to prepare for a time when other life might be detected. In the meantime, by approaching familiar themes from new angles, Davison's volume stretches and enriches our existing theology.

ANDREW DAVISON is the Starbridge Professor of Theology and Natural Sciences at the University of Cambridge, where his work has inspired the arts and humanities programme at the groundbreaking Leverhulme Centre for Life in the Universe. One of the foremost scholars working between theology, philosophy, and the natural sciences, he is fellow in theology and Dean of Chapel at Corpus Christi College, University of Cambridge. His work on life elsewhere in the universe has been covered by news outlets around the world, in more than twenty languages. Davison is the author of *Participation in God: A Study in Christian Doctrine and Metaphysics; Blessing; The Love of Wisdom: An Introduction to Philosophy for Theologians*; and *Why Sacraments?*

CURRENT ISSUES IN THEOLOGY

General Editors:
Iain Torrance
Pro-Chancellor of the University of Aberdeen

David Fergusson
University of Cambridge

Editorial Advisory Board:
David Ford   *University of Cambridge*
Bryan Spinks   *Yale University*
Kathryn Tanner   *Yale Divinity School*

There is a need among upper-undergraduate and graduate students of
theology, as well as among Christian teachers and church professionals, for a
series of short, focussed studies of particular key topics in theology written by
prominent theologians. Current Issues in Theology meets this need.

The books in the series are designed to provide a 'state-of-the-art'
statement on the topic in question, engaging with contemporary thinking as
well as providing original insights. The aim is to publish books which stand
between the static monograph genre and the more immediate statement
of a journal article, by authors who are questioning existing paradigms or
rethinking perspectives.

Other titles in the series:

ANDREW DAVISON
University of Cambridge

Astrobiology and Christian Doctrine

Exploring the Implications of Life in the Universe

Shaftesbury Road, Cambridge CB2 8EA, United Kingdom

One Liberty Plaza, 20th Floor, New York, NY 10006, USA

477 Williamstown Road, Port Melbourne, VIC 3207, Australia

314–321, 3rd Floor, Plot 3, Splendor Forum, Jasola District Centre, New Delhi – 110025, India

103 Penang Road, #05–06/07, Visioncrest Commercial, Singapore 238467

Cambridge University Press is part of Cambridge University Press & Assessment, a department of the University of Cambridge.

We share the University's mission to contribute to society through the pursuit of education, learning and research at the highest international levels of excellence.

www.cambridge.org
Information on this title: www.cambridge.org/9781009303163

DOI: 10.1017/9781009303187

First published 2023
First paperback edition 2024

A catalogue record for this publication is available from the British Library

Library of Congress Cataloging-in-Publication data
NAMES: Davison, Andrew, 1974– author.
TITLE: Astrobiology and Christian doctrine : exploring the implications of life in the Universe / Dr Andrew Davison, University of Cambridge.
DESCRIPTION: New York : Cambridge University Press, 2023. | Includes bibliographical references and index.
IDENTIFIERS: LCCN 2022043209 | ISBN 9781009303156 (hardback) | ISBN 9781009303187 (ebook)
SUBJECTS: LCSH: Religion and science. | Exobiology. | Theology.
CLASSIFICATION: LCC BL240.3 .D384 2023 | DDC 201/.6576839–dc23/eng20230327
LC record available at https://lccn.loc.gov/2022043209

ISBN   978-1-009-30315-6   Hardback
ISBN   978-1-009-30316-3   Paperback

With gratitude for the
welcome and support of Dr William Storrar
and the Center of Theological Inquiry, Princeton

Theological principles tend to become torpid for lack of exercise, and there is much to be said for giving them now and then a scamper in a field where the paths are few and the boundaries undefined; they do their day-by-day work all the better for an occasional outing in the country.

–Eric Mascall[1]

Christin the Universe

–ALICE MEYNELL[2]

With this ambiguous earth
His dealings have been told us. These abide:
The signal to a maid, the human birth,
The lesson, and the young Man crucified.

But not a star of all
The innumerable host of stars has heard
How He administered this terrestrial ball.
Our race have kept their Lord's entrusted Word.

Of His earth-visiting feet
None knows the secret, cherished, perilous,
The terrible, shamefast, frightened, whispered, sweet,
Heart-shattering secret of His way with us.

No planet knows that this
Our wayside planet, carrying land and wave,
Love and life multiplied, and pain and bliss,
Bears, as chief treasure, one forsaken grave.

[1] E. L. Mascall, *Christian Theology and Natural Science: Some Questions on Their Relations* (London: Longmans, Green and Co., 1956), 45.

[2] Alice Meynell, *Collected Poems* (London: Burns & Oates, 1913), 114–15.

Nor, in our little day,
May His devices with the heavens be guessed,
His pilgrimage to thread the Milky Way
Or His bestowals there be manifest.

But in the eternities,
Doubtless we shall compare together, hear
A million alien Gospels, in what guise
He trod the Pleiades, the Lyre, the Bear.

O, be prepared, my soul!
To read the inconceivable, to scan
The myriad forms of God those stars unroll
When, in our turn, we show to them a Man.

Contents

Acknowledgements

The foundations for this book were laid during time in residence (2016–2017) at the Center of Theological Inquiry, Princeton, as a participant in their programme on 'Societal Implications of Astrobiology'. I am deeply grateful for my place in that community for those nine months, and to Dr William Storrar and Dr Joshua Maudlin, the Director and Associate Director, respectively, for having offered me that opportunity; to those responsible for academic leadership during my time there: Professors Robert Lovin, Frank Rosenzweig, and Doug Ottati; and to NASA and the John Templeton Foundation, which funded the programme. My colleagues for those nine months offered both scholarly conversation and friendship. I was fortunate indeed to have as my neighbours Professors Gerald McKenny and Jesse Couenhoven, and their families. I was delighted, while I was in Princeton, to reconnect with Dr Bill Barry, then Chief Historian of NASA, and have been glad of his kindness and friendship since.

Among my colleagues in the Faculty of Divinity at the University of Cambridge, I extend particular thanks to Professor David Fergusson (not least as editor of this series), Dr Simon Zahl, Professor Catherine Pickstock, and Professor Ian McFarland, as well as to Professor Christopher Kelly, Dr Marina Frasca-Spada, Mrs Jenny Raine, and the Revd Dr Matthew Bullimore at Corpus Christi College. More recently, I have had the good fortune to be involved in the work of the Cambridge Initiative for Planetary Science and Life in the Universe, and now in the Leverhulme Centre for Life in the Universe. I value the welcome that so many scientists offered to someone from the School of Arts and Humanities, and extend particular thanks to Professors Didier Queloz and Nicholas Tosca, and Drs Emily Mitchel, Paul Rimmer, and Oliver Shorttle.

Not for the first time, the ever-impressive community of scholarship and formation at the Seminary of the Southwest in Austin, Texas, extended hospitality to me, as a place for writing in the Fall of 2019. I thank their Dean and President, the Very Revd Dr Cynthia Briggs Kittredge; their Academic Dean, Professor Scott Bader-Saye; and their Professor of Systematic Theology, Anthony Baker, for the opportunity to talk to faculty and students about these ideas.

The two readers for Cambridge University Press wrote perceptively about the manuscript. The final version is the better for their comments.

Even before I spent time in Princeton, astrobiology was a topic of theological interest to me, with a place in my third-year undergraduate paper at Cambridge. I therefore have a deep debt of gratitude to acknowledge towards the students who have discussed many of these subjects with me in supervisions over the past eight years.

Dr Austin Stevenson provided detailed and unfailingly perceptive comments on a draft. He also made the diagram in the introduction to the section on sin, redemption, and Incarnation. Dr Beatrice Rehl has been the most encouraging of editors. I thank the Very Revd Professor Iain Torrance for his encouragement, some time ago, that I should think of submitting this book to the *Current Issues in Christian Theology* series.

I recognise, in particular, the support and encouragement of my family, and of the group of priest friends from my days at Westcott House, who have been such a central part of my life for twenty years.

Introduction

The scale of the universe cannot be fathomed with the human eye, but the night sky offers a start. If you live in or near a city, you only ever have seen a few stars. We need to travel away from built-up areas to see the heavens in their glory.[1] Someone with good eyesight (or glasses) would then be able to see around nine thousand stars, at least if she travelled to observe the sky first from one hemisphere of the Earth, then from the other. Binoculars would increase the tally of stars to maybe two hundred thousand, while even a cheap portable telescope would expand even that ten- or twentyfold. That, however, takes us only a tiny fraction of the way towards apprehending the whole. Our best scientific telescopes, pitched on mountains in Chile or Hawaii, or launched into space, allow us to estimate that there are around one hundred billion stars in our Milky Way galaxy: 100,000,000,000 stars.[2]

---

[1] For suggestions about amateur astronomy and photographing the night sky, see Valerie Stimac, *Dark Skies: A Practical Guide to Astrotourism* (Carlton, Victoria: Lonely Planet, 2019); Sarah Barker and Maria Nilsson, *Fifty Things to See in the Sky*, illustrated by Maria Nilsson (London: HarperCollins, 2019); and Sten Odenwald's *Guide to Smartphone Astrophotography*, written for NASA and widely available online.

[2] Jean-René Roy, Pierre-Yves Bely, and Carol Christian, *A Question and Answer Guide to Astronomy*, 2nd ed. (Cambridge: Cambridge University Press, 2017), 133; David H. Levy, *David Levy's Guide to the Night Sky* (Cambridge: Cambridge University Press, 2001). The Biblical image of a multitude, 'like the stars in the heavens', is well justified as meaning a great many. The other Biblical phrase for such a large quantity is sand upon the shore. The reader may be interested in a calculation of the number of grains of sand on Earth as around 7.5×10^{18}: around 2,700 stars in the observable universe for every grain of sand (although a lot of grains of sand for every star if we stick only to the Milky Way). The figure for sand comes from David Blatner, *Spectrums: Our Mind-Boggling Universe from Infinitesimal to Infinity* (New York: Bloomsbury, 2014).

Until we observed planets around other stars, we could not be sure that there were any. Planets could have been common, or extraordinarily rare. According to one theory for how solar systems form, planets would be routine, coalescing alongside stars from the same cloud of dust, or nebular.[3] The rival theory envisaged that planets are formed by the collision of one star with another, or of a star with a comet.[4] That would make planetary systems vanishingly rare, since the immense size of stars dwindles almost to nothing compared to the distance between them. Collisions would happen a great deal less often than the mid-air encounter of one ball with another on a golf course.[5] By the 1960s, the consensus among scientists was shifting towards the nebular hypothesis, but it took observation to settle the matter.[6] The epochal moment in recent science, which has done so much to provoke further research, was the announcement by Michel Mayor and Didier Queloz in 1995 they had uncovered a planet orbiting another star like our own sun. Since then, the number of these 'exoplanets' in our human catalogue has grown apace. On

[3] Immanuel Kant (1724–1804) was an early exponent in *Allgemeine Naturgeschichte und Theorie des Himmels* (Königsberg: Johann Friederich Petersen, 1755), translated as *Universal Natural History and Theory of the Heavens or an Essay on the Constitution and Mechanical Origin of the Whole Universe Treated According to Newton's Principles*, trans. W. Hastie (Ann Arbor: University of Michigan Press, 1969).

[4] Georges Louis Leclerc, Comte de Buffon (1707–1788), proposed collision of the sun with a comet in *Les Époques de la Nature*, published in *Histoire Naturelle: Générale et Particulière, Contenant Les Époques de La Nature* (Paris: de l'Imprimerie Royale, 1778).

[5] As Hannu Karttunen et al. have written, 'assuming a typical star density of 0.15 stars per cubic parsec and an average relative velocity of 20 km/s, only a few encounters would have taken place in the whole of the galaxy during the past 10^9 years'. On that view, 'the solar system could be a unique specimen' (*Fundamental Astronomy*, 6th ed. (Berlin: Springer, 2016), 168).

[6] This book is not the place for detailed exposition of how planets are found. Many recent books set out the science with admirable clarity. See Shawn D. Domagal-Goldman et al., 'The Astrobiology Primer v2.0', *Astrobiology* 16, no. 8 (August 2016): 561–653; David A. Rothery et al., eds., *An Introduction to Astrobiology*, 3rd ed. (Cambridge: Cambridge University Press, 2018); Wallace Arthur, *The Biological Universe: Life in the Milky Way and Beyond* (Cambridge: Cambridge University Press, 2020).

5 October 2021, *The Extrasolar Planets Encyclopaedia* listed 4,846 planets, in 3,582 planetary systems (with 798 of those solar systems known to possess more than one planet).[7] Those numbers are the provocation for this book, even more so once we extrapolate them to the galaxy as a whole, or even to the entire observable universe.[8]

The discovery of a first planet outside our solar system ranks among the most momentous feats of science, and a good deal has been written by theologians in response, chiefly with the prospect of extraterrestrial life in view. While theological interest has intensified, however, it would be a mistake to think that it is entirely new. As we will see, thinking in Christian theology about the implications of life elsewhere in the cosmos goes back almost six hundred years.

For a conservative estimate of habitable planets, we might concentrate only on the solar systems of sunlike stars. That can be defined in a few different ways, but we might end up classifying around 4 per cent of the stars in the Milky Way that way. That gives us 4 billion sunlike stars in our galaxy. Observations over the past twenty-five years suggest that most stars are encircled by planets, but many of those planets are not likely sites for life: some are composed of liquified or solid gas, like Jupiter, Saturn, Uranus, and Neptune; others are rocky but burnt to a crisp, like Mercury, or partly rocky but a very long way from the star, and cold, like Pluto (demoted to status of a 'dwarf planet' in 2006). To work out the proportion of stars with habitable planets, the two main criteria are a rocky composition (rather than gas), and a temperature at which any water present on the surface would be a liquid. Earlier

---

[7] http://exoplanet.eu/catalog/. It is likely that many of these systems contain additional planets, that we are currently unable to detect.

[8] We speak of the 'observable universe' as that which we could possibly observe. It marks out the distance that light could travel to date across the entire age of the cosmos. Since the universe is expanding, however, more would exist beyond that horizon. Indeed, on views of early cosmology that envisage an early period of unimaginably rapid inflation, one suggestion has the universe as a whole containing as many as 10^{100} stars (Tomonori Totani, 'Emergence of Life in an Inflationary Universe', *Scientific Reports* 10, no. 1 (December 2020): 1671).

estimates had about one in five sunlike stars with habitable Earth-like planets. Recently, that has been revised upwards, to between 0.37 and 0.60 such planets per sunlike star.[9] These figures will no doubt shift. For instance, we are beginning to make progress in understanding the capacity of a star to have several habitable planets in its orbit.[10] Habitable moons are also possible. However, if our estimate of the proportion of sunlike stars with Earth-like planets remained at about a half, that gives us two billion such planets in the Milky Way.

Two billion is an incomprehensibly large number, but even that is only a start. Our galaxy is not alone. In fact, by a strange coincidence, the number of galaxies in the observable universe seems to be about two hundred billion (200,000,000,000): almost identical to the number of stars in our galaxy.[11] If our galaxy is more or less average in terms of the number of stars it contains, that puts the number of stars in the observable universe at something like 2×10^{22}: twenty thousand billion billion stars, or two followed by twenty-two noughts. That in turn would suggest around 8×10^{20} sunlike stars, and perhaps 4×10^{20} rocky planets of the right temperature circling them: four hundred billion billion.

Of course, water will not be present on every rocky planet capable of harbouring it in liquid form, and all sorts of factors may be particularly conducive to the evolution of life, which may or may not apply to this or that planet. For instance, the presence of a moon may be significant, if life evolved in tidal pools, or underwater hydrothermal vents, if not. Other features may be significant for protecting any

---

[9] Steve Bryson et al., 'The Occurrence of Rocky Habitable-Zone Planets around Solar-like Stars from Kepler Data', *Astronomical Journal* 161, no. 1 (22 December 2020): 36.

[10] Stephen R. Kane et al., 'Dynamical Packing in the Habitable Zone: The Case of Beta CVn', *The Astronomical Journal* 160, no. 2 (27 July 2020): 81.

[11] Roy, Bely, and Christian, *Guide to Astronomy*, 177. Recent calculations may justify increasing this estimate by a factor of around ten, to about two trillion galaxies (Christopher J. Conselice et al., 'The Evolution of Galaxy Number Density at Z < 8 and Its Implications', *The Astrophysical Journal* 830, no. 2 (13 October 2016): 83).

life that does evolve: a giant neighbouring planet, like Jupiter, may be useful for hoovering up asteroids that would otherwise collide with an inhabited planet. Even lowering the figure of four hundred billion billion by several orders of magnitude, that still leaves us with an astonishing number of potential cradles for life, and that, to my mind, changes everything. The number of places where life could evolve and take hold seems to be extraordinarily large. Those calculations, moreover, say nothing about the billions of billions of habitable planets that may already have been and gone, or are yet to be.

The evolution of life is not impossible. I am sufficient evidence of that, as are you. Life can evolve, and there look to be billions of billions of planets where that might have happened. The emergence of life is a remarkable thing, and perhaps not at all common. But is it so uncommon as to happen only once in, say, four hundred billion billion opportunities? Extrapolation from one example is a perilous business, but we do have one more piece of information. Life got started on Earth surprisingly early: it stretches back maybe 3.8 billion years. The planet is 4.5 billion years old, and it spent around 0.5 billion years in the Hadean eon: the literally Hades-like first period, during which it was bombarded by meteorites, covered in volcanoes, and bathed in the radiation of elements with short half-lives. Life began only a short time later – 0.2 billion years later – and it has been going for 3.8 billion years since. That rapid arrival may offer one suggestion that life is not too difficult to get going.[12]

At present we are far more able to estimate whether a planet might be broadly habitable than we are at assessing whether it is

---

[12] Some recent work on the distinctive chemistry of this Hadean eon, however, has suggested that it was well placed for producing the sort of combination of molecules that might lie at the origins of life. On that view, it is not surprising that life got going in such seemingly inhospitable conditions: they would, in fact, be particularly productive (Bhavesh H. Patel et al., 'Common Origins of RNA, Protein and Lipid Precursors in a Cyanosulfidic Protometabolism', *Nature Chemistry* 7, no. 4 (April 2015): 301–7; John D. Sutherland, 'Opinion: Studies on the Origin of Life – the End of the Beginning', *Nature Reviews Chemistry* 1, no. 2 (February 2017): 12).

inhabited, but we stand at the cusp of a significant leap. Already to some extent, and soon with much greater accuracy, we will be able to analyse the atmospheric composition of planets around other suns. The James Webb space telescope is a significant addition here. Even the meagre absorption of a star's light by a planet's atmosphere (microscopic in comparison to the star) as the planet passes in front is enough to yield information as to which gases are present. If the combination of gases we see is thermodynamically anomalous – if the combination is not likely to form a stable mixture – that may serve as a sign of life. The Earth would appear anomalous in just this way if seen from elsewhere, since it contains a highly reactive combination of methane alongside oxygen.[13] This capacity to analyse atmospheres is set to change the stakes when it comes to detecting other life. Up to now, the emphasis has been on waiting for signs from an advanced civilisation (in radio transmissions, for instance, or by detecting the traces of how an advanced civilisation might engineer an entire solar system). Soon, however, we will be able to look for signs of life before it has reached an advanced state (if it ever does), given away simply by how it perturbs the chemistry of the planet it inhabits and shapes. That expands the range of living planets we could detect enormously. In terms of Earth, it would mean being able to detect life as it had been present for perhaps three billion years, not as it has been present for one hundred.

In recent decades, scientific study in the area of this book has shifted in the direction of thinking about the universe as a whole as a place where life can evolve and flourish. We see this in a shift

---

[13] The combination of carbon dioxide with methane, in the absence of carbon monoxide, is another marker, if seen from afar, that would have suggested the presence of life on Earth during some earlier periods (Joshua Krissansen-Totton, Stephanie Olson, and David C. Catling, 'Disequilibrium Biosignatures over Earth History and Implications for Detecting Exoplanet Life', *Science Advances* 4, no. 1 (January 2018): eaao5747; David C. Catling and Kevin J. Zahnle, 'The Archean Atmosphere', *Science Advances* 6, no. 9 (February 2020): eaax1420).

of terminology. For a period, the language of 'exobiology' predominated, as the name for scientific speculation about life beyond ('exo') Earth (or on 'exoplanets'). Today we more often talk of 'astrobiology', which is the scientific study of the place of life in the cosmos. The shift is from concentrating on life other than terrestrial life (of which, as yet, we know none) to thinking about place of life in the cosmos *per se*, of which terrestrial life is part. That goes hand-in-hand with the integration of 'planetary science' (previously seen as being about other planets) with 'Earth science', with each discipline enriching the other. In this book I will use 'exobiology' when addressing other life, and 'astrobiology' when I am thinking about the place of life in the universe.

Astrobiology and Christian Doctrine

Little in recent science outshines the discovery of planets around other stars. Results pouring in since the mid-1990s have transformed our understanding of the universe, which turns out to be strewn with planets, a fair proportion of them potentially habitable. That makes astrobiology – the scientific study of life as a phenomenon of the cosmos as a whole – a discipline *de jour*. Renewed theological discussion of other worlds, and life elsewhere, has followed, although as a topic for Christian theology *per se*, that is not new. Theologians have been writing about the theological implications of biological life beyond Earth since the mid-fifteenth century.[14] The attitude of those early Renaissance theologians was typical of much that would follow: they were unphased by the prospect of other life, but also brisk in their discussions, leaving us only a paragraph at most on the topic. They acknowledged the possibility of life elsewhere, thought that it posed no particular problem

---

[14] For further discussion of Ray, Wilkins, and Trollope, with quotations and citations, see Chapter 1.

for Christian belief, and moved on to some other topic. Examples
of this sort of response into Early Modernity could be multiplied at
length. We see it, for instance, in John Ray's classic combination of
biological survey and theological wonderment, in which he throws
off, more or less in passing, a single, unthreatened mention of life
on other planets in relation to God. In this period, theology often
features in works approaching life beyond Earth from a scientific
perspective (such as one from John Wilkins, Bishop of Chester).[15]
Again, however, those theological comments tend to be as notably
brief as they are unruffled.

Christian rumination on other life remained a significant topic in
the centuries that followed, even if it was not explored in any detail.
When Anthony Trollope, for instance, wanted to depict a group
of characters talking about a modish topic of the day in *Barchester
Towers* (1857), he had them talking about life elsewhere in the solar
system, and its theological implications. In 1920, Frank Weston
(1871–1924), Bishop of Zanzibar, saw his contribution on the topic
as joining an already lively scene, in which 'it is *often* argued that if
other planets are dwelling-places of rational beings the incarnation
with its atoning work cannot be true'. (He found this conclusion
'unwarranted'.)[16]

A succession of familiar theological names commented on extraterrestrial life in the twentieth century, if only in passing, among
them Yves Congar, Hans Küng, Eric Mascall, Wolfhart Pannenberg,
Karl Rahner, and Paul Tillich. Some of that writing expanded the
bundle of theological discussions of the theme, but they still rarely
exceeded a few paragraphs in length. Towards the end of the century, and into the twenty-first, chapter-length surveys of themes in
theology and astrobiology became common, and were published

---

[15] John Wilkins, *The Discovery of a World in the Moone. Or, A Discovrse Tending to
Prove, That 'tis Probable There May Be Another Habitable World in the Moon*, 5th ed.
(London: J. Rawlins for John Gellibrand, 1684).

[16] Frank Weston, *The Revelation of Eternal Love: Christianity Stated in Terms of Love*
(London: A. R Mowbray and Co., 1920), 128, emphasis added.

in multidisciplinary edited collections.[17] That genre allows only a limited scope, however, and writing for a non-theological audience tends to restrict the author's capacity to go into detail. Nonetheless, these contributions are witness to the enduring place of theology among the arts and humanities, and to recognition of the role that religion plays for many in interpreting the world, not least if life elsewhere were to be confirmed.

Over the past two decades, edited collections have appeared, devoted to theological discussions of other life in the universe, plus a few single-author volumes.[18] Nonetheless, room remains for development in several directions, to which I hope this book will be a contribution. One would be to move writing further from commentary upon what I described above as the 'bundle of theological discussions', accumulated from historical sources. However distinguished those authors might be thought to be, their insights are typically sparse and offered – as I have said – for the most part

[17] Examples include chapters by Ernan McMullin, Celia Deane-Drummond, Cynthia Crysdale, Richard Randolph, and Francisca Cho, in *Exploring the Origin, Extent, and Future of Life: Philosophical, Ethical, and Theological Perspectives*, ed. Constance M. Bertka (Cambridge: Cambridge University Press, 2009), and essays by Robin Lovin and Guy Consolmagno, in *The Impact of Discovering Life beyond Earth*, ed. Steven J. Dick (Cambridge: Cambridge University Press, 2015).

[18] Steven J. Dick, ed., *Many Worlds: The New Universe, Extraterrestrial Life, and the Theological Implications* (Philadelphia: Templeton Foundation Press, 2000); Ted Peters et al., eds., *Astrotheology: Science and Theology Meet Extraterrestrial Life* (Eugene, OR: Cascade, 2018); Kenneth J. Delano, *Many Worlds, One God* (Hicksville, NY: Exposition Press, 1977); Marie George, *Christianity and Extraterrestrials?: A Catholic Perspective* (Bloomington, IN: iUniverse, 2005); Thomas O'Meara, *Vast Universe: Extraterrestrials and Christian Revelation* (Collegeville, MN: Liturgical Press, 2012); Keith Ward, *Christ and the Cosmos: A Reformulation of Trinitarian Doctrine* (Cambridge: Cambridge University Press, 2015); Jacques Arnould, *Turbulences Dans l'univers: Dieu, Les Extraterrestres et Nous* (Paris: Albin Michel, 2017); Olli-Pekka Vainio, *Cosmology in Theological Perspective: Understanding Our Place in the Universe* (Grand Rapids, MI: Baker Academic, 2018). David Wilkinson's *Science, Religion, and the Search for Extraterrestrial Intelligence* (Oxford: Oxford University Press, 2013) contains two theological chapters. Giuseppe Tanzella-Nitti's encyclopaedia article 'Extraterrestrial Life' remains an ideal introduction to topics of theological importance, accessed 1 February 2018, https://inters.org/extraterrestrial-life.

in passing. Far more valuable is attention to existing theological writing that bears upon questions raised by astrobiology, for all the implications for other life would have been entirely absent from the author's mind. Chapter 14 of this book provides an example. Down Christian history we find discussion about what difference (if any) the Incarnation has upon the relation of the Word to the rest of creation. In the Reformation, and debates stemming from it, this typically had to do with Christ's presence in the Lord's Supper. There is obviously much in that material that bears upon the question of multiple Incarnations elsewhere in the universe, even though that topic was not historically in view. In this fashion, a central task for theological consideration of life elsewhere in the universe is to expand the range of the historical material, such as this, that can be brought to bear on the topic.

Another expansion would address the range of doctrinal topics under discussion, whether in turning to topics previously little considered at all (such as eschatology), or in bringing topics together that have otherwise mainly been treated separately, with the hope of cross-fertilisation. Alongside such expansions of breadth, there will also be value in an increase in academic depth or focus. Much that has been written theologically about life elsewhere in the universe, historically and to some extent today, has been conceived with a wide or popular religious readership in mind. The motivations for that are often admirable, but a degree of technical precision can be lost as a result. That is particularly to be seen in discussions of Christology. For instance, where the idea of more than one Incarnation has been denied, what is meant by 'Incarnation' is often difficult to pin down, or else set out very much at variance with the sort of formulations of Christological thinking that are foundational to Catholic, Orthodox, Anglican, and Protestant traditions. Any attempt to engage astrobiology with greater theological precision will likely also entail a deeper grounding of our discussions in a specific theological tradition: Augustinian, Bonaventurian, Calvinist, Thomist, or whatever.

Addressing questions of purpose, one motivation for a book such as this is a desire to help the human community (and specifically, the Christian community) to be more ready to receive, process, and respond to any future signs of life elsewhere. Detection might come in a decade, centuries hence, or perhaps never, but if it does, it will be useful to have thought through the implications in advance. Large numbers of people will turn to their religious traditions for guidance – as to what other life means for the standing and dignity of human life, for instance – and work done in advance will surely pay off.

A second motivation aligns with a theme familiar from literature and poetry in the twentieth century, namely that after a journey – physical or intellectual – in unfamiliar territory, one can return home with fresh eyes.[19] As an example, while theology has previously been carried out with human beings in view, it has recently found itself (and its reflections on humanity) enlivened by attention to non-human animals. In the same way, our theology can find useful provocation, even invigoration, by having life beyond our planet in mind for a spell. I have already quoted Eric Mascall (1905–1993) in the frontispiece, writing – indeed – on our topic:

> Theological principles tend to become torpid for lack of exercise, and there is much to be said for giving them now and then a scamper in a field where the paths are few and the boundaries undefined; they do their day-by-day work all the better for an occasional outing in the country.[20]

The text quoted alongside Mascall is a now quite famous poem by Alice Meynell (1847–1922), which offers an example of what

---

[19] For istance, G. K. Chesterton, *Charles Dickens: A Critical Study* (New York: Dodd Mead and Co, 1906), 45–48; T. S. Elliot, 'Little Gidding', V in *Four Quartets* (London: Faber and Faber, 1974); J. R. R. Tolkien, 'On Fairy-Stories', in *Essays Presented to Charles Williams*, ed. C. S. Lewis (London: Oxford University Press, 1947), 38–89.

[20] Mascall, *Christian Theology and Natural Science*, 45.

invigoration can look like, in which several aspects of Christian belief shine in new ways once placed in different light.

My emphasis is largely on the repercussions for Christian theology of other *intelligent* life. Among any planets that do harbour life, intelligence would almost certainly be present on only a small proportion of them, but that is still naturally where most of the theological interest will lie: with the prospect of creatures that can know, love, pursue the good, fall prey to the curtailment of evil, know redemption, and stand in that remarkable relation to God in which, for all the infinite qualitative difference, creature and creator each address the other as a person. From time to time, I will consider life lacking memory, intellect, or will (or with only its first flickerings), but my interest is generally on the sort of life for which the categories of knowledge and revelation, sin and redemption, grace and the beatific vision, could be in view. With the launch of a new Leverhulme Centre for Life in the Universe at Cambridge, non-sentient life, and the transition from the non-living to the living, is set to feature prominently in my research in coming years. Those questions will be a topic for a further monograph.

Not every topic that might attract the interest of scholars of theology and religion concerning other life will receive attention here. That is in part because of the constraints of space, but also, and less arbitrarily, because they fall outside the areas in which I can claim even marginal expertise. Nor have I considered the question of 'what next' steps, following the imagined arrival of evidence of other life. There is nothing here, for instance, about evangelism, mission, or inter-planetary comparative theology (all popular themes for novelists). Indeed, situations of future 'contact' between us and other life are not in view at all. Nor is there anything about the Search for Extraterrestrial Intelligence (SETI), or its more recent counterpart, involving active broadcast of our presence (Messaging Extraterrestrial Intelligence, or METI). The latter has provoked discussion in recent years as to its ethics and advisability. Are we unwise to give our presence away? That theme is beginning to receive some theological attention, as are questions about what we should physically send into space, but the theological ethics of space exploration and messaging is not a topic for this book.

Also of interest to scholars of religion are traditions where extra-terrestrial life features among the tenets of the faith. There is a galac-tic or inter-planetary dimension, for instance, to both Mormonism and Seventh Day Adventism, while religions such as Scientology and Raëlianism are even more fully grounded on extraterrestrial themes.[21] Also of interest to social scientists is the recent phenom-enon of interpretating existing religions in terms of alien life and visits (these receive only a brief mention, in Chapter 2), and empir-ical studies, such as those of Ted Peters and Julie Louise Froehlig, to investigate what challenges might or might not be posed to mem-bers of religious communities by the prospect of other life.[22] The headline findings are that adherents of a range of religious tradi-tions report that they can take the idea in their stride. Non-religious people also seem to over-estimate the challenges that religious peo-ple think they would experience if faced with evidence of alien life. The social sciences can also offer perceptive analysis of the work and world of space exploration, as itself a cultural phenomenon, as in the work of my colleague Timothy Jenkins.[23]

From time to time, I have drawn on writings and perspectives of other religions, not least from a paper by the rabbi Norman Lamm that remains fresh after several decades. I have also begun leading sessions on this topic at interfaith summer schools. By and large, however, I both recognise the potential for fruitful inter-faith dia-logue around topics covered in this book, and confess to not having

[21] For a survey, see Benjamin E. Zeller, ed., *Handbook of UFO Religions* (Leiden: Brill, 2021).

[22] Ted Peters, 'The Implications of the Discovery of Extra-Terrestrial Life for Religion', *Philosophical Transactions of the Royal Society A: Mathematical, Physical and Engineering Sciences* 369, no. 1936 (13 February 2011): 644–55.

[23] Jenkins' book on this topic is forthcoming.

the knowledge, expertise, or space to pursue that here.[24] Also standing largely outside the scope of this book would be detailed work
with specialist Biblical scholars. I indicate in Chapter 17 that attention to what the Biblical writers might or might not have meant
(or could or could not have meant) by terms such as 'whole world'
is significant. Such questions would be useful topics for discussion
across theological disciplines.

Theologically, the book largely comes from a particular perspective, namely Thomism. I offer that particularity as a strength, wishing to see conversations between theology and the sciences engage
as much with the specificities of theology as with the specificities of
science. Indeed, any deepening of theological engagement with science will, to my mind, more or less necessarily involve greater specificity in the theological position from which it is being addressed.
Happily, work between theology and science today has by and
large set aside generalised questions about the relation between
theology-in-general and science-in-general, thinking instead about
more particular scientific topics (here astrobiology), and doing so
by drawing from the deep wells of particular traditions or schools
of theological thought.[25]

Throughout the book, I have included footnotes to passages in
the works of Aquinas. Sometimes that serves to identify the source
of a text that I both quote and consider (usually for the sake of its
strengths, but sometimes in relation to what I see as weaknesses).
On other occasions, a citation points to a text that I do not discuss.
Those are not offered as if the passage will answer or foreclose all

---

[24] Norman Lamm, 'The Religious Implications of Extraterrestrial Life', *Tradition: A
Journal of Orthodox Jewish Thought* 7/8 (1965): 5–56. David Weintraub has offered a
survey from a wide range of religious traditions in *Religions and Extraterrestrial Life:
How Will We Deal with It?* (Cham: Springer International Publishing, 2014).

[25] Andrew Davison, 'More History, More Theology, More Philosophy, More Science:
The State of Theological Engagement with Science', in *New Directions in Theology
and Science: Beyond Dialogue*, ed. Peter Harrison and Paul Tyson (London:
Bloomsbury, 2022), 19–35.

further questions, but because I want to indicate where relevant material can be found in the works of this author, which – with all its strengths, and no doubt some weaknesses – could inform the reader in thinking further about the topic in hand.

Of all authors, I find Aquinas the most useful for fruitful theological consideration of the natural sciences. I hope that this book offers an illustration of that, and therefore a commendation of his writings, and of later Thomism, for the attention of those who engage in that sort of work. More specifically, I hope that this book will illustrate and commend the value of an approach to Aquinas and his legacy that was nicely summarised by Mascall:

> I do not consider *Thomas locutus, causa finita* [Thomas has spoken, the case is closed] as the last judgement to be passed on any theological problem; though my approach might be summed up in the words, *Thomas locutus, causa incepta* [Thomas has spoken, the matter is begun].[26]

Such a Thomism, seeking to be neither defensive nor revisionary, and valuing both openness and confidence, offers a form of theology that is both appealing on its own terms, and particularly open to conversations about scientific topics.

---

[26] E. L. Mascall, *He Who Is: A Study in Traditional Theism* (London: Longmans, Green and Co., 1943), ix.

Part I | Creation

The doctrine of creation addresses all that exists within the universe and its relation to the creator. The emphasis is not on origins in a temporal sense – what happened some long time ago – but on God as the originator of creation and the constant dependence of all things on God for their existence. Given that no created thing had to exist, creation is fundamentally an undeserved act of generous giving on the part of God, which would apply equally to everything beyond Earth, and therefore to whatever other life the universe might contain.

To varying degrees, theologies of creation have considered not only *that* creatures exist, but also the significance of *how* they are, thinking doctrinally about themes such as life, form, diversity, materiality, and relation, and how all of that is grounded in the underlying dependence of creatures upon God, and their imitation of the One who gives all things their being. That will also be relevant to thinking about possible exobiology.

Only relatively rarely have theologies of creation addressed life elsewhere directly. Nonetheless, even when inhabitation of other regions of space was not in view, Christian theology has typically thought about other intelligent life in the form of the angels. It has also grappled with the question of whether God could, or had, created 'worlds' beyond the one we know. Among the topics gathered under the doctrine of creation, it is to that final question we turn first.

1 | Many Worlds

In this chapter, I consider Christian responses to the proposal that our world is one of many.[1] From this, among other things, will emerge the surprising lesson about relations between 'theology and science' that what sometimes held people back was the science of the day, not the theology. As the subject for a first chapter, it also usefully presents us with an area where the story is now settled: there *are* other planets – what these authors would call worlds – whether or not there is other life.[2] We will also see how discussion of a topic that remains limited to this globe – whether there would be humanity on the other side of the equator, and whether it would be related to us or not – provides a parallel to interest in other worlds, reaching back into the patristic period.

Questions about the extent of the cosmos, and whether life is to be found elsewhere within it, have been posed by philosophers and scientists for as far back as Western philosophy is recorded. Anaximander (c. 610–c. 546 BC) held that the cosmos is eternal, and

---

[1] On this topic, see Michael J. Crowe, *The Extraterrestrial Life Debate, 1750–1900* (Mineola, NY: Dover, 1999); Michael J. Crowe, ed., *The Extraterrestrial Life Debate: Antiquity to 1915 – A Source Book* (Notre Dame, IN: University of Notre Dame Press, 2008); Arnould, *Turbulences Dans l'univers*; Pierre Maurice Marie Duhem, *Medieval Cosmology: Theories of Infinity, Place, Time, Void, and the Plurality of Worlds*, trans. Roger Ariew (Chicago: University of Chicago Press, 1985).

[2] Recognising Peter Harrison's work in *The Territories of Science and Religion* (Chicago: University of Chicago Press, 2015), we may do well to recognise that categories like 'religion' and 'science' are not unvarying over time. Nonetheless, the point I make here stands, that we will observe some unexpected relations between attention to theological sources and reflection on the character of physical reality in this story.

that it contains an infinite number of worlds, continually perishing and coming to be.[3] Belief in the presence of countless worlds (known as 'pluralism' in this context), even an infinite number, was revived by atomist philosophers such as Democritus (c. 460–c. 370 BC) and Epicurus (341–270 BC).[4] They held that some of these worlds were inhabited, as the Christian theologian Hippolytus of Rome recorded:

> Democritus ... spoke as if the things that are were in constant motion in the void; and that there are innumerable worlds, which differ in size. In some worlds there is no sun and moon, in others they are larger than in our world, and in others more numerous. The intervals between the worlds are unequal; in some parts there are more worlds, in others fewer; some are increasing, some at their height, some decreasing; in some parts they are arising, in others failing. There are some worlds devoid of living creatures or plants or any moisture.[5]

Epicurus, however, departed from Democritus in supposing that every one of these worlds would be inhabited. Early Christian writers were aware of some of this tradition. Basil the Great refers to them, for instance, in his *Homilies on the Six Days of Creation*, writing that 'There are among them ['Greek sages'] some who say there are infinite heavens and worlds'.[6]

---

[3] The sources for Anaximander's position include Simplicius, *Commentary on Aristotle's Physics*, 1121, 5–9 and Cicero, *On the Nature of the Gods* (I, 10, 25). Cited by Mark Brake, *Alien Life Imagined: Communicating the Science and Culture of Astrobiology* (Cambridge: Cambridge University Press, 2012), 12.

[4] Jacques Arnould considers antiquity in *Turbulences Dans l'univers*, 35–45. Michael Crowe collects and discusses texts from antiquity in *Extraterrestrial Life Debate – Source Book*, 3–13. For a brief survey of secondary literature, see Klaas J. Kraay, 'Introduction', in *God and the Multiverse: Scientific, Philosophical, and Theological Perspectives* (London: Routledge, 2014), 15, n. 6.

[5] On Democritus and Epicurus, see Brake, *Alien Life Imagined*, 24.

[6] Basil, *Homilies on the Six Days of Creation*, III.3, translation from *The Treatise de Spiritu Sancto, the Nine Homilies of the Hexaemeron and the Letters of Saint Basil the Great*, trans. Blomfield Jackson (Edinburgh: T&T Clark, 1895), 66. A translator's footnote (66, n. 1) gives Anaximander (Diogenes Laertius, *Lives of Eminent Philosophers*, II.1,2) and Democritus (*Lives*, IX, 44).

Plato offered a different view of cosmic life, which would be influential among many Christian writers: that the cosmos as a whole is a living being, animated by a world soul.[7] However, he also held the world to which we belong to be the only one, out of likeness to its architype (which must itself be single and unique, since multiplicity in the archetype would then call for a yet more ultimate exemplar).[8] This is rather an unusual argument for Plato to make, given that his account of exemplarity more generally imagines many physical copies of each perfect exemplar. He also held the stars to be living beings or 'heavenly gods': the 'fixed stars' are 'living beings divine and everlasting', and the 'wandering stars', or planets, are 'visible and generated gods'.[9]

Aristotle followed Plato in holding to only one world, on the physical basis that he could not imagine more than one centre of gravity to which all solid matter would be drawn, nor more than one worldly circumference that the element of fire would seek.[10] He was more circumspect than Plato about the stars and planets as living beings, but wrote nonetheless that 'We think of the stars as mere bodies ... entirely inanimate; but we should rather conceive of them as enjoying life and action ... We must, then, think of the action of the stars as similar to that of animals and plants'.[11] Among later classical writers, Lucretius (c. 99–c. 55 BC) proposed multiple

---

[7] *Timaeus* 34A–37C. Kepler wrote that 'we freely enquire what the nature of each mind may be, particularly if in the heart of the world it plays the part of the soul of the world, and is more tightly tied to the nature of things' (*The Harmony of the World*, trans. Eric J. Aiton, Alistair Matheson Duncan, and Judith Veronica Field (Philadelphia: American Philosophical Association, 1997), 495).

[8] Plato, *Timaeus*, 31a–b.

[9] Plato, *Republic*, 508a, translation from *Republic*, trans. Robin Waterfield (Oxford: Oxford University Press, 1994), 234; *Timaeus* 40b, 40d, translation from *Plato's Cosmology: The Timaeus of Plato*, trans. Francis Macdonald Cornford (Indianapolis, IN: Hackett, 1997), 118, 135.

[10] Aristotle, *On the Heavens*, I.8, 276b and, more widely, I.8–9.

[11] Aristotle, *On the Heavens*, II.12, 292a. Translation from 'On the Heavens', in *Complete Works of Aristotle: The Revised Oxford Translation*, ed. J. Barnes, trans. J. L. Stocks, vol. 1 (Princeton, NJ: Princeton University Press, 1984), 481.

inhabited worlds in *De rerum natura*, while Lucian of Samosata (AD c. 125–after 180) explored ideas of multiple inhabited planets, with travel and war between them, in his novel *A True Story*.[12]

Theology and Science: Openness and Limitation

In turning to Christian writers (or indeed Jewish and Muslim writers), it is tempting to view their opinions on these matters as driven by theology rather than scientific concerns. In fact, they were often deeply interested in knowing and thinking about the nature of the physical world. For example, the Jewish philosopher and theologian Maimonides (Moses ben Maimon, 1135 or 1138–1204) was well-informed about aspects of astronomy, appreciating the scale of the solar system, for instance. He estimated the distance between the Earth and Jupiter to be around 125,000,000 miles.[13] He was close: the distance is 365,000,000 to 600,000,000 miles, depending on the relative positions of the Earth and Jupiter on their orbits. As another example, Aquinas, while generally not as directly interested in matters of science as his teacher, Albert the Great (c. 1200–1280), appreciated that 'as astronomers say, there are many stars larger than the moon'.[14]

The question of multiple worlds – taken at the time to mean a concentric system of spheres centred on Earth (or on another 'Earth') – had come to new prominence in the thirteenth century

---

[12] 'You are bound to confess that there are other worlds in other regions and different races of men [*varias hominum gentis*] and generations of wild beasts' (Lucretius, *De Rerum Natura*, trans. W. H. D. Rouse and Martin F. Smith (Cambridge, MA: Harvard University Press, 1924), book 2, lines 1075–76, pp. 178–79; Lucian, *A True Story* in *Lucian: Volume 1*, trans. Austin Morris Harmon (Cambridge, MA: Harvard University Press, 2006).

[13] Moses Maimonides, *The Guide of the Perplexed*, trans. Shlomo Pines, vol. 2, 2 vols (Chicago; London: University of Chicago Press, 1974), III.14, quoted by Lamm, 'Religious Implications', 6.

[14] *Summa Theologiae* (hereafter *ST*) I.70.1 *obj.* 5. On this not contradicting the description of the moon as a 'great light' (Gen. 1.16), see *ad* 5, and I.70.1 *ad* 3.

with the rediscovery of Aristotle. Strikingly, when that idea was rejected, as it often was, that was as much on scientific as theological grounds. Aristotle's science was thought to preclude the existence of other worlds. Theological principles, however, might go either way on this question: on the one hand, there seemed to be something appropriate about there being only one world, its singleness reflecting the one God; on the other, a greater, perhaps even infinite, number of worlds seemed to reflect the plenitude of God, and fit well with the reluctance of theologians to suggest any impediment to the power of God – a reluctance that would only grow with time.

Across the thirteenth century and into the fourteenth, we see a gradual softening towards the idea of many worlds.[15] For an early medieval thinker such as William of Auvergne (c. 1180/90–1249), God simply could not have created any other worlds, whether finite or infinite in number, and 'this impossibility is not a defect in God, nor a defect issuing from God, rather it is a defect on the part of the world, which cannot exist in multiples'. He likened this to the 'impossibility' for God to know the square root of two ('the relation of the diagonal of a square to its side'), which might strike us today as placing an odd and unnecessary limit on God's knowledge.[16]

Albert was only slightly more open. His discussion of this topic in his *Commentary on Aristotle's Concerning the Heaven and the Earth* opens with the arresting claim that 'Since one of the most wonderful and noblest questions concerning nature is whether the world is one, or whether there are many words, and this is a question the human mind desires to understand per se, it seems fitting for us to

---

[15] O'Meara lists four church fathers who may seem to discuss 'the divine power creating other worlds or with the existence of intelligent beings in or on heavenly bodies' (Thomas O'Meara, *Vast Universe*, 67). These passages, however, are in fact each either obscure or almost certainly about angels, and therefore offer little in terms of an acceptance of other, distinct physical dwelling places for life in the cosmos.

[16] William of Auvergne, 'De Universo', in *Guilielmi Alverni Episcopi Parisiensis, Opera Omnia*, vol. 1 (Frankfurt am Maine: Minerva, 1963), prima pars principalis, pars I, ch. 16, fol. 100a–b (facsimile of Hotot, 1679). Translation from Duhem, *Medieval Cosmology*, 444.

inquire about it'.[17] His argument is somewhat circuitous, but not complicated. He grants the cogency of those who argue for more than one world on the basis of divine power: 'there could be many worlds, although there are not, because God could have made them, had he wished to, and still could make them if he wished: again this I do not dispute'.[18] The impediment to multiple worlds would again lie not on the side of God, but on the side of physical reality: in its 'parts, and its essential and proximal causes'.[19] For instance, Albert thought that the rotating spheres of many worlds would come to touch one another, and therefore impede each other's motion.

Albert concluded that 'on account of what belongs to the nature of the world' – a scientific consideration, rather than a theological one – 'it is not possible for multiple worlds to come about, even if we to hold that God were to have the power to do it'.[20] Presumably, it could happen as a miracle, maybe an ongoing one, or if God had created a different sort of universe. A distinction between what is impossible on the part of the character of creation as it is, in contrast to what is possible as an express exercise of the power of God, had been set out earlier by Michael Scot (1175–c.1232): 'God can do this, but nature cannot withstand it. The impossibility of the plurality of worlds results from the nature of the world itself, from its proximate and essential causes; God, however, can make several worlds if he so wishes'.[21] (Such comments, however, seem to lack the last word in clarity.) Later, as we will see, writers would come to discount any sense of the impossibility of multiple worlds on the part of physics.

For Albert, even were a universe of many worlds possible, it would lack fittingness – a theme that will recur across this book – since it would

---

[17] Albert the Great, *Commentary on De Caelo et Mundo*, book 1, tr. III, ch. 1, in *Opera Omnia*, ed. Borgnet, vol. 9 (Paris: Vives, 1890), 65, my translation here and below.

[18] Albert, *Commentary on De Caelo et Mundo*, book 1, tr. III, ch. 6, p. 80.

[19] Ibid., p. 81.

[20] Ibid.

[21] Michael Scot, *Eximii atque: excellentissimi physicorum motuum cursusque* (Bologna: Justinianum de Ruberia, 1495), vol. 2, 146, translation from Duhem, *Medieval Cosmology*, 443.

set up a plurality of places or communities between which exchange would not be possible, yet the good of the whole is constituted by the interrelation of its parts. In writing this, Albert appears to assume that any other worlds would be inhabited, since isolation would stand particularly against 'civic interchange' (*commercione civium*).[22]

In Aquinas we again find *scientific* arguments against many worlds, not least that bodies are attracted to one another – or, rather, he thinks, to the centre of our Earth – such that a multiplicity of worlds would eventually produce a collision.[23] Other arguments are more theological. Like Albert, he objected to worlds between which there could be no relation or interchange, since 'whatever things come from God, have relation of order to each other, and to God Himself'.[24] To deny that the world is one would therefore be to deny that it is an interrelated whole, and therefore that that there is an 'ordaining wisdom'. He notes that for atomists such as Democritus, many worlds come about by chance, precisely without providence.

As I have noted, however, theological arguments could also seem to run the other way. Aquinas considered the fascinating objection that 'nature does what is best and much more does God. But it is better for there to be many worlds than one, because many good things are better than a few. Therefore many worlds have been made by God'.[25] His reply was that more is not actually a good in itself (what he calls a 'material multitude'): more is only better if it serves some purpose beyond extent (such as the augmentation of the excellence of the thing itself – its form). Indeed, offering a *reductio ad absurdum*, he points out that the more-is-better approach would 'tend to infinity', which he thought undid itself, since 'the infinite is opposed to the notion of end'. That statement illustrates just how suspicious mediaeval Aristotelians were of the notion of a realised infinitude. Aquinas also distrusted the

[22] Albert, *Commentary on De Caelo et Mundo* book 1, tr. III, ch. 6, p. 81.
[23] *ST* I.47.3 *ad* 3.
[24] *ST* I.47.3.
[25] *ST* I.47.3 *obj.* 2.

idea of multiple worlds on the basis that duplication of this world seemed futile, while additional novel worlds would not actually be new 'worlds' as much as additional parts of what would then count as a single wider whole:

> If God were to make other worlds, He would make them either like or unlike this world. If entirely alike, they would be in vain – and that conflicts with His wisdom. If unlike, none of them would comprehend in itself every nature of sensible body; consequently no one of them would be perfect, but one perfect world would result from all of them.[26]

Other figures would also deny that God could create many worlds, but that denial became increasingly controversial as the thirteenth century drew on.[27] This is the crucial juncture for the acceptance of the possibility of multiple worlds in Western Christianity. That God had not created other worlds remained uncontroversial, but that God *could* not – a position advanced by Aristotle's most forthright and total advocates – provoked a backlash, most notably in the list of 219 propositions condemned by Étienne Tempier, Archbishop of Paris, in 1277. Among them we read that it must be denied that 'the first cause cannot make more than one world', as also that one must not deny the possibility of newness on the part of the action of God.[28]

---

[26] Aquinas, Thomas, *Exposition of Aristotle's Treatise on the Heavens*, trans. Fabian R. Larcher and Pierre H. Conway (Columbus, OH: College of St Mary of the Springs, 1963), book I, ch. 9, lect. 19, n. 197.

[27] Arnould lists Michael Scott, William of Auvergne, and Roger Bacon as other thirteenth century deniers (*Turbulences Dans l'univers*, 49).

[28] Propositions 27 and 22. Numbering from Pierre Mandonnet, *Siger de Brabant et l'averroisme Latin Au XIIIe Siècle*, vol. 2 (Louvain: Institut Supérieur De Philosophie, 1908), 175–91. In an earlier numbering system, these are proposition 34 and 48. The condemnations are translated in Ralph Lerner and Muhsin Mahdi, eds., *Medieval Political Philosophy: A Sourcebook* (Ithaca, NY: Cornell University Press, 1972), 335–54. For a discussion, see Rik van Nieuwenhove, 'The Condemnations of 1277', ch. 15, in *An Introduction to Medieval Theology* (Cambridge: Cambridge University

Although at least one prominent Franciscan, Francis Bacon, would oppose belief in many worlds, others were central to a trend to respond to the Parisian condemnations by embracing the possibility of a plurality of worlds.[29] Bonaventure (1221–1274) taught emphatically that God could create a plurality of worlds. He took it for granted that God could also make another world in another place, and indeed could 'make a hundred worlds in different locations'.[30] Richard of Middleton (c. 1249–1308) illustrates a significant ease with the prospect of worlds that are independent from each other, in contrast to Albert and Aquinas and their worries on that score. Richard could write that 'I understand by universe a set of things a single surface contains'. On that basis, 'In the same fashion that the earth of our universe rests naturally in the centre of the first universe, the earth of the second universe would rest naturally in the centre of the universe to which it belongs'. They would be happily and distinctly bounded, and matter placed anywhere within a 'universe' (or discrete portion of it) would tend towards the local centre.[31]

Press, 2012) and Edward Grant, 'The Condemnation of 1277, God's Absolute Power, and Physical Thought in the Late Middle Ages', *Viator* 10 (1979): 211–44. Among those holding to the 'non-impossibility' of multiple worlds in the thirteenth century, Arnould lists Geoffrey of Fontaine, Henry the Great, Richard of Middleton, William of Ware, John of Bassols, and Thomas of Strasbourg, followed by John Buridan and William of Ockham in the fourteenth (*Turbulences Dans l'univers*, 51–53).

[29] Duhem, *Medieval Cosmology*, 444–46.

[30] *Commentaria in Quatuor Libros Sententiarum*, I, D. 44, art 1, q. 4, Opera Omnia, 1882, I, 780, quoted by Grant McColley and H. W Miller, 'Saint Bonaventure, Francis Mayron, William Vorilong, and the Doctrine of a Plurality of Worlds', *Speculum* 12, no. 3 (1937): 387.

[31] Richard of Middleton, *Commentary on the Sentences*, book 1, dist. 43, art. 1, q. 4, from *Magistri Ricardi de Mediavilla, Seraphici Ord. Min. Convent. Super Quatvor Libros Sententiarvm, Petri Lombardi Quaestiones Subtilissimae*, vol. 1 (Brescia: Vincentium Sabbium, 1591), 392b–393a, translation from Duhem, *Medieval Cosmology*, 452. As Duhem notes, at stake here, in the later Middle Ages, are notions of gravity and attraction, between the Aristotelian idea of bodies moving to their own 'proper place' – such as the Earth, for the element of earth – and a more general account of attraction, which Duhem diagnoses as more Platonic (Ibid., 472–79).

Richard's contemporary William of Ware (or William Varon) made a useful distinction between meanings of the term 'world'. It can mean 'the universality of creatures taken all together', in which case, there could be no other worlds: they would be 'only a portion of the [wider] universe'. Alternatively, it can mean 'another celestial sphere', which is how he chooses to use it.[32] William also offers a helpful analysis of the non-impossibility of plural worlds (in the second sense) approached variously in terms of 'the Producer', 'what is produced' anew, and 'the world already created'.[33]

William of Ockham (1285–1347) again held that God could make other worlds, and indeed could 'make a world better than this one'. He offered a pair of refutations to counterarguments from Aristotle that would turn up across this literature. The first is that while our cosmos might contain all the matter *of this cosmos*, that does not prevent God from creating other matter elsewhere, and thus other things. God can make any number of individuals of a given species on Earth, and since 'God is not constrained to produce them in this world; He can produce them outside this world, and thereby make another world in the same fashion that He made this world'.[34] The second angle is the one we saw in Richard of Middleton, about the non-attraction of independent universes. Matter in one world is attracted within that world, and matter in another, within that one.[35]

Among these Franciscans, we should consider finally William of Vaurouillon (c. 1392–1463/64).[36] He distinguished two questions,

[32] William of Ware, *Guillelmi Varronis Seu de Waria in IV Sententiarum Libros Commentarius* (Bibliothèque Municipale de Bordeaux, MS 163), book 2, q. 8, fol. 96, col. C, translation from Duhem, *Medieval Cosmology*, 455.

[33] William of Ware, ibid., translation from Duhem, ibid.

[34] William of Ockham, *Scriptum in Librum Primum Sententiarum (Ordinatio), Distinctiones 19–48*, ed. Girard Etzkorn and Franciscus Kelley (St Bonaventure, NY: Franciscan Institute, 1979), dist. 44, q. unica, p. 655, translation from Duhem, *Medieval Cosmology*, 462–63.

[35] Ockham, *In Librum Primum Sententiarum*, dist. 44, q. unica, pp. 657–58.

[36] McColley and Miller, 'Plurality of Worlds', 386, n. 2. They call him William Vorilong.

answering positively to both: whether God could create an infinite number of worlds, and whether God could make an infinitude of worlds better than this one.

> If it be inquired whether a whole world is able to be made more perfect than this universe, I answer that not one world alone, but that infinite worlds, more perfect than this one, lie hid in the mind of God. If Democritus, who posits actual infinite worlds, rightly understood this fact, he would have understood rightly. If it then is asked how the second world cleaves to this one, I answer that it would be possible for the species [i.e. character – not living 'species'] of this world to be distinguished from that of the other world. If it be further inquired where it could exist, I answer that it would be able to be placed above any part of the heaven, south, or north, east or west …[37]

Vaurouillon is often cited in theological discussions of astrobiology as the first theologian to discuss themes such as sin, salvation, and multiple Incarnations (however briefly).[38] I will return to him in Chapter 13.

The fifteenth century also brings us to Nicholas of Cusa (1401–1464), Cardinal and Bishop of Brixen, notable in *On Learned Ignorance* (completed in 1440) not only for his advocacy of a plurality of worlds but also for his relativisation of the Earth: 'Therefore, the earth is a noble star which has a light and a heat and an influence that are distinct and different from [that of] all other stars, just as each star differs from each other star with respect to its light, its

---

[37] Guillermus Vorrilong, *Guillermus Vorrillong Super Quattuor Libris Sententiarum Nouiter Correctus [et] Apostillatus*, 1502, book 1, dist. 44, f72r, translation from McColley and Miller, 'Plurality of Worlds', 387.

[38] McColley and Miller write that de Vaurouillon 'was sufficiently impressed by this probability [the existence of more than one world] to so re-interpret fundamental Christian beliefs that they were not in conflict with the idea of more than one inhabited globe' (McColley and Miller, 'Plurality of Worlds', 389). This goes too far: he does not reinterpret doctrine to fit the possibility of another world; he makes assumptions about another world (for instance that there would be no sin) to fit with existing doctrine. They also seem to me to go too far when they suggest that his text 'indicates a tendency toward belief in an actual plurality of populated worlds' (ibid.). That underestimates the capacity of the scholastic mind to ask hypothetical questions, and to give hypothetical answers.

nature, and its influence'.[39] Nor did he consider inhabitation only hypothetically, writing that 'The regions of the other stars are similar to this, for we believe that none of them is deprived of inhabitants'. We see this in his argument that we should not imagine that life beyond Earth is necessarily more capable than we are.

[We cannot rightly claim to know] that our portion of the world is the habitation of men and animals and vegetables which are proportionally less noble [than] the inhabitants in the region of the sun and of the other stars. For although God is the center and circumference of all stellar regions and although natures of different nobility proceed from Him and inhabit each region (lest so many places in the heavens and on the stars be empty and lest only the earth – presumably among the lesser things – be inhabited), nevertheless with regard to the intellectual natures a nobler and more perfect nature cannot, it seems, be given (even if there are inhabitants of another kind on other stars) than the intellectual nature which dwells both here on earth and in its own region.[40]

As Duhem notes, there is something remarkable going on here, namely that

the first time in Western Christianity that one heard someone speak about the plurality of inhabited worlds [actual worlds, actually inhabited] it was proposed by a theologian who has spoken at an ecumenical council a few years before. The person who sought to reflect upon the characteristics of the sun and moon … had the confidence of the popes; the highest ecclesiastical honours were bestowed upon him. There can be no greater proof of the extreme liberality of the Catholic church during the close of the Middle Ages towards the meditations of the philosopher and the experiments of the physicist.[41]

[39] Nicholas of Cusa, *Nicholas of Cusa on Learned Ignorance: A Translation and an Appraisal of De Docta Ignorantia*, trans. Jaspar Hopkins (Minnesota, MN: Arthur J. Banning Press, 1985), II.12, p. 94. Interpolations in Hopkins' translation.
[40] Ibid., II.12, pp. 95–96.
[41] Duhem, *Medieval* Cosmology, 510.

Into Modernity

A century and a half later, Giordano Bruno (1548–1600) also upheld the thesis of many worlds, but whereas Cusa was to receive high office in the church, Bruno was burnt at the stake. On that account, he has achieved of the status of being something of a martyr for science, not least for the idea of a widely inhabited universe.[42] Recent scholarship has been more cautious, suggesting that the deviation of his thought from received Christian orthodoxy on doctrinal maters more easily explains the animosity of church authorities. Among the recusals he was forced to make, one concerned having identified God with matter (the theme is addressed in five out of the eight statements he was made to reject).[43] He also taught that God acts of necessity. The reports of the investigation of Bruno by the Inquisition record him saying at one point that 'as a consequence of my philosophy, since God's power is infinite it must necessarily produce effects that are equally infinite'.[44]

Despite the thirteenth-century condemnations, which stressed that God *could* create other worlds, insisting that God *had* done so remained a position censured as heretical in Gregory XIII's Corpus of Canon Law, as Alberto A. Martinez has pointed out. Bruno's advocacy of actual, and inhabited, multiple worlds crossed that line, and so may have constituted part of what stood against him after all.[45] That Cusa fared differently likely rests on his more general alignment with traditional orthodoxy (although often in a highly creative way), and perhaps simply on the fact that the church was more confident and at peace in the mid-fifteenth century than it was at the cusp of the seventeenth.

[42] Giordano Bruno, *De l'infinito universo et Mondi: All'illustrissimo Signor di Mauuissiero* (Venetia [London]: Charlewood, 1584).

[43] I am grateful to Dr Lucas Mix for this point.

[44] Concerning the second censured proposition.

[45] Alberto A. Martinez, *Burned Alive: Bruno, Galileo and the Inquisition* (London: Reaktion, 2018), 61.

Into the seventeenth century, the sense that the idea of multiple worlds threw up doctrinal questions was not lost on the churches. Martinez points to a Catholic index of heresies dating from shortly after the time of Bruno, stating that 'we cannot assert that two or many worlds exist, since neither do we assert two or many Christs'.[46] Among the Protestant Reformers, both Martin Luther (1483–1546) and John Calvin (1509–1564) rejected the heliocentrism of Copernicus (1473–1543). In his *Table Talk*, Luther is reported to have seen the new science as a modish bid to grab attention:

> There was mention of a certain new astrologer who wanted to prove that the earth moves and not the sky, the sun, and the moon. This would be as if somebody were riding on a cart or in a ship and imagined that he was standing still while the earth and the trees were moving. [To this Luther remarked] 'So it goes now. Whoever wants to be clever must agree with nothing that others esteem. He must do something of his own. This is what that fellow does who wishes to turn the whole of astronomy upside down. Even in these things that are thrown into disorder I believe the Holy Scriptures, for Joshua commanded the sun to stand still, and not the earth'.[47]

Calvin's rejection is even more striking, given his otherwise generally outspoken advocacy of attention to science. In Chapter 5, we will see him taking up the position that the Bible is not to be treated as a text-book of astronomy, for which one needs to turn to those trained in that field. In a sermon on 1 Corinthians 10:19–24, however, he accuses those who 'say that the sun does not move, and that it is the earth which shifts and turns' of derangement and demonic possession:

---

[46] *Antidotum contra diversas omnium fere seculorum haereses* (Basel, 1528), p. 248; rev. L. Ricchieri, Haereseologia (Basel, 1556), 715, here quoting the *Contra Acephalos* of Rustici Diaconi, written between 553 and 564, published in *Rvstici Diaconi contra Acephalos*, ed. Sara Petri, 100 (Turnhout: Brepols, 2013).

[47] Martin Luther, *Luther's Works, Volume 54 – Table Talk*, ed. Theodore Gerhardt Tappert, trans. Helmut T. Lehmann (Philadelphia: Fortress Press, 1967), 358–59. He cites Josh. 10.12.

When we see such minds we must indeed confess that the devil possess them, and that God sets them before us as mirrors, in order to keep us in his fear. So it is with all who argue out of pure malice, and who happily make a show of their imprudence. When they are told: 'That is hot,' they will reply: 'No, it is plainly cold.' When they are shown an object that is black, they will say that it is white, or vice versa. Just like the man who said that snow is black; for although it is perceived and known by all to be white, yet he clearly wished to contradict the fact. And so it is that they are madmen who would try to change the natural order, and even to dazzle eyes and benumb their senses.[48]

Luther's protege Phillip Melanchthon (1497–1560) went beyond astronomy, to address the prospect of other life, offering a stiff denunciation on grounds that echo the Christological concerns of the Catholic index of heresies just mentioned:

The Son of God is one: our master Jesus Christ, coming forth in this world, died and was resurrected only once. Nor did he manifest himself elsewhere, nor has he died or been resurrected elsewhere. We should not imagine many worlds because we ought not imagine that Christ died and was risen often; nor should it be thought that in any other world without the knowledge of the Son of God that people would be restored to eternal life.[49]

Similarly aware of the potential Christological implications of life elsewhere was Galileo's Dominican defender Tommaso Campanella. In his *Apology for Galileo* (1622), he went out of his

[48] John Calvin, 'Sermon on 1 Corinthians 10:19–24', in *Ioannis Calvini opera quae supersunt omnia*, ed. Edouard Cunitz, Johann-Wilhelm Baum, and Eduard Wilhelm Eugen Reuss, vol. 49 (New York: Johnson, 1964), 677, translation from Robert White, 'Calvin and Copernicus: The Problem Reconsidered', *Calvin Theological Journal* 15, no. 2 (1980): 236–37.
[49] *Initia Doctrinae Physicae: Dictata In Academia Witeberg*ensi. Vitebergae: Crato, 1565. The text was republished in the *Corpus Reformatorum*, edited Carlos Gottlieb Bretschneider (Halis Saxonus, apud C. A. Schwetschke et fildum, 1846), columns 220–21, passage here from column 221, translation from Thomas O'Meara, *Vast Universe*, 6.

way to defuse any tension on that front, by arguing that if there are 'humans living on other stars, they would not have been infected by the sin of Adam since they are not his descendants'.[50]

Among outspoken opponents to the idea of multiple worlds, we also encounter the French Calvinist Lambert Daneau (c. 1530–c. 1590), who wrote 'Fie upon this infinity or multitude of worlds. There is one and no more'. He thought the idea to be at least 'foolish and childish' and even 'blasphemous', since scripture recounts 'the special visible works of God' and it does so speaking of 'this one world only'.[51] English writers who opposed multiple worlds included Thomas Heywood ('Manifest it is, that there is but one world'), John Swan, and George Hakewill.[52] By the middle of the seventeenth century, however, 'the conviction that our world alone was inhabited' was 'generally in retreat'.[53]

In contrast to this, astrobiological discussion by Richard Baxter (1615–1691) deserves attention, both because it shows this much-loved writer fully embracing the idea of widespread life and because, far from worrying that this demotes human beings and the Earth, the idea is able to achieve significant positive theological work for him. On account of that, and of its picturesque style, I will quote it at some length:

> it greatly quieteth my mind against this great objection of the numbers
> that are damned and cast off for ever, to consider how small a part

---

[50] Tommaso Campanella, *A Defense of Galileo, the Mathematician from Florence*, ed. and trans. Richard J. Blackwell (Notre Dame, IN: University of Notre Dame Press, 1994), 112. Campanella goes on to write that the inhabitants would not, in fact, be 'humans' but rather 'beings of a different nature, who are similar to us but not the same as us' (112–13).

[51] Lambert Daneau, *The Wonderful Workmanship of the World* (London: Andrew Maunsell, 1578), 25–27.

[52] Thomas Heywood, *The Hierarchie of the Blessed Angels* (London, 1635), 153–54; John Swan, *Speculum Mundi; or, A Glasse Representing the Face of the World* (Cambridge, 1635), 210–28; George Hakewill, *An Apologie of the Power and Providence of God in the Government of the World*, 3rd ed. (Oxford, 1635) – citations from David Cressy, 'Early Modern Space Travel and the English Man in the Moon', *American Historical Review* 111, no. 4 (1 October 2006): 965.

[53] Cressy, 'Early Modern Space Travel', 965.

this earth is of God's creation, as well as how sinful and impenitent. Ask any Astronomer, that hath considered the innumerable number of the fixed Stars and Planets, with their distances, and magnitude, and glory, and the uncertainty that we have whether there be not as many more, or an hundred or thousand times as many, unseen to man, as all those which we see (considering the defectiveness of man's sight, and the Planets [moons] about Jupiter, with the innumerable Stars in the Milky way, which the Tube [telescope] hath lately discovered, which man's eyes without it could not see,) I say, ask any man who knoweth these things, whether all this earth be any more in comparison of the whole creation, than one Prison is to a Kingdom or Empire, or the paring of one nail, or a little mole, or wart, or a hair, in comparison of the whole body. And if God should cast off all this earth, and use all the sinners in it as they deserve, it is no more sign of a want of benignity or mercy in him, than it is for a King to cast one subject of a million into a Jail, and to hang him for his murder, or treason, or rebellion; or for a man to kill one louse, which is but a molestation to the body which beareth it; or than it is to pare a mans nails, or cut off a wart, or a hair, or to pull out a rotten aking tooth. I know it is a thing uncertain and unrevealed to us, whether all these Globes be inhabited or not: but he that considereth, that there is scarce any uninhabitable place on earth, or in the water, or air, but men, or beasts, or birds, or fishes, or flies, or worms and moles do take up almost all, will think it a probability so near a certainty, as not to be much doubted of, that the vaster and more glorious parts of the Creation are not uninhabited; but that they have Inhabitants answerable to their magnitude and glory (as Palaces have other inhabitants than Cottages): and that there is a connaturality and agreeableness there as well as here, between the Region or Globe, and the inhabitants ... I make no question but our number to theirs is not one to a million at the most.[54]

[54] Richard Baxter, *The Reasons of the Christian Religion* (London: R. White, for Fran. Titon, 1667), 388–89. In a marginal note, he cites the French Roman Catholic priest, philosopher and astronomer Pierre Gassendi (1592–1655): 'Of the probability of the habitation of the Planets, see *Gassendus* [his name in Latin], and his reasons, that

Such open-mindedness is seen in the work of John Wilkins (1614–1672), Master of Wadham College, Oxford and then Trinity College, Cambridge. Eventually Bishop of Chester, he was a keen experimentalist and a founding member of London's Royal Society. His book of 1638, *A Discovery of a New World: Or a Discourse Tending to Prove, that 'tis Probable There May be another Habitable World in the Moon* (to give around a third of the title) is a remarkable work of scholarship. Alongside extensive scientific treatments, page after page is filled with discussions, not only of Biblical texts and the Church Fathers, but also of Thomas Aquinas, Nicholas of Cusa, contemporary Jesuits, and the pagan writers of antiquity. Wilkins' work on the nature of scriptural revelation, and how it bears – or not – upon scientific questions offers valuable lessons for the relation between science and theology today. We will turn to that in Chapter 5.

The English clergyman John Ray (1627–1705), sometimes called the father of British natural history, stands as another example. In his *Wisdom of God Manifested in the Works of the Creation* (1691), extraterrestrial life features as an uncontroversial aside:

> Every fix'd star [in number 'next to infinite' or 'innumerable as to us, or their number prodigiously great'] ... is a Sun or Sun-like Body, and in like manner incircled with a Chorus of Planets moving about it ... [and is] in all likelihood furnished with as great variety of corporeal Creatures, animate and inanimate, as the Earth, and all as different in Nature as they are in Place from the Terrestrial, and from each other.[55]

From here on, books would continue to be published on theology and astronomy, some of which discussed the possibility of life

---

the inhabitants are not men of our species, but that the inhabitants are diversified as the habitations are, and other things in the universe' (388). The reference seems to be to Petri Gassendi, 'Syntagmatis Philosophici', in *Opera Omnia*, vol. 4 (Florence: Cajetanum Tartini et Sanctem Franchi, 1727), 8–9.

[55] John Ray, *The Wisdom of God Manifested in the Works of the Creation* (London: Samuel Smith, 1691), part I, 18–19.

elsewhere, although without a great deal of theological depth.[56] As Jacques Arnould has written, 'the plurality of worlds passed from a status of heresy to that of a powerful argument for the rhetoric of natural theology'.[57] As an example of how much the topic of life elsewhere remained in public view, consider this exchange from Anthony Trollope's (1815–1882) *Barchester Towers* (1857). Wanting his characters to appear up-to-date and sophisticated, reflecting the conversations of the drawing rooms of their time, he has them discuss life elsewhere in the solar system and its theological ramifications.

"Are you a Whewellite or a Brewsterite, or a t'othermanite, Mrs. Bold?" said Charlotte, who knew a little about everything, and had read about a third of each of the books to which she alluded.

"Oh!" said Eleanor; "I have not read any of the books, but I feel sure that there is one man in the moon at least, if not more."

"You don't believe in the pulpy gelatinous matter?" said Bertie.

"I heard about that," said Eleanor; "and I really think it's almost wicked to talk in such a manner. How can we argue about God's power in the other stars from the laws which he has given for our rule in this one?"

"How, indeed!" said Bertie. "Why shouldn't there be a race of salamanders in Venus? and even if there be nothing but fish in Jupiter, why shouldn't the fish there be as wide awake as the men and women here?"

"That would be saying very little for them," said Charlotte. "I am for Dr. Whewell myself; for I do not think that men and women are

[56] Principal examples include William Derham (1657–1735), *Astro-Theology: Or a Demonstration of the Being and Attributes of God, from a Survey of the Heavens* (London: W. Innys, 1714); William Whiston (1667–1752), *Astronomical Principles of Religion, Natural and Reveal'd* (London: J. Senex and W. Taylor, 1717); and Christian Huygens, *Cosmotheoros* (The Hague: Adriaan Moetjens, 1698), translated as *The Celestial Worlds Discover'd* (London: Timothy Childe, 1698), with no translator identified.
[57] Arnould, *Turbulences Dans l'univers*, 83, my translation.

worth being repeated in such countless worlds. There may be souls in other stars, but I doubt their having any bodies attached to them."[58]

Theological ruminations on other worlds or the implications of life elsewhere in the universe, then, are not new; indeed, they go back, more or less continually, to the middle of the fifteenth century. A great many responses, often from writers of considerable note in their own time, have been receptive, confident, and positive. Alongside that, we encounter contentions that such life would pose a threat to the principal tenets of the faith, but these arguments cannot be said to have had the upper hand since the seventeenth century. This is little appreciated. Consider Carl Sagan, for instance, a significant scientific figure in the development of astrobiology, and someone whose writing and broadcasting helped to define the role of the contemporary scientific public intellectual. In his influential *Pale Blue Dot*, he was still able to ask

> How is it that hardly any major religion has looked at science and concluded, 'this is better than we thought!' The universe is much bigger than our prophets said, grander, more subtle, more elegant. Instead they say, 'no, no, no'. My god is a little god and I want him to stay that way. A religion, old or new, that stressed the magnificence of the universe as revealed by modern science might be able to draw forth reserves of reverence and awe hardly topped by the conventional faiths.[59]

Acknowledging Sagan's standing as a scientist, as a statement about history this is simply wrong, and seems to betray a complete

---

[58] Anthony Trollope, *Barchester Towers*, ed. John Bowen (Oxford: Oxford University Press, 2014), ch. 6. Trollope's characters will have been reading Whewell's *Of the Plurality of Worlds* (London: John W. Parker and Son, 1853) and the reply by Sir David Brewster, *More Worlds Than One: The Creed of the Philosopher and the Hope of the Christian*, Corrected and Enlarged Edition (London: Murray, 1854). Whewell writes about 'boneless, watery, pulpy creatures' (183) and 'aqueous, gelatinous creatures' (185) on Saturn and Jupiter. On this exchange, see Arnould, *Turbulences dans L'Univers*, 98–101. Whewell had initially supported the idea of extraterrestrial life, but later rejected it on Christological and soteriological grounds.

[59] Carl Sagan, *Pale Blue Dot: A Vision of the Human Future in Space* (London: Headline, 1995), 50.

unawareness of a tradition of theological writing that stretches (among Christians) from the fifteenth century and before, right up to Sagan's own time. Judaism has its own deeply considered discussion of the question, stretching back even further.[60]

The Antipodes

In closing this chapter, I will turn to the fascinating case of the antipodes. This posed questions to writers from quite early in Christian history about the possibility of life elsewhere, without requiring their imagination to leave the Earth.

For Biblical and Patristic writers, the cosmos was the sum of the earthly realm within which we live, plus the encircling vault of heaven. Whether there could be more to physical reality than that, actually or potentially, was not a matter of any great deal of speculation. Even supposing the cosmos to consist only of the Earth and the heavens, however, the question of life elsewhere presented itself to early Christian writers in the form of the antipodes. As Richard J. Blackwell recounts, the term has its roots in '"what is across from our feet," and referred to both the people and the places located in what we now call the Western hemisphere'.[61] The idea finds its origin in Western thought among the Pythagoreans, who proposed a world corresponding to our own on the other side of the Earth.[62] The word 'antipodes' itself seem to have been

---

[60] See Lamm, 'Religious Implications'; Howard Smith, 'Alone in the Universe', *Zygon* 51, no. 2 (June 2016): 497–519; Norbert M. Samuelson, 'Jewish Theology Meets the Alien', in *Astrotheology: Science and Theology Meet Extraterrestrial Life*, ed. Ted Peters et al. (Eugene, OR: Cascade, 2018), 208–15.

[61] Translator's note in Campanella, *Defense of Galileo*, 138, n. 60. Its etymology is not, as some have written, a reference to creatures with feet at the other end of their bodies from us, but to those who dwell opposite to where our feet stand.

[62] 'There are also antipodes, and our "down" is their "up"' (Diogenes Laertius, *Lives of Eminent Philosophers*, book 8, ch. 2, n. 25, on Pythagoras), translation from Diogenes

coined by Cicero (106–43 BC).[63] As a realm often thought to be entirely cut off from the regions known to European writers, it would truly be an 'other world', possibly with its own life.

Among Christian writers, antipodean inhabitants were discussed and dismissed by Lactantius (AD c. 250–c. 325), on the grounds that look rather ridiculous today, given our appreciation that gravity draws all towards the centre of the Earth, without any other absolute sense of up or down. 'Is there any one so senseless as to believe that there are men whose footsteps are higher than their heads?', Lactantius asks, 'or that the things which with us are in a recumbent position, with them hang in an inverted direction? That the crops and trees grow downwards? that the rains, and snow, and hail fall upwards to the earth?'[64] He records precisely a gravitational solution to this challenge, offered by advocates for the antipodes: 'they reply that such is the nature of things, that heavy bodies are borne to the middle, and that they are all joined together towards the middle, as we see spokes in a wheel; but that the bodies which are light, as mist, smoke, and fire, are borne away from the middle, so as to seek the heaven'. Unfortunately, he considered such ideas to be the work of those who 'when they have once erred, consistently persevere in their folly, and defend one vain thing by another'.

Lactantius thought that universal inhabitancy would follow were the Earth spherical but – unlike a good many ancient writers – he denied that it was.[65] If the heavens were spherical, then

Laertius, *Lives of Eminent Philosophers*, trans. Robert Drew Hicks, vol. 2 (Cambridge, MA: Harvard University Press, 2005), 343.
[63] Cicero, *Academia*, II.123.
[64] Lactantius, *Divine Institutes* III.24, translation from Alexander Roberts and James Donaldson, eds., *Ante-Nicene Fathers – Volume VII: Fathers of the Third and Fourth Centuries*, trans. William Fletcher (Edinburgh: T&T Clark, 1994), 94.
[65] For a summary of the principal sources through which Christianity inherited the idea of a spherical Earth from antiquity, see Alison Peden, 'The Medieval Antipodes', *History Today*, December 1995.

the earth also itself must be like a globe; for that could not possibly be anything but round, which was held enclosed by that which was round... And if this were so, that last consequence also followed, that there would be no part of the earth uninhabited by men and the other animals. Thus the rotundity of the earth leads, in addition, to the invention of those suspended antipodes.[66]

Lactantius might therefore have been warmer towards the idea of the Antipodes, if he could have been convinced that the Earth is round.

Later, Augustine wrote in the *City of God* that 'As for the fabled "antipodes", men, that is, who live on the other side of the earth, where the sun rises when it sets for us, men who plant their footsteps opposite ours, there is no rational ground for such a belief'.[67] He supposed that if the other half of the Earth were geographically no different from the half we know, then it 'cannot be devoid of human inhabitants'.[68] He did not, however, accept the premise. We need not, for instance, assume that there is dry land there: the seas may cover all of the land on the other half of the Earth. Augustine considered two principles to settle the matter: the truth of scripture, and the absurdity of supposing that anyone could cross that 'vast expanse of ocean' on a ship. The second point rules out the possibility of inhabitation from the stock of Adam and Eve, and he took the Biblical account to rule out an origin for human life distinct from the primordial parents of Genesis.[69]

The idea of antipodeans was also rejected by Bede (672/3–735) and Isidore of Seville (c. 560–636).[70] In a letter to Boniface of 748, Pope Zachary threatened a priest named Vergil, later Bishop of Salzburg,

---

[66] Lactantius, *Divine Institutes* III.24, p. 94.

[67] Augustine, *City of God*, XVI.9, p. 664.

[68] Both he and Lactantius are adopting here something like the principle of mediocrity: that it is better to assume that things alike in one respect (e.g. geography) are also alike in another (e.g. in being inhabited).

[69] He also rejected that there might be people whom the Church could not reach to evangelise (*Letter* 199.12).

[70] Peden, 'Medieval Antipodes', 29.

with excommunication for teaching that 'there is another world and other men beneath the earth'.[71] Aquinas, to the best of my knowledge, did not address the topic,[72] although his renowned teacher, Albert the Great, did. As one of the great scientifically inclined minds of the Middle Ages, we may not be surprised to read that he accepted that the antipodes could be habitable, and quite likely were.[73] Moreover, since one might get there by means of a sufficiently long journey, none of that need present any particular theological problems.[74] He also recognised that 'up' and 'down' are relative.

Conclusion

The message from discussions of the antipodes, as with other topics treated in this chapter, is again that questions that may seem to be novel are rarely entirely new to Christian thought. We have also seen that while Christian theology took a long time to come to the idea of many worlds – as much on the basis of faulty science as on theological grounds – when that was finally reversed, the idea was widely embraced by the end of early modernity. Alongside the antipodes, the other great analogy for life beyond Earth in Christian theology would be belief in angelic beings. We turn to that in the next chapter.

[71] Ibid.

[72] The Latin word *antipodes* does not occur in his corpus in any grammatical form. The antipodes are discussed by Peter of Auvergne (1240–1304) in his continuation of Aquinas's *Commentary on De caelo et mundo* (book 4, ch. 1), and in two commentaries – on Boethius's *De consolatione philosophae* (book 2, ch. 3) and the Pseudo-Boethian work *De disciplina scholarium* (ch. 3) – by William Wheatley (d. after 1317), both for a time attributed to Aquinas.

[73] Albert the Great, *De natura locorum*, tract. I, ch. 6–10, in Albertus Magnus, *Opera Omnia*, 9:538–50, especially ch. 10, pp. 549–50. On this, see Daniel Joseph Kennedy, *St Thomas Aquinas and Medieval Philosophy* (New York: Encyclopedia Press, 1919), 42–43.

[74] Later, the topic was discussed by Campanella in *Defense of Galileo*, 53, 138, nn. 61, 62, nn. 63–6, who mentions Aquinas in the *ST* (presumably I.102.2 *ad* 4, where Aquinas quotes Aristotle, *Meteorology*, II.5), Avicenna, Ephrem, Anastasius of Sinai, and Moses of Syria (with no reference given for these).

2 | Angels

Theological writing on angels offers something valuable in relation to astrobiology: not direct equivalence, but a case, nonetheless, where the theologian has acknowledged diversity to creation and the possibility of intelligent life beyond human beings and the confines of Earth.

Christianity inherited belief in angels from Judaism, although the sense that our world is inhabited by spirits also characterised the surrounding pagan culture of the Early Church, and it aligns with human instincts more universally. While some theological accounts of angels differ profoundly from the idea of extraterrestrial intelligence (ETI), others provide a clear equivalence. At their most continuous, we have writers – if not perhaps from an academic stable – who simply identify ETI with angels, or vice versa. More generally, the stress will be on the difference between angels and ETI. By extraterrestrial life we mean biological beings, whereas angels are not biological, and have often been thought to be immaterial (especially in my own Thomist tradition). By extraterrestrial life we also imagine something occupying a place in created, spatial reality; with the angels, religious communities have understood beings sometimes coming and going in our midst, but mainly dwelling in the presence of God, outside of our physical order altogether.[1]

---

[1] One of the principal traditional distinctions between orders of heavenly powers is between those who serve bodily creation and impinge upon it, and those that do not (Sergius Bulgakov, *Jacob's Ladder: On Angels*, trans. T. Allan Smith (Grand Rapids, MI: Eerdmans, 2010), 81).

43

My approach in this chapter will often stress the difference between what has been said about angels and what we might think about ETI. The value in thinking about the place of angels in Christian theology would be to be reminded that the tradition has entertained belief in a diversity of created things, with human beings not the only creatures possessing intelligence and will. That value follows, whether or not a particular reader today holds that angels exist, although I imagine that a good many more will do so today than a few decades ago.

Theologians have often accorded human beings a special status within the created whole for one reason or another, for instance, as representing a microcosm, or because of the Incarnation. Nonetheless, the angels have typically been taken to stand above human beings in power and excellence.[2] This reminds us of an established theological vision in which, already, humans are not the most elevated or advanced beings within creation.

More broadly, the idea of angels has furnished thought experiments, by which we have explored and honed our sense of what it means to be human or biological, by comparison to that which is neither. As an example, the much-maligned question of angels dancing on pin heads addresses the nature of intellectual presence.[3] Angels have also proved useful in thinking about the nature of the *imago dei*,

[2] Karl Barth offered an unusual account of angels in *CD* III.3, such that both material creatures and angels have their own distinct 'advantage', §51 (*Church Dogmatics: The Doctrine of Creation (III/3)*, trans. Geoffrey W. Bromiley and J. R. Ehrlich (Edinburgh: T&T Clark, 1961), 480). For his criticism of Aquinas on angels, see 391–93.
[3] Dorothy L. Sayers, *The Lost Tools of Learning* (London: Methuen and Co., 1948), 11–12 and Mortimer Jerome Adler, *The Angels and Us* (New York: Touchstone, 1993), 129–30. See Dominik Perler, 'Thought Experiments: The Methodological Function of Angels in Late Medieval Epistemology', in *Angels in Medieval Philosophical Inquiry: Their Function and Significance*, ed. Isabel Iribarren and Martin Lenz (London: Routledge, 2016), 143–53 and Tiziana Suárez-Nani, 'Angels, Space and Place: The Location of Separate Substances According to John Duns Scotus', in *Angels in Medieval Philosophical Inquiry: Their Function and Significance*, ed. Isabel Iribarren and Martin Lenz (London: Routledge, 2016), 89–111.

how intellect relates to the senses, the difference between immediate knowledge and discursive reason, and the dynamics of 'individuation': what makes this lion or angel different from that lion or angel?[4] From time to time in this book, even beyond this chapter, they will continue to fulfil this role, provoking us to think by way of contrast.

Theological Bearings

Within the Old and New Testaments, we encounter a variety of beings that later theologians have grouped together as angels. Their place in these texts is also varied, appearing in narrative, in writings associated with praise, in apocalyptic literature, and in the Epistles. The Hebrew noun *mal'āk* and Greek *angelos* both mean 'messenger', which is often how they appear in the Bible. Sometimes they are pictured as a throng, or heavenly court, as in Isaiah and Job, while in other places they appear alone.[5] Sometimes a reference to an angel (especially 'the angel of the Lord') seems to be a way of talking about an appearance of God.[6] Biblical scholarship suggests that some of these beings may first have been understood as distinct deities, and were later subsumed into a monotheistic picture.[7] The theologian ought not to fear such histories of the clarification of thought.

In doctrinal writing, angels generally feature much as they do in the Bible: rarely as the central focus of attention, but with a certain

---

[4] For instance, *ST* I.50, 58, 85.1, 93.3.

[5] Isaiah 6; Job 1.6. For individual appearances, see, for instance, Dan. 6.22; 1 King 19.5; Luke 22.43; Acts 12.7, and references to individual named angels in footnote 11.

[6] Paul Quay provides a window on theologians towards the end of the twentieth century who wished to downplay the place of angels in the dogmatic confession of the faith on this basis ('Angels and Demons: The Teaching of IV Lateran', *Theological Studies* 42, no. 1 (March 1981): 20–45, 22, n. 7.

[7] Yehezkel Kaufmann, *The Religion of Israel: From Its Beginnings to the Babylonian Exile*, trans. Moshe Greenberg (New York: Schocken Books, 1972); Mark S. Smith, *The Origins of Biblical Monotheism: Israel's Polytheistic Background and the Ugaritic Texts* (New York: Oxford University Press, 2001).

background ubiquity nonetheless. In creedal terms, angels would be included as part of 'heaven' in the phrase 'maker of heaven and earth' (Apostles' Creed), and they are likely a prominent part of what was being proposed as 'invisible' in '[maker] of all things, visible and invisible' (Niceno-Constantinopolitan Creed). Within Western Christianity, their part in the doctrinal whole was underlined at the Fourth Lateran Council (1215).[8] That angels did not receive any extensive attention from previous councils indicates not that their place within the created order was contested, but rather that it was not in doubt.

Angels feature across the writings of patristic authors, who sometimes treated them somewhat systematically, not least in gathering them into groups within a hierarchy. The now-familiar nine-fold order was elaborated from the lists within the Pauline Epistles: principalities; powers; virtues and dominions;[9] and thrones, dominions, principalities, and powers,[10] combined with the angels and archangels,[11] cherubim,[12] and seraphim.[13] The order of the hierarchy differs, for instance, between Augustine, Gregory the Great, Pseudo-Dionysius, and John of Damascus.[14] Among mediaeval

[8] Lateran IV, Constitution 1, in Norman P. Tanner and Giuseppe Alberigo, eds., *Decrees of the Ecumenical Councils: From Nicaea I to Vatican II*, vol. 1 (Washington, DC: Georgetown University Press, 1990), 230.

[9] Eph. 1.21.

[10] Col. 1.16.

[11] References to angels are too numerous to list. The idea of named archangels appears in Judaism in post-Biblical literature. The New Testament contains two references to an 'archangel' (1 Thess. 4.16 and Jude 9). The latter names Michael, who appears by name elsewhere (Daniel 10, 12; Rev. 12), as does Gabriel (Daniel 8, 9; Luke 1), without that designation. Tobit lists Raphael among the 'seven angels' (Tobit 12.15).

[12] Gen. 3.24; Ps. 18.10; Ezek. 10.1–20, 26.14, c.f. Ezek. 1 and Rev. 4.6–7. A pair of carved cherubim are presented as framing the ark of the covenant (Ex. 25.17–20), meaning that it is sometimes difficult to tell if an invocation of these refer to something angelic or to their physical depiction on the ark (e.g. 1 Sam. 4.4; Isa. 37.16; Ps. 80.1, 99.1; Heb. 9.5).

[13] 'Fiery ones': Isa. 6.1–3; c.f. Rev. 4.8.

[14] Augustine, *Confessions*, 12.22, and various sections of *City of God* and *Literal Commentary on Genesis* (see Elizabeth Klein, *Augustine's Theology of Angels* (Cambridge: Cambridge University Press, 2018)); John Chrysostom, various

writers, Bernard of Clairvaux, Hugh of St Victor, Thomas Gallus, Alan of Lille, Albert, Aquinas, Bonaventure, and Duns Scotus all wrote extensively about angels.[15] They were treated systematically by Calvin in the *Institutes*, and discussed by Luther across his career.[16] In the past century, significant treatments come from Karl Barth, Jean Daniélou, Eric Mascall, and Sergei Bulgakov.[17]

Angels as Exobiology

As I noted above, religious writers have occasionally made a direct identification between angels and extraterrestrial life. In one

sermons (see Jean Daniélou, *The Angels and Their Mission: According to the Fathers of the Church* (Notre Dame, IN: Christian Classics, 2011)); Gregory the Great, *Sermons on the Gospels*, 34 (on the Feast of St Michael); Pseudo-Dionysius, *Celestial Hierarchies*; John of Damascus, *On the Orthodox Faith*, II.3. Many of these patristic and mediaeval texts are collected in Steven Chase, ed., *Angelic Spirituality: Medieval Perspectives on the Ways of Angels* (New York: Paulist Press, 2002).

[15] Albert, *Commentary on the Celestial Hierarchy of Dionysius*; Aquinas, *ST* I.50–64, and other passages, including I.65.3 and I.103–119, and *On Separated Substances*; Bonaventure, *Breviloquium* II.6–8 and passages in *Commentary on the Sentences*, book 2 (see David Keck, 'Bonaventure's Angelology', in *A Companion to Bonaventure*, ed. Jay M Hammond, J. A. Wayne Hellmann, and Jared Goff (Leiden; Boston: Brill, 2014), 289–332); Scotus, passages from the *Ordinatio* (see Étienne Gilson, *Jean Duns Scot: Introduction à Ses Positions Fondamentales* (Paris: J. Vrin, 1952), ch. 5). Dante's *Paradiso* would also have a profound influence. On this period, see David Keck, *Angels and Angelology in the Middle Ages* (Oxford: Oxford University Press, 1998).

[16] Calvin, *Institutes of the Christian Religion*, book 1, ch. 16, nn. 3–20, and see Andrew Sulavik, 'Protestant Theological Writings on Angels in Post-Reformation Thought from 1565 to 1739', *Reformation & Renaissance Review* 8, no. 2 (2006): 210–23. On Luther, see Philip M. Soergel, 'Luther on the Angels', in *Angels in the Early Modern World*, ed. Peter Marshall and Alexandra Walsham (Cambridge: Cambridge University Press, 2006), 64–82.

[17] Jean Daniélou, *Les Anges et Leur Mission, d'après Les Pères de l'Église*, second edition (Paris: Éditions de Chevetogne, 1953), translated as *Angels and Their Mission*; E. L. Mascall, *The Angels of Light and the Powers of Darkness* (London: Faith Press, 1954); Barth, *Church Dogmatics: The Doctrine of Creation (III/3)*, §51, 367–531; Bulgakov, *Jacob's Ladder*.

popular approach, we find attempts to explain Biblical and other descriptions of angelic encounters as being, in fact, encounters with ETI and ET technology. This came to particular prominence in the late 1960s with a series of books – highly mythological works of demythologisation – by Erich von Däniken (born 1935), beginning with *Erinnerungen an die Zukunft* ('Memories of the Future'), translated as *Chariots of the Gods*.[18] Von Däniken's corpus is of little value to academic systematic theology, but it has a significant place in the sociological study of recent and contemporary religion.[19]

The opposite approach sees reports of encounters with ETI as encounters with angels. While he is not an academic theologian, Billy Graham has been influential on this score within recent Protestant Christianity. Graham viewed 'UFO sightings' as possibly angelic. While that remained only a suggestion for him, he was less reserved over the existence of ETI *per se*, writing 'I firmly believe there are intelligent beings like us far away in space who worship God. But we would have nothing to fear from these people. Like us, they are God's creation'.[20] Other interpretations represent

[18] Erich von Däniken, *Erinnerungen an die Zukunft* (Econ-Verlag, Düsseldorf 1968); *Chariots of the Gods? Unsolved Mysteries of the Past*, trans. Michael Heron (London: Souvenir, 1969). Kenneth Delano surveyed other attributions of religious traditions to extraterrestrial origins in *Many Worlds, One God*, 68–85, commenting 'Only if a person feels free to dispense himself from the need of good, firm evidence can he hold that the religions of mankind originated with the arrivals from other worlds of superior beings piloting UFOs' (67). According to Delano, 'the first person to expound the God-as-spaceman hypothesis at any great length was a British writer, B. Le Poer Trench [Brinsley Le Poer Trench, 8th Earl of Clancarty]', in *The Sky People* (London: Neville Spearman, 1960), according to whom religions have arisen from misunderstandings of such visits (*Many Worlds*, 69).
[19] Additional examples of this genre include Jean Sendy, *The Moon: Outpost of the Gods*, trans. Lowell Bair (New York: Berkley, 1975); Lee Gladden and Vivianne Cervantes Gladden, *Heirs of the Gods: A Space Age Interpretation of the Bible* (Beverly Hills, CA: Bel-Air Publishing Corporation, 1982), and a series of books by W. Raymond Drake.
[20] Billy (William Neil) Graham, *Angels: God's Secret Agents*, second edition (Nashville: W Publishing, 1994), 9–12, 15; *National Enquirer* (30 November 1976), quoted by

proposed encounters with ETI as meetings with angels in a fallen or demonic form, which has come to some prominence in Eastern Orthodox theology.[21]

The direct connection between ETI and angels has a deeper, if not now particularly influential, theological history. Mortimer Adler noted, for instance, that throughout the nineteenth-century German theological project to think about the possibility of life elsewhere in the physical universe, 'some attempt [was] made to relate the hypothesis of superior intelligences inhabiting other parts of the physical universe with the Biblical doctrine of God's heavenly host of holy angels'.[22] More recently, in *The Christian Faith,* the Dutch Reformed theologian Hendrikus Berkhof (1914–1995) considered exobiology in relation to angelic life, albeit in passing.[23] His interest is perhaps not surprising, given that an earlier work, *Christus en de Machten,* dealt with spiritual powers in the wake of the Second World War.[24] In the later book, Berkhof speculated that in some angelic encounters, including perhaps some of those in the scriptures, God had made use of 'extra-terrestrial beings'.[25] While

Ted Peters, *Science, Theology, and Ethics* (Aldershot: Ashgate, 2003), 126. One might reply, of course, that human beings are also 'God's creation', and that does not prevent them from sometimes doing harm. Implied here is probably 'God's unfallen creation'.

[21] Seraphim Rose, *Orthodoxy and the Religion of the Future* (Platina, CA: St. Herman of Alaska Brotherhood, 2004). The position has been endorsed by Metropolitan Hilarion, head of the Russian Orthodox Synodal Department for External Church Relations, in 2020 ('Russian Orthodox Church equates aliens with demons', *Interfax,* 20 April 2020, https://interfax.com/newsroom/top-stories/68479). For similar Orthodox interpretations in terms of the demonic, see Weintraub, *Religions and Extraterrestrial Life,* 116–17.

[22] Adler, *Angels and Us,* 9.

[23] Hendrikus Berkhof, *Christelijk geloof: Een inleiding tot de geloofsleer* (Nijkerk: Callenbach, 1973), with several subsequent editions. Quotations here are from *Christian Faith: An Introduction to the Study of the Faith,* trans. Sierd Woudstra (Grand Rapids, MI: Eerdmans, 1979), translating the Dutch fourth edition of 1978.

[24] Nijkerk: Callenbach, 1952; translated as *Christ and the Powers,* trans. John Howard Yoder, Scottdale: Herald Press, 1962.

[25] Berkhof, *Christian Faith,* 176.

it is not entirely clear what he had in mind, he seems to be talking about the sort of ETI envisaged in this book: the sort at least theoretically open to scientific investigation.

From discussions of angelic visitations in 'the Israelite-Christian faith', Berkhoff elaborates three useful principles:

> (a) God's world, including those beings who are consciously subject to him, is far richer than what can be seen on our planet; (b) outside this provisional and alienated world there are other realities which already now are fully and perfectly filled with his glory; and (c) these worlds do not look down with contempt on our darkened planet but possess a genuine willingness to be used in the service of God's love for man to help our work reach its destination.[26]

The third of these comments underlines Berkhoff's willingness to think about the entanglement of human and extraterrestrial stories, coming closer to generally far less academic writing, which I am otherwise not considering in this book. Between the other two principles, his less controversial proposal is that the presence of the angels in the Christian story stresses that there is more to creation than the human dimension and what is readily presented to our view. More contested is the idea that sin and the fall are not the only trajectory that life could take. As we will see in Chapter 10, much depends on one's views about freedom and the fragility of materiality. While his writing is too compressed to make this clear, Berkhoff was possibly thinking of life elsewhere which had fallen but was already fully redeemed.

Angelic Bodies

Theological writing on angels holds open a useful perspective on exobiology, witnessing as it does to the long-standing sense that

[26] Ibid.

human beings do not monopolise either intelligence or the attention of God. Nonetheless, quite how close an analogy angels offer depends on how we think of them, especially since the Christian tradition has been divided over whether to think of them as bodily or not. For some, they are pure spirit or intelligence: forms without matter.[27] For others, they have bodies and matter, albeit in a sense different from our own.[28] Lateran IV seems to have cultivated a certain ambiguity, distinguishing between angels as 'spiritual' and other creatures as 'corporeal' and 'sensible' (*mundanam*), while avoiding a contrast between angels and that which is material (*materialem*).[29]

Some scriptural writers seem to have a form of embodied existence in mind. After all, the 'sons of God', who lie with human women in Genesis 6, are usually interpreted as angels, and begetting is a bodily affair: 'the sons of God saw that they [female human beings] were fair… [and] the sons of God went in to the daughters of humans, who bore children to them'.[30] Later Jewish writing on angels is complex, and where they are said to be without bodies, that might mean that they do not have bodies as human beings do. For others, angels can take on the appearance of a human body for the sake of communication: a position that Aquinas would also support, writing that angels form bodies from air for the purpose of appearing.[31] Post-scriptural Jewish writing will tend to associate angels with

---

[27] In Aquinas, for instance, see *ST* I.50.1–2.

[28] For instance, John of Damascus, *On the Orthodox Faith*, II.3.

[29] Lateran IV, Constitution 1, in Tanner and Alberigo, *Decrees of the Ecumenical Councils*, 1:230. In the assessment of Paul Quay, this caution in wording reflected Pope Innocent III's hope of an end to the schism between East and West, given that the East had 'long spoken of the angels as both "spirits" and "material"' (Quay, 'Angels and Demons', 20, n. 2, 50, n. 38).

[30] Gen. 6.1–2, 4.

[31] Aquinas, *ST* I.51.2. Bulgakov, however, wrote that 'To fabricate some sort of luminous envelopes or gaseous bodies as an explanation for the possibility of this vision is a misunderstanding. The very forms in themselves simply become visible, as ideal forms' (Bulgakov, *Jacob's Ladder*, 146).

bodies of a less substantial form than those of human beings, often closer to basic elements, especially fire, although sometimes they are changed *into* fire or wind.[32] This association between angels and fire is also found in Psalm 104.4, and is picked up in Heb. 1.7.

In Christian theological writing, a certain angelic bodiliness, although of an ethereal form, is found in several of the Fathers, although there can be ambiguity (for instance, from Origen), and Augustine considers the matter undecided.[33] It remained a topic of lively discussion through to the seventeenth century.[34] Among Eastern Orthodox authorities, Bulgakov singles out the influence of Makary of Egypt here.[35] While the liturgy of the Eastern Church traditionally refers to the angelic host as the 'bodiless powers', its theology typically has them possessing some form of ethereal materiality.[36] Ultimately, even in the East, Bulgakov concluded that 'opinions are usually divided' between the position that angels have bodies somewhat comparable to those of human being, however 'subtle' those bodies may be, and that they do not. Indeed, Bulgakov concluded, the Eastern tradition contains 'seemingly contradictory propositions'.[37] For his part, Bulgakov considered the opinion

---

[32] 2 Enoch 29.3; 2 Baruch 21.6; Apocalypse of Abraham 15; 2 Esdras (sometimes knowns as 4 Esdras) 13.21.

[33] For instance, Tertullian, *On the Flesh of Christ*, ch. 6; Gregory the Great, *Moralia on Job*, II.3. On Origen, compare *On First Principles*, I.6.4 and I.7.7; Augustine, *City of God*, 15.23.

[34] See Anja Hallacker, 'On Angelic Bodies: Some Philosophical Discussions in the Seventeenth Century', in *Angels in Medieval Philosophical Inquiry: Their Function and Significance*, ed. Isabel Iribarren and Martin Lenz (London: Routledge, 2016), 201–14.

[35] Bulgakov, *Jacob's Ladder*, 143.

[36] John A. McGuckin, 'Angels', in *Encyclopedia of Eastern Orthodox Christianity*, ed. John A. McGuckin (Chichester: Wiley-Blackwell, 2010), vol. 1, 28–30. Thus, in a prayer from the Synaxis of the Archangel Michael and the Other Archangels, the Byzantine asks them 'beneath your wings of immaterial glory shelter us'.

[37] Bulgakov, *Jacob's Ladder*, 143. As an example, he refers to the seventh ecumenical council (Nicaea II, specifically session 5). See also Sergius Bulgakov, *Icons, and the Name of God*, trans. Boris Jakim (Grand Rapids, MI: Eerdmans, 2012), 96, n. 131.

that 'angels are corporeal' to be 'highly dubious',[38] writing that 'it is completely impossible to allow … for any sort of body whatsoever, even the most subtle, that would be indissolubly bound to an angelic spirit and clothe it'.[39]

In the Western Middle Ages, angelic materiality was the common position among Franciscan theologians, as an example of their 'universal hylomorphism': the contention that every creature without exception is composed of both form and matter (respectively *morphē* and *hylē* in Greek), angels included.[40] The contrasting perspective, that angels are pure spirit without bodies or matter, was typical among Dominicans, for instance, in the writings of Albert and Aquinas.[41] Despite being controversial in its day, Aquinas' position on angelic non-materiality would eventually become the generally accepted Roman Catholic perspective following his elevation as the 'common doctor' of the Church. More recently, from a Protestant perspective, Robert Jenson advocated universal materiality, maintaining that, while creatures may be more or less material in comparison to one another, they are all definitely material in comparison with God.[42] The danger there might be to conflate divinity too closely with immateriality.

[38] Ibid., 96.

[39] Bulgakov, *Jacob's Ladder*, 144.

[40] John F. Wippel, 'Metaphysical Composition of Angels in Bonaventure, Aquinas, and Godfrey of Fontaines', in *A Companion to Angels in Medieval Philosophy*, ed. Tobias Hoffmann (Leiden: Brill, 2012), 45–78. Much rested on whether the necessary contrast of creation (in its complexity) with divine simplicity could be upheld simply by pointing to the distinction in creatures between being and essence, or whether it was necessary also to be able to point to the difference between form and matter. More widely, see Franklin T. Harkins, 'The Embodiment of Angels: A Debate in Mid-Thirteenth Century Theology', *Recherches de Théologie et Philosophie Médiévales* 78, no. 1 (2011): 25–58.

[41] Albert, *In II Sent.* dist. 1A, art. 4; Aquinas, *ST* I.50.2. See James A. Weisheipl, 'Albertus Magnus and Universal Hylomorphism: Avicebron. A Note on Thirteenth-Century Augustinianism', *Southwestern Journal of Philosophy* 10, no. 3 (1979): 239–60; Wippel, 'Metaphysical Composition of Angels'.

[42] Robert Jenson, *Systematic Theology – Volume 2: The Works of God* (New York: Oxford University Press, 1999), 48–49.

In sum, the Christian tradition represents a variety of views as to whether angelic life is characterised by any form of materiality or embodiment. Even where that prospect has been most thoroughly entertained, however, angels have still been seen as strikingly different from what I mean in this book by material, biological ETI. Yet, even where the difference is most clearly articulated, as in Thomism, the point remains that including angels within one's picture of the world reflects an openness to the idea that human beings are not the only intelligent life in creation.

Beyond that, especially if one follows a strictly disembodied account of angelic existence, the angels may seem to offer little as a parallel for thinking about material life elsewhere in the universe. That turns out not entirely to be the case. In the next chapter, we go on to think about the nature of life, and later about questions of human uniqueness, and angles can play a useful contrasting role in thinking that through. Before closing this chapter, however, I will turn to two other ways in which life very different from our own has been considered within a theological picture, first beyond our planet, and then within it.

Living Astronomical Bodies

The provocation for this book is the prospect that many astronomical objects (planets and moons) could offer a dwelling for life. For much of human history, rather a different picture was often imagined, with astronomical objects seen not as places where other life might dwell, but as themselves alive. We have already encountered this in Plato and Aristotle. For the most part, the Biblical tradition seems to buck this trend, describing the sun and moon in Genesis 1 simply as lights, greater and lesser. However, the account of creation in Job has it that 'the morning stars sang together and all the heavenly beings shouted for joy',[43] and that may suggest some

---

[43] Gen. 1.16; Job 38.7.

relation or conflation between angels and stars. Similarly, the name Lucifer comes from the tradition of associating the principal fallen angel with the 'morning star'.[44]

Ancient and scholastic thought associated stars and planets with life on account of their movement. The heavenly bodies seemed to move relative to a stationary Earth, whether in the rotation of the heaven of the 'fixed stars' or in the motion of the planets (from the Greek for 'to wander'), and such seemingly purposeful movement seemed to imply life. While the resulting idea, of ensouled heavens and planets, seems an odd proposal to contemporary ears, it may be the closest analogy we have in the Christian theological tradition to material extraterrestrial life before the fifteenth century. With it, we are presented with the notion of distant heavenly bodies as living and even intelligent beings.

For those influenced by Aristotle, the tendency was to think of spiritual beings as animating principles (more like the soul, or *anima*), infusing the heavenly bodies, rather than as separate beings pushing them around. As Cornelio Fabro put it, 'above the material world [Aristotle admitted] the existence of spiritual substances, whether Intelligences or souls, as moving principles of the stars'.[45] Augustine also addressed this topic.

> The question is also commonly asked whether these visible luminaries are solely and simply bodies, or whether they have their own kind of spirits to direct them; and if they do, whether they are also 'inspirited' by them into living beings, as fleshly bodies are 'ensouled' by the souls ... or [whether] without any such mixture are just directed on their courses by the presence of them alone.[46]

---

[44] Isa. 14.12 seems to refer to a human being, but this passage was read alongside Ezek. 28, where the human/other-than-human distinction seems blurred, and alongside elaborations on this tradition in Luke 10.18 and Rev. 9.1.

[45] Cornelio Fabro, 'The Intensive Hermeneutics of Thomistic Philosophy: The Notion of Participation', trans. B. M. Bonansea, *Review of Metaphysics* 27, no. 3 (1974): 457, citing Aristotle, *De caelo* III, 2, 285a 25 ff.

[46] Augustine, 'Literal Meaning of Genesis', in *On Genesis*, trans. Edmund Hill (Hyde Park, NY: New City Press, 2002), II.18.38, 228.

Nothing, he thought, 'can easily be grasped on this point', one way or the other, although he hoped that 'study of the scriptures' might yet turn up passages to help him form an opinion. In the *Enchiridion*, he wrote, 'Nor am I certain whether the sun and the moon and all the stars belong to that same society [of the angels], although some people think that there exist shining bodies that do not lack sense or intelligence'.[47]

Both Aristotle and Augustine would influence Aquinas here, who surveyed various positions in *De Potentia*: 'Augustine leaves in doubt whether some immaterial substances have been united to heavenly bodies, although Jerome and Origen seem to assert it'.[48] In contrast 'several modern [i.e. mediaeval] authorities' reject it on the basis that the scriptures present us with human beings and angels, and living astronomical bodies are in neither class. For his part, Aquinas recognised that there could be a 'material' or purely physical dimension to the seemingly erratic movement of the heavenly bodies (such as epicycles).[49] Nonetheless, he was also guided by the belief that life and movement on Earth required the stirring influence of heavenly movement ('the heavenly bodies cause life in the world below'), and since nothing can produce an effect of a greater order than its own nature ('nothing acts beyond [the capacity of] its species'), and life is greater than non-life, the source of movement of the heavens must be living, one way or another. Rather than

---

[47] *Enchiridion*, §58, translation from *Augustine Catechism: Enchiridion on Faith Hope and Charity*, ed. Boniface Ramsey, trans. Bruce Harbert (Hyde Park, NY: New City Press, 2008), 87–88.

[48] *De Potentia*, 6.6, citing Augustine, *Literal Commentary on Genesis*, II.18.38; Jerome, *Commentary on Ecclesiastes*, on 1.6; Origen, *On First Principles*, I, 7, translation from *The Power of God*, trans. Richard J. Regan (Oxford: Oxford University Press, 2012), 179–80. Jerome likens the sun to a living animal. Origen holds both that the heavenly bodies are living (I.7.3) and that their souls were created prior to their bodies (I.7.4). See also *De Potentia*, 3.11 *ad* 13, where Aquinas states that heavenly bodies are not themselves animate, but are moved by 'an angel or God', discussed in relation to whether there is more than one form of rational animal in Chapter 9.

[49] *De Potentia*, 6.6 *obj.* 9.

supposing that the heavenly bodies were themselves alive, however, he preferred to interpret them as inanimate bodies moved by the will and power of incorporeal spirits.[50]

Today, as I have said, Biblical scholars are likely to point in rather the opposite direction, to the naturalism of the opening chapter of Genesis, according to which the sun and the moon are simply 'lights', not supernatural entities such as gods to be worshipped.[51] Compared to the typical assumptions of the ancient Near Eastern world, the sun and moon have been dethroned, and are claimed as simply one more part of God's creation: good, but not divine. However, the mediaeval vision of astronomical objects as ensouled beings is not as far from that as we might imagine. After all, angels and spiritual intelligences were seen to be every bit as created as earthworms: created beings that do God's will, and resolutely not objects of worship. It may also be anachronistic to suppose that the ancient Hebrew mind, in its striking naturalisation of astronomical objects, saw those objects in an equivalent way to us: as a lump of rock, or a ball of plasma.

Be that as it may, this naturalising tendency flowered with the discoveries of early modern science (perhaps even fostering them), which established the heavenly bodies to be as mundane as anything upon earth. A rapid succession of observations dispensed with the antique and mediaeval astronomical model, with its idea of incorruptible, unchanging celestial matter and animating spirits. For one thing, the movements of the heavens were found not to be 'perfect': which is to say – according to the standards of perfection at the time – that they are not circular but rather elliptical. Also important were observations of change among objects beyond the moon, since the lunar orbit had previously been thought to mark the boundary

---

[50] *De Potentia*, 6.6 *resp.*, and *ad* 10. We will return to animated astronomical bodies when we turn to Aquinas on whether there is more than one species of rational animal, in Chapter 9.

[51] Gen. 1.14–19.

of mutability. The discovery of sunspots offers a striking example, revealing change in even the most godlike of the heavenly bodies.[52] This implied that the heavens are made from material just like the Earth, and not of an incorruptible 'fifth element'. Already, Kepler had written in the conclusion of his *Harmonies of the World* that neither 'Intelligences as gods' nor 'innumerable armies of planetary spirits' were any more necessary to explain the motions of planets or the perceived motions of stars.[53] However, Kepler's dismissal of living beings as heavenly motors was no dismissal of life elsewhere in the cosmos. He encouraged his readers to enquire 'even if some intelligent creatures, of different nature from the human, happen to inhabit a globe [other worlds] which is in that way animated, or will inhabit it'.[54] Before closing his book with a prayer, he writes that God

> has created species to inhabit the waters, though there is no place under them for air, which livings things draw in; He has sent into the immensity of the air birds propped up by feathers; He has given to the snowy tracts of the north white bears and white foxes, as food the monsters of the sea to the one, the eggs of the birds to the other; He has given lions to the deserts of burning Libya, camels to the far spread plains of Syria, and endurance of hunger to the one, of thirst to the other. Has he then used up all His skill on the globe of the Earth so that He could not, or all His goodness, so that He would not wish to adorn with suitable creatures other globes also ...?[55]

Kepler thought not, and in that way, just as the idea of living stars and planets was waning, the prospect of life *on* other astronomical bodies began to be taken increasingly seriously.

---

[52] Galileo Galilei, *Istoria e dimostrazioni intorno alle macchie solari* (Rome: G. Mascadi, 1613).

[53] Kepler, *Harmony of the World*, 495.

[54] Ibid.

[55] Ibid., 497. Kepler also a wrote novel, in Latin, which was published after his death, describing a journey to the moon, which is inhabited (*Somnium, seu opus posthumum de astronomia lunari* (Sagan and Frankfurt: Sumptibus haeredum authoris, 1634)).

Other Creatures on Earth

In this chapter, I have principally pointed to angels as holding open a place in the Christian imagination (as in that of other religions) for the prospect of intelligent life beyond the human. In concluding this discussion, we might also remember that a variety of intelligent creatures besides angels and human beings have been entertained in Christianity and other religions, even if their place has primarily been within popular belief and lore, rather than scholarly reflection.

In Islam, one encounters the jinn, while within European Christianity we have the faery. A fascinating text here comes from the Scottish Presbyterian minister Robert Kirk (1644–1692), whose *The Secret Commonwealth* (published by Walter Scott in 1815) describes the place of fairy creatures in the thought and practice of his parishioners in the Scottish Highlands.[56] If angels are not much considered in contemporary academic theology (although they are by no means routinely denied), these other beings – fairies, mermaids, elves, trolls, boggarts, brownies, and so on – have been eclipsed almost entirely, not only in the academy, but also in the popular imagination, although they persisted longer in ritualised communal habit than in outright belief. My Lancastrian maternal grandmother (born in 1917) would always crush eggshells before discarding them, to prevent fairies from using them for boats. I doubt that she consciously believed that to be true, but the practice was formed in childhood. I mention such beings here not to endorse earlier beliefs, but as another example of how cultures steeped in Christian theology have readily entertained that there is more to the sum of sentient life than the human species. In at least one sense contemporary science is returning to this even on our own planet, with exploration of other 'diverse intelligences', among which the octopus and other cephalopods are perhaps emerging

---

[56] Robert Kirk, *The Secret Commonwealth of Elves, Fauns, and Fairies* (New York: New York Review Books, 2007).

as the most striking.[57] Recently, some theologians have argued that it is healthy to retain some sense of there being more in heaven and earth than can be found in any tidy philosophy, or at least that preserving such stories represents a sane holism. Among writers wanting to keep bonds to history and local custom intact, we find Stephen Clark, David Bentley Hart, and John Milbank.[58] Recalling belief in such beings, even if it is now largely banished from theological thought, further reminds us that Christian theology has long entertained a wide view of what might exist and be of value to God, with a picture of a varied and sometimes strange splendour of creation, much of it quite separate from, and tangential to, human existence.

[57] Peter Godfrey-Smith, *Other Minds: The Octopus, the Sea, and the Deep Origins of Consciousness* (New York: Farrar, Straus and Giroux, 2016).

[58] John Milbank, 'Fictioning Things: Gift and Narrative', *Religion & Literature* 37, no. 3 (2005): 1–35; John Milbank, 'Stanton Lecture 8: The Surprise of the Imagined' (Faculty of Divinity, University of Cambridge, 8 March 2011); David Bentley Hart, 'The Secret Commonwealth', in *A Splendid Wickedness and Other Essays* (Grand Rapids, MI: Eerdmans, 2016), 23–27; Stephen R. L. Clark, 'How to Believe in Fairies', *Inquiry* 30, no. 4 (January 1987): 337–55.

3 | Life

Astrobiology and theology are each concerned with life, even if they approach it in different ways. In this chapter, we explore those congruences and differences. In doing so, more than in any other chapter, we will find theology offering philosophical resources that may aid the scientist in her quest to understand life and its qualities. Moreover, in theological traditions of thinking about analogy, our sources also offer a deep and well-considered approach to how we might speak of many different things as living, but not all in an identical way.

Biology is focused on measurement and external assessment; theology is concerned with the experience of life from the inside, and with its value and meaning, in a way that goes beyond the professional concerns of the scientist. However, while biology and theology approach life differently, we can take those differences too far. Both disciplines address *life*, with no fallacy of equivocation there. Biology has more than molecules in view: we cannot understand life without reference to organs and organisms, and indeed to community, and to dwelling in an environment. Terrence Deacon points this out in relation to something as seemingly simply chemical as haemoglobin.[1] We can treat it in purely chemical terms, and that is

[1] Terrence W. Deacon, 'Emergence: The Hole and the Wheel's Hub', in *The Re-Emergence of Emergence: The Emergentist Hypothesis from Science to Religion*, ed. Philip Clayton and P. C. W Davies (Oxford: Oxford University Press, 2006), 111–50. On the phenomenal unlikeliness of any particular protein sequence ever existing, consider an analysis by Stuart Kaufmann. Imagine a protein consisting of two hundred units, each of which could be one of the familiar twenty amino acids. The shortest period in which anything can happen is the Planck time of 10^{-43} second,

indispensable, but it is not the whole story, not even for the scientist. We can also ask why such a molecule, enormously complex as it is, should occur in the world, and not some other arrangement of amino acids of equal chemical validity. To understand why there is haemoglobin in the world at all we need to understand it within the wider order of things. That takes in how this molecule functions presently within the physiological whole of the organism in its environment; it also takes in the history of how evolutionary processes have placed this particular molecule in nature, whittling down the 'space' of conceivable options to this particular configuration.

Biology's concern with life, then, cannot be reduced to genes and molecules without missing much of prime scientific interest. Nor should we say that theology attends to life only at a distance from biology, since theology and religion are profoundly concerned with flesh, birth, and death, among other themes. One only has to recall the role of the church in the development of the hospice movement, with figures such as Cicely Saunders and the All Saints' Sisters of the Poor. Many writers have commented that to the same extent that someone attends to the doctrine of the Incarnation, he or she should be invested in the provision of good drains.

Both theology and biology attend to life. At least sometimes, the study of biology makes use of categories familiar to the theologian, such as intention, form, or desire. Conversely, the study of theology often requires us to think concretely about the nature of this 'flesh', and its life. This has not always been obvious on either side. Mary Midgley, among others, observed the molecular-focussed biology of the mid- to late twentieth century, and pointed to the spectacle of biology – the

the universe is about 10^{17} seconds old, and the visible universe contains perhaps 10^{80} atoms. Even if all those atoms had been 'doing nothing since the Big Bang except making proteins in parallel at every tick of the Planck time clock', it would still take 10^{39} times the current age of the universe 'to make all the possible proteins of the length of 200 amino acids, *just once*' (*A World beyond Physics: The Emergence and Evolution of Life* (Oxford: Oxford University Press, 2019), 3). That it should come to be that any particular protein is routinely synthesised by a cell, compared to the unfathomably large number that are not, is a fact of stupefying specificity.

science of *bios* (life) – trying its 'damnedest to reduce life's distinctive patterns to ones found in things that are lifeless'.[2] Similarly, traditions of theology have not always shown interest in biology, or even in the category of life. Note, for example, how many reference works in theology include no entry on life: we are more likely to find an entry on 'eternal life' than on 'life' in a more biological sense.[3]

A proper concern with life requires that the theologian attend to what the scientist has to say. At the same time, they should be reluctant to cede the study of life in its entirety to biologists, as if life belonged primarily to natural science and only derivatively beyond that, as a borrowed term. I disagree, therefore, with the judgment of Holmes Rolston III that 'Life is literally a biological term but extend[s] by metaphor across a spectrum of key concepts in philosophy and religion'.[4] Not so.

Definitions of Life

Definitions of life are important for astrobiologists, not least as a guide for what to look for.[5] NASA has set the running in recent

---

[2] Mary Midgley, *The Solitary Self: Darwin and the Selfish Gene* (Durham: Acumen, 2010), 22. A return from this position is discussed in Daniel J. Nicholson, 'The Return of the Organism as a Fundamental Explanatory Concept in Biology', *Philosophy Compass* 9, no. 5 (May 2014): 347–59.

[3] We find no entry on 'life', for instance, in Jean-Yves Lacoste's three-volume *Encyclopaedia of Christian Theology* (London: Routledge, 2004), nor in the *Oxford Dictionary of the Christian Church* up to the third edition (Oxford: Oxford University Press, 1st ed. 1957, 3rd ed. 2005), although I have supplied one for the fourth. The *Anchor Bible Dictionary* contains entries on the 'tree of life', and one on the 'author of life', but none on life as such. The *New and Enlarged Handbook of Christian Theology* of 2003 stands out (Nashville, TN: Abingdon Press), edited by Donald W. Musser and Joseph L. Price, with an article on life by Daniel C. Maguire (306–7).

[4] Holmes Rolston III, 'Life, Biological Aspects', in *Encyclopedia of Science and Religion*, ed. J. Wentzel Van Huyssteen (New York: Macmillan Reference, 2003), 527.

[5] Steven A. Benner, 'Defining Life', *Astrobiology* 10, no. 10 (December 2010): 1021–30; Carol E. Cleland, *The Quest for a Universal Theory of Life: Searching for Life as We Don't Know It* (Cambridge: Cambridge University Press, 2020). Cleland has

years, describing life as 'a self-sustaining chemical system capable of Darwinian evolution'. While the theologian might well find such scientific definitions of life lacking, she also has theological reasons for humility and forbearance. Life in its fullest and truest sense is ascribed properly to God, whose life inexpressibly surpasses that of any creature. If we view life as a creaturely likeness to something truly divine, we may not be surprised to find it difficult to fathom.

As a guide for spotting something, definitions of life are more difficult to set out than one might expect. In searching for life elsewhere in the universe, we want a definition that touches upon the essence of life, but we currently have only the experience of life on one planet to go on. Perhaps there are no sufficient conditions for being alive, and even necessary conditions may prove slippery. In that case, we might want to approach the matter in terms of 'family resemblance,' as put forward by Ludwig Wittgenstein. In this way we could identify a cluster of characteristics, many or most of which might be found in each living thing, even though any one of them could be missing.[6] It is possible, given a sufficiently rich list, that we could avoid too many false positives or negatives.[7] Theology has its own history of thinking about life (even if reference works suggest otherwise), some of which may be of use to the scientist. Returning to NASA's definition – 'a self-sustaining chemical system capable of Darwinian evolution' – the theologian might raise an eyebrow at both 'chemical system' and 'capable of Darwinian evolution'. Life is said of both God and angels,

anthologised a wide range of discussions of the nature of life, with Mark A. Bedau, in *The Nature of Life: Classical and Contemporary Perspectives from Philosophy and Science* (Cambridge: Cambridge University Press, 2010). Lucas John Mix, who has written on astrobiology from a theological perspective, addresses life more generally in *Life Concepts from Aristotle to Darwin: On Vegetable Souls* (Cambridge: Palgrave Macmillan, 2018).

[6] Ludwig Wittgenstein, *Philosophical Investigations: The German Text, with a Revised English Translation*, trans. G. E. M. Anscombe, 3rd ed. (Oxford: Blackwell, 2001), I.65, 27.

[7] Edward N. Trifonov surveyed 123 definitions of life, and suggested 'nine groups of defining terms' in 'Vocabulary of Definitions of Life Suggests a Definition', *Journal of Biomolecular Structure and Dynamics* 29, no. 2 (October 2011): 259–66.

neither of which are 'chemical systems', nor 'capable of Darwinian evolution'. In one sense, the point hardly matters: it is not the purview of NASA to think about either God or angels. The concern, however, can be illuminating, since from a theological perspective neither evolution nor chemistry are definitive of life as such.

Take the idea of digital or 'artificial' intelligence, either produced *de novo* by some other intelligent life-form, or as a state to which earlier, carbon-based life has migrated: the view (which I find far-fetched) that human memory and consciousness could be 'uploaded' onto some sort of computer system. Such putative post-biological life may not reproduce, or it may do so in a non-Darwinian way, but that would not prevent it from being alive. Again, angels offer a useful thought experiment. If they either cannot or do not reproduce, that would not prevent them from being alive.[8] Indeed, some biological organisms are alive while also standing outside an evolutionary pathway. Sterile hybrids, such as mules or hinnies, are one example. If we are going to invoke evolution, then we should recognise that it characterises the past – and how something has come to be as it is – rather than the present or the future. Life, perhaps, always comes about by evolution, but it need not later be capable of evolution itself: it makes more sense to say that a living thing must have had parents than to say that it must be capable of having offspring. Here the discussion might move into the sort of ethical or political register familiar to the theologian, who may be wary of any definition of life that would exclude from its scope (even if only implicitly) anyone who is unable to bear children congenitally or on account of injury.

Turning to 'chemical system', while an imagined digital life would exist on circuits made of chemicals – silicon and various rare metals, perhaps – the theologian familiar with Aristotle might want to point out that the life it sustains would not be grounded primarily in the reactions of a 'chemical system'. The direct underlying substrate

---

[8] If that is what we are to understand by the statement that they 'neither marry nor are given in marriage' in Matt. 22.30.

for such life could be silicon-as-logic-gates, or the code that runs on those logic gates. As a parallel, consider that the words on this page are composed more fundamentally of letters than they are of ink, not least because the letters are indispensable for writing, but they can be realised equally well either in ink or in pixels. The scholastic theologian would comment that life is inherently a formal category, not a material one, such that the nature of the material or 'stuff' out of which it is constituted is strictly secondary.[9] The essence of life lies in the pattern, we might say, not in that which is patterned. That is not to deny that the life we are talking about is a phenomenon in matter; it is just to insist that the life lies in how the matter is, rather than in its materiality. Again, as a question of form, life is definitively one of those features that rests in the relation of the parts, and is destroyed when the parts are no longer conditioned each by the others.

This is the territory of hylomorphism: the distinction between form (that which emerges and coordinates) and matter (that out of which it emerges, and that which is coordinated). Life is formal: it is a property of the cohering and emerging whole. As formal, it is realised in matter but underdetermined as to what sort of 'matter' – what sort of substrate – that involves. It can be a chemical system, which is the only kind of substrate we know, but in theory it could be some other kind of system, such as a digital one. Some writers on artificial intelligence have suggested that the majority of intelligent extraterrestrial life, if it exists, would be in the sort of 'post-biological' state mentioned above: digital, perhaps, or something else that lies beyond our imagination.[10] The theologian need not be convinced by such suggestions, but they illustrate that a tradition of philosophy of which theologians have often been custodians – the Aristotelian

---

[9] The category of form aligns closely with definitions for life – including elements such as movement or the processing of information, for instance – while the category of matter aligns with the conditions for life: that *out of which* life might emerge.

[10] Susan Schneider, 'Superintelligent AI and the Postbiological Cosmos Approach', in *What Is Life? On Earth and Beyond*, ed. Andreas Losch (Cambridge: Cambridge University Press, 2017), 178–98.

distinction between form and matter – offers a good deal for the analysis of life. Even just among chemically based life (my focus), this distinction reminds us that formal concepts such as information and thermodynamics lie at the heart of what life consists in, and that they can be realised in different substrates or settings.

In this way, while the theologian might criticise existing definitions of life, her critique can play a positive role, offering additional resources for thinking about the nature of life, drawn from the riches of theological traditions. In this section, I will consider two additional philosophical resources of this kind that are familiar to theology: the relation of life to self-preservation, and to intentional self-movement.

Life, Self-Preservation, and Movement

To approach life in terms of self-preservation is to observe that life is intrinsically orientated towards life, and its continuance.[11] Among philosophical sources, we might consider Cicero: 'Every natural organism aims at being its own preserver, so as to secure its safety and also its preservation true to its specific type.'[12] Augustine also took this dynamic to be axiomatic about life:

> Mere existence is desirable in virtue of a kind of natural property. So much so that even those who are wretched are for this very reason unwilling to die ... Why, even the irrational animals, from the immense dragons down to the tiniest worms, who are not endowed with the capacity to think on these matters, show that they wish to

[11] We find this expressed across a great many philosophical and theological sources, as we will see, but also in domestic settings and rituals, such as the tendency for toasts to refer to the preservation and perpetuation of life, whether *salud, salute, santé*, or *Gesondheid* ('health') or, perhaps even more explicitly, *l'chaim* ('to life' or 'for life'). Self-preservation is gestured towards by the 'self-sustaining' element in the NASA definition, although my instinct is to say that this is offered primarily with metabolic elements in mind.

[12] Marcus Tullius Cicero, *De Finibus Bonorum et Malorum*, trans. Harris Rackham, 2nd ed. (Cambridge, MA: Harvard University Press, 1931), VI.16, 319.

exist and to avoid extinction. They show this by taking every possible action to escape destruction. And then there are the trees and shrubs. They have no perception to enable them to avoid danger by any immediate visible movement ... [and yet, they also act so as to] preserve their existence.[13]

We find a similar emphasis in Aquinas. Expounding the idea that the first and fundamental object of practical or moral reason is the search for that which is good, he considered three ways in which this can apply to human beings: that which applies to us solely as rational beings (such as 'a natural inclination to know the truth about God, and to live in society'), that which applies to us more broadly as animals (including propagation and the care for offspring), and that which applies to everything. Significantly for our purposes, Aquinas articulated the last of these in terms of self-preservation: 'in the human being there is first of all an inclination to good in accordance with the nature which he has in common with all substances: inasmuch as every substance seeks the preservation of its own being, according to its nature'.[14] As he puts it in the *Summa Contra Gentiles*, 'every thing loves its own being and desires its preservation, an indication of which is the fact that every thing resists its own dissolution.'[15] In a sense, that applies even to inanimate things ('all substances'), since something like self-preservation is fundamental to any formed thing. Even a vase is able, by virtue of its form, to push back against onslaughts that would challenge its integrity. In another sense, however, this applies particularly to life, which is why Aquinas would see living things as the best examples of what we mean by

---

[13] Augustine, *City of God*, 11.27.1, translation from *Concerning the City of God against the Pagans*, ed. G. R. Evans, trans. Henry Bettenson (London: Penguin, 2003), with a parallel in Augustine, 'Literal Meaning of Genesis', in *On Genesis*, ed. John E. Rotelle, trans. Edmund Hill (Hyde Park, NY: New City Press, 2002), 157–581, III.16.25, p. 247.

[14] *ST* II-I.94.2, with another discussion in II-I.85.6.

[15] *Summa Contra Gentiles* (hereafter *SCG*)II.41.5.

a 'substance'. With life, existence and self-preservation become an intention.[16]

Many of these ideas spring from Aristotle, for whom life was crucially characterised by an impetus to remain. He approached that in part under the concept of *entelécheia*, which Joe Sachs (in his 2011 translation of Aristotle's *Physics*) renders as 'being-at-work-staying-the-same'.[17] With our appreciation of both homeostasis and immune systems, modern science has made us even more acutely aware of how right Aristotle was to see, at the heart of life, this tendency for living things to resist the buffeting onslaught of their environment, making internally led adjustments to iron out perturbations and withstand insults.[18]

If we turn to consider movement as a definitive property of live, Aristotle again stands as the well-spring. Movement lies at the root of his distinction between animate and inanimate. To be living is to be animate, or self-animated: to have *within oneself* the principle, or source, of one's own movement.[19] A round stone can roll, but only because it is pushed, or drawn by gravity down a slope. In contrast, a mouse – or even moss – can move itself. This capacity for self-movement renders it animate: it reveals or involves possession of a soul, or *anima*. 'Soul', here, obviously, means something different from its common theological or popular sense. In the Aristotelian tradition, to speak of a soul is not to talk about something extraneous to a material thing, nor of something inherently immortal, but to say that the form of such a thing – what defines it, and what it adds up to as a coordinated whole – is characterised by self-initiated movement.

Developments in our understandings of metabolism over the past century or so again suggest that Aristotle had recognised in

[16] Kauffman, *A World beyond Physics*.
[17] Aristotle, *Aristotle's Physics: A Guided Study*, ed. and trans. Joe Sachs (New Brunswick, NJ: Rutgers University Press, 2011), 245.
[18] Lee Smolin discusses this feature life, which calls the ability to withstand 'bumps', in *The Life of the Cosmos* (Oxford: Oxford University Press, 1997), 155.
[19] Aristotle, *De Anima* I.2, where he writes that the two marks that, above all, distinguish life from non-life are movement and sensation.

movement something more profoundly characteristic of life than
he could have known. Not only do living things move spatially, they
also move internally. The metabolic warp and weft of life is characterised by movement: atoms moving through cycles of synthesis and degradation, molecules moving from one internal cellular
partition to another, and ions flowing through channels. Internally,
then, as well as externally, Aristotle's association of life with movement – duly extrapolated to take in biochemistry – seized upon
something truly fundamental to life.

In following Aristotle by associating life with movement, theologians are not grafting a purely philosophical idea onto a theological
system that otherwise knew nothing of it. The authors of both Old
and New Testament texts saw a close connection between life and
movement, as can be seen, for instance, in the tradition of speaking
of moving water as 'living'.[20] Movement also likely undergirds the
association of life with breath.[21]

The movement that is characteristic of life is not simply movement
of any form; it is self-directed movement. Even with the simplest
bacterium, its internal movements, and to some extent its external
movements and effects, have a responsive quality, making sense in
relation to some end or ends.[22] In this way, the theologian may wish
to say that in all life – even at its most basic – a spark of freedom is
to be found, a flicker of what a philosopher working from the perspective of phenomenology might call 'intentionality'. To be alive
is to be oriented towards the world, and to have an interest in one's
environment; it is to respond to that environment with something
at least analogous to desire. Moreover, this is not a mere responsiveness to one's environment, taken simply as a given. To at least some
degree, all living organisms respond to their environments with

---

[20] For instance, Num. 19.17; Jer. 2.13, 17.13; Zech. 14.8; John 4.14.

[21] For instance, Gen. 2.7, 6.17; 1 Kings 17.17; Psalm 104.29; Job 27.3; Acts 17.25.

[22] I have discussed this in 'All Creatures That on Earth Do Make a Dwelling: Ecological
Niche Construction and the Ubiquity of Creaturely Making', *Philosophy, Theology
and the Sciences* 7, no. 2 (2020): 181–204.

purposeful attempts to adapt them, a point which I will discuss in terms of 'niche construction' in the next chapter.

The theologian, then, has much to say about life as such. Speaking from my own Thomist tradition, I have stressed the value of thinking about life hylomorphically, and in terms of self-preservation and self-movement (within which I have included intentionality, and life as a will-to-life). These angles are closely linked. On the one hand we have the ability to resist being moved, or changed, by another. On the other, we have self-movement and an ability to effect change. In one sense, self-movement and responsiveness seem to come first, in that self-movement allows for the pursuit of self-preservation. In another, self-preservation seems to be more fundamental, as a good or end: self-movement and responsiveness are exercised for the sake of self-preservation.

Life and Analogy

The subject of astrobiology is life, yet an unambiguous definition of life eludes us, largely on the basis that we have only one set of examples to consider. However convinced one might be by ideas of convergence in evolution (see Chapter 9), any life elsewhere in the universe is likely to be diverse, not least since life on Earth is also varied. Faced with such a plurality of things to speak about, theology has something conceptually useful to offer with an account of analogy, already well illustrated by its sense that a wide variety of things may be described as living. Alongside plants and animals, with human beings among them, theologians consider angels to be alive, although in a mode quite different from physical creatures, and they maintain that God is most alive, albeit unthinkably differently.[23]

---

[23] 'The word "life" is also applied to the Creator himself, and his life is life in the highest degree' (Augustine, *On Free Choice of the Will*, trans. Thomas Williams (Indianapolis, IN: Hackett, 1993), II.17, 63).

The theologian, and especially the scholastic theologian, might readily turn to the category of *analogy* as offering a fruitful way to think about how things can be alike but not identical or, indeed, be much different, yet still show flickers of a comparability worth speaking about.[24]

Indeed, life presents us with particularly fascinating cases for analogical thinking, stretching beyond biological beings. We speak analogically by talking about a living ecosystem, or a living cosmos. Indeed, we can go further still, and ask what sort of relationship applies between our terminology when we speak also about a lively debate, the vitality of a poem, living water, or the common life of a nation.[25]

Analogy deals with how we might use the same word in different circumstance. In doing so, it sits between two outlying positions. One of those extremes is equivocity, when we use the 'same' word in more than one situation, but only accidentally, as when we might talk about the 'bark' of a tree and the 'bark' of a dog. The other extreme is univocity, when we use a word in different contexts and mean exactly the same thing by it, as when we describe both a lion and a panther as a 'cat'. In contrast to univocity, analogy recognises difference; in contrast to equivocity, it recognises kinship.

On the relation of all life to God, the source of life, we might turn to Pseudo-Dionysius, as one of the relatively few 'household name' theologians to have written explicitly about life, and with a strong sense of analogy, in book six of *On the Divine Names*.[26] The variety found within created life, he writes, reflects a gradation of reception from God, who is the source of life: 'From this Life [God's life] … every living being and plant, down to the last echo of life,

---

[24] For a more extensive discussion of analogy than space allows here, see my *Participation in God: A Study in Christian Doctrine and Metaphysics* (Cambridge: Cambridge University Press, 2019), ch. 7, and 'Machine Learning and Theological Traditions of Analogy', *Modern Theology* 37, no. 2 (April 2021): 254–74.

[25] See my 'Living Worlds in Christian Theology', in *Life as a Planetary Phenomenon*, ed. William Storrar and Joshua Mauldin (forthcoming, 2023).

[26] Pseudo-Dionysius, *On the Divine Names*, VI.1, translation from *The Complete Works*, trans. Colm Luibheid and Paul Rorem (Mahwah, NJ: Paulist Press, 1987), 103.

has life'. Everything he lists lives, but its life ranges from the fullness of the angels, down to 'the last echo of life'. In the drier language of Bernard Wuellner, those degrees within life would be 'analogical levels of immanent perfection in the ranks of living things, namely plants, animals, men, angels, and God'.[27]

Analogy combines a note of similarity with one of difference. However great the difference one might wish to stress between divine and creaturely life, the Abrahamic traditions have still wanted to say both that creatures are alive and that God is alive and, outside of a few examples, they intend more than equivocation.[28] God is described as the 'living God' across a notably wide range of Biblical books.[29] God is also called the source, or giver, of life. In the Book of Acts, for instance, Christ is described as 'the Author of life', and God as the one who 'gives to all mortals life and breath and all things', such that 'In him we live and move and have our being'.[30]

God, truly and absolutely, is alive; creatures are alive by imitation, receiving life, as everything else, from God, yet both God and creatures are properly said to live. The relation between those uses is analogical, which can name likeness against the backdrop of a still greater unlikeness. No organism could monopolise what it means to live. Indeed, if God is the primary analogate for life – the one in whom the meaning of 'life' finds its fullest, indeed perfect, expression – that opens the way for us to speak all the more readily about living planets, or about the cosmos as living or animated, or for that

---

[27] Bernard Wuellner, *A Dictionary of Scholastic Philosophy*, 2nd ed. (Milwaukee, WI: Bruce Publishing Company, 1966), 'Degrees of Life', under 'Life', 171, emphasis added. I would have a concern here about placing God alongside creatures on any graded scale, even at the top.

[28] Maimonides, for instance, treats language about God equivocally, and divine life in particular, in *Guide of the Perplexed*, I.57–58. See my *Participation in God*, 177–78, 195.

[29] Examples include Deut. 5.26; Josh. 3.10; 1 Sam. 17.26; 2 Kings 19.4; Ps. 84.2; Jer. 10.10; Dan. 6.20; Hos. 1.10; Matt. 16.16; Rom. 9.26; 2 Cor. 3.3; 1 Thess. 1.9; 1 Tim. 3.15; Heb. 12.22; with variants such as Isa. 57.15; Dan. 4.34; Rev. 4.10.

[30] Acts 3.15; Cf. Acts 17.25, 28 and Gen. 2.7; Ps. 104.30; Job 33.4; John 1.4.

matter about living water and music as full of vitality.[31] All of that would also be a witness, in yet more disparate ways, to the Living God as the giver of life. We might even say that the vitality of life is seen not only in the paradigmatic cases of life itself (in biology), but also in the analogically related breadth of how it is realised. Indeed, so fundamental has been the belief that God abounds in life, and that the cosmos is marked by that characteristic of God as its exemplar, that theological discussions have often assumed that the universe contains much life, even that wherever there is habitability, there is habitation. It is to that conjunction that we turn, having in this chapter demonstrated that our theological traditions have a good deal to say about the nature of life, as well as resources for setting out how something – here, life – might be recognised and named analogically as similar but across cases also marked by difference.

---

[31] Aquinas discusses the idea of water as 'living' in *ST* I.18.1 *ad* 3.

4 | Emptiness and Plenitude

Our search for life in the universe has, until recently, focused on *habitability*. We have been interested in places that could have a liquid solvent (typically, but not necessarily, water), a source of energy, and the absence of conditions that seem prohibitively destructive. While cells, for instance, can evolve to be more resilient to radiation than we once imagined, it is unlikely that life could survive constant, intense bombardment by gamma rays. As we saw in the introduction, technology has now put us at the cusp of being able to identify the composition of gases in the atmospheres of planets around other stars with sufficient precision to reveal perturbations due to life. That will transform our search from guesses at habitability to a search for *inhabitation*. In this chapter we will find that Christian theology, shaped by an inherently teleological outlook, has often found it difficult to imagine habitable places other than as being for habitation, and therefore also as inhabited.

Consult passing discussions of the life elsewhere in the universe written by theologians down the centuries, and we commonly find the inclination not only to accept that life could be present elsewhere in the universe, but even to expect it. This expectation is not just that life exists somewhere out there, but that it will be present *wherever it can be*. Here they echo the perspective of the Greek astronomer of antiquity Cleomedes (dates unclear, possibly second century AD), albeit in his case writing not about different planets, but regions of the Earth: 'Nature loves Life, and Reason requires that all of the Earth, where possible, be filled with animal life, both rational and irrational'.[1]

Our focus in this chapter is a common set of theological arguments and assumptions about why those expectations have been in place. One stems from the purpose of creation, supposing that if the cosmos was created for the sake of life, large-scale emptiness would not befit it. It starts with the prospect of emptiness and rejects it. The other starts with absolute fullness, in the life and being of God, and sees that too as pointing towards a universe full of life and variety. These two approaches are not incompatible.

Historical Arguments: The Unsuitability of Emptiness

Historically, right through to the eighteenth and nineteenth centuries, we encounter arguments for widespread inhabitation on the basis of habitability. Once other stars were recognised as equivalent to our own sun, the assumption followed that these stars also possessed their own solar systems of planets. Even where other star systems were not in view as possible homes for life, other planets in our solar system were, based on a mistaken assumption of similarity between them. Where there was habitability, there was assumed to be habitation. In his influential book of 1854, *More Worlds Than One*, David Brewster wrote that 'Wherever there is matter there must be Life; Life Physical to enjoy its beauties – Life Moral to worship the Maker, and Life Intellectual to proclaim His wisdom and His power'.[2]

---

[1] *Cleomedes' Lectures on Astronomy: A Translation of The Heavens*, trans. Alan C. Bowen and Robert B. Todd (Berkeley: University of California Press, 2004), I.1, 37.

[2] Brewster, *More Worlds Than One*, 171. Theodore Hesburgh suggested that there should be a profusion of that which best reflects God ('intelligence and freedom') and not simply a profusion of matter, which reflects God less well ('Foreword', in *The Search for Extraterrestrial Intelligence: SETI*, ed. Philip Morrison, John Billingham, and John Wolfe (Washington, DC: Government Printing Office, n.d.), vii, quoted in Thomas O'Meara, *Vast Universe*, 15). Earlier than any of these writers, Christiaan

One foundation here is sometimes known as 'the principle of mediocrity': the assumption that what is true of Earth is not an exception. More likely than not, what applies here also applies elsewhere.[3] Many of our theological forebears held that the universe was large and contained a great many habitable planets, and from this assumption of habitability they inferred habitation: if there are cradles for life, they could not imagine them to be empty. We might discern here the influence of a line from the forty-fifth chapter of Isaiah:

> For thus says the Lord,
> who created the heavens
>   (he is God!),
> who formed the earth and made it
>   (he established it;
> he did not create it a chaos,
>   he formed it to be inhabited!):
> I am the Lord, and there is no other.[4]

Approached in purely scientific terms, the proposal that if a place is habitable then it will be inhabited is fallacious. A more modest or probabilistic approach fares better: given that the evolution of life is possible, and we already know of a great many places where it might have happened, the larger we take the universe to be, the less plausible a wholesale lack of life beyond Earth begins to look. The principle of mediocrity returns here: better to suppose that our planet is not strikingly unusual.

These were theological discussions, however, as much as they were scientific, and their authors viewed the cosmos teleologically:

Huygens had written that 'no reason would permit' that a universe of other planets should contain 'but vast Deserts' (Huygens, *Celestial Worlds Discover'd*, 21 – the translation is anonymous).

[3] Numerically speaking, the tendency was an over-estimation of the proportion of stars with habitable planets, compared to what we know today, although that assumption is offset by our knowledge of quite how large our galaxy is (with its approximately 100 billion stars), not to mention that we now know our galaxy to be only one of many.

[4] Isa. 45.18, emphasis added.

they saw the universe, and its habitability, as being for the sake of inhabitation, and inhabitants.[5] Richard Bentley (1662–1742) had made a parallel argument based on usefulness, that just as heavenly bodies close to Earth are useful to human beings, those elsewhere were created for 'like uses' by other 'intelligent minds'.[6] Others argued that God created so that his works could be seen, and be a cause of rejoicing and praise to God. On that view, a universe that exceeded the capacity of human beings to observe it, on account of either its size or age, or both, would call for additional observers. In the words of the Jesuit L. C. McHugh, for instance,

> Does it not seem strange to say that His power, immensity, beauty, and eternity are displayed with lavish generosity through unimaginable reaches of space and time, but that the knowledge and love which alone give meaning to all this splendor are confined to this tiny globe where self-conscious life began to flourish a few millennia ago?[7]

Another perspective considered the limited array of life on Earth compared to the vastness of the universe, and thought it unlikely that that Earthly life, even human life, could be all there is. The French theologian Jean Guiton wrote in 1956 that there would be something preposterous in supposing that the universe, in all its size and splendour, is simply a backdrop for human beings: 'Le socle est trop grand pour la statue' – the plinth is too large for the sculpture.[8]

[5] Even outside an explicitly religious perspective, in recent decades at least some variants of the 'anthropic principle' in contemporary cosmology have addressed the question as to whether the cosmos is inherently poised to produce life.

[6] Richard Bentley, *A Confutation of Atheism from the Origin and Frame of the World* (London: H. Mortlock, 1693), part III, 6.

[7] L. C. McHugh, writing in *America* 104 (1960), 296, quoted by Kenneth Delano, *Many Worlds, One God*, 14. The argument had been made earlier by Januarius De Concilio, *Harmony between Science and Revelation* (New York: Fr Pustet, 1889), 219–20.

[8] Jean Guitton, *Jésus* (Paris: B. Grasset, 1956), quoted by Ludwik Kostro, 'Some Philosophical and Theological Implications of Modern Astrobiology', in *The History and Philosophy of Astrobiology: Perspectives on Extraterrestrial Life and the Human Mind*, ed. David Duner et al. (Newcastle upon Tyne: Cambridge Scholars Publishing, 2013), 264.

Although I am warmly disposed towards the suggestion of life elsewhere in the universe, I find this argument weak, and at the same time both too anthropocentric and insufficiently invested in the remarkable character of life, and of rational life in particular. While the argument is ostensibly put forward to avoid supposing the cosmos fundamentally to be about humans, it nonetheless assumes that cosmic inorganic reality, in all its vastness and variety, could at best play a supporting role to human life.[9] In contrast to Guiton, I would rather say that star clusters and frozen moons, neutron stars and supernovae, gravitational waves and the aurora borealis in the skies of uninhabited planets are part of the 'sculpture', and not simply a 'plinth'.

Thinking of life as the statue, and the inorganic world as its plinth, as Guiton did, also risks too much of a separation of life from matter, and the Gnosticism of supposing that matter *qua* matter is of no consequence. Nothing that exists fails to participate in God, receiving a likeness to at least some divine nobilities. Inanimate matter is not without form, beauty, or value. Life certainly possesses a new and remarkable quality, compared to the inanimate – the climbing hydrangea on the wall outside my window may outshine the sun when it comes to life, as I outshine that plant as to reason (as a further intensification of the divine likeness) – but we are all creatures: the human being, the hydrangea and the wall, alongside suns or dwarf planets. We are all creatures, and God is not.

A first argument against the 'too large a plinth' position, then, is that it does not take the dignity of inanimate things sufficiently seriously. At the same time, it suffers the opposite fault of not taking seriously enough the remarkable character of life, and of

---

[9] Edward Milne, in a passage to be discussed below, seems to share this position, in that he thinks that 'God could scarcely find the opportunities to enjoy himself, to exercise his Godhead, if a single planet were the seat of His activities' (*Modern Cosmology and the Christian Idea of God* (Oxford: Clarendon Press, 1952), 152). By this, tellingly, he means a single inhabited planet, namely our own. Nothing else in creation seems to count when it comes to God's delight.

rational life most of all: 'of all knowable things, knowledge itself is by far the most amazing thing there is'.[10] The rest of creation is of enormous dignity, even that which is simply and only inorganic, but that does not prevent us from saying, on top of that, that there is something additionally extraordinary about life, even if we find it only on this planet, and supremely with life that is rational and self-aware, with knowledge and capacity to will and to love. For that, no 'plinth' (if we were to use that language) would be too large or grand.

Turning back to the sun, the hydrangea, and the human being, words of W. Norris Clarke come to mind, setting this out in terms of an 'intensity of being':

> [Life] infuses [the living thing] with an increased perfection, a more intense degree of being. We may say, therefore, that living things exist more intensely; they have a higher pitch of being: they are more. The flower growing unobserved and hidden in a crevice upon the highest mountain has a greater interiority and intensity of being; it is more than the mountain, greater in its inner perfection than the giant and majestic beauty of the physical universe: it is more. In this light we may read Aquinas' remark: *nobilitas cuiuscumque rei est sibi secundum suum esse* [Every excellence in any given thing belongs to it according to its being].[11]

Anselm had written much the same in the *Monologion*. Thinking of the contrast between the inanimate, the living-but-irrational, and the living-and-rational, he wrote that 'some natures exist more than

---

[10] Étienne Gilson, *The Spirit of Thomism* (New York: Kenedy and Sons, 1964), 16. Both Augustine and Aquinas, as O'Meara notes (*Vast Universe*, 33), wrote that the justification of a single sinner is a greater work than even the creation of the universe (*ST* II-I.113.9). It is an interpretative jump, however, for O'Meara to go from that to saying that a 'single free, intelligent creature touched by God's grace' is 'more valuable than the entire material universe'.

[11] Fran O'Rourke, 'Virtus Essendi: Intensive Being in Pseudo-Dionysius and Aquinas', *Dionysius* 15 (1990): 68–69, quoting *SCG* I.28.2, *correcting cuiusque to cuiuscumque*.

others [*magis minusue sint*] ... [and the] comparative excellence ... [of something is found in] its comparative proximity, through its natural essence, to superlative excellence'.[12]

The emergence of life within the realm of the non-living is a shift of the highest significance. It is so profound, on a qualitative level, as to render quantitative comparisons otiose, such as contrasting the size or mass of what lives in the cosmos to the size or mass of what does not. Moreover, to see the rest of creation, were it without life, as somehow 'empty' may be an additionally unfortunate way to describe a cosmos that contains even one living planet. Even were Earth the only place to harbour life, the cosmos would not be 'empty' of life, since it would contain our planet, and its inhabitants. To say that the rest of the cosmos is empty would be like going to a concert hall to hear a cellist of the first rank playing Bach's suites and complaining that, apart from that performer, the stage was 'empty'. In one sense it would be true, but it would radically miss the point. The cellist, and Bach's music, would command the stage, and what stage, what auditorium – what cosmos, indeed – would be too grand for such music? Above all, the Christian theologian would want to say that the Incarnation, even more than the presence of human life, crowns the extraordinary dignity of life on Earth, or the dignity of even the entire cosmos.

Life and Fullness

When the prospect of life elsewhere in the universe has been approached in terms of the doctrine of creation, authors have often, even typically, been open to it. That, as we have seen, can be pursued in 'negative' terms, by rejecting the idea that creation could be characterised as widespread emptiness (even if I would argue that

---

[12] *Monologion*, §31, translation from Anselm, *The Major Works*, ed. Brian Davies and G. R. Evans (Oxford: Oxford University Press, 2008), 47.

a universe devoid of life beyond Earth is hardly 'empty'). The alternative approach is not to start from creation, and its qualities, but from God as its creator, and from divine plenitude.

If the premise of the first approach is that the cosmos is for life, this second approach adds that the cosmos is for the communication and display of divine excellences (among which life is particularly significant). That, in turn, is seen to entail (or at least suggest) multiplicity and diversity, and therefore to undergird an expectation that life would be widespread and, perhaps, diversely realised.

The basic proposal has been set out often, by writers as different as the contemporary Dominican Thomas O'Meara and the twentieth-century astronomer Edward Arthur Milne, but it will be worthwhile to elaborate upon it here.[13] Aquinas – admittedly never far from discussion in this book – is of particular value, since ideas of multiplicity and variety are so central a concern to his writing on creation.

Consider, for instance, this passage from the first part of the *Summa Theologiae*.

> The distinction and multitude of things come from the intention of the first agent, who is God. For he brought things into being in order that his goodness might be communicated to creatures, and be represented by them; and because his goodness could not be adequately represented by one creature alone, he produced many and diverse creatures, that what was wanting to one in the representation of the divine goodness might be supplied by another. For goodness, which in God is simple and uniform, in creatures is manifold

---

[13] O'Meara wrote that 'God artistically creates the cosmos… and intends a universe that is diverse' (*Vast Universe*, 31). See also Milne's comment in n. 9 above, although it is not ideally well phrased from the perspective of a doctrine of God. On a traditional view, God is perfectly and eternally fulfilled by virtue of enjoyment of God's own perfect life. Creation is entirely gratuitous, and while God delights in it, creation does not add anything to God's own perfect joy, not even were creation infinite.

and divided and hence the whole universe together participates the divine goodness more perfectly, and represents it better than any single creature whatever.[14]

In some passages, Aquinas set this out in the quasi-quantitative terms of the relation between finitude and infinitude.[15] On other occasions, he used the more qualitative language of the (non-)comparison between divine and creaturely perfection, or the perfection of the one divine exemplar and the many particular and partial creaturely likenesses.

> Since every created substance must fall short of the perfection of divine goodness, in order that the likeness of divine goodness might be more perfectly communicated to things, it was necessary for there to be a diversity of things, so that what could not be perfectly represented by one thing might be, in more perfect fashion, represented by a variety of things in different ways.[16]

An important aspect of this analysis rests on the difference between two kinds of likeness between causes and effects. On the one hand, an effect can be equal to its cause, when both cause and effect are the same kind of thing (of the same 'species', as he put it). This is 'univocal causation', and human generation is an example, since a child is equal in humanity to its parents. With the other sort of causation, an effect falls short of its cause as a full expression of its reality, being of a different kind, as when the print left in mud by a dog's paw expresses a likeness to the animal, but only a very partial one. This is non-univocal causation.[17]

---

[14] *ST* I.47.1, and see *SCG* II.45.3.

[15] *SCG* II.45.5; *De Veritate*, 23.1 *ad* 3 and 23.4 *co*. I think an argument can be made, however, that Aquinas' conception even in these passages is not fundamentally quantitative.

[16] *SCG* III.97.2. Bonaventure writes on the same theme in *Breviloquium* II.3.

[17] What I am calling 'non-univocal' causation here might often be called 'analogical'. In scholastic writing it is often called 'equivocal causation', but that does not imply a complete disjunction, or merely accidental relation of effect to cause. On the distinction

Creation is eminently an example of the second sort of relation of likeness between cause and effect. Aquinas saw creaturely multiplicity as a direct consequence of this.

> Created things cannot attain to a perfect likeness to God according to only one species of creature. For, since the cause transcends the effect, that which is the cause, simply and unitedly, exists in the effects in composite and multiple fashion – unless the effect attain to the species of the cause; which cannot be said in this case, because no creature can be equal to God. The presence of multiplicity and variety among created things was therefore necessary that a perfect likeness to God be found in them according to their manner of being.[18]

This finds crystalline expression in *De Potentia*, where creation is helpfully contrasted with the eternal begetting of the Son. Eternal generation, alongside the spiration of the Spirit, is the paradigmatic example of univocal causation ('God from God, Light from Light, True God from True God', as the Nicene Creed has it), whereas creation is profoundly non-univocal as an effect in relation to its cause.[19]

This approach to creation, as finite likenesses of divine plenitude, expressed in multiplicity and variety, places a strong emphasis on diversity. That may not be a sufficient basis for the theologian to make predictions about exobiology, but it does at the very least accord with a universe containing a multiplicity and variety of life beyond the Earth. Writing about providence, Aquinas went so far as to say that multiplicity, or what he called 'the numerical plurality of things', stands near the summit of the divine plan for creation. First place belongs to 'divine goodness as the ultimate end' of all of God's works, but next comes 'numerical plurality of things', which

---

between these forms of causation, see *ST* I.4.2–3; *On the De Trinitate of Boethius* 1.2; *Commentary on the Metaphysics of Aristotle*, book 7, 8, n. 1448. On other occasions, one form is discussed alone, as in *SCG* I.29. McInerny treats the distinction in *The Logic of Analogy: An Interpretation of St. Thomas* (The Hague: Nijhoff, 1971), 126–35.

[18] *SCG* II.45.2. C.f. *ST* I.75.5 *ad* 1.

[19] *On Power* 3.16 *ad* 12, translation modified. There is a parallel discussion in *ST* I.33.2 *ad* 4.

is 'the first rational principle in creatures', such that to its 'establish-ment and conservation … all other things seem to be ordered'.[20] Today, our sense of the expanse of the canvas on which this numer-ical plurality might be worked out is so much larger.

Aquinas commented that more is added to creation's imitation of God's perfections by a diversity of species than by a multiplica-tion of individuals within a species.[21] Even more significant for him is the presence of variety among the 'grades' of being. Indeed, he went so far as to write that the universe would be fundamentally lacking, and imperfect, if any of the particular grades of being that it might possess were missing.[22] His underlying sense of those 'grades' was ultimately influenced by Porphyry's commentary on Aristotle's *Categories* (the *Isagoge*), distinguishing between that which is only material (inanimate things, or 'minerals'), those things which add life (vegetables), those which add sensation (animals), and those which add rationality (human beings).[23] The angels also belong in this picture, sharing rationality with human beings, but not their materiality, and reflecting many gradations among them.

Nothing is necessarily implied about extraterrestrial life from an argument about realisation of gradations of creation, unless it were to exemplify some addition grade, which we might not be able to imagine.[24] However, the point about a variety of species (rather

[20] *SCG* III.97.11.
[21] *SCG* II.93.5, c.f. II.84.5.
[22] 'All possible natures are found in the order of things; otherwise, the universe would be imperfect' (*SCG* II.91.6).
[23] '"Substance" itself is a genus. Under this is "body", and under "body", "animated body", under which "animal", under "animal" "rational animal", under which "human being"' (*Isagoge* section 2, translation from Richard Bosley and Martin M. Tweedale, eds., *Basic Issues in Medieval Philosophy: Selected Readings Presenting the Interactive Discourses among the Major Figures* (Orchard Park, NY: Broadview Press, 1997), section 2 ('on species'), 359). 'Under' here (*sub*) does not mean 'less than', but 'falling under the broader category of'.
[24] In the discussion of the *imago dei* below, that would align with the possibility of a form of likeness to God that is simply different in kind from our own, rather than only in degree.

than more course-grained grades) better reflecting divine perfection than a diversity of individuals does bear upon the question about life beyond Earth. Additional species, with what might be in many ways fundamentally different forms of life, would expand the fullness of creation's capacity to reflect divine perfection in a creaturely way. That applies not only to diversity of phenotype, as a biologist might put it, but also to additional diversity through the cultures that such creatures would create, not least in forms of artistic, moral, and religious life.

The Cosmos as Finite or Infinite

For some thinkers, such theological considerations have weighed so strongly in favour of an expectation of life elsewhere in the universe that the logic was pushed in the direction of an *infinitude* of creaturely expressions of divine perfection: both animate and inanimate.[25] If divine plenitude leads to creaturely variety, then divine infinitude might seem to suggest an infinite diversity of creatures. That is not to say that an actual infinity of diverse creatures would, when taken together, completely reflect divine infinitude, but that it would do better than any finite range of variety.

Aquinas addressed this, and rejected it, based on an Aristotelian repulsion at the idea of an 'actual infinitude', which – he thought – would destroy order and proper boundedness. A useful passage here deals with whether the universe is, or could be, of infinite age.[26] Since

[25] Bruno, *De l'infinito universo et Mondi: All'illustrissimo Signor di Mauuissiero* Whether Nicholas of Cusa held the universe to be infinite in *On Learned Ignorance* is disputed. See Tyrone Tai Lun Lai, 'Nicholas of Cusa and the Finite Universe', *Journal of the History of Philosophy* 11, no. 2 (1973): 161–67.

[26] I have discussed this topic in relation to contemporary cosmology in 'Looking Back towards the Origin: Scientific Cosmology as Creation Ex Nihilo Considered "from the Inside"', in *Creatio Ex Nihilo: Origins and Contemporary Significance*, ed. Markus Bockmuehl and Gary Anderson (Notre Dame, IN: University of Notre Dame Press, 2017), 367–89.

'all things participate in God's goodness so far as they have being', he wrote, it would seem that 'the more enduring they are, so much the more do they participate in God's goodness'. It may appear 'proper' to divine goodness not to create a universe that would exist for 'some limited time only', but rather that 'some created things should have existed from eternity'.[27] Against this, Aquinas offered a robust defence of the suitability of a finite universe,[28] returning us to the distinction between univocal and non-univocal causation. While the universe was created such that 'by its likeness to him the creature might show forth his goodness', nonetheless that showing forth would always involve a non-univocal rather than univocal likeness, because creation is not God. The likeness to God that creatures bear cannot work 'in terms of equality'. Although that would be as true of an infinite universe as a finite one (here in duration), there is something particularly fitting about finitude. A finite cosmos bears witness to God's perfections in its diversity, and to God's transcendence in its finitude, that is more 'in keeping with the way in which the transcendent is manifested by that which is transcended'.[29]

Such arguments might also apply to discussions of the spatial extent of the universe and to the diversity of its creatures. Variety, even riotous variety, befits divine plenitude, but there is also a fittingness to finitude, since a creaturely likeness is just that: a likeness, and not an attempt at equality with God. A finite cosmos offers a created likeness to divine plenitude in its diversity, but also underlines that no likeness can be equal to God, either in part or taken together.

In anticipation of a discussion that I will follow in far greater detail in Chapter 16, it may be useful to comment on the sort of argument that Aquinas is offering here. He does not argue in terms

[27] *SCG* II.32.9.
[28] *SCG* II.35.8.
[29] *SCG* II.35.8. Aquinas returned to this topic a little later, arguing that (temporal) finitude is 'entirely fitting [*convenientissimum*]' because that makes it all the more obvious that the cosmos is not self-grounded (*SCG* II.38.15).

of necessity, supposing that from some belief about God certain features of the universe necessarily follow or that God being as God could only act one way.[30] Neither is it simply a matter of shapeless will or divine possibility. Aquinas would certainly recognise some limits on what it was possible for God to do, on the basis that God's actions are consistent with God's nature, or because certain forms of words are simply nonsense and not to be dignified with the prefix 'God can'.[31] His mode of argument regarding the nature of creation was typically neither one of possibility nor of necessity, however, but of suitability or fittingness, given the nature of God. What God does is neither unfree and determined, on the one hand, nor random and unconnected to the divine nature, on the other. God's actions exhibit *convenientia*, to use the Latin term. God is free, but what God does is always consistent with who God is.[32] I will return to the topic of freedom in Chapter 16.

Niche Construction and Living Planets

As we have seen, theologians have frequently found a sharp distinction between habitability and habitation more difficult to maintain than we might expect, finding the idea of an inhabitable place without inhabitants odd or unnatural. Although the automatic

---

[30] While Aquinas will sometimes write that 'multiplicity and variety among created things' is 'necessary' (for instance, *SCG* II.45.2.), this is a case of a 'necessity given', not a necessity of an absolute form. See, for instance, *On Power* 3.16, where he argues that God is free to create a universe one way or another, but that in creating it a particular way, certain features naturally follow. In particular, the sort of universe that God has created is intrinsically and inescapably characterized by 'both diversity and multitude in things'. God is not obliged to create; creation is gratuitous.

[31] *SCG* II.25.

[32] It is something of a truism that freedom is difficult to define, and that definitions are contested. One purpose, or meaning, to saying that God is free when it comes to creation – that it is, and how it is, including how it unfolds – is to stress that creation does not enjoy the absoluteness or *aseity* that God does. The statement 'God is'

assumption that habitable places are inhabited is scientifically problematic, it is not only theologians who have blurred the distinction between habitability and inhabitancy. Recent work on the relationships between organisms and their environments has shown a more dynamic, two-way affair than had previously been appreciated. It is not simply that organisms are adapted by evolution to 'fit' or flourish in their ecological niches; organisms also work to adapt those environments to their own better advantage, in a phenomenon known as 'niche construction'. While some organisms are obviously seen to build things, such as beavers, spiders, and human beings, all organisms modify their environments to some extent, even if that is only in pH or some aspect of chemical composition.[33]

An environmental niche is not a static thing. Organisms do not simply find a location (on a smaller or larger scale) to be habitable or not; they also render more habitable what was previously less so. In this way, all organisms participate in the work of forming a habitable creation, and the categories of habitation and inhabitancy are shown to be interwoven. On these grounds, the planetary scientist David Grinspoon has argued that any life lastingly established on a planet will have managed to transform that planet on a deep level of habitability. On his view, 'a living planet … is not the same as a planet with life on it …. Because life is not a minor afterthought on

expresses a truth incomparably more ultimate than saying 'This is' of creation, which is marked instead by contingency. Another angle touches on the absolute perfection of God, which totally fills and satisfies the will, whether divine or creaturely, in a way that no creature can, such that nothing that was filled with the knowledge of God would have any inclination to anything other than God. The will would be captivated by God's own self in a way that no creaturely good could so compel it (that angle explored in *ST* I.19.3). One might also want to say that God is free in the sense that what God does could have been otherwise, and I think that touches on something important, for all I recognise the difficulties in speaking counterfactually about God and eternity. At the least, this angle lines up with the first point above, that to suppose creation might not have been, or might have been different, does not offend theological principles in the way that supposing that God might not have been, or might have been different, would do so forcefully.

[33] For some of the science, alongside theological commentary, see my 'All Creatures'.

an already functioning Earth, but an integrated part of the planet's evolution and behavior'.[34] (Clearly, by attributing life on a 'living planet' we do not mean quite the same thing as when we attribute life to an organism, as we saw in the discussion of analogy in Chapter 3.)[35]

In the words of Carl Goldblatt, 'habitability and inhabitancy are inseparable'.[36] On Earth, not only the atmosphere and hydrosphere (the interconnected system of all the planet's water) but even the lithosphere (meaning, here, the Earth's crust as well as all mountains and surface soil and rocks) has been fundamentally changed by life, in ways that make the planet more habitable. This, we might note, offers something of an exorcism of the deep gloom of those writers who have, from time to time, described Earth's life as a thin scum or slime upon the face of the planet, or something equivalent. Stephen Hawking was among those who have described life (or here human life) in this way: 'The human race is just a chemical scum on a moderate size planet, orbiting round a very average star in the outer suburb of one among a billion galaxies'.[37] Life, however, turns out to be more integral and transformative than that. Living things

[34] David Harry Grinspoon, *Earth in Human Hands: The Rise of Terra Sapiens and Hope for Our Planet* (New York: Grand Central, 2016), 71–72.

[35] I have explored this point in 'Living Worlds in Christian Theology', where I also consider the relevance of the theological notion of a 'world soul' to this question, as an idea with a surprisingly long and well-established pedigree in strands of Christian theology.

[36] Colin Goldblatt, 'The Inhabitance Paradox: How Habitability and Inhabitancy Are Inseparable', in *Conference Proceedings of Comparative Climates of Terrestrial Planets II* (Moffett Field, CA, 2015), https://arxiv.org/abs/1603.00950. On this, see also Smolin, *The Life of the Cosmos*, 146–49.

[37] *Reality on the Rocks*, Windfall Films, 1995. The idea goes back at least as far as Arthur Schopenhauer, *The World as Will and Representation*, vol. 2 (New York: Dover, 1969), 3. The idea, as put forward here by Hawking, is discussed by Raymond Tallis in 'You Chemical Scum, You", in *Reflections of a Metaphysical Flaneur: And Other Essays* (London: Routledge, 2014), 163–68, and by Rowan Williams in *Being Human: Bodies, Minds, Persons* (London: SPCK, 2018), 22–23. I am grateful to Matthew Fell for drawing these discussions to my attention.

are present far deeper than the 'scum' image suggests – beneath surface deposits, deep into the Earth's crust – and the processes of life have transformed processes such as plate tectonics at an even greater depth, for instance, through chalk deposits (laid down from the shells of microscopic sea creatures) which lubricate the movement of one plate against another.[38]

Providence

This chapter has told the perhaps unexpected story of theological arguments *for* the widespread habitation of the cosmos, with habitability and habitation thought not be as distinct as we might imagine. Turning to the largest scale, we can also ask what it takes for the cosmos as a whole to be even possibly habitable. In closing this chapter, that takes us towards the doctrine of providence, which should not be unexpected: where the doctrine of creation is in view, the doctrine of providence is sure to follow.[39]

We see this topic broached, for instance, in discussions of the size and age of the universe, which has sometimes been supposed necessarily to be of enormous size and age if God wishes for there to be life within it. For Edward Arthur Milne, for instance, this was about the improbability of life evolving in any one place. Indeed, Milnes went so far as to suggest that the universe is infinite in extent for that reason, as 'an infinite number of scenes of experiment in evolutionary biology'.[40] An infinite universe would overcome any worries about unlikely probabilities; within it, the creator could be sure to achieve any given outcome.

[38] Ed Yong, 'Life Found Deep under the Sea', *Nature*, 14 March 2013, nature.2013.12610; Grinspoon, *Earth in Human Hands*, 73–75.
[39] This area of theology is set out from a range of perspectives in David Fergusson, *The Providence of God: A Polyphonic Approach*, Current Issues in Theology (Cambridge: Cambridge University Press, 2018).
[40] Milne, *Modern Cosmology*, 151.

Several concerns might be raised about this. While it provides a way for the creator to achieve a desired outcome with surety, it does so at the cost of also achieving every other possible outcome, many of them presumably not so palatable: in an infinite universe there would also be every variation on every possible horror. Also problematic, to my mind, are the underlying assumptions here about the relation of the creation to the creator. In ways that have often been endemic to theology for the past few centuries – today often much criticised – God seems to feature here as an agent among agents, a thing among things, a cause among causes, cleverly devising a fool-proof scheme, as a creaturely agent might devise one within the world. A god who has to operate that way is not the God of the Christian tradition.[41] A more Thomist or participatory perspective, especially, would say that God acts in all action, and that God's action differs so profoundly from that of creatures that an action can be entirely the work of the creature in one sense, and entirely the work of the creator in another. Milne himself invoked providence.[42] The way this is done, however, with the language of 'God continually intervening', serves to underline the flat, univocal vision of God as a being among beings.

Making the universe large, or infinite, to ensure certain outcomes is problematic from the perspective upon which this book stands, but reflections about the size or age of the universe need not entirely be set aside. An idea put forward by John Polkinghorne is worth working through:

> a universe that was much smaller than ours would not have lasted long enough to have been able to evoke carbon-based life of our kind

---

[41] On problems with the language of intervention, see my 'Creation and Divine Action', in *The Oxford Handbook of Creation*, ed. Simon Oliver (Oxford: Oxford University Press, 2023), where I also discuss accounts of divine action offered from a participatory perspective.

[42] '[God] *tended* his creation in guiding its subsequent evolution on an infinite number of occasions in an infinite number of spatial regions. That is of the essence of Christianity, that God actually intervenes in History' (Milne, *Modern Cosmology*, 153, emphasis added).

of complexity. In a real sense, all that vast multitude of stars is necessary for the possibility of our being here as the inhabitants of Earth.[43]

Much has happened in cosmology since Polkinghorne wrote that in 2009, but his overall principle is a good one: not just any universe would survive long enough for life to evolve, simply because it would not survive long enough for solar systems to form, or even for heavier elements to be produced. Indeed, as we now famously know, only very particular combinations of fundamental constants yield a cosmos that gets far at all down the path of forming atoms, stars, and heavier elements (leading to discussions of 'fine-tuning', 'anthropic principles', and the idea of a multiverse). In the words of Martin Rees,

> The initial conditions that could have led to anything like our present Universe are actually very restrictive, compared to the range of possibilities that might have been set up. We know that our Universe is still expanding after 10^{10} years. Had it recollapsed sooner, there would have been no time for stars to evolve … The expansion rate cannot, however, be too fast – or the expansion kinetic energy would have overwhelmed gravity, and the clouds that developed into galaxies would never have been able to condense out [later forming stars and solar systems].[44]

A connection between size and age, and the possibility of the formation both of elements and of stars with their solar systems, is well established.

---

[43] John Polkinghorne, *Theology in the Context of Science* (New Haven: Yale University Press, 2010), 51.

[44] Martin J. Rees, 'Black Holes, Galactic Evolution and Cosmic Coincidence', *Interdisciplinary Science Reviews* 14, no. 2 (June 1989): 155. Moreover, for life to be possible, the universe must have been around for sufficiently long for elements to have been formed over time within stars and, especially for the heaviest elements, by the violent death of stars. Matter must have gone through at least one cycle, and likely two, of stars exploding and the debris recoalescing before sufficient quantities of heavier elements are around for life to emerge from.

For my part, providence is not something to be related to or squared with natural science, as if they were parts of the same jigsaw. Science is science, and providence embraces everything without needing to overturn nature. Science seeks to understand how and why things happen in the way they do, according to the natural processes of created reality. Theology holds that God acts in all of that: indeed, that the existence and action of every creature is God's act. The divine purpose is achieved in a way that respects, and indeed upholds, the integrity of creaturely entities and processes. There is not a great deal to say about providence and science: not because they are incompatible, but because they are so completely compatible, each is allowed simply and fully to be what it is.

The history of the universe matters to the theologian, nonetheless, leading as it has to subsequent generations of stars, heavier elements capable of catalytic chemistry, and planets. If God's purpose for matter and life is to be achieved through the processes of nature acting in their usual way, then limitations on what could or could not happen naturally are relevant. If God is going to create life through the processes of nature, the cosmos must be such that the processes of nature could bring life forth, meaning that the universe has to reach the stage of heavy elements and planets. One does not need to think that the evolution of life in the cosmos was a hit or miss affair to suppose that it was necessary for the universe to be of such a size and age for that to have happened. The universe can be marked by certain forms of necessity, not because God had to create one sort of universe (although we would rule some 'options' out as incompatible with divine goodness), but because God has chosen to create in such a way, and the emergence of life in that fashion rests on certain preconditions.[45] For it to be possible for life to emerge naturally, there are constraints to the age of the universe: how old, and therefore how large, it would have to be, and therefore how old and large its parameters ever allow it to be.

---

[45] We find a particularly eloquent discussion of this principle in *ST* I.21.4.

Conclusion

Not surprisingly, many themes of interest are thrown up when we look at astrobiology from the perspective of a doctrine of created things. My focus here has been on the nature of life. In Part III, we will turn to the related theme of the *imago dei*, the relation between habitability and habitation, and the claim (which will not quite go away) that the position of a planet in the universe is significant. We may be struck by how willingly the authors discussed here and in those chapters have typically embraced the prospect of life beyond Earth. Indeed, as I suggested above, my instinct – although I am not quite sure how one would go about proving it – is that those authors or traditions with a well-developed doctrine of creation have usually also been able to take on an astrobiological perspective.

Among the theological questions thrown up by these chapters that would benefit from further theological work, my emphasis would be on the origin and nature of life. As I commented in Chapter 3, it is surprising how little the topic of life-as-such, and of what the sciences have to say about its origins, has been explored as a topic of overlapping interest between theologians and scientists.

In the next section we move from themes in the doctrine of creation and providence, and turn to revelation, knowledge, and language.

Part II | Revelation and Theological Knowledge

Whether in the past or today, the prospect of exobiology throws up epistemological questions. From early modern times, in works such as John Wilkin's treatise dealing with life on the moon, authors have felt it necessary to reply to objections that thought of other life is impious, because it is not mentioned in the Bible. Attention to that topic remains useful, as the charge is repeated today, but so is the way in which it encourages us to think what the scriptures are for: to what end the theologian might think they were written, and what that means about how they are to be interpreted. Down Christian and Jewish history, we find this explored in terms of 'accommodation', the idea that however theologically one might treat ideas of divine inspiration, that does not take the texts out of their context; consequently, they should be understood as speaking in the language and concepts of their time.

More generally, considerations of astrobiology frequently throw up questions about diversity and difference, and how that is to be held alongside what might be shared in common. As my fixed point in this book, I have taken most of all a traditional Christian doctrine of God. I have done that, in part, simply on account of my aim to write a work of Christian theology, but also because a central contention of that faith is that God is the same in all places, as well as at all times. Even with that said, however, questions remain about difference and similarity, not in asking if God is different elsewhere, but in asking how understanding of God may be marked out by those dynamics of variation as well as commonality, the one God being known by different creatures according to their distinct settings and capacities for understanding.

In the second of these two chapters, I lay particular emphasis on the doctrine of the Trinity, again for more than one reason. That doctrine is the definitive form taken by the Christian understanding of God. It has also been challenged, as contingent and terrestrial in expression, in a book by Keith Ward. He does not suppose that God is other than One and Three, but he does argue that our sense of the threefoldness of God will not extrapolate well beyond Earth, particularly as expressed as Father, Son, and Holy Spirit.

In response, I turn to a Thomist account of analogy, which we have already encountered as a way for thinking about multiplicity and commonality in relation to life in Chapter 3. I emphasise the underpinnings of Aquinas' account of analogy, particularly in his doctrine of creation. I argue that this gives us reasons to suppose that the language of Father, Son, and Holy Spirit (or, more promisingly, the Spirit as love and gift) is not simply a matter of certain earthly categories being pressed into somewhat arbitrary service. Rather, the words we have – the words with which we speak about God – have the capacity to be used that way because they name features of creation that mirror the characteristics of God about which we speak.

5 | Revelation

There is no mention of other planets in the Bible, never mind life
on them. Is that significant? Would we expect it, if there were other
life? Such questions encourage us to ask what revelation is for. In
thinking about that, exobiology turns out to be an ideal case study.

Readers may not think that the absence of exobiology from
Biblical texts poses any problem, even if the cosmos were to abound
with life. They might think, as I do, that there is no more reason
to expect mention of exobiology in the historic revelation to Jews
and Christians than to find mention of the duck-billed platypus,
which is found only in Australasia. As Rabbi Norman Lamm wrote
in 1965, 'Nothing is said of other races, for indeed Torah was given
to man on earth and its concern is limited to terrestrial affairs'.[1]
Earlier, Martin Luther had written that 'God does many things that
he does not disclose to us in his word; he also wills many things
which he does not disclose himself as willing', or we might consider
Richard Bentley, who had pointed out that the opening of Genesis
says nothing of the creation of the angels, although they are mentioned elsewhere in the Pentateuch.[2] Asking 'in what respect ... the
Canonical books [are] inspired', John Henry Newman replied that

---

[1] Lamm, 'Religious Implications', 32.
[2] Martin Luther, *The Bondage of the Will: Luther's Works – Volume 33: Career of the
Reformer III*, trans. Philip Saville Watson and Benjamin Drewery (Philadelphia:
Fortress Press, 1972), 140; Bentley, *A Confutation of Atheism from the Origin and
Frame of the World*, 6. Aquinas discussed the absence of mention of the creation of
the angels in Gen. 1 in *ST* I.61.1 *ad* 1.

it seems unworthy of Divine Greatness, that the Almighty should, in His revelation of Himself to us, undertake mere secular duties, and assume the office of a narrator, as such, or an historian, or geographer, except so far as the secular matters bear directly upon the revealed truth.[3]

In contrast, some recent Christian writers (from what is called a 'conservative' perspective, rightly or not) have claimed that life simply cannot exist beyond Earth, as the Bible makes no mention of. In the view of Metropolitan Hilarion of the Russian Orthodox Patriarchate, for instance, 'If civilizations really existed on other planets, our Holy Scripture, the Bible, would definitely say something about that. If it doesn't say anything about it, we assume that they don't exist'.[4] The evangelical 'Young Earth Creationist' Jonathan D. Sarfati agrees, writing that 'Scripture strongly implies that no intelligent life exits elsewhere ... The Bible says nothing indicating that God created life anywhere but Earth'.[5] Judging by

---

[3] John Henry Newman, 'Inspiration in Its Relation to Revelation', in *Stray Essays on Controversial Points* (Birmingham: [Privately Printed], 1890), 9, reprinted in *On the Inspiration of Scripture*, ed. J. Derek Holmes and Robert Murray (London: Geoffrey Chapman, 1967), 108. The essay was written in 1884. Yves Congar also wrote appealingly on the topic of what is and is not in the Bible in 'Has God Peopled the Stars?', in *The Wide World My Parish*, trans. Donald Attwater (Baltimore: Helicon Press, 1964), 184–85.

[4] Metropolitan Hilarion, speaking as head of the Russian Orthodox Synodal Department for External Church Relations, transcribed and translated in 'Russian Orthodox Church Equates Aliens with Demons', *Interfax*, 20 April 2020, https://interfax.com/newsroom/top-stories/68479.

[5] Jonathan D. Sarfati, 'Bible Leaves No Room for Extraterrestrial Life', *Science and Theology News* 4, no. 7 (March 2004): 5, quoted by Weintraub, *Religions and Extraterrestrial Life*, 140. Other examples include Luther Tracy Townsend, *The Stars Not Inhabited* (New York: Eaton and Mains, 1914); Stuart Burgess, who writes that 'we can be certain that there is no extraterrestrial life' on Biblical grounds (*He Made the Stars Also: What the Bible Says about the Stars* (Leominster: DayOne, 2008), 139, with a discussion of 'Biblical reasons' on pp. 139–47; and Dave Hunt, *Cosmos, Creator and Human Destiny: Answering Darwin, Dawkins, and the New Atheists* (Bend, OR: Berean Call, 2010), cited by Wilkinson, *Search for Extraterrestrial Intelligence*, 150. In the sixteenth century we have Lambert Daneau: 'when the holie Scripture doeth

David Weintraub's assessment of attitudes towards exobiology within 'Evangelical and Fundamentalist Christianity', arguments within this constituency against life elsewhere fall broadly into three categories: that the Bible is silent on the matter; that ideas of other life are put forward on the basis of evolution, which is taken to be false; and that it causes inextricable theological problems, largely to do with sin and redemption.[6]

While Lamm himself was happy for the Hebrew scriptures to make no mention of life beyond Earth, we might note in passing that not every commentator has agreed. In some Jewish traditions, an enigmatic saying in Judges 5.23 has been interpreted as referring to life on other planets: 'Curse Meroz, said the angel of the Lord, Curse bitterly the inhabitants thereof because they did not come to the help of the Lord, to the help of the Lord against the mighty ones'.[7] Given that heavenly bodies were mentioned fighting for the people of God three verses earlier ('The stars fought from heaven, from their courses they fought against Sisera'), a passage in the Talmud sees one possible interpretation of 'Meroz' as a planet with inhabitants. From a Christian perspective, a few years ago Lucas Mix suggested that John 10.16 'may include alien life' ('I have other sheep that do not belong to this fold').[8] As a direct reference to other life from Christ, I find that implausible, given that Gentiles are so obviously his meaning, but the principle of a broad divine embrace and ingathering is not irrelevant to our discussion.[9] For my part, I take it that Biblical texts are silent on extraterrestrial life.

diligently reckon vp the special visible works of God … hee maketh mention of this one worlde only, and not of any other. Whiche if there had bine many, doubtlesse hee would haue made mention of them' (*Wonderful Workmanship*, 26).

[6] Weintraub, *Religions and Extraterrestrial Life*, 135–44. The life in question is taken to be rational.

[7] *Moed Katan* 16a, translation from Willem F. Smelik, *The Targum of Judges* (Leiden: Brill, 1995), 471, discussed in Weintraub, *Religions and Extraterrestrial Life*, 77.

[8] Lucas Mix, 'Other Sheep in the Universe', *Living Church*, 19 November 2017, 14.

[9] This is the perspective in Congar, 'Has God Peopled the Stars?', 185–86.

The Scope of Revelation

The question 'What is in the Bible, and why?' can be approached in at least two ways. One proceeds as it were from the side of God, supposing providence to have directed what is discussed and what is not. It can also be addressed from the side of humanity, thinking about the human process of writing. In the first case, our starting point would be the idea that certain truths were to be communicated so that certain divine purposes could be fulfilled. That, however, need not involve playing down the human dimension of composition, editing, and transmission, which provide our jumping off point in the second case. To focus, in that way, on that human dimension is to place providence in the background, at least for the moment, although a believer may also hold, out of theological conviction, that this human dimension mediates the revelation of God.

These two perspectives – broadly a theological one, which starts with what God wishes to communicate, and one from Biblical studies, which starts with the story of composition and editing – need not lie as far apart as they might seem, especially if we attend to that useful category of divine *accommodation*. However 'high' a view one might have of scriptural inspiration, Christian theologians are likely to agree that revelation is given for the sake of the recipient. Attention to the human dimension of scripture is therefore far from secondary, even for a markedly theological approach to revelation. If what God does, God does well, and if God's purpose here is revelation, then revelation will be 'accommodated', or suitable, for its recipients, with all their limitations and cultural specificities. The Rabbis wrote that the 'Torah speaks in human language' or in the words of the tenth-century Jewish scholar al-Qirqisani, that 'God addresses mankind in a manner adapted to their minds and accessible to their understandings'.[10] Christians might think of the Day

---

[10] S. Horovitz and I. A. Rabin, *Mekhilta De-Rabi Yishma'el*, 2nd ed. (Jerusaelm: Sifre Vahrman, 1970), Va-yisa 4, 168, quoted by Stephen D. Benin, *The Footprints of God:*

of Pentecost, with each person hearing the message of God in his or her own language.[11] As Glenn Sunshine puts it, "For an infinite, perfect, and holy God to interact with finite, fallible and fallen humanity, he must accommodate himself to our ability to understand him, coming down to our level so that we can grasp what he says and does'.[12] Dante had made the point in relation to Biblical metaphors: 'Scripture condescends [*condescende*]/to your capacities, and says that God/has hands and feet – though meaning otherwise'.[13]

Both Jewish and Christian authors have likened divine speech addressed to human beings to the speech of adults to children, in which we descend to their level and use the sort of language and images that children naturally understand. Calvin, for instance, asks,

> Who even of slight intelligence does not understand that, as nurses commonly do with infants, God is wont in a measure to "lisp" in speaking to us? Thus such forms of speaking do not so much express clearly what God is like as accommodate the knowledge of him to our slight capacity.[14]

Irenaeus invokes the parallel image, already used by Paul, of giving milk to children,[15] while Bonaventure makes the link between accommodation in Biblical revelation and Incarnation through infancy:

Divine Accommodation in Jewish and Christian Thought (Albany: State University of New York Press, 1993), 141 (and see 142–45, and Glenn S. Sunshine, 'Accommodation Historically Considered', in *The Enduring Authority of the Christian Scriptures*, ed. D. A. Carson (Grand Rapids, MI: Eerdmans, 2016), 246).

[11] Acts 2.8.

[12] Sunshine, 'Accommodation Historically Considered', 238.

[13] Dante Alighieri, *Paradiso*, canto 4, lines 43–45, translation from *Paradiso*, trans. Robin Kirkpatrick (London: Penguin, 2007), 33, Italian quoted by Benin, *Footprints of God*, 93.

[14] *Institutes* I.13.1, quoted by Sunshine, 'Accommodation Historically Considered', 254, who also cites I.17.13, on God repenting. For a Jewish example see Dov Baer, *Magid Devaraṿ Le-Yaʻakov*, ed. Rivka Schatz Uffenheimer (Jerusalem: Magnes Press, Hebrew University, 1976), 296–97, on Hosea 11.1, cited by Benin, 176. Calvin's other favourite image is communication with rustic and unlettered people (*Institutes*, I.11.1), quoted Sunshine, 254.

[15] 1 Cor. 3.1–1, with a parallel in Heb. 5.12.

Christ the teacher, lowly as He was in the flesh, remained lofty in His divinity. It was fitting, therefore, that He and His teachings should be humble in word and profound in meaning: even as the Infant Christ was wrapped in swaddling clothes, so God's wisdom is wrapped in humble images.[16]

Among the church fathers, John Chrysostom particularly pursued these matters, his interest in accommodation driven not only by an attention to human limitations, but also by consideration of divine transcendence, which comes through especially in his arguments with the Anomoeans, who claimed to know the essence of God.[17]

The sense that accommodation is necessary, resting on the mismatch between God and our capacities, will also be central in the next chapter, where we turn to consider that God's unchanging reality might be mediated differently to diverse recipients. Looking further ahead, we have also begun to turn up matters that bear upon whether we might expect more than one Incarnation as the ultimate, and perhaps also context-specific, form of divine condescension or accommodation.

Accommodation, Exegesis, and the Purpose of Scripture

Having surveyed some points relating to the idea of accommodation, we can turn more particularly to the absence of discussions of exobiology in the Bible (alongside other aspects of now firmly established astronomy). Approached from the human side – from Biblical studies – the argument is so straightforward as to seem

---

[16] Bonaventure, *Breviloquium*, trans. José de Vinck (Paterson, NJ: St Anthony Guild Press, 1963), prologue, 4. The image is also found in Calvin (*Commentary on 1 Peter*, on 1 Pet. 1.20, quoted by Sunshine, 'Accommodation Historically Considered', 253 and the Vatican II document *Dei Verbum* (n. 13); in Irenaeus, see *Against Heresies*, 4.38, quoted by Sunshine, 240).

[17] John Chrysostom, *On the Incomprehensibility of God*, III.3, quoted by Benin, *Footprints of God*, 68–69.

banal: the human authors of the scriptures did not know about other life, so they did not write about it. From the more doctrinal perspective, good communication is focused communication, and the inspiration of the scriptures would therefore be expected to have a clear and limited focus. For a Reformation treatment of the idea, consider the Thirty-Nine Articles of Religion of the Church of England (with parallels in other Reformed confessions), and their claim that the scriptures 'contain all things necessary to salvation', which implies a focus of attention,[18] while both the Council of Trent and the First Vatican Council taught 'the object and promise' of scriptural inspiration to be 'faith and moral conduct'.[19]

Augustine saw that focus as explicitly a matter of accommodation, even of divine shrewdness, given the human capacity for evasion or distraction: 'the Spirit of God who was speaking through them [the authors of the Scriptural books] did not wish to teach people about such things which would contribute nothing to their salvation'.[20] These authors showed 'good sense' in passing over such matters 'as not holding out the promise of any benefit to those wishing to learn about the blessed life, and, what is worse, as taking up much precious time that should be spent on more salutary matters'.[21]

Such perspectives informed John Wilkins' contention that little can be learned from what the Bible *does not* discuss: 'the Negative Authority of Scripture is not prevalent in those things which are not the Fundamentals of Religion'.[22] There is no mention of other life, any more than there is mention of planets, which we now know to encircle the sun. On such matters, the silence of the Bible directs us to the work of natural science, which is a fitting comment, coming from a founder, and first secretary, of the Royal Society (the early and prestigious English body for scientific study).

[18] Article 6 (following Augustine, for instance, *Literal Commentary on Genesis*, 2.9.20).
[19] Newman, 'Inspiration in Its Relation to Revelation', 108.
[20] Augustine, 'Literal Meaning of Genesis', II.9.20, 202.
[21] Augustine, 'Unfinished Literal Commentary on Genesis', II.9.20, 212.
[22] Wilkins, *Discovery of a World*, 20.

Now if the Holy Ghost had intended to reveal unto us any Natural Secrets, certainly would never have omitted the mention of the Planets [which he has noted are not discussed in the Bible] ... And therefore you must know, that 'tis beside the Scope of the Old Testament or the New, to discover any thing unto us concerning the Secrets in [Natural] Philosophy; 'tis not his [God's] intent in the New Testament, since we cannot conceive how it might any way belong either to the Historical, Exegetical, or Prophetical parts of it; nor is it his intent in the Old Testament'.[23]

Wilkins quotes Edward Wright (1561–1615), who used a now-familiar nursery simile: 'Tis not the endeavour of Moses, or the Prophets, to discover any Mathematical or Philosophical Subtilties, but rather to accommodate themselves to Vulgar Capacities, and ordinary Speech, as Nurses are wont to use their Infants'.[24]

Calvin had written much the same in his *Commentary of Genesis*: 'It must be remembered, that Moses does not speak with philosophical [i.e. scientific] acuteness on hidden mysteries, but relates those things which are everywhere observed, even by the uncultivated, and which are in common use'.[25] The creation of the 'two great lights', the sun and the moon, offers a good example (as we saw with Aquinas in Chapter 1). The moon is not the second largest object in the solar system. Saturn and Jupiter, for instance, are much larger than the moon, and indeed even the Earth.[26] Calvin thought that of no consequence, the purpose of scripture not being to teach us astronomy, but

---

[23] Ibid., 21–22.

[24] Edward Wright, preface to William Gilbert's *De Magnete, Magneticisque Corporibus, et de Magno Magnete Tellure* (1600), trans. Wilkins, 22. The identification of 'Mr Wright' here comes from Hans Aarsleff, 'John Wilkins (1614–1673): Life and Work', in *John Wilkins and 17th-Century British Linguistics*, ed. Joseph L. Subbiondo (Amsterdam: J. Benjamin, 1992), 30.

[25] Jean Calvin, *Commentaries on the First Book of Moses, Called Genesis*, trans. John King, vol. 1, 2 vols (Edinburgh: Calvin Translation Society, 1847), 1.14, p. 84, amending 'occult' to 'hidden'.

[26] Aquinas remarks on this in *ST* I.70.1 *obj.* 5 and *ad* 5.

to exhort readers as regards their standing before God: 'as it became a theologian, he [Moses] had respect to us rather than to the stars ... [thus] he deemed it enough to declare what we all may plainly perceive, that the moon is a dispenser of light to us'.[27] Moses is not to be censured 'for not speaking with greater exactness',[28] and anyone 'who would learn astronomy, and other abstruse arts [or hidden arts – *alias artes reconditas*], let him go elsewhere. Here the Spirit of God would teach all men without exception'.[29] In a passage worth quoting at length, Calvin goes on to praise the work of astronomers in terms likely to cheer the scientifically minded reader today.

Astronomers investigate with great labour whatever the ingenuity of the human mind can comprehend. Nevertheless, this study is not to be rejected, nor this science to be condemned, because some frantic persons are wont boldly to reject whatever is unknown to them. For astronomy is not only pleasant, but also very useful to be known: it cannot be denied that this art unfolds the admirable wisdom of God. Wherefore, as ingenious men are to be honoured who have expended useful labour on this subject, so they who have leisure and capacity ought not to neglect this kind of exercise. Nor did Moses truly wish to withdraw us from this pursuit in omitting such things as are peculiar to the art [of astronomy]; but because he was ordained a teacher of the unlearned and rude, as well as of the learned, he could not otherwise fulfil his office than by descending to this grosser method of instruction. Had he spoken of things generally unknown, the uneducated might have pleaded in excuse that such subjects were beyond their capacity ... Let the astronomers possess their more exalted knowledge; but, in the meantime, they who perceive by the moon the splendour of night, are convicted by its use of perverse ingratitude unless they acknowledge the beneficence of God.[30]

[27] Calvin, *On the First Book of Moses*, I.15, p. 86.
[28] Ibid., I.15, p. 85.
[29] Ibid., 1.6, pp. 79–80.
[30] Ibid., 1.16, pp. 86–87, with some modernisation. Benin notes the parallel with ST I.68.3 (*Footprints of God*, 279, n. 95).

Calvin and Wilkins between them provide ample reason for understanding why life elsewhere in the universe, if it exists, might not be revealed to human beings by God.

We might note how much latitude Wilkins allowed in scriptural interpretation when he thought empirical findings called for it:

> when the Words of Scripture shall seem to contradict common Sense or Experience, there, are they to be understood in a qualified Sense, and not according to the Letter. And 'tis observ'd, that for want of this Rule, some of the Ancients have fastened strange Absurdities upon the Words of the Scripture [of which he provides examples].[31]

Here he followed a tradition well illustrated by Augustine, citing a passage from the *Literal Commentary on Genesis* that has come to justified prominence in discussions of the relationship between theology and science.[32] Lamm had something similar to say: 'if the literal reading of this position of the Torah [the opening of Genesis] contradicts what reason tells us to be the truth, it means that we must not have properly understood the divine teachings and must return to the sacred text and probe deeper into it in order to discover what is, after all, a single and unified truth'.[33]

The significant shift in outlook since Wilkins' time is not over what the Bible should or should not contain, but over whether its authors knew more about science than they wrote. Calvin assumed both that Genesis was written by Moses and that he knew the full scientific picture, but held it back.[34] That was a uniform assumption among theologians, the Biblical writers being God's agents of accommodation. Augustine had said the same.[35] Over the course

[31] Wilkins, *Discovery of a World*, prop. 2, p. 24.
[32] Augustine, 'Literal Meaning of Genesis', I.19.39, p. 195.
[33] Lamm, 'Religious Implications', 20.
[34] Calvin, *On the First Book of Moses*, 1.15, p. 86.
[35] Augustine, 'Literal Meaning of Genesis', II.9.20, p. 213.

of the seventeenth and eighteenth centuries, this perspective began to shift among scholars, from supposing that the Biblical writers shrewdly condescended to their audience, towards seeing them as inherently thinking according to the views of their times, however much what they wrote might have been guided or inspired by God.[36] The contemporary theologian is unlikely to find that unexpected or problematic.

Conclusion

If God accommodates himself to us in Scripture, using the concepts and understandings common to the original audience, and if the purpose of Scripture is shrewdly focused on that which is necessary for salvation, then arguments from silence will bear little weight. This is true whether we suppose (as theologians used to) that accommodation was the work of the Biblical authors who knew more than they wrote, or only of God, who guided the writing of otherwise historically limited individuals. The question of what the Bible is for, and how its contents should speak to us today, not least in topics with a scientific dimension, is of perennial significance. Thinking about astrobiology turns out to offer an ideal example of a topic with which to think that through.

The theme of accommodation, which has featured prominently in this chapter, will return in the discussion of the Incarnation in Part 4 of this book, where it will serve as the basis for my own argument in favour of the idea of multiple Incarnations. Ideas of divine accommodation and condescension also relate to the discussion, in Chapter 16, of the idea that the saving actions of God work with the shape or nature of human (and other) life rather like a great artist works with her materials.

---

[36] Hoon J. Lee, *The Biblical Accommodation Debate in Germany: Interpretation and the Enlightenment* (Cham: Springer, 2017).

In the next chapter, we will look at another of the central points that Christians hold to be revealed in the scriptures – the doctrine of the Trinity – and consider the claim that this doctrine is so accommodated to human language and experience that it could be understood elsewhere only if stripped of much that is most distinctive about its Christian expression.

6 | Knowledge of God and the Language of the Trinity

This is not a work of interstellar comparative theology. We have no examples of extraterrestrial religion or theology to compare with ours, and any signs of life that might turn up in the atmospheric spectrum of an exoplanet will tell us next to nothing about what sort of life is there. Nor am I concerned here with communication or contact. Nonetheless, even the prospect of theology elsewhere raises a question that is worth addressing, as to whether any non-human conception of God would necessarily be different from ours, perhaps profoundly so: not because God is different, but because of the different biology, culture, and history of those other creatures. This question helpfully challenges us to think about the contingency and situatedness of our own religious and theological life. A provocation to thought here comes from Keith Ward's book-length treatment of this question, *Christ and the Cosmos: A Reformulation of Trinitarian Doctrine* (2015). Ward's focus is on the doctrine of the Trinity (which is also mine in this chapter), and therefore also on the Incarnation (to which I turn in the next section of this book).

I should begin this Trinitarian discussion by stressing that the Christian doctrine of the Trinity is monotheistic. A non-Trinitarian monotheism found elsewhere would not necessarily be problematic from a Christian perspective, even if the Christian might suppose such a form of monotheism also to omit saying something of first significance. There would be a parallel there with saying that Jewish and Islamic monotheisms are correct and honourable in their confession of God as One, even if the Christian thinks that there is also something to be said about God as Three-in-One.

Contingency and Divergence

The confession of the Trinity is foundational for Christianity. Within it, the most hallowed place has gone to the names Father, Son, and Holy Spirit. By means of an exobiological thought experiment, Ward argues that these names are particularly contingent, human, and local.

> God is truly Father, Son, and Holy Spirit as God truly relates to human beings. But just suppose there are non-human beings in existence, whether angels or alien life forms. Would God truly be to them a male member of the species *Homo sapiens*, his male offspring, and a being which often takes the form of a bird? ... These symbols could only apply where there was bisexual reproduction and winged flight.[1]

In Jesus, Ward writes, we see God revealed 'in the fullest way that is possible in a human life', and 'Trinitarian belief is founded upon the revelation of God in the face of Jesus Christ'.[2] Nonetheless, for Ward this finite encounter 'cannot license claims that such revelation discloses the essential nature of God as it is in eternity and as it is unchangeably bound to be throughout all times and places':[3] God is eternally and essentially threefold, but 'only takes Trinitarian form as Father, Son, and Spirit in relation to humans on this planet'.[4]

---

[1] Ward, *Christ and the Cosmos*, 137.

[2] Ibid., 39. This is about the strongest claim that Ward makes to the fullness of revelation in Christ. Otherwise, he is more inclined to stress an incompleteness, compared to what God is. Moreover, Ward seems to suggest that particularity and accommodation to createdness is not simply to be said of Jesus of Nazareth, and any other Incarnation, but even of God-as-Word: 'God is the infinitely greater reality from which the pattern (the Word) of the cosmos is generated, a pattern which Jesus expresses in human form' (ibid., 69).

[3] Ward, *Christ and the Cosmos*, 100. This is a 'capacity essential to the divine nature' (141).

[4] Ibid., 141.

Ward makes it clear that his sense of the limited application of those names – Father, Son, and Holy Spirit – does not rest on modalist or Sabellian convictions. While he sees those names as merely part of the story of God's dealings with human beings, God is nonetheless really three, and not only when it comes to modes of appearing.[5] Nonetheless, Ward stresses that God will be known differently by different creatures. In that, he tends to want to downplay any sense of a complete revelation in Christ.[6]

For my part, I would begin by recognising that any revealed knowledge of God that is comprehensible to creatures of different forms will respect those differences. Ward's point that human language and understanding of God does not exhaust what God is also needs to be taken seriously. The revelation or mediation of the nature of God into the language, culture, and understanding of species and civilisations with different biology, patterns of life, and culture will also be limited in its own characteristic ways. At the same time, I want to explore the theological case for an underlying similarity of confession, first, because there are alternative (if usually subordinate) names for God as Trinity in Christian theology that have good grounds for universality (and Ward, indeed, makes this point) and because I will argue that what Ward sees as the most limited of human Trinitarian language – Father, Son, and Holy Spirit – could be more universal than he will allow.

The story of how Christians came to speak of God in Trinitarian terms is deeply historical twice over. First, it is the product of Christian

---

[5] 'The position I hold is not modalist, in this meaning of the word, because God is essentially threefold. I have said, however, that God might not be known as "Father, Son, and Spirit" in worlds where there were no fathers, sons, atmospheres, flames, or birds'. Ibid., 248, and see 131–32, 141–42, 252.

[6] Ibid., 100. While, as Aquinas has it, not even the encounter with Christ could tell us 'what God is' (*ST* I.12.13 *ad* 1), I would want to place the emphasis on the Person of Christ being the Person of the Son, such that even if Christ does not show us 'what God is', he shows us who God is, at least to the extent that that can be done in a human and finite manner.

deliberations unfolding in history, and within particular cultures. To hold certain creeds and formulations to be authoritative does not require us to deny that they emerged over time, entangled with the contingencies of history and human agents, by turns both noble and base. Belief in providence does not require us to de-historicise anything, and an appreciation of history will often enrich our doctrinal understanding. Second, those discussions, and the confessions they produced, are also historical in that they did not primarily grow from consideration of abstract or propositional material, but of the narrative and historical texts of the Old and New Testaments, especially the story of Christ. Pre-eminently, we have the language of Father, Son, and Holy Spirit because of what Jesus is recorded as having said, and because of what the Gospels present of the shape and character of his life. The story of the Church coming to a Trinitarian faith is one of interpretation of the story about Jesus Christ, and the growing conviction that the man encountered there is divine, and related to God as a son to a father, and that he sent Holy Spirit, who is also divine.

For reasons I will explain in the chapters on Christology, my instinct is to suppose that were life elsewhere to have come to the fullest knowledge of God of which it is capable, it would have been led there by encounters with God in its own flesh, that is to say by means of its own Incarnation, with divine accommodation to bodiliness and cultural forms taken to the ultimate degree. Whether other life would know of God as Trinity in that way, however, or only by revelation outside of any direct experience of an Incarnation, the concerns we are navigating here would still apply as to the limitations impressed by biology, and forms of life and culture.

Convergence

There are grounds for a contingent variety in what, and how, different creatures might know of God. As I have said, if God communicates to other civilisations, there would have to be accommodation for it to be good communication for that species, just as we take the dealings of God with us to be good communication for us. While there would therefore be a diversity to how God is comprehended, I also take there to be grounds for convergence in Trinitarian understanding, as in other things that might be known about God.

One way to seek continuity between how very different species might understand God as threefold would be to move away from the language of 'Father', 'Son', and 'Holy Spirit', as Ward suggests. The tradition, after all, offers a range of alternative Trinitarian triplets. Ward's selections – and his book is full of them – generally reflect his inclination towards philosophical idealism, and align with his preference for 'psychological' understandings of God as Trinity, and his dislike of social Trinitarianism.[7] In the following sample, terms or phrases relating to the First Person are in ordinary Roman type, those to the Second Person are italicised, and those to the Third Person are in bold:

source, *support*, and **goal**;[8] transcendent, *manifest*, and **uniting**;[9] primordial, *expressive*, and **unitive**;[10] primal origin, *expressed thought*, and **beatific love**;[11] envisagement, *actualisation*, and **love**;[12] unlimited, *unitive wisdom*, and **love**;[13] subjectivity, *creativity*, and **unitive love**;[14] primordially personal and ontological being, with *knowledge* and **intention**;[15] origin, *ideal*, and **realiser of the ideal**;[16]

---

[7] Ward goes so far in the psychological direction as to say that the Son has no act of thinking, but is the thought of the Father, and the Spirit has no act of loving, but is the love of the Father. Here we might contrast Augustine, for instance.

[8] Ward, *Christ and the Cosmos*, 260, citing John Macquarrie, *Principles of Christian Theology* (London: SCM Press, 1966), 198.

[9] Ward, *Christ and the Cosmos*, 230.

[10] Ibid., 258, citing Macquarrie, *Principles of Christian Theology*, 198. Similar triplets can be found in Ward, *Christ and the Cosmos*, 252, 260.

[11] Ward, *Christ and the Cosmos*, 256.

[12] Ibid., 225.

[13] Ibid., 106.

[14] Ibid., 256.

[15] Ibid., 183.

[16] Ibid., 62.

thinker, *intelligible thought*, and **creative power of being**;[17] primal source of being, *expressed in the actualisation of supreme value*, and **blissful contemplation of that value**;[18] origin, *one proceeding through*, and **one perfected in**.[19]

These triplets illustrate something of the breadth of historical Trinitarian thought, with its additional ways to speak of God as Three-in-One, alongside the distinctly 'personal' categories of Father, Son, and Holy Spirit. We could add others beyond Ward's lists. Sarah Coakley has suggested an inherently threefold characteristic to the Christian experience of prayer drawing on Paul, particularly in Rom. 8.[20] Karl Barth explored a threefold character to God's self-revelation, as 'Revealer, Revelation, and Revealed-ness'.[21] Augustine linked memory with the Father, the Son with intellect, and the Spirit with will or love.[22]

Elsewhere, I have explored a tradition going back to Patristic writers of appropriating to Father, Son, and Holy Spirit various triplets aligned with three of Aristotle's dimensions of causation as well as with three of the 'transcendental' characteristics of being. This associates efficient causation and unity with the Father, formal (or exemplary) causation and truth with the Son, and final causation

[17] Ibid., 65. Here and with the previous reference, he is commenting on John's Gospel.

[18] Ibid., 127.

[19] Ibid., 222. This is based on a discussion of Gregory of Nyssa's thought by William Alston, 'Substance and the Trinity', in *The Trinity*, ed. Stephen T. Davis, Daniel Kendall, and Gerald O'Collins (Oxford: Oxford University Press, 2002), 192; and see 237, which quotes 'Not Three Gods'.

[20] Sarah Coakley, *God, Sexuality and the Self: An Essay 'on the Trinity'* (Cambridge: Cambridge University Press, 2013), 101–51.

[21] Karl Barth, *Church Dogmatics: The Doctrine of the Word of God (I/1)*, ed. G. W. Bromiley and Thomas F. Torrance, trans. G. W. Bromiley, 2nd ed. (Edinburgh: T. & T. Clark, 1975), 339. In have commented upon this threefold designation in relation to other triplets grounded in efficient, formal, and final causation, in *Participation in God*, 51–52.

[22] John of the Cross associated this triplet with the theological virtues: memory with hope, intellect with faith, and will with charity (*The Ascent of Mount Carmel*, book 2, ch. 6).

and goodness with the Spirit.[23] That suggests features within being-as-such that might furnish notions through which another form of rational creature might also talk about God in a threefold manner: that every being, for instance (and being as such) is marked by unity, truth, and goodness, or that causation has four dimensions, of which three can be applied (by analogy) to the act of God as creator.[24] Whether or how those triplets (and any from Ward's lists that we might call into service) would lend themselves to speaking about One God in Three Persons is a significant question. In particular, while one might place the emphasis on natural theology here, I would place it on revelation, and the tutorship that revelation gives to subsequent thought. These triplets have not come to feature within Christian theology as if Christians simply found and applied them to God by reflection on the properties of creatures, the structure of revelation, or the experience of prayer. Rather, those characteristics, coming from God in creation, were there for God to speak through, or to be recognised *after* God has spoken. In this way, the theologian may wish to go so far as to insist, with Bonaventure and Aquinas, that creatures can arrive at knowledge of God as 'in three Persons' only by means of a gift of grace, beyond nature.[25]

Bonaventure addressed this in his *Commentary on the Sentences*.[26] Each creature has a unity, truth, and goodness, and associated with

---

If memory, intellect and will are converged towards, and if their perfection intrinsically involves hope, faith, and charity, then those virtues (possibly as divinely infused, or as having natural analogues) would offer three further associations with the Persons.

[23] On this see my *Participation in God*, 42–64, and an essay in a forthcoming edited volume on Trinitarian ontologies.

[24] The fourth dimension – material causality – cannot be attributed to God as creator, since God is not 'that out of which' creation is formed, as the doctrine of creation *ex nihilo* stresses.

[25] Bonaventure, *Commentary on the Sentences*, book I, dist. 3, part 1, single article, q. 4 (Bonaventure, *Commentary on the Sentences: Philosophy of God*, trans. R. E. Houser and Timothy B. Noone (Saint Bonaventure, NY: Franciscan Institute, 2013), 83–84); Aquinas, *SCG* I.3.2.

[26] For a discussion of this in Aquinas, we could turn to *ST* III.45.7.

these come strings of other aspects. Unity sees the creature divided from others and undivided within itself, coming from God as the agent of creation (or efficient cause); both distinctiveness and coming forth relate to memory. Truth means that the creature is distinguishable from others, derived from God as its exemplar (or formal) cause, and able to be known. Goodness means that it is linked and ordered to other creatures, that it is directed to God as its goal (or final cause), and that it can be loved. All of that, Bonaventure writes, can be known 'by philosophy', which is to say by general application of common reason. He sees this, for instance, in the threefold distinction of philosophy itself into ontology, epistemology, and ethics.[27] Only by faith, however – by which he means revelation, or Christian instruction – can one see that any of this points to God as three Persons. Nonetheless, Bonaventure was open to the possibility of divine enlightenment outside of Christianity: 'through reason the philosophers never knew the Trinity of persons' unless they came in some way to possess 'something of the habit of faith'.[28] In speaking in ways pregnant with Trinitarian understanding, these philosophers said more than they knew or – if they did begin to have a sense of what it meant – it was 'because they had been illuminated by the enlightening rays of faith'.

Following Bonaventure, we could say that an alien culture might recognise an innate threefoldness to being and, if they speak about God, they might trace that threefoldness back to God as creator. Without revelation, however, at least on this view, that would get them to God as the cause of creation in its threefoldness, or even to God as characterised by the threefold perfections given to creatures, but not to the idea that God is three Persons in one Being. That

---

[27] Bonaventure, *Itinerarium Mentis in Deum*, III.6, translation from *Itinerarium mentis in Deum*, trans. Zachary Hayes (St. Bonaventure, NY: Franciscan Institute Publications, 2002), 90–93; Bonaventure, *On the Reduction of the Arts to Theology*, trans. Zachary Hayes (St Bonaventure, NY: Franciscan Institute, 1996), IV, 40–42, following Augustine, *City of God*, VIII.4, XI.25.

[28] Bonaventure, *Commentary on the Sentences*, book 1, dist. 3, part 1, single article, q. 4, *conclusio*, translation from *Philosophy of God*, 83–84.

said, we should perhaps be wary of divisions that are too watertight: all reason is already a participation in divine reason, and God can lead whomsoever he wills to a fuller knowledge of himself. Here, we might think of the intimations of a threefoldness to God found across religious traditions.[29]

By turning to abstract categories, rather than to the personal names of 'Father, Son, and Holy Spirit', Ward sees some possibility for a shared Trinitarian confession between different species, and he suggests that consideration of this possibility might also protect the Christian accounts from becoming too attached to what he sees as their human frame of reference. The personal names would remain in the bedrock of our theology, but there would be no expectation of them finding parallels elsewhere.

> There is indeed a cosmic Trinity and it has disclosed itself to us in ways suited to our understanding – as Father, Son, and Spirit. Whatever we discover, and whatever hitherto unimagined worlds we may confront in future, this can remain an unchanging ground of Christian faith. But it does not entitle us to say that the way in which God truly appears to us is the way in which God must appear to all possible beings or the way in which God is in the divine being itself, apart from any creation.[30]

Ward is not a modalist, as I have said: he does not suppose that the threefoldness of God *per se* is merely an appearance, behind which

---

[29] In *The Experience of God: Being, Consciousness, Bliss* (New Haven: Yale University Press, 2013), David Bentley Hart observes that many other religious traditions, beyond Christianity, have a sense of a threefoldness to God, not least in terms of 'sat-chit-ananda' (being, consciousness, and bliss) from Brahmin traditions of Hinduism, which plays a structuring role in Hart's book. Ward notes that 'there exist non-Christian versions of a threefold movement of a supreme Spirit, from conception through expression to liberation and unity' (*Christ and the Cosmos*, 259–60). On ancient Platonisms and a threefoldness to God, see Andrew Radde-Gallwitz, 'The One and the Trinity', in *Christian Platonism: A History*, ed. Alexander Hampton and John P. Kenney (Cambridge: Cambridge University Press, 2020), 53–78.

[30] Ward, *Christ and the Cosmos*, 106–7.

there is God as One. He nonetheless goes further than many theologians might wish, certainly further than I would go in supposing that God-as-Trinity lies ineffably behind a surface idea of God as Father, Son, and Holy Spirit. In contrast, I do not think that consideration of Trinitarian theology from an astrobiological perspective, with human contingencies therefore in mind, need make us see the traditional language of the Persons as so completely human and contingent.

Although 'anthropological' in reference, Christians have not thought it accidental that these names, which have enjoyed the highest honour – Father, Son, and Holy Spirit – are *personal*. That is most obvious with the names of the First and Second Persons but for the Holy Spirit the name is also taken to designate a Person and not a characteristic, or facet, of divine action. The confession of God as three 'Persons' does not mean three personalities, but the language of personhood remains central: God is personal, and the well-spring of personhood. If God is properly said not to be 'a person' in some flatly anthropomorphic sense, that is not because God is less than personal but rather, to use the language of Pseudo-Dionysius, it is because God is hyper-, exceedingly, or eminently personal.[31] More supposedly 'universal', seemingly less 'anthropological' language, such as speaking about God as 'being and origin, expression or appearance' is not untrue, but it does not bear sufficient witness to divine Personhood.[32]

Questions about the language of persons bears directly on the relation of divine names and titles to gender. Theology will err if it forgets (as even as conservative a document as the *Catechism of the Catholic Church* has it) that 'God transcends the human distinction between the sexes'. God 'is neither man nor woman: he is God. He also transcends human fatherhood and motherhood, although he is their origin and standard'.[33] The danger in forgetting

---

[31] Pseudo-Dionysius, across the *Divine Names*, but, for instance, II.3.

[32] Ward, *Christ and the Cosmos*, 252, emphasis added.

[33] *Catechism of the Catholic Church: Revised in Accordance with the Official Latin Text Promulgated by Pope John Paul II*, 2nd ed. (Vatican City: Libreria Editrice Vaticana, 1997), §239, 63.

that is part of why Ward sees value in leaving behind personal categories such as 'Father' and 'Son', and turning to ungendered but more abstract categories, such as source, support, and goal, or envisagement, actualisation, and love.[34] As Janet Soskice has written, however, taking leave of personal names may not be the best answer to feminist concerns, not least because use of these terms in the Bible is often provocative, full of theological freight, and indeed often subversive of easily assumed gender conventions, and because it may be a pyric victory from a feminist perspective to lose the centrality of relation that personal language for the Trinity teaches and reinforces.[35] Sarah Coakley, for instance, follows Aquinas in distinguishing between the metaphorical use of 'Father' in our address of God, and the deeper sense in which the language of 'Father', 'Son', and 'Spirit' teaches something fundamental about the life of the Trinity as relation.[36] It is not my place to speak for women about their experience of the traditional Trinitarian names, but in drawing attention to comments of these two recent colleagues, I will at least echo their contention that moving from personal to abstract language, in a way that shifts the emphasis away from relation and relationality, may not be simply and only a good thing.

A further defence of the personal names is perhaps a paradoxical one: that in using language with such a clear human reference we usefully draw attention to the fact that our speech about God is inescapably human. Calling God 'Father, Son, and Holy Spirit' provokes us to acknowledge that there is nonetheless no older or younger within the Godhead, and that God-as-God is not male. We might again recall Pseudo-Dionysius, who praised language for God (such as 'God is a rock') that comes bearing a warning about

---

[34] Ward, *Christ and the Cosmos*, 260, 225.

[35] Janet Martin Soskice, *The Kindness of God: Metaphor, Gender, and Religious Language* (Oxford: Oxford University Press, 2008), 78–79, 115, 122–24.

[36] Coakley, *God, Sexuality and the Self*, 324.

its creatureliness.[37] In contrast, were we to concentrate on naming God after human faculties, or – especially – after forms of causation, we might feel unduly confident, and gloss over the mismatch present even there between human speech and divine reality, thinking that in speaking in these abstract ways we understood God as God is. In contrast, the personal names draw attention to their context-laden qualities, and alert us that they are both true and inescapably human in their reference.

My third, and perhaps most significant, contention is that the language of God as Father, Son, and Spirit is likely not as bound to earthly reference and contingencies as Ward supposes. If we imagine that other life is generated and generative, or characterised by what Hannah Arendt called 'natality',[38] then that 'coming forth' of life from life would be an image within the world of something about the eternal life of God ('God from God, light from light, Very God of Very God'), just as the coming forth of creation as a whole has been said to rest upon the 'coming forth' of Person from Person within the Godhead, and follow from it.[39] That is not to say that the experience of creaturely begetting automatically opens up the life of the Trinity to us, but it does mean that wherever there is begetting, revelation could use that language, could point to it as that within the world which reflects something profound about the life of God as Trinity. Indeed, in Chapter 8, we will see Aquinas mention this sort of coming forth as one way in which the image of God is more perfectly to be found in human beings than in angels (although they generally surpass humans in that regard).

When it comes to the Third Person, Ward's analysis is somewhat impeded by his tendency to associate theological thinking with the

---

[37] Pseudo-Dionysius, *Celestial Hierarchies*, II.3.

[38] Hannah Arendt, *The Human Condition* (Chicago: University of Chicago Press, 1958), 8–9, 247. For discussion of the idea in other works by Arendt, see Wolfhart Totschnig, 'Arendt's Notion of Natality: An Attempt at Clarification', *Ideas y Valores* 66, no. 165 (2017): 327–46.

[39] *ST* I.45.6 *ad* 1, as set out in the body of the article.

physical forms by which the Spirit is manifest in the New Testament: 'As for the Spirit, it obviously does not exist as a bird of any sort or as a tongue of fire'.[40] No one claims, however, that God is a bird or a flame in the same sense that God is Father or Son. Aquinas could distinguish here between an analogy (human fatherhood imitates the Fatherhood of God, although the Father entirely exceeds my father in his fatherhood), and a metaphor (a dove is a dove, and the Holy Spirit is not, although the image can be communicative).[41] He also distinguishes between the Trinitarian processions (eternally in God) and the missions (in the created world), such that God is neither a bird nor even human in the same sense that God is Spirit or Son. He also makes the distinction, within the visible missions, between that of the Son and that of the Spirit, since the presence of the Spirit is only signified visibly by a sign (such as the dove in John 1.32), while the divine person of the Son is truly present and tangible as the Word made flesh.[42]

To place our consideration of the Holy Spirit on equivalent territory to that of speaking about Father and Son, we might therefore say that the Spirit is love (the love that proceeds from two as a third), or gift, moving us from metaphor to analogy. The Holy Spirit is the truest and originary love and gift,[43] of which every creaturely love or gift is an image: 'Every generous act of giving, with every perfect gift, is from above, coming down from the Father of lights'.[44] Any creaturely experience or embodiment of gift or love, anywhere, would be a participation in that eternal truth of the nature of God as Three, as to the Third Person. It would again be that in creation everywhere from which God could be named.

---

[40] Ward, *Christ and the Cosmos*, 140.

[41] *ST* I.13.3 *ad* 1.

[42] *ST* I.43.7.

[43] 'If taken personally it [love] is the proper name of the Holy Ghost; as Word is the proper name of the Son' (*ST* I.37.1); 'Gift, taken personally in God, is the proper name of the Holy Ghost' (*ST* I.38.2).

[44] James 1.17.

The Augustinian triplet of memory, intellect, and will (or love) as a reflection of the Father, Son, and Holy Spirit is a further avenue for establishing a shared Trinitarian confession. Whether this would stand as a ground for a threefold appreciation of God elsewhere in the universe depends on whether one thinks these faculties are constitutive of personhood as such, and on whether one sees them, and personhood, as something upon which evolution would converge. I will consider that question in the chapter on the *imago dei*, and make an argument in favour of convergence, grounded in the relation of these three faculties to the threefold structure of time: memory relating to the past, intellect to the present, and will to the future. Of course, if one held to a direct divine origin to personhood, human or otherwise, as something imposed into creation outside of or beyond evolution, then parallel faculties would likely come with it, wherever it is to be found. (Personally, I would wish to chart the course of seeing miraculous invocations as unnecessary, although the divine infusion of the soul remains the official teaching of the Roman Catholic Church, for instance.) In that case, questions of evolutionary convergence to these faculties may be seen as beside the point, or indeed as impossible without that divine aid (although, even then, faculties such as memory and the senses are understood as something bodily, and therefore the subject of evolutionary trajectories, and possibly convergence). Either way, if memory, intellect, and will are shared, they offer another common basis for expressing faith in God as Three-in-One.

In summary, I think that we have reasons to suppose that the confession of God as Trinity could be expressed in terms that are comparable to what Christians have wished to say, even by different creatures, in different settings and circumstances, both because part of that Christian confession has been set out in terms that are metaphysically basic (facets of causation, transcendental qualities of being, and so on), but also because the language that Christians have set above all others, that of Father, Son, and Holy

Spirit (or Gift), is not unconnected to that which would be shared in generating, being generated, and that which is given.[45]

Analogy, Metaphor, Participation, and Language

Ultimately, one's view of religious language, and not least how contingent it may be, depends on one's metaphysics. My foundations – in notions of participation, with the idea that all things are constituted as some sort of sharing from God, along with ideas of analogy that characteristically go with it – have already been in view here. That particularly explains why I differ from Ward, in not supposing that our traditions of speaking about God, elaborated on the basis of revelation, need be as fundamentally contingent as he supposes, nor therefore as divergent from what other creatures might know or express.

Ward does not spell out his theory of religious language explicitly, but it appears to be one by which God makes best use of what happens to be to hand in terms of language, experience, or reference. In describing God as 'a compassionate Father, a redemptive and self-sacrificial Son, and a sanctifying Spirit', Ward holds that we are 'rightly describing',[46] since

> good fathers on earth are a source of the being of their children, and they care for them and for their good. In speaking of God as father, then, we are pointing to an aspect of the divine being which is the source of the whole physical universe and which cares for the good of what it has generated.[47]

[45] Just because those more philosophical titles are valid, however, does not mean that they should be adopted in our Earthly situation in preference to the traditional names. As John of St Thomas put it, for instance, while it may be valid to baptise in the name of 'the One Generating, the One Generated, and the One Proceeding', it is rash, in a matter of such gravity, needlessly to cause confusion or to sow doubt (John of St Thomas, *Cursus Theologicus D. Thomae* (Colonia Agrippina: Metternich, 1711), In II-Iae, q. 21, disp. 12, art. 3, vol. 4, 519.

[46] Ward, *Christ and the Cosmos*, 255.

[47] Ibid., 249.

On this view, there is something that ought to be said about God and, happily, as a reasonably good way to do so, we can make use of notions of fatherhood, since among human beings – generally, or at least ideally – our experience and language of fatherhood at least somewhat aligns with what is to be said about God. Ward's method moves from the earthly to the divine: we – or the biblical authors, or Jesus, or God in revelation – use the words we have for what lies around, and apply them to God: 'The terms used for these three aspects – Father, Son, and Spirit – are terms drawn wholly from, and dependent for their meaning upon, items in a specifically human world'.[48] More generally, for Ward,

> these are all symbols for God drawn from things common on this planet. Other worlds may find other symbols, which we cannot be expected to imagine, that are more appropriate for them. The question is whether these symbols are appropriate symbols for some real underlying threefoldness in God.[49]

In contrast, the account of religious language offered by Aquinas is rather the inverse of this, or at least what has been said so far is only half the story.[50] Human words can be used to speak of God because what they name among creatures comes from God in the first place.

Ward picks up some of the epistemological outcomes from Aquinas's discussion, but he passes over their metaphysical

---

[48] Ibid.

[49] Ibid., 248.

[50] Ward quotes Aquinas on analogy, but does not follow the participatory logic of that account (ibid., 129–30). We might also note Ward's tendency to univocal (or at least seemingly non-analogical) use of language in relation to God, for instance, in his discussion of intra-Trinitarian relations: the Persons 'might know each other completely and admire each other tremendously. But all the rich texture, the hurt, and the forbearance and forgiveness required by human love would be missing. They need no help, need to learn nothing, do not need to put up with another's foibles' (179). The lack of analogical reticence here risks presenting rather a domesticated picture of divine life.

KNOWLEDGE OF GOD AND THE LANGUAGE

foundations.[51] Those foundations come in his account of creation as a participation in, or sharing from, God. On this view, words for creaturely things can have bearing for talking about God because everything that is good or noble about any creature is a reflection of divine perfection. Certainly, we only first *learn* the meaning of something like goodness or justice from finite, creaturely examples; only later, if at all, do we come to realise that they are finite receptions or reflections of qualities that *originate* and abound perfectly in God. In this way, when we use a creaturely word to speak about God, the quality signified (such as goodness or justice) belongs more truly to God than to the creaturely contexts from which we learned its sense, although the 'mode of signifying' – how our context both allows and colours our sense of the meaning – applies more to creaturely cases than to God.[52]

We have seen Ward writing that 'the terms used for these three aspects – Father, Son, and Spirit – are terms drawn wholly from, and dependent for their meaning upon, items in a specifically human world'.[53] The scholastic-minded theologian can affirm this as far as it goes. When it comes to the 'mode of signifying', the words we use of God are 'dependent' on 'items in a specifically human world'. Why, however, are there things in creation whose qualities, and our names for them, can be used to speak of God? Only because those things,

---

[51] I discuss Aquinas' account of analogy in *Participation in God*, 171–97, and expand it, with reference to later scholastic writers, in 'Machine Learning and Theological Traditions of Analogy'.

[52] *ST* I.13.6. Ward makes many references to the second Person as pattern or archetype for creation, but he does not bring that to bear on an account of religious language. He writes that 'God is capable of taking form within the created world and of enabling that world to participate in the divine life' (*Christ and the Cosmos*, 252). This participation looks like an overlay or a second act: something is chosen or taken up and *in that*, rather than in anything foundational about origin in God, it comes to participate in God and to be able to speak of God. Elsewhere Ward uses the language of God participating in the world by becoming one of its players, and – unlike the participatory tradition – being changed by it (77–78).

[53] Ibid., 249.

and their qualities, come from God as creator, offering finite and creaturely reflections of something that is boundless and perfect in God.[54]

Ward's account of religious language starts with what we have around us, as if it all just happens to be there, and its relation to God is more or less accidental. That explains Ward's sense of only a weak and contingent force to the traditional Trinitarian names. The language of Fatherhood, Sonship, and Spirit stretches something from creatures to refer to God, with all of the limitations that this implies: limitations that Ward is not slow to point out, writing 'I am inclined to say that the representation of God as a male human is grossly inadequate, if not actually idolatrous'.[55]

In contrast, an analogical or participatory angle understands good ways to speak about God as good because they take up created images that are already a reflection of God. The author of the Letter to the Ephesians seems to make this point in relation to the language of fatherhood, in writing 'I bow my knees before the Father [*Patéra*], from whom every family [*pâsa patriá*] in heaven and on earth takes its name'.[56] Commenting on this passage, J. Armitage Robinson was alert to its participatory logic:

> God is not only the universal Father, but the archetypal Father, the Father of whom all fathers are derivatives or types. So far from regarding the Divine fatherhood as a mode of speech in reference to the Godhead, derived by analogy from our conception of human fatherhood, the Apostle maintains that the very idea of fatherhood exists primarily in the Divine nature, and only by derivation in every other form of fatherhood … The All-Father is the source of fatherhood wherever it is found.[57]

---

[54] Ward may gesture to this in his comment about God as 'source of the whole physical universe' (249), but an exemplarist logic is not drawn out.

[55] Ward, *Christ and the Cosmos*, 139. In keeping with his generally idealist philosophy, he prefers 'mental' or 'spiritual' qualities as ways of taking about God (ibid.).

[56] Eph. 3.15.

[57] Armitage Robinson, *St Paul's Epistle to the Ephesians: A Revised Text and Translation with Exposition and Notes*, 2nd ed. (London: James Clarke and Co.,

In this way, the language of Father, Son (or Parent and Child), and Holy Spirit (or Gift) is seen to refer to God using names drawn from aspects of creation because those aspects of creation are marked by a derived likeness to the nature of God. That would make them not so arbitrary after all, and also more likely also to be at hand elsewhere, wherever there is life, begetting, love, the giving of gifts, and so on, as imitations of God. The commonality of creation provides a common repertoire of ways, across the cosmos, by which language that is grounded in the excellences of creatures, as derived from God, could provide ways to speak of God.

I have negotiated the territory of this chapter as a metaphysical realist. When it comes to knowledge, that commits me to the general principle that something objective underlies any true sense of things, whether in knowledge of a creature, or in a creature's witness to God. It does not, however, require a denial of contingency or mediation when it comes to knowing. The way any person, tradition, or culture expresses truth will be shot through with the contingencies, specificities, and particularities of language, experience, history, and so on. However, none of those elements of contingency, mediation, or particularity need undo the realist sense that, at root, knowledge is a witness to reality, based on a reception from that reality. To be true, knowledge does not need to be an identical repetition of what is known; indeed, that would be impossible. It need only be a faithful participation in it, a faithful reception from it. That will always be contingent, partial, and

---

1969), 84, Greek transliterated. He cites Athanasius making the same point: 'God does not make human beings His pattern; but rather God is properly, and alone truly, Father of His Son, [and] we human beings are also called fathers of our own children; for of Him "is every fatherhood in heaven and earth named"' ('Four Discourses against the Arians', discourse I, ch. 27, n. 23, in *Nicene and Post-Nicene Fathers: A Select Library of the Christian Church – Second series*, Vol. 4, ed. Archibald Robertson, trans. John Henry Newman and Archibald Robertson (Grand Rapids, MI: Eerdmans, 1980), 320, translation slightly amended).

specific, since what is known is in the knower after the manner of the knower.[58] Such mediatory realism weaves together the themes of similarity and divergence in relation to instances of knowledge of God: similar in that they receive from, and bear witness to, the same reality; different in that the truth of what is known is received into, and expressed in terms of, the different, contingent particularity of the knower.

A Terrestrial Parallel in W. B. Yeats

In a poem from the mid-1880s ('The Indian upon God'), W. B. Yeats treats many of the interests of this chapter, only in his case they are not approached in terms of multiple perspective across the cosmos, but in the imagined outlooks of different terrestrial creatures.[59] The poem is reproduced at the end this chapter, and comes from a period when Yeats' religious interests had been fired by contact with Indian thought.

Yeats imagines a range of creatures speaking about the form in which they know and relate to God. Each is refracted through the distinctive form of life of its own species. First, we hear from a moorfowl:

… [I] heard the eldest speak:
Who holds the world between His bill and made us strong or weak
Is an undying moorfowl, and He lives beyond the sky.
The rains are from His dripping wing, the moonbeams from His eye.

---

[58] *ST* I.14.1 *ad* 3. On this idea, see my *Participation in God*, 306–7.

[59] For dating, see Snežana Dabić, *W. B. Yeats and Indian Thought* (Newcastle upon Tyne: Cambridge Scholars Publishing, 2015), 34. It was first published as 'From the Book of Kauri–/Section V. On the Nature of God' (*Dublin University Review*, October 1886), as 'Kanva, the Indian, on God' in 1889, and with its lasting title in 1895 (ibid., 39); Peter McDonald, ed., *The Poems of W. B. Yeats*, vol. 1 (London: Routledge, 2020), 433.

KNOWLEDGE OF GOD AND THE LANGUAGE

After the fowl's perspective come three further three-line meditations, from a lotus, a roebuck, and a peacock, each expressing how
God is understood: as a lotus, a roebuck, and a peacock. Seen with
a twenty-first-century eye, perhaps trained in suspicion or cynicism, the mood here may look scathing, and the reference to the
'Indian' derogatory, or xenophobic: a Victorian equivalent, perhaps,
to Xenophanes' jibe that if horses or oxen could draw, they would
depict gods that look like horses and oxen– 'Who made the grass
and made the worms and made my feathers gay, / He is a monstrous
peacock'.[60] Given Yeats' reverence towards Indian religious thought,
however, and – more particularly – the powerful influence on Yates
of Mohini Chatterji (especially around the time that this poem was
written),[61] something more positive is clearly intended. As Jacqueline
Genet has it, 'Rather than being an attack on the anthropomorphic
conception of God, it is simultaneously an affirmation of both the
divine and of the subjective character of the truth'.[62]

I am not in a position to comment upon this poem from the
perspective of the Hindu ideas that inspired it.[63] There are themes
here, however, that are shared by Abrahamic writers, particularly
around creation and participation, with their notes of dependence
and exemplarity. God is seen by the moorhen as the one who 'holds

---

[60] Xenophanes, fragment B17. He is underlining a point he has just made about human
beings anthropomorphising the gods, for instance, as to clothing (B14) and vices
(B11–12). Kenneth Delano assumes that Yeats' poem offers a criticism of a 'naively
anthropocentric' view of religion 'in a similar vein' to Xenophanes (*Many Worlds,
One God*, 111), whereas I see it as more positive about mediation, diversity, and
representation.

[61] Sushil Kumar Jain, 'Indian Elements in the Poetry of Yeats: On Chatterji and
Tagore', *Comparative Literature Studies* 7, no. 1 (1970): 82.

[62] Jacqueline Genet, *William Butler Yeats: Les Fondements et l'évolution de La Création
Poétique* (Villeneuve-d'Ascq: Publications de l'Université de Lille, 1976), 86, my
translation.

[63] Jain ('Indian Elements', 88) identifies the most direct influence as a passage from the
Bhagavad Gîtâ (ch. 10, particularly vv. 19–42) in Chatterji's translation *The Bhagavad
Gîtâ or the Lord's Lay* (Boston: Ticknor and Co, 1887), 163–66.

the world between His bill' and 'made us strong or weak'; the lotus turns to the Lotus 'Who made the world and ruleth it', knowing itself to be 'in His image made'; the roebuck is born of the divine ideas of the great 'Scamper of the Skies'; three times in rapid succession the peacock speaks of what the 'monstrous peacock' has made. What is going on among the characters in the poem is much more than anthropomorphism (or its equivalent for these creatures). Whether read alongside the Bhagavad Gîtâ or the Bible, God is recognised here as the boundless origin and exemplar, with each creature bearing some different finite witness to some of the perfections of its maker. As the speech of the lotus particularly makes clear, in terms resonant for a Thomist, it can speak of God in terms drawn from its own being and experience because everything good and noble about its existence was in God before it was in the creature. This need not simply be an imagined exercise in natural theology. It would also apply to revelation, expressed in the terms they could comprehend. The moorhen's knowledge that 'The rains are from His dripping wing, the moonbeams from His eye' could come from inspired scripture, and not only as some extrapolation from nature.

The vista upon God afforded for each of these creatures by the mediating possibilities of their distinct creaturehood is particular, and none exhaust what God is (nor would all of them taken together). Each perspective is in a certain sense radically incomplete, both in that it does not include everything that the other creatures apprehend, but most of all in that no creaturely knowledge of God matches up to God as God is. In another sense, however, we might see an element of completeness in each case. The knowledge of God in each creature's tradition could be sufficient to guide them both as to how to live now, and to an eternal homeland.[64]

Genet's description of the character of the truth in view here as 'subjective' need not mean that it is without grounding, but rather that it needs to be expressed, mediated, translated, or produced

---

[64] *ST* I.1.1, 4, 5.

in and for each setting. Alongside that, we can also note, despite the differences, the capacity illustrated here for certain ideas, especially that of creation, to be expressed in parallel ways across different creaturely traditions, albeit inflected within a different frame of reference or 'mode of signification'. In Yeats' 'Indian upon God', we have a remarkable meditation on the idea that the one God, boundless and creative, can be known in different but not incommensurable ways by different creatures – possibly across the cosmos – refracted and accommodated to their own distinct way of knowing.

Conclusion

Any knowledge of God that is comprehensible to creatures of different forms will respect and reflect those differences. That is not to say, however, that difference will be absolute, and we can have good reasons to suppose that the doctrine of God as Trinity could be expressed by different creatures in terms comparable to traditional Christian formulations. This is true not only of terms that speak of causation or transcendental qualities of being, but also of the language of Father, Son, and Holy Spirit which, in referring to generation, coming forth, and gift, is more universal than we often recognise. Here, is it helpful to distinguish between terms used by way of analogy and those used metaphorically, or those which refer to the divine processions and those to the divine missions. So, for example, 'love' and 'gift' will be more universal conceptions of the Spirit than 'flame' or 'dove'. Whether threefoldness in God is something known by reason, or only by divine revelation, it can be expressed in creaturely terms not simply because there neutrally just happen to be terms at hand for us to use, but because a trace is found, in creaturely perfections, of that which is perfect in God. The fittingness of the human terms 'Father (or Parent)', 'Son (or Child)', and 'Holy Spirit (or Gift)' as theological categories comes from their derived likeness to the nature of God, the source and exemplar of all creaturely generation, reception, and generosity. As such, our consideration of astrobiology need not lead us to abandon these personal categories in favour of more abstract terms. This is fortunate, given the way they uphold and point to the centrality of relation in the life of God.

Paradoxically, it may be that by retaining these more obviously human categories, we are less likely to lose sight of how inescapably limited and human all of our theological terms and categories are. That is no tragedy. The work of human theology is to speak to humans in a human way. Following the line offered in Yeats' poem, Christian theology can suppose that God can be known in diverse but commensurable ways by different cultures and creatures in terms accommodated to their mode of being and knowing.

--

W. B. Yeats, 'The Indian Upon God'

I passed along the water's edge below the humid trees,
My spirit rocked in evening light, the rushes round my knees,
My spirit rocked in sleep and sighs; and saw the moorfowl pace
All dripping on a grassy slope, and saw them cease to chase
Each other round in circles, and heard the eldest speak:
Who holds the world between His bill and made us strong or weak
Is an undying moorfowl, and He lives beyond the sky.
The rains are from His dripping wing, the moonbeams from His eye.
I passed a little further on and heard a lotus talk:
Who made the world and ruleth it, He hangeth on a stalk,
For I am in His image made, and all this tinkling tide
Is but a sliding drop of rain between His petals wide.
A little way within the gloom a roebuck raised his eyes
Brimful of starlight, and he said: *The Stamper of the Skies*,
He is a gentle roebuck; for how else, I pray, could He

Conceive a thing so sad and soft, a gentle thing like me?
I passed a little further on and heard a peacock say:
Who made the grass and made the worms and made my feathers gay,
He is a monstrous peacock, and He waveth all the night
His languid tail above us, lit with myriad spots of light.

Part III | *Imago Dei* and Uniqueness

The three chapters in this section will address our sense of ourselves, and the difference that the prospect of life elsewhere in the universe may or may not make to that. Among doctrinal topics, this is where I consider the idea that human beings are made in the *imago dei*, or image of God, and ask how that might also apply to life beyond Earth. In teaching theology and astrobiology for almost ten years, I have been struck that the bearing of intelligent life elsewhere in the universe on human worth and dignity is the topic that has most challenged religiously minded students. Not every student with confessional commitments reacts that way, not even the majority, but it is common, nonetheless.

As we might now expect, discussion of the image in relation to life elsewhere in the universe will open vistas upon terrestrial questions. What do we mean by the image, and how do its various meanings relate to one another? How might the image, or other forms of similitude to God, apply to non-human creatures on Earth? How is the image related to uniqueness, and how is uniqueness related to value? However, before we get to the *imago dei*, I will consider a larger scale question, again to do with value, arising from the size of the universe and the position of the Earth. We will ask whether seeing the Earth as simply a 'wayside planet' (in Alice Meynell's words) has affected (or should influence) our sense of its dignity and ours, or its place in the purposes of God.

7 | A Copernican Demotion?

The value and standing of human beings, were there to be life beyond Earth, calls for attention to theological anthropology. Before we turn to consider such theological detail about humanity, however, we might usefully think about the position of the Earth itself in the cosmos, since the claim has often been made that Copernicus demoted human beings by demoting the Earth from a position at the centre of the universe. In this short chapter, we will see that this is not quite so simple. Theologically, our traditions were never so quick to associate position with dignity, and they contained plenty that speaks of human insignificance, physically speaking, well before we get to Copernicus. Approached in terms of the philosophy of science, early modern science did not so much maintain an old paradigm and change a couple of things, swapping the sun and the Earth: one now more central than we thought, another more peripheral. Rather, it changed the whole sense of what heavenly bodies are thought to be, and what spatial relations in the cosmos are taken to mean.

The suggestion that the presence of life elsewhere in the universe would undermine human significance is widespread in popular literature on exobiology, not least cast in terms of planetary position. In the assessment of Stephen Jay Gould, that comes as one more demotion in a long line of demotions, with successive advances in scientific knowledge coming at 'the almost intolerable price' of our 'progressive dethronement from the center of things, and increasing marginality in an uncaring universe. Thus, physics and astronomy relegated our world to a corner of the cosmos, and biology shifted our status from a simulacrum of God to a naked, upright ape'.[1]

Thomas Kuhn had gone beyond Gould, bringing other life explicitly into this chain of demotions, and suggesting that it bears on a range of Christian doctrines:

> If, for example, the earth were merely one of six planets, how were the stories of the Fall and of the Salvation, with their immense bearing on Christian life, to be preserved? If there were other bodies essentially like the earth, God's goodness would surely necessitate that they, too, be inhabited. But if there were men on other planets, how could they be descendants of Adam and Eve, and how could they have inherited original sin? … Again, how could men on other planets know of the Saviour who opened to them the possibility of eternal life? … Worst of all, if the universe is infinite … where can God's Throne be located?[2]

As Kuhn had it, the process of marginalisation began with Copernicus 'demoting' the Earth from the centre of the cosmos,[3] then the recognition that the stars are other suns, Darwin bracketing human beings with the rest of life, followed by an extraordinary expansion to our sense of the number of stars within our own galaxy, and recognition that our galaxy is itself only one of extraordinarily many.[4]

---

[1] Stephen Jay Gould, *Wonderful Life: The Burgess Shale and the Nature of History* (London: W. W. Norton & Company, 1989), 44. John Donne expressed something of this disorientation – 'And new philosophy calls all in doubt' – in his poem 'An Anatomy of the World: The First Anniversary' (1611).

[2] Thomas S. Kuhn, *The Copernican Revolution: Planetary Astronomy in the Development of Western Thought* (Cambridge, MA: Harvard University Press, 1957), 193. Kuhn saw these as answerable but disruptive questions. These matters are also Alexandre Koyré's territory in *From the Closed World to the Infinite Universe* (New York: Harper and Brothers, 1958).

[3] In reading such claims, it is good to be on guard against the anachronism of claims that 'scientists' raised challenges for 'theologians', as if these were simply and easily distinct guilds or groups of people in this period. Peter Harrison's *Territories of Science and Religion* bears directly upon this.

[4] Freud named three decenterings or demotions – by Copernicus, Darwin, and Freud himself – which John Lucas Nix calls the decentering of the planet, the species, and

The triumphs of early modern astronomy have, indeed, profoundly changed our sense of the universe and our position within it. What that has or should mean for human self-understanding, however, is a matter of considerable dispute. The association of place – being at the centre – with value is complex. Indeed, in a pre-modern conception of the universe, Earth's position at the centre was not necessarily an exalted one. The centre was where things fall; the Earth could more reasonably be considered as the rubbish dump of the cosmos than its summit.[5] Perfection lay above, away from the Earth; only beyond the moon did one pass into immutable materiality. In the words of C. S. Lewis, 'the geocentric universe is not in the least anthropocentric … We watch "the spectacle of the celestial dance" from its outskirts. The Medieval Model is, if we may use the word, anthropo-peripheral. We are creatures from the Margin'.[6]

One can as well claim, then, that Copernicus elevated the Earth, exhaling us from the position of refuse tip to take a place among the other planets. This idea underlies John Wilkins' playful claim, in the treatise discussed in Chapter 1, that a new planet had been discovered – a new moving or wandering body, namely the Earth – since

the ego ('Life-Value Narratives and the Impact of Astrobiology on Christian Ethics', *Zygon* 51, no. 2 (June 2016): 521). Victor Stenger expands this, placing weight on the theory that our cosmos is part of a multiverse ("Faith in Anything Is Unreasonable," in *Is Faith in God Reasonable? Debates in Philosophy, Science, and Rhetoric*, ed. Corey Miller and Paul Gould (New York: Routledge, 2014), 66–67).

[5] This is particularly well set out by Martinez Hewlett in 'The Copernican Revolution That Never Was', in *Astrotheology: Science and Theology Meet Extraterrestrial Life*, ed. Martinez Hewlett et al. (Eugene, OR: Cascade, 2018), 90–105. See also Lamm, 'Religious Implications', 27–28; John Hedley Brooke, *Science and Religion: Some Historical Perspectives* (Cambridge: Cambridge University Press, 1991), 89–94.

[6] C. S. Lewis, *The Discarded Image: An Introduction to Medieval and Renaissance Literature* (Cambridge: Cambridge University Press, 1994), 55. His sources are Chalcidius (a fourth-century Christian translator and commentator on Plato's *Timaeus*), and the twelfth-century theologian Alan of Lille. I discuss this further, with Jacob Sherman, in 'Science and Christian Platonism', in *Christian Platonism: A History*, ed. Alexander Hampton and John P. Kenney (Cambridge: Cambridge University Press, 2020), 376–77.

it was now to be included among their number.[7] Perhaps more accurately, we should say that modern science led more to the demotion of the other planets than to either the demotion or exaltation of the Earth. Heavenly bodies beyond the moon turned out to be mutable, made from the same sort of matter as the Earth, not from an elevated and immutable fifth element. That was the significance of Galileo's observation of heavenly change, with sunspots on the sun, moons orbiting other planets, and supernovae (transient phenomena involving the death of stars, recorded, for instance, in 1572, 1600, and 1604).[8] Or, perhaps more accurately still, we should not say that these discoveries constituted either a promotion or a demotion, but rather the replacement of one entire frame of reference by another. The Earth is no longer the centre, *and* the centre is no longer base (or exalted); the Earth joined the heavens, but the heavens are no longer a realm of immutable glory.[9]

None of that is to deny that scientific developments have shown the universe to be successively and extraordinarily larger than we had previously imagined, with a significantly different structure from what had previously been proposed. The eighteenth century, for instance, saw the proposal that our sun is not the centre of the

---

[7] Wilkins, *Discovery of a World*.

[8] Already, we might note, Ambrose of Milan had written that the same elements that are found on Earth are also found in the heavens (*Hexameron* book 1, homily 1, ch. 6, n. 20), in *Hexameron, Paradise, and Cain and Abel*, trans. John J. Savage (New York: Fathers of the Church, 1961), 19.

[9] Thomas Kuhn notes the shift in interpretive paradigm here, but in different terms: 'the men who called Copernicus mad because he proclaimed that the earth moved ... were not either just wrong or quite wrong. Part of what they meant by "earth" was fixed position. Their earth, at least, could not be moved. Correspondingly, Copernicus' innovation was not simply to move the earth. Rather, it was a whole new way of regarding the problems of physics and astronomy, one that necessarily changed the meanings of both "earth" and "motion". Without those changes, the concept of a moving earth was mad' (Thomas S. Kuhn, *The Structure of Scientific Revolutions* (Chicago: University of Chicago Press, 1970), 149–50, and see Kuhn, *The Copernican Revolution: Planetary Astronomy in the Development of Western Thought*, ch. 3, 4, and 7.

cosmos, but in fact one of a great many stars circling a centre of gravity.[10] Our sense of being one-among-many on an astronomical scale was further expanded by work to show that the collection of stars (or the galaxy) to which we belong, the Milky Way, is one alongside many others. Here, plaudits go principally by the North American astronomers Heber Doust Curtis (1872–1942) and Edwin Hubble (1889–1953). All that led to our present sense of the size of the observable universe, as containing around 200 billion galaxies of around something like 100 billion stars each.

The question to ask in response to all of that is simply whether size or position has any significance when it comes to value or meaning at all. Rabbi Norman Lamm responded forthrightly in his 1965 paper:

> The claim by a race to spiritual dignity and intrinsic metaphysical value does not depend on a 'good' cosmic address. It depends only upon the ability of members of that race to enter into a dialogue with the Creator of all races. God makes Himself available to His creatures wherever they are in His immense universe; He is not a social snob who will not be seen in the cosmic slums and alleys.[11]

His provocation was a comment by the astronomer Harlow Shapley that the prospect of finding intelligent extraterrestrial life elsewhere in the cosmos offers 'intimations of man's inconsequentiality'.[12] In

---

[10] Put forward by Thomas Wright (1711–1786) in *An Original Theory or New Hypothesis of the Universe* (London: H. Chapelle, 1750). Immanuel Kant (1724–1804) took this as an inspiration for his exposition of these ideas in *Allgemeine Naturgeschichte und Theorie des Himmels*.

[11] Lamm, 'Religious Implications', 32. Lamm offers a survey within Judaism of the discussion as to whether or not human beings are central to creation, not least in the contrast between the tenth-century Egyptian-born Rabbi Saadia, as 'the most illustrious systematic exponent of anthropocentrism', and Maimonides, who took 'a position diametrically opposed to Saadia's theory of man's superiority in the universe' in his mature work, despite having concurred with Saadia in his *Commentary on the Mishnah* from his youth (24–29).

[12] Lamm, 6, quoting Harlow Shapley, *The View from a Distant Star* (New York: Basic Books, 1963).

reply, Lamm turned the tables, suggesting that it was in fact Shapley who was erroneously attached to the idea 'that geography determines metaphysics'.[13] Instead, Lamm thought, we would do better to deny that position has anything at all to do with worth: '[man's] actions and his destiny are of significance to a Creator who, in His infinity, is not bewildered by numbers'.[14] Along similar lines, G. K. Chesterton had earlier suggested that associations of size with value are foolish:

> I do not believe in dwelling upon the distances that are supposed to dwarf the world; I think there is even something a trifle vulgar about this idea of trying to rebuke spirit by size ... I shall not stoop to the ... trick of making it [Earth] a small planet in order to make it insignificant'.[15]

Furthermore, although astronomers since Copernicus have much expanded our knowledge of the size of the universe, we might also ask whether that is quite the same thing as having expanded our felt sense of such matters. It is one thing to have newly enlarged numbers to hand, even enlarged by several orders of magnitude, and another to be able to bring that scale into our imagination.[16] Nor did human beings before modernity, theologians among them,

[13] Lamm, 'Religious Implications', 31. Similarly, Thomas Morris has written that 'Critics often accuse Christian theologians of being anthropomorphic in their thought. But here it seems to be the critics who are anthropomorphizing, or better, anthropomorpathizing, with the assumption that if they were a God, he would not deign to notice or value anything as small and insignificant on the cosmic scale as the earth and its inhabitants ... Modern critics' are 'making the same mistake with respect to value theory as the ancients whose views they deride' (*The Logic of God Incarnate* (Ithaca, NY: Cornell University Press, 1986), 166–67).

[14] Lamm, 'Religious Implications', 54.

[15] G. K. Chesterton, *The Everlasting Man* (San Francisco: Ignatius Press, 1993), 23. As Olli-Pekka Vainio has put it, 'Things like spatial location, size, and distance are axiologically insignificant categories in this context' (*Cosmology in Theological Perspective*, 115). In his poem 'The Death of Copernicus', Aubrey de Vere wrote, 'The small, the vast, are tricks of earthly vision:/To God the Omnipotent All-in-Each,/ Nothing is small, is far' (*Poems from the Works of Aubrey De Vere*, ed. Margaret Domvile (London: Catholic Truth Society, 1904), 170).

[16] C. S. Lewis comments perceptively on the 'vertiginous' size that the universe had for the medieval mind, suggesting that expansions beyond that, quantitatively, hardly

suppose the universe to be small. Ptolemy (died 168 AD) – of the much-derided Ptolemaic cosmos – had estimated the distance from the Earth to the edge of the cosmos (the fixed stars) to be 57,340,000 miles.[17] Maimonides went further, reporting Saturn to be about 125 million miles from the Earth.[18] Can the human imagination really embrace the difference between 125 million miles and 1.4 billion?

On the structure and scale of the universe, at least one mediaeval theologian was even ahead of early modern astronomy. In the fifteenth century, as we have seen, Nicholas of Cusa at least raised the possibility that the Cosmos is infinite on theological grounds, since its creator is infinite. He also denied that the Earth is at the centre in any absolute sense, and suggested that our sun is one more star among innumerable stars.[19] From a couple of millennia earlier, we might consider familiar lines from Psalm 8.[20] In numerical terms, the ancient Hebrews no doubt lacked even the sense of expansiveness found in Ptolemy or Maimonides, and yet the underlying point (which might once have been called 'existential', and now perhaps 'phenomenological') is an awe at the night sky that we can recognise today.

---

expand the psychological sense of the scale of the human, or even the terrestrial, in comparison (*The Discarded Image: An Introduction to Medieval and Renaissance Literature*, 92–121, especially 98).

[17] Vainio, *Cosmology in Theological Perspective*, 51, citing Claudius Ptolemaeus, *Ptolemy's Almagest*, ed. Gerald J. Toomer (Princeton, NJ: Princeton University Press, 1998), 1.5; Stephen Webb, *Measuring the Universe: The Cosmological Distance Ladder* (London: Springer, 1999), 34–35. Vainio points out that this is approximately 'the distance from Mars to Earth', by which I take him to mean the difference between the average distance of these two planets from the sun.

[18] Maimonides, *Guide for the Perplexed*, 3.14, quoted by Vainio, *Cosmology in Theological Perspective*, 51. Maimonides underestimated the distance, which varies between 1.2 and 1.7 billion miles across the circuit of its orbit.

[19] Nicholas of Cusa, *On Learned Ignorance*, II.1, in *Nicholas of Cusa on Learned Ignorance: A Translation and an Appraisal of De Docta Ignorantia*. The difficulty in interpreting Cusa on this point is discussed in Lai, 'Nicholas of Cusa and the Finite Universe'. Cusa did not make the same distinction that we do between stars and planets.

[20] 'It is not really possible to date the psalm with any degree of certainty' (Leonard P. Mare, 'Psalm 8: God's Glory and Humanity's Reflected Glory', *Old Testament Essays* 19, no. 3 (2006): 931).

> O Lord, our Sovereign,
> how majestic is your name in all the earth!
> You have set your glory above the heavens ...
> When I look at your heavens, the work of your fingers,
> the moon and the stars that you have established;
> what are human beings that you are mindful of them,
> mortals that you care for them?[21]

This ancient Israelite bard had a profound sense of the smallness of the human being in comparison to the rest of the cosmos, however different his cosmology was to that of Aristotle, Ptolemy, Copernicus, or our own. His text demonstrates that no one need know that the Earth is about 100 million miles from the sun, or that there are about 100 billion stars in our galaxy, to feel insignificant on purely material terms. Likewise, the affirmation of human worth found later in the psalm has nothing to do with astronomy – faulty or otherwise – but stems rather from theology.

> Yet you have made them a little lower than God,
> and crowned them with glory and honour.
> You have given them dominion over the works of your hands;
> you have put all things under their feet.[22]

We now recognise that the 'works of God's hands' run to 100 billion stars in our galaxy, and to about as many galaxies. Even stressing that human dominion does not run to them seems unlikely to have surprised the writer, or his readers. The human remit extends to 'sheep and oxen ... the beasts of the field, the birds of the air, and the fish of the sea, [and] whatever passes along the paths of the seas'. The list is an extensive one, but not exhaustive: it does not extend to the heavens – to sun, moon, and stars.[23]

---

[21] Ps. 8.1, 3–4.
[22] Ps. 8.5–6.
[23] Ps. 8.8.7–8.

This psalm may also remind us that the Jewish and Christian (and indeed Islamic) imagination already assumed that human beings were not the only creatures with an elevated spiritual dignity, and perhaps not the highest. While the NRSV translates the word *elohim* in verse 5 as 'God' ('a little lower than God'), the Hebrew is a plural, and so it could be translated as 'gods', which is to say as 'heavenly beings'. Such beings, within an eventually more fully integrated Jewish monotheism, came to be called angels, and indeed, the Septuagint renders this word as *angeloi*, the Vulgate – following it – as *angelis*, and the Authorised Version as 'angels'.

Scientific Concerns over Heliocentrism

When we considered mediaeval discussions around a plurality of worlds in Chapter 1, we saw that that reluctance to move away from earlier perspectives – especially the idea that there would only be one world, which meant something like one solar system – was often grounded in the science of the day, and not in some theological objection to a newer proposal. The shift to a heliocentric vision of the cosmos offers a similar story, closer to our time, in this case dealing with the move to a heliocentric picture, where a major impediment was not theological but scientific.

The ancient world had bequeathed Ptolemy's geocentric model, with the sun, moon, and other planets orbiting the Earth. It was generally accepted in the thought of the Abrahamic faiths until the sixteenth century, although it was not without critics, such as the Iranian Arabic polymath Nasir al-Din al-Tusi (1201–1274), since Ptolemy's model does not quite fit what we observe, requiring some arbitrary tweaks, called epicycles.

The great upheaval came with Nicolaus Copernicus, and his suggestion that the Earth and other planets circle the sun, rather than the sun, moon, and other planets circling the Earth. Copernicus' proposal was modified and placed on a stronger theoretical framework by Johannes Kepler, who established the basic characteristics of planetary motion, encapsulated in his three laws. One, for instance, recognises that planets travel in elliptical paths, not circular ones. A rigorous mathematical basis would have to wait for the development of calculus: one of the central contributions of Isaac Newton, alongside his laws of motion, and his mathematical account of gravitational attraction. Even without the benefit of telescopes, the Danish astronomer Tycho Brahe (1546–1601) amassed painstaking observations, later deployed by Galileo Galilei (1564–1642), adding far greater numerical detail to Kepler's work and turning up significant qualitative discoveries. Among these, the observation of moons circling Jupiter was important, since it offered decisive proof that not all the bodies in motion in the solar system orbited the Earth, or anything else at the centre. His work on sunspots, as I have already mentioned, helped to demonstrate that the rest of the solar system was made from the same sort of mutable matter as the Earth.

That is the story of the triumph of early modern astronomy, and a triumph it is. It does not mean, however, that a heliocentric model had been established beyond doubt, on scientific grounds, by the end of Galileo's career, with the church serving only as an obstacle. For one thing, as is now widely appreciated, Galileo received a mixture of approval and disapproval from church leaders, and he was a man of significant religious conviction. So were other figures in the story: Copernicus, for instance, was a canon of the cathedral in Frauenburg (now Frombork, in present-day Poland) until his death. Just as worthy of note, however, and less well known, are objections to a heliocentric model from scientific quarters.[24]

---

[24] Dennis Danielson and Christopher M. Graney, 'The Case against Copernicus', *Scientific American* 310, no. 1 (January 2014): 72–77; Christopher M. Graney, 'The Telescope against Copernicus: Star Observations by Riccioli Supporting a Geocentric Universe', *Journal for the History of Astronomy* 41, no. 4 (November 2010): 453–67; 'Stars as the Armies of God: Lansbergen's Incorporation of Tycho Brahe's Star-Size Argument into the Copernican Theory', *Journal for the History of Astronomy* 44, no. 2 (May 2013): 165–72.

The chief problem was that stars appeared to be of appreciable size in the sky when observed through a telescope. If the Earth really does move around the sun, however, then we know that the stars must be enormously far away, since their position in the sky does not appear to change. The combination of those two observations would suggest that the stars must be of an astonishing size. In order to appear to a viewer on earth to be of finite, measurable size, while existing at such a distance from us as not to shift in the night sky as the Earth moves, each star would need to be larger than our entire solar system. That, however, offends the very principle that Copernicus' work suggests, namely that there is nothing particularly unusual about the Earth or our solar system (the 'principle of mediocrity'). Only in the 1800s was the mistake in this argument discovered. It turns out that, when viewed through a telescope, stars appear far larger than they actually are. They should appear as infinitesimal points, but they do not because of the way in which their light is dispersed by glass lenses.[25] Only with this appreciation was the scientific objection to heliocentrism properly answered.

Heliocentrism was then fully established, and yet we might sum up our discussion in this chapter with the conclusion that cosmological shifts over the size of the universe, and the position of the Earth, are ultimately not particularly significant. In thinking about our place in the universe, the theological tradition has placed little emphasis on either. Instead, it has often been highly invested in the idea, found at the opening of Genesis, that human beings bear the 'image of God', and it is to that claim and idea that we turn in the next two chapters.

---

[25] Our understanding as to why this is so rests with George Biddell Airy (1801–1892), who also set Greenwich as the prime meridian.

8 | Uniqueness and Sharing the *Imago Dei*

In asking whether the presence of other life in the cosmos would compromise or threaten our human significance or standing, not least in relation to God, the idea of the human being as made in the image of God (the *imago dei*) is obviously central. In my experience of teaching, students often associate the image with distinction from other life, and a sense of superiority. The presence of other rational life would tend to threaten that. For my part, I cannot see why the *imago dei* should be comparative or competitive, or lessened in us were it also to be found elsewhere. Such topics raise much to discuss, not least since treatments of the *imago dei* are varied and because the ideas of uniqueness invoked here are more complex than we might at first suppose.

I begin this discussion by turning to that idea of 'uniqueness', for which the *Oxford English Dictionary* suggests two distinct senses.[1] Historically, the word initially referred to that 'of which there is only one'; a meaning close to the etymological roots in the Latin *unicus*, meaning 'single, sole, alone of its kind'. 'Unique' in this sense is principally descriptive. In contrast, the second sense is more evaluative or value-laden: it is to be better. That meaning has emerged only relatively recently, as a matter of 'standing alone in comparison with others, *frequently by reason of superior excellence*'.[2] Unlike

---

[1] 'unique, adj. and n.', *Oxford English Dictionary Online*. Oxford University Press, March 2015. www.oed.com/view/Entry/214712 (accessed 9 April 2015).
[2] Emphasis added.

the first meaning, it admits more by way of degree than the first, such that the otherwise odd phrase 'very unique' starts to make more sense.[3]

On a first look, it would seem that uniqueness in either of these senses would be undermined or forfeit if other creatures are comparable to us (first sense) or superior to us (second sense), but much rides on those words 'comparable' and 'superior', and each is complex. How complete does comparability have to be before it compromises uniqueness in the first sense, for instance? Two different forms of rational animal would both be rational animals, but a good deal could still distinguish them: much that is to be prized and celebrated, 'unique'. Moreover, even where they can be directly comparable, we can ask whether uniqueness is really correlated with value at all, or for that matter with the *imago dei*. Is anything less valuable because something else is like it? Does being in the *imago dei* in any way require that other things are not? Intellectual powers have been the supreme mark of excellence among creatures for much of Christian theology, yet while angels have been said to exceed us there, that has not prevented those same theologians from saying that human beings are made in the image of God. Turning to the second sense of uniqueness (unique-as-better), superiority might be less easy to define than one would think.

I do not see that value need be aligned either with being different from other things, or with being superior. Back in 1914, L. T. Townsend wrote, 'If he [the human being] is not the greatest, the grandest, the most important of created things, the one to whom all else is made to contribute, then the Bible writers have misrepresented

---

[3] 'The usage [of 'unique'] in the comparative and superlative, and with adverbs as *absolutely, most, quite, thoroughly, totally,* etc., has been objected to as tautological' (*OED Online,* 'unique'). The association of the phrase 'very unique' with estate agents (or real estate brokers) is attested at the turn of the twentieth century by Kenneth Grahame: '"Toad Hall", said the Toad proudly, "is an eligible self-contained gentleman's residence, very unique"' (*The Wind in the Willows* (London: Methuen and Co, 1908), ch. 6).

entirely man's relation to God and the universe'.[4] But why should that be so? Why should human value be diminished just because other creatures share that upon which it rests? We could pose that question without having to think of life beyond Earth. Why should we suppose that anything valuable or glorious about human beings would be less valuable or glorious just because it turned out that dolphins, for instance, had a rich intellectual, communal, religious, and artistic life? Someone may think that value rests on being different from other things, or being better than them, but that would be a philosophical, moral, or ideological stance. Whether it is contestable is open to question: I suspect that convictions like this are more argued from than argued to, and more a part of one's psychological fundamental makeup than items for debate.

Accounts of the Image

Other questions remain but, before turning to them, it may be useful to rehearse some of the accounts of the *imago dei* that have been given. Although many readers will be familiar with such discussions, this book seeks to be of value to those outside theology who wish to appreciate how questions about astrobiology might impact religious thought (here Christian thought), so an introduction to some of the main schools of interpretation within contemporary Christian theology as to the nature or location of the *imago dei* may be in order.

Discussion of the *imago dei* has long been a contested area. As Calvin wrote, 'Interpreters do not agree concerning the meaning of these words'.[5] I aim for an integrative view, thinking that our

---

[4] L. T. Townsend, *The Stars Not Inhabited: Scientific and Biblical Points of View* (New York: Eaton and Mains, 1914), quoted without page number in Delano, *Many Worlds, One God*, 9.

[5] Calvin, *On the First Book of Moses*, 1:93, in Gen. 1.26, quoted by David S. Cunningham, 'The Way of All Flesh: Rethinking the Imago Dei', in *Creaturely*

theology will be stronger for it, not seeing different accounts as necessarily in conflict, or lined up against one another. Different theologians, and different theological traditions, may put the emphasis on one interpretation over another without requiring the conquest of that account over all the others. From my own participatory viewpoint, I would expect the realisation of the image to be multifaceted precisely because it is an image of the infinite within the finite. While monolithic claims have sometimes been made, with one account of the image routing the others, the different accounts of the image are generally complementary, even co-implicating, and flounder when set in competition with one another, as we will see.

I will focus on three broad interpretations of the image of God in human beings: in human constitution, in the human role, and in human relations. The 'constitution' (or 'structural') approach locates the image in what human beings *are*, and often in the possession of certain faculties. Within this broad framework, the stress may be laid more on one facet than another: on reason, moral sense, freedom, creativity, or personhood, for instance.[6] As we saw in Chapter 8, Augustine set out a constitution-based account of the *imago dei* in Trinitarian terms, with memory, intellect, and will (reflecting the Father, Son, and Holy Spirit, respectively).[7] Augustine's example teaches us to be wary about how we use language of 'faculties' or 'constitution', since for him (as for others after him, including Aquinas) the image is not so much found in particular capacities as in their exercise. That is to say, the human being exhibits the image of God not so much in being-able-to-remember, but in the act of remembering, and similarly with knowing and willing (or

Theology: On God, Humans and Other Animals, ed. Celia Deane-Drummond and David Clough (London: SCM Press, 2009), 109.

[6] See a summary in Claus Westermann, *Genesis 1–11: A Commentary*, trans. John J. Scullion (Minneapolis, MN: Augsburg, 1994), 149.

[7] This finds its fullest expression in book XIV. The idea appears earlier, but alongside a profusion of other triplets, some more closely associated with memory, intellect, and will, some less so.

loving).[8] Indeed, more specifically, the image would find its fullest form in remembering, knowing, and loving *God*.[9] Recognising that nuance goes a good way towards addressing the accusation, sometimes made against 'constitution' accounts of the *imago dei*, that they are inherently 'static'.[10] Such an approach to the image may be possible, but that is not what is offered by Augustine or Aquinas, for instance, with their emphasis on facilities-in-action. The emphasis is not on an atemporal capacity-to-know, for instance, but on the act of knowing.

Seeing human beings as exhibiting the *imago dei* through faculties-in-action brings us into the territory of the second broad category, thinking about the image of God in terms of activity and 'role'. Recent years have seen considerable interest in how the idea of the *imago dei* is introduced in Genesis in terms of role or function, through notions of 'dominion': 'Then God said, "Let us make humankind in our image, according to our likeness; and let them have dominion over the fish of the sea, and over the birds of the air, and over the cattle, and over all the wild animals of the earth, and over every creeping thing that creeps upon the earth"'.[11]

Useful here is recognition that the language of an 'image' was deployed in the ancient Near Eastern world (forming a background to the Old Testament) to describe the relation of a local ruler to a regional overlord. As representative or viceroy, the local ruler was the 'image' of the more ultimate power.[12] Genesis 1 presents just such a combination of the language of image and of delegated authority. That helpfully qualifies the meaning and limits of

[8] Such an account raises questions about disability. A Thomist will likely say that the *imago dei* plays out at the level of specific natures, such that someone who lacks the capacity to reason in a certain way, for instance, nonetheless has the dignity proper to a human being on account of being human.

[9] Augustine, *De Trinitate*, XIV.12.15.

[10] I have discussed this in *Participation in God*, 108.

[11] Gen 1.26.

[12] Westermann, *Genesis 1–11*, 151–54; J. Richard Middleton, *The Liberating Image: The Imago Dei in Genesis 1* (Grand Rapids, MI: Brazos Press, 2005), 93–146.

'dominion', since while authority is granted to a vassal ruler in that locality, that place, and its people, are held in trust. The viceroy who despoils his or her charge is liable to discipline. To be in the image of God according to function would therefore be to act as God's representative within the surrounding creation, with responsibilities as well as privileges. A 'functional' account of the *imago dei*, however, does not exclude other approaches. Accounts based on role mesh nicely with accounts based on constitution, for instance. Human beings can fulfil their role precisely because of what they are: knowing, loving, remembering, creative, free, and so on. Unless we imagine that a rock or a rosebush could serve as God's viceroy, the *imago dei* as function is inherently entangled with the *imago dei* as constitutional or structural.

This brings us to the third broad category for describing the *imago dei*, set out in terms of relationships. Here Karl Barth, for instance, laid stress on the plurals – both divine and human – in the Genesis text quoted above, as also to the plurality of human beings as male and female.[13] The *imago dei* would not consist simply in that plurality, but in relatedness. For Barth, that was particularly between men and women, though it does not exhaust the bounds of human plurality and relation. This interrelatedness between persons constitutes the analogy in human beings to the Trinitarian interrelatedness within God. More recently, the Barthian Robert Jenson has drawn out the element of address in a relational account, asking 'Who then were Adam and Eve? They were the first hominid group

---

[13] Gen 1.26, 27. Karl Barth, *Church Dogmatics: The Doctrine of Creation (III/1)*, trans. O. Bussey and H. Knight (Edinburgh: T&T Clark, 1958), §41, 191–206. Biblical scholars are more likely today to suggest that the plural here ('let us') refers to God addressing a heavenly council. Perhaps in the depths of earlier traditions this may have carried a sense of polytheism, but this language would morph in later Hebrew thought to being understood as referring to the company of angels. See the comment on Ps. 8.5 in this regard in Chapter 7. Bill Arnold sees the plural as 'a pregnant way of saying that God deliberated with himself about the creation of humankind' (*Genesis* (Cambridge: Cambridge University Press, 2013), 49).

that in whatever form of religion or language used some expression that we might translate 'God', as a vocative ... Who were Adam and Eve? They were the first hominid group who by ritual action were embodied before God'.[14]

Again, this account need not be seen as being in competition with others. We can accept that human plurality and relationships bear witness to the life of God as Three-in-One, without supposing that relationality exhausts the meaning of the image. Human relationality, for instance, is grounded in what we are, and vice versa: 'constitution' accounts of the image need to take relationality on board; 'relation' accounts should recognise that their insights are grounded in the nature of human creatures as human creatures. Similarly, relationality and role reinforce one another. Rarely do we accomplish anything of significance alone: human action is usually joint action. Similarly, human relatedness is intrinsically bound up with action and joint projects, a point that Aquinas underlined in stressing that marriage, for all it is about the relation of one person to another, naturally gives rise to participation in social projects, or 'an entire communion of works'.[15]

Other Creatures on Earth

One of our questions is whether the *imago dei* necessarily involves being different from other creatures. In recent years, burgeoning theological interest in animals has led some to question whether the association of human beings with the image of God prevents other animals from being described that way. David S. Cunningham, for instance, has written that

---

[14] Jenson, *Systematic Theology: The Works of God*, 59–60.
[15] *ST* III, *suppl.* 49.2, posthumously constructed from the fourth book of his *Commentary on the Sentences*.

the biblical text never denies the attribution of 'image of God' to any other element of creation ... anyone who attempts to make the theological claim that some (or all) other creatures are not created in God's image in any sense of the term must depend upon an *argumentum e silentio* [an argument from silence].[16]

Certainly, the opening chapters of the Bible do not paint a picture of human beings as simply and only distinct from other creatures. Human beings are created along with other land animals on the sixth day, for instance, and they too are of and from the earth.[17] On the other hand, even if made on the same day, human beings do close the sequence of making, which is hardly without significance. Similarly, Adam names the animals, and not vice versa, and none among them is found to be a suitable helpmeet, hence the creation of Eve.[18] Moreover, the language of image and likeness *is* used only of the human, and that strikes me as more than an 'argument from silence'. Here Lamm suggested a sensible balance: on the one hand, 'man's creation at the end of the six days, at the apex of an ascending order of creatures, implies man as the end not only chronologically but also teleologically'; on the other, 'opposing this is God's majestic address to Job out of the whirlwind, which leads us from a consideration of the mystery and immensity of creation to an appreciation of man's triviality and his moral and physical and intellectual inadequacy' (although, personally, I would not want 'triviality' to be the last word on humanity).[19] I take it that Genesis

---

[16] Cunningham, 'Way of All Flesh', 106.
[17] This bears upon discussion of 'Deep Incarnation', to which I turn in Chapter 12, and the point that in the Incarnation God takes up flesh (*sarx*), which is shared certainly by all animals, and could be said to name the bodies of all that live. The perspective of the writer of Ecclesiastes is also worth bearing in mind: 'For the fate of humans and the fate of animals is the same; as one dies, so dies the other. They all have the same breath, and humans have no advantage over the animals; for all is vanity' (Eccl. 3.19).
[18] Gen. 2.18–24.
[19] Lamm, 'Religious Implications', 23. Lamm refers to God's address from the whirlwind (Job 38.1–40.2). He notes the presence of dignity and insignificance side

1 does associate the *imago dei* only with human beings and – like Lamm – it would be to Job that I would turn for a de-centering complement. That said, even if human beings alone stand in the image of God in Genesis 1, that does not mean that the image *consists* in a difference from every other creature and thus can only apply to one species, such that if another turned out to bear it, that would prove that we are not made in the image of God after all. Nor does it mean that creatures not in the image bear no likeness to God as creator.

Restricting the Image but Sharing the Trace

Cunningham's proposal, in fact, is not so much to flatten out the distinction between human beings and other animals entirely as it is to deny that creaturely likeness to God comes down to being either an image or nothing: 'the word "image" is not a Boolean operator (like true-or-false); we use it more like we ordinarily use words for a certain colour (say, "yellow")'.[20] Turning to scholastic theological traditions, Cunningham's point would be partially accepted and partially recast. There too, we encounter the idea that every creature is related to God as its exemplar and therefore constituted by some likeness or similitude to God. The difference from Cunningham would be still to reserve the language of image for creatures of a certain kind – for instance, for those

---

by side in Ps. 8.4–9, as we saw in Chapter 7. William Brown has written perceptively about astrobiology in relation to the Book of Job in 'Knowing God in Light of Job and Astrobiology', in *Knowing Creation: Perspectives from Theology, Philosophy, and Science*, ed. Andrew B. Torrance and Thomas H. McCall (Grand Rapids, MI: Zondervan, 2018), 141–54.

[20] Cunningham, 'Way of All Flesh', 111. David Clough suggests something similar, in a discussion of other creatures and the *imago dei* that places the idea in a strongly Christological framework (*On Animals: Volume I: Systematic Theology* (London: Bloomsbury, 2012), 100–2).

with memory, intellect, and will – and to use other terms for more widely shared forms of likeness to God, to which we will now turn.

Both Aquinas and Bonaventure offered the distinction between a more and less specific form of creaturely likeness to God which they called an image, and a broader trace (or vestige), and for both writers, a Trinitarian perspective is in view.[21] Bonaventure, in fact, began with a further form of likeness, called a 'shadow'. Writing in his *Commentary on the Sentences*, he described every creature as bearing the 'shadow' of a divine likeness. Every creature proceeds from God according to what belongs alike to all Three Persons, for instance, in as much as the being of the creature bears witness to the being of God, from whom it comes. Beyond this shadow, Bonaventure also described every creature as coming from God bearing a trace. This brings us to the territory of the triplets that are familiar from Chapter 6: each creature bears the likeness-as-trace as *one* and unified in itself, as characterful and *true*, and as *good* and in relation.[22] Again, each aspect here comes from, and belongs to, all three Persons, but this trace has a Trinitarian angle, which the 'shadow' lacks, in that we can properly associate (or 'appropriate') these characteristics with the Father, Son, and Holy Spirit, respectively. In that way, although only with the eyes of faith, one can see an appropriated likeness to the Trinity (a trace) in all creatures.

---

[21] For instance, Bonaventure, *Commentary on the Sentences*, book 1, dist. 3, part 1, single article, q. 2, translation from *Philosophy of God*, 77–78; *Breviloquium*, II.1, 71; *Itinerarium*, I.14, pp. 57, 59; V.7, p. 119. I discuss this in relation to these and other texts in Bonaventure in 'Bonaventure's Trinitarian Ontology' in a contribution to a forthcoming edited collection on Trinitarian ontologies. In Aquinas, see *ST* I.39.8, 45.7, with a treatment in my *Participation in God*, 60–61, 101–3. This is the territory of the threefold perfections appropriated to the Persons of the Trinity discussed in relation to Aquinas and Bonaventure in Chapter 6.

[22] The middle aspect, in the characterfulness of each creature, provides a particularly significant basis for speaking about every creature as constituted by a certain form of likeness derived from God, whether we associate that with the likeness of the creature to a divine idea, or with the way in which it shows forth in creation some combination of likenesses to divine excellences (as I discuss below).

On top of this, some creatures, though not all, are then said not only to bear a shadow and trace of divine likeness, but also to be made in the image of God. This is again a Trinitarian point. The perfections of unity, truth, and goodness, which are reflected as traces in creation, are only *appropriated* to the three Persons, but the distinction between memory, intellect, and will – found in human persons – is an image of what truly *distinguishes* the divine Persons. For Bonaventure, as for Aquinas, rational creatures are set apart in this way, as an image, and not only a trace (and shadow).[23]

Having this wider, more general language to place alongside the language of image allows us to describe human beings as in the image of God without by any means cutting other creatures adrift, since they too bear a trace and shadow. As the doctrine of creation *ex nihilo* stresses, the whole of every creature comes from God. Even if human beings are distinct, as having been made in the image of God, that does not undo all they share with other creatures. Nor does the language of image, trace, and shadow exhaust all that has been said about divine exemplarity, with each creature also imitating God in some entirely specific way: copying a divine idea, and imitating a particular combination of divine excellences.[24] We have categories, then, that allow us to speak about the human being (and other rational creatures) as distinct, while also recognising their place in the wider ensemble of creatures, each of which are also valuable: as exhibiting the divine trace, imitating divine excellences, and embodying a distinct divine idea.

---

[23] Bonaventure adds the eschatological category of likeness, to which a creature that bears the image is elevated by grace (*Breviloquium*,II.12.1). I have discussed this passage, along with *ST* I.45.7 and Aquinas's *Commentary on Colossians*, ch. 1, lect. 4, n. 31, in *Participation in God*, 101–3.

[24] On this in Aquinas, see Gregory Doolan, *Aquinas on the Divine Ideas as Exemplar Causes* (Washington, DC: Catholic University of America Press, 2008); Mark McIntosh, *The Divine Ideas Tradition in Christian Mystical Theology* (Oxford: Oxford University Press, 2021), and my discussion in ""He Fathers-Forth Whose Beauty Is Past Change', but 'Who Knows How?': Evolution and Divine Exemplarity"', *Nova et Vetera* 16, no. 4 (November 2018): 1067–102.

Even thinking about life on Earth, the one planet we know, the characteristics, roles, and relationships that we associate with the *imago dei* did not burst upon the scene with human beings as if totally new, unconnected to what went before. Every organism, down to the simplest bacterium, exhibits some form of what a philosopher might call 'intentionality': every creature, even that bacterium, has something like an 'interest' in the world around them. It has some sense of what the environment is like, and it can exercise some agency in relation to how it finds that environment to be – some minimum of motility, perhaps, or even simply the ability to open and close ion channels selectively in response to its external environment.[25] There is also a sense of memory across all living organisms: in genetics and epigenetics, for instance, and in the widespread ability of organisms to respond to stimuli after the fashion of counting, as with insects that emerge from the earth after only a certain number of winters, or of carnivorous plants which close in on an insect only on the second trigger of a sensitive hair. At least judging by organisms on Earth, then, memory, intellect, and will are foreshadowed across the living world, however much human beings stand out in the way they exhibit these powers (to the extent, indeed, that the scriptural writers can talk about the human being becoming a 'friend' of God).[26] While memory, intellect, and will, as we find them in human beings, might be found only relatively rarely on the astrobiological scene, some analogical sense of them likely belongs to life as such.

Christian theology can be hierarchical about creatures without being dismissive of any of them. Any notion of a hierarchy of

---

[25] See the comments on niche construction in Chapter 4, and my paper 'All Creatures'.

[26] Exod. 33.11; Isa. 41.8; James 2.23. As Gregory of Nazianzus had it, the goal of life for the Christian is 'To be, rather than to seem to be, a friend of God' (*De Vita Sua*, II.1.11, translation from Franz Jozef van Beeck, *God Encountered – Part III: Finitude and Fall* (Collegeville, MN: Liturgical Press, 1995), 9.

species must rest on a prior sense of a hierarchy of attributes, even if that remains unarticulated. For a swathe of Christian writing, including much scholasticism, the structure of that hierarchy has been expressed clearly (as we saw in Chapter 4): to be alive is more exalted than to be inanimate; to possess a greater degree of sensing and responsiveness is more elevated still (as in the difference between a plant and an animal); finally, to be able to understand and reason about the world in general terms is the highest perfection of all.[27] Despite some criticisms that could be made, this seems correct to me. Nonetheless, I would want to concede that there are varied ways to map excellence. Even if I outstrip an eagle in reason and creativity, it outstrips me in swiftness and clarity of sight; a rock surpasses both me and the eagle in solidity, although we both surpass the rock when it comes to life. Such a multi-dimensional vision of excellence may be useful when it comes to thinking about astrobiology. For one thing, the excellences of whatever does not possess reason are truly excellent, and they display something glorious that is derived from God. Just as I have not wanted to write off vast regions of inanimate matter across the cosmos – stars, planets and moons, nebulae and so on – as simply the 'plinth' for the 'statute' that is life, neither would I want to say that life has no value if it lacks abstract reason, or the flowering of memory, intellect, and will that we see in human beings.[28] Nor would I want to say that creatures that possess only the trace have value only as a step on the way towards those with the image.

Christian traditions have been right to rejoice in the particular glories of different sorts of creatures. Nonetheless, I would still also want to uphold the sense of a hierarchy of perfections: reason, swiftness, solidity, and clarity of sight all are good, but reason stands out, not least because it can encompass the others in a way that they cannot. We can reason about the rock and its solidity, but it cannot reason about us.

---

[27] See Chapter 4, on the roots of this distinction in Porphyry.
[28] See Chapter 4.

Variegation and Non-Competition in the Metaphysics of Likeness

We can suppose the human being to be set apart without denying the God-givenness of every other creature's particularity. To say that human beings are unique-as-distinct on Earth, however, on account of the image of God, is not to say that they are the only creatures in the cosmos that could possesses it. Nor is it to say that the image they bear consists in their difference from every other creature, as if the image would be compromised or lessened if other life were comparable to them and bore it too. Again, Lamm is useful here, setting out, in his own idiom, what I have explored here in more metaphysical terms:

> It is true the doctrine of man's creation in the divine Image bestows transcendent value upon him, lifting him out of the order of the purely natural; but it is by no means necessarily an exclusivist principle. It is quite possible that homo sapiens on this planet and other equivalent races elsewhere represent the interpenetration of the natural and the supernatural.[29]

Lamm sees that 'interpenetration' as lying at the heart of otherwise varied accounts of the image of God. He also makes the point that the image need be no more 'exclusivist' or exclusionary between species as it is between multiple human beings: 'If the Image of the Absolutely One God can be impressed upon the manifold individuals within the human race, it can be similarly bestowed upon a multitude of races'.[30]

For the image to be competitive, with more here meaning less somewhere else, seems at odds with the very idea of an image. Just because one thing bears a likeness to an exemplar, that does not prevent anything else from doing so. Exemplarity is not attenuated by

[29] Lamm, 'Religious Implications', 22.
[30] Ibid., 23.

imaging: Queen Elizabeth II was painted many times, and that did not use up her likeness; a couple can have many children, passing on their likeness to each (a fully Biblical notion), and be no less able to pass on their likeness to a further child.[31] If a human being is not attenuated by the passing on of her likeness, how much less could finite likenesses diminish the infinite God? Even with mundane examples, no likeness fully represents the origin: parents can have many children, and each receives something of their likeness in a way that another does not; a painter might treat the same subject many times without producing the same portrait. Even within creation, we find an inexhaustible depth in the passing of the finite into the finite. How much more would that apply to the relation of the finite to the infinite? Similarly, if we take the image to be about representation by action and authority, it need not be competitive, especially if we are talking about different regions. Even in human terms, one person may be the King's image or representative in Cambridge, as Lord Lieutenant of Cambridgeshire, and that will not impede someone else being Lord Lieutenant of Norfolk. A caveat on that front might be the possibility of tensions over shared responsibility for a place occupied in common. That might raise questions about places with more than one species functioning as the image of God, but that would not in any relevant sense apply to human beings, since the distance between stars (and even more, between any inhabited planets) precludes the suggestion that the stewarding role of human beings could apply on a galactic or cosmic scale.[32]

In closing this discussion, we can note that a likeness points away from itself, from the image to the exemplar. Whatever good or noble character, relation, or role we might mean by the *imago dei*, it comes from God. As Augustine was fond of asking, taking up a rhetorical question from Paul, 'What do we have that we did

---

[31] Gen. 5.3.

[32] Interstellar travel might change that, but in that case, I would be inclined to suppose that the role of divine representation belongs to the native inhabitant, not the visitor.

not receive?' As the Letter of James has it, every 'perfect gift is from above'.[33] This should urge us all the more not to be proprietorial about the *imago dei*. It is not ours by dint of ingenuity or striving. It is a gift in creation, elevated yet further by grace. The *imago dei* (or for that matter, the *vestigium dei*) is something God shares with us, and perhaps with other creatures, in making them what they are. It is not ours to horde or begrudge to others. What God gives freely on Earth, God may also give freely elsewhere. This emphasis on the giver also cautions us against belittling the excellence of any other creature simply because it is not of the same glory as the *imago dei*. Indeed, even if a creature bears only a trace or vestige of God, it too is of great worth, since its exemplar is God.

Analogy and the *Imago Dei*

Scholastic traditions have set out different forms of likeness to God, not least with the distinction between the trace and image of God. Even in relation to the latter, however, and concentrating on creatures to which we might attribute memory, intellect, and will (or elevated and self-aware forms of relationality or stewardship), we can imagine different forms of divine likeness, and do so without treating them in a stiffly hierarchical fashion. As I intimated above, any sense that the image of God is a finite reflection of boundless divine perfection already suggests that the image need not be one thing only, or identical wherever it is found. To put this another way, if the relation between God and creatures is one of analogy, not univocity, then the image would also be related analogically between one creature and another. Even among human beings, all bearing the image of God, the image is inflected in particular ways.

[33] 1 Cor. 4.7; James 1.17.

If we say that God has (or is) 'reason' and that a creature has 'reason', we are not using those words in the same way: we are using them by way of analogy. God is reason itself – superabundant and perfect – whereas creatures simply embody some limited likeness or fragmentary imitation of divine reason. Different rational creatures could, and I think would, possess diverse forms of finite intelligence. The relation of finitude to plenitude suggests as much. Across the vast history of the universe, and its measureless expanse of space, there may be, or have been, thousands of forms of rational being, or millions, or more. Even all taken together, in their unfathomable variety, they would not exhaust the perfection of what they gesture towards: the superabundant reason of God, which we call *Logos*. The Son is the perfect image of the Father. Creatures may participate in some aspects of that image, but they are not the Son's equal. Creation's homage to plenitude is its multiplicity, and I would stress that same variety in the realisation of the *imago dei*: whether according to a structural, relational, or role-focused account of the image. Being a creaturely representative of God, or bearing the image in relation to a particular role, stretches across a variety of forms even on Earth (parenthood, teaching, government, gardening, and so on), none of which alone, or together, exhaust how the functional dimension of *imago dei* could be expressed in the world. The variation across the cosmos would no doubt be greater still.

Aquinas, for his part, indicated a pluriformity to what the image might mean in response to the question of whether the image is to be found more perfectly in human beings or in angels.[34] As his overall answer, angels outstrip human beings, since 'their intellectual nature is more perfect' than ours. Nonetheless, he could identify at least two ways in which human beings embody a likeness to God that the angels cannot share. The first is 'that man proceeds

---

[34] Not every theologian has attributed the *imago dei* to angels, but the Thomist tradition has, and I think with good reason: they are conscious and intelligent, free, and able to make moral choices; they are at least somewhat communal (they

from man, as God from God'. In that, human life reflects something of the eternal generation of the Son: a human child is from human parents, in some way after the fashion that the Son is 'God from God'. A second unique feature of the human expression of the *imago dei*, at least compared to the angels, in that 'the whole human soul is in the whole body'. This, Aquinas thought, is an apt similitude for the relation of God to the world, who is 'in every part … in regard to the whole world'. (I find this angle less compelling than the first.) Here, in what could simply seem a quirky aside, Aquinas offered an important endorsement of a multi-dimensional understanding of the image. Also notable in this passage is his departure from a purely intellectual account of the image, since both examples are directly bodily. Alongside human beings and angels, biological creatures elsewhere could bear the *imago dei* in other, variegated ways, some common (or at least analogous) to the way we bear it, but perhaps in other respects unlike anything we could imagine. To suppose otherwise would be to risk idolatry by suggesting that God is just like his human image.

Conclusion

In summary, I suggest that Christian theology has nothing to lose in accepting that other creatures could bear the image of God. Likeness is of its nature not a competitive matter. Moreover, the boundlessness of God's perfection likely sets up the *imago dei* to take varied forms, as finite reflections of the infinite. Even in respect to any single aspect of the image we might expect a variety of inflections. Every aspect of divine perfection – we call them 'aspects', but in

rejoice together); they are described metaphorically as God's 'sons'; they act as God's representatives and envoys; and they undertake forms of stewardship. Whatever definition one takes of the *imago dei*, it will be found in that list, and often to a greater degree than with human beings.

God they are all one – has a boundlessness to it. Human beings do not exhaust what it means to bear even *one* aspect of the *imago dei*, nor do we each bear any single aspect in the same way. This offers another forceful reason not to treat the image in a competitive matter, or to suppose that we would be any less remarkable, or loved by God, were we not to be the only creatures to bear God's image.

9 | Uniqueness, Convergence, and Embodied Cognition

In the previous chapter, I looked at ideas of uniqueness and the *imago dei* largely from a philosophical perspective within theology, asking what some of the main categories might mean, and how they might function if put to work in relation to a multiplicity of life. In this chapter, I turn to more specific characteristics of human life (and possibly other life) and especially to what it means to be rational, moral, and bodily. Among the more intriguing aspects of the thought of Aquinas that this book will turn up, here we will encounter his idea that there could only be one sort of rational animal such as ourselves. That is not so much because rational life is impossible beyond what we call *Homo sapiens*, but because he thought that all rational animals would be fundamentally the same sort of thing. Aquinas based that, in part, on consideration of the sort of body that would be necessary for such a rational being, which brings him surprisingly close to contemporary accounts of embodiment in cognition and convergence in evolution.

Convergence and Contingency in Evolution

Thinking about different angles on what it could mean to bear the image of God brings us to the territory of convergence and contingency in evolution. Convergence is the phenomenon, widely observed on Earth, of seeing evolution press closely similar solutions into play independently when different species have faced similar challenges or environments. When we see different species exhibiting equivalent features, that need not mean that they inherited it in common from a shared ancestor that also possessed that feature; it can be because evolutionary trajectories have converged on it independently. We see this in areas as distinct as forms of chemistry and structures of proteins, the shape and function of bodies and organs, means of propulsion, and patterns of behaviour.[1] The camera eye (with a lens) is a commonly cited example.[2] It has evolved independently several times, while eyes more generally have evolved down even more parallel trajectories.[3] Among the traits that have evolved convergently on Earth, we find many that are of interest to the theologian: forms of social relation, tool use, agriculture, and communication, for instance. Some degree of intelligence – although that is a fraught term – seems to have evolved independently in apes, corvids and dolphins.[4]

Admittedly, as far as we know, evolution has not converged elsewhere on Earth on a capacity for abstract thought: the ability to think about universals (such as the idea of a tree, and not just this or that tree), or to think about thought, or about the good that underlies every good, rather than only this or that thing as desirable.[5] Some writers judge this to be because reason and consciousness, as we see them in human beings, do not represent enough of a 'solution' to be converged upon, for instance, in view of the countermanding energy demands of the advanced brain. For my part, however, reason and consciousness strike me as the ultimate

---

[1] I have discussed this at greater length in 'He Fathers-Forth'.

[2] Simon Conway Morris discusses a wide range of convergences in *Life's Solution: Inevitable Humans in a Lonely Universe* (Cambridge: Cambridge University Press, 2008), 147–228.

[3] Richard Dawkins, *The Ancestor's Tale: A Pilgrimage to the Dawn of Life* (London: Weidenfeld & Nicolson, 2004), 673–74; Joram Piatigorsky, 'A Genetic Perspective on Eye Evolution: Gene Sharing, Convergence and Parallelism', *Evolution: Education and Outreach* 1, no. 4 (2008): 403–14.

[4] Corvids include crows, ravens, and magpies. Octopuses are also a candidate.

[5] Indeed, Aquinas would deny that these capacities are, or could be, the result of a natural process. I am reluctant to go down that road unnecessarily.

'meta-solution', bearing upon any number of potential problems or challenges, since the mind can range across the whole of what is thinkable. Aquinas commented on this directly in the opening of his treatise on rule and kingship:

> For all other animals, nature has prepared food, hair as a covering, teeth, horns, claws as means of defence or at least speed in flight, while man alone was made without any natural provisions for these things. Instead of all these, man was endowed with reason, by the use of which he could procure all these things for himself by the work of his hands.[6]

Given that intelligence has served human beings so well in evolutionary terms (at least up to now), my instinct turns towards the idea that there could be convergence towards it elsewhere. Whether or not that comes about easily or often is a different matter.

Turning to relation-based accounts of the *imago dei*, and away from a capacities approach, we can note that the study of biology also shows evolutionary convergence towards forms of sociality and social behaviour, even if they have not elsewhere on Earth reached a form that that we would call the *imago dei* properly speaking.[7] We know of many broadly parallel examples of close-knit relationality that have evolved convergently, for instance, among ants or termites and other social insects, meerkats and primates, not to

---

[6] *De Regno*, book 1, ch. 1, n. 5. We might also think here of Aquinas' thoroughly Aristotelian praise of human hands, as the 'tool of tools' (*Commentary on the De Anima of Aristotle*, book III, lect. 13, n. 790, commenting on *De Anima*, III.8), which are so integral to the life of a rational being as to be 'due' to them (*ST* I.21.4). The hand can produce, diversely and by art, what other animals have limitedly and determinately. Aquinas links this idea directly (in this passage in the *Commentary*) to the mind's undetermined openness as to what it can know.

[7] Conway Morris lists communities and eusociality, alongside aggression, agriculture, communication, courtship behaviour, culture, cultural transmission, dialects, disgust, expressions of surprise, farming, maternal care, matrilineal social systems, music, parental care, social systems, song, speech, temperaments, and vocalisations (*Life's Solution*, 457–61).

mention the convergent ubiquity of cross-species relations, many of which are profitable to both parties.[8]

If evolution converges towards intelligence elsewhere, many questions nonetheless remain concerning the variety of forms it might take.[9] On the side suggesting contingency and variety we have Ludwig Wittgenstein's insight that meaning expressed in language is closely bound up with 'forms of life': that 'words have meaning only in the stream of life', or, as he put it elsewhere, that 'to imagine a language means to imagine a form of life'.[10] Contingent differences, therefore, as to 'forms' and 'streams' of life might rather profoundly shape rationality to take divergent forms.[11] Of course, if there are also convergences when it comes to those forms of life, even if not exact parallels, there may then also be convergences over forms of rationality, even with Wittgenstein's principle in mind. The metaphysical

---

[8] See my 'Biological Mutualism: A Scientific Survey', *Theology and Science* 18, no. 2 (24 May 2020): 190–210; 'Christian Doctrine and Biological Mutualism: Some Explorations in Systematic and Philosophical Theology', *Theology and Science* 18, no. 2 (24 May 2020): 258–78.

[9] In a paper from 2016, 'Human Uniqueness: Standing Alone?', *The Expository Times* 127, no. 5 (2016): 217–24, I argued that contingency and variety as to the bodily forms taken by life would tend towards contingency and variety in forms of intelligence. Now, as I set out below, I can see arguments in that direction, but also in a more convergent and unified direction.

[10] Ludwig Wittgenstein, *Remarks on the Philosophy of Psychology*, ed. G. E. M. Anscombe and G. H. von Wright, trans. H. Nyman and C. G. Luckhardt, vol. 2 (Oxford: Basil Blackwell, 1980), 687, quoted in Kerr, *Theology after Wittgenstein* (London: SPCK, 1997), 134; Wittgenstein, *Philosophical Investigations*, §19. See also Ludwig Wittgenstein, *Culture and Value*, ed. G. H. von Wright and Heikki Nyman, trans. Peter Winch, amended 2nd ed. (Oxford: Basil Blackwell, 1980), 85.

[11] The relation of exobiological cognition to its 'lifeworld' is discussed by Mathias Osvath in 'Astrocognition: A Cognitive Zoology Approach to Potential Universal Principles of Intelligence', in David Dunér *et al.* (eds.), *The History and Philosophy of Astrobiology: Perspectives on Extraterrestrial Life and the Human Mind* (Newcastle: Cambridge Scholars Publishing, 2013), 49–66, with brief discussions in relation to language and signs, respectively, in this volume, from Arthur Holmer, 'Greetings Earthlings! On Possible Features of Exolangauge', 157–84, and Göran Sonesson, 'Preparations for Discussing Constructivism with a Martin (the Second Coming)', 185–200.

realist, who thinks of thought as an openness to the reality of things – a typical scholastic position – might incline towards an expectation of convergence winning out over contingency and difference, since what is ultimately known is *being*, and being is ultimately unified.

While on that we can do no more than speculate, it is intriguing to ask whether the capacities so famously associated by Augustine with the *imago dei* – memory, intellect, and will – are simply contingent, or whether they are grounded, or called forth, by some non-arbitrary aspect of reality. In exploring the second possibility, I would point to the structure of time according to past, present, and future,which might provide reason for thinking that what we know of conscious personhood as humans, characterised by memory, intellect, and will, is more than merely contingent, and may therefore be converged towards. Memory bears the stamp of the past. Will is oriented towards the future, aspiring to a state of affairs that has not yet come to be. Intellect relates to the present.[12] On this account, there would be a basis for memory, intellect, and will in the tensed character of existing in the flow of time. On that view, wherever the evolving capacity for consciousness is open to the temporal nature of the reality in which it finds itself, we might see something like those three faculties, so fundamental to Augustine's account of the human being.

Embodied Cognition

Another important angle on the dynamics of convergence and contingency comes in the study of 'embodied cognition', where scholars have argued, and increasingly demonstrated, that thought is

---

[12] Admittedly, in turning to the past, intellect blends into memory, and in turning to the future, it blends into will in the form of imagination. If the essence of intellect, however, rests in openness to reality beyond oneself, then intellect belongs most properly in the present, since it is in the present moment that the world primarily appears to us.

grounded in the particularity of our bodily experience of the world. A recurrent motif in this literature is that thought is shaped and embedded in its 'encompassing biological, psychological, and cultural context', through both *perception* and *action*:[13] in perceiving the world, but also acting within it – in pushing upon it, and having it push back at us.[14] A sense of this turned up in the failure of early attempts to establish 'computer cognition' in terms abstracted from embodied experience, highlighting the ways in which seemingly abstract matters of human 'knowing about' are not disconnected from the body, but are grounded in experience and interaction with the world.[15]

That being true, different bodily forms, giving rise to different forms of embodied interaction with the world, might again profoundly affect the forms of rationality found in different creatures, not least if we recognise that rationality is not simply logic-crunching, but also deeply aligned or integrated with hopes, desires, intentions, and emotions (from which we cannot abstract the body and its variations). Even with convergence on memory, intellect, and will, there may be considerable differences as to what those look like, based on bodily and related social differences. Perhaps, however, there is convergence towards some of what underlines the specificity of the embodiment of cognition. Even on Earth, Simon Conway Morris points to some evidence of convergence on bipedalism, and we have examples of convergence in vision, and in sound-based echolocation.[16]

---

[13] Francisco J. Varela, Evan Thompson, and Eleanor Rosch, *The Embodied Mind: Cognitive Science and Human Experience* (Cambridge, MA: MIT Press, 1991), 173.

[14] Indeed, perception and action are often spoken about together, as 'sensorimotor capacities', since they 'are fundamentally inseparable in lived cognition' (Varela, Thompson, and Rosch, *Embodied Mind*, 173). Cognition is 'rooted in the bodiliness of the 'pre-conceptual structures of our sensibility (i.e., our mode of perception, or [of] orienting ourselves and of interacting with other objects, events, or persons)' (Mark Leonard Johnson, *The Body in the Mind: The Bodily Basis of Meaning, Imagination, and Reason* (Chicago: University of Chicago Press, 1992), 14).

[15] Varela, Thompson, and Rosch, *The Embodied Mind*, 148; Tobias Tanton, *Corporeal Theology* (Oxford: Oxford University Press, 2022).

[16] Morris, *Life's Solution*, 162–63, 181–82, 269–70.

Standing against contingency and variation, however, is the scholastic analysis of material reality according to form and matter (or hylomorphism). From that perspective, we could justifiably say that the powers of rationality and consciousness are 'formal', and are therefore underdetermined as to the ways in which they are physically realised (which, as the corresponding 'material' principle, could be varied in many different ways: as to physiology, chemistry, architecture, and so on).[17] Or, to put it differently, the same powers of rationality, as formal qualities, could be realised in different material ways.

As should by now be clear, it is easier to identify factors that might point in one direction or another than to be able to say to what extent either apply, or prevail, in any life beyond Earth. Convergence on Earth may suggest convergence elsewhere, while rationality's relation to embodiment and forms of life highlight that unless those are highly converged towards, differences there might underlie differences in forms of mental and social life. Further to that, from a scholastic perspective, it may be that what most concerns us are formal categories, rather than material ones, and that there can be convergence at the level of form, even where the underlying materiality is different.

Aquinas on Multiple Rational Animals

Rather remarkably, Aquinas considered many of these questions in respect to the relation of variability of body to variability of mind. We find this in three texts composed at roughly the same time, in which he asks whether there could be more than one species (or kind) of rational animal. His response in all three places was that there could not. As we will see, however, rather than denying the

---

[17] Alternatively, one could point to receptivity of the intellect as a material quality, but then say that the mode of existence that allows for that capacity is a formal matter.

possibility of other instantiations of rationality, the logic of his argument pushes more towards saying that any variety of examples would amount to a single kind of thing. Moreover, in each text, he was also willing to entertain an intriguing counterexample, with the notion of living and rational heavenly bodies as other rational material things, even if they are not quite rational animals.[18] In looking at these passages, it is also worth recognising that Aquinas was seeking to explore what he took to be the case on the basis of his Earthly experience – namely that there was only one form of rational animal – rather than addressing an open-ended question in more absolute terms.

The first of these discussions is from the second book of the *Summa Contra Gentiles* (c. 1259–1265), where Thomas' argument rests on the sort of body that befits a rational being.[19] A rational soul, he writes, could not belong with just any kind of body so as to be its substantial form. It would need to be the form of a mixed body, for instance (i.e. not of a pure element), for reasons Aquinas considered it necessary to discuss at considerable length. Among mixed bodies, various further considerations would apply. First, something as noble as a rational soul could only properly belong to a body that possesses a 'harmonious quality to the highest degree'. The body belonging to the soul of a rational animal also ought to have sensitive flesh and a keen sense of touch since, like Aristotle, Aquinas saw those properties as closely related to mental sensitivity.[20] Discussing this passage, Marie I. George offers a somewhat

[18] *Disputed Questions on Spiritual Creatures*, 8 *ad* 10; *Commentary on the De Anima of Aristotle*, book 2, ch. 3, lect. 5, n. 293; *SCG* II.90.1.

[19] *SCG* II.90. Gilles Emery, in 'Brief Catalogue of the Works of Saint Thomas Aquinas', in *Saint Thomas Aquinas – Volume 1: The Person and His Work*, ed. Jean-Pierre Torrell, trans. Robert Royal, rev. ed. (Washington, DC: Catholic University of America Press, 2005), 332–33, suggests 1260 as a more definite date for book two of the *SCG*.

[20] *ST* I.76.5; 91.3 *ad* 1.

more neurological gloss, noting that Aquinas comes close here to thinking about the sorts of trajectories down which evolutionary convergence would need to go in order to bring forth something that could be as rational as a human being is.[21]

Provided that all such necessary characteristics are present, Aquinas explicitly wrote that he could imagine there being other cases where 'an intellectual substance is united to [such] a ... body'. The body of such a creature would be 'of the same nature as the human body' and its form would be 'of the same nature as the human soul'. On that account, 'there would be no specific difference between the animal so constituted and man'. In other words, his conviction that there could only be one sort of rational animal is not a denial of the existence of non-human cases, but the affirmation that they would be the same sort of thing as us. This aligns with one of the perspectives I mentioned above, that if there were convergence in bodily form, rationality might also be more rather than less convergent across the cosmos.

In the *Commentary on the De Anima of Aristotle* (1267–1268), likely written seven or eight years later, Aquinas offered a fascinating counterpoint to the discussion in the *SCG*.[22] As we have seen, his earlier position was that only a specific sort of body would befit, or be compatible with, rationality. In contrast, his focus in the *De Anima* commentary was on the relative and unusual *peculiarity* of the form of a rational thing (the soul) in relation to its body.

---

[21] George upholds the Roman Catholic position that human personhood does not emerge organically from the body or its evolution, but is created separately by God, and given to the body as its substantial form. As such, her question is not so much about the characteristics of the body of a creature that has evolved to be rational, but rather about what the evolved bodily characteristics would have to be for a creature to then be suitable as the recipient of a separately created rational soul. Despite the difference, the questions are closely related.

[22] The dates given here come from the Brian Davies and Eleonore Stump, eds., *The Oxford Handbook of Aquinas* (Oxford: Oxford University Press, 2014), and are in close agreement with Emery, 'Brief Catalogue'.

Fundamental to Aquinas's anthropology is the idea that a rational soul serves as the form of a material body in a different way from the forms of other material things.[23] In every other case, we have straightforward hylomorphism: the notional distinction between form and matter (*morphe* and *hyle*), which are nonetheless inseparable. We could not have matter without form, nor vice versa: neither the stone-ish-ness of a stone (its form) outside of matter, nor matter undetermined by some form or other, which would make it a stone, or a frog, or something else.[24] In contrast, Aquinas thought of the form of a human being – a rational soul – as the sort of thing that could exist separate from its matter, as it does after death (even if that is an unnatural state, since its nature is to inform the matter of a human being).[25] That conviction belongs alongside his belief that each human soul is created separately and individually by God, rather than emerging in the natural process of things, and that the highest pitch of rational activity (namely reasoning about universals) is undertaken without the involvement of any bodily organ (although that about which it reasons does come to it in a bodily way).[26] Aquinas drew on that final point in arguing that there is only one sort of rational animal: 'For as intellect has no bodily organ, intelligent beings cannot be differentiated according to a physical diversity in the constitution of their bodily organs, as are the different species of animals (whose different constitutions cause them to sense in different ways)'.[27] According to this line of analysis, when

[23] *Commentary on the De Anima of Aristotle*, book 2, ch. 3, lect. 5, n. 294.
[24] In a certain sense, Aquinas' account of cognition requires us to finesse these statements, although not in a way that undermines the argument being made here, since to know something would be to receive its form, although, crucially, in a different mode. See my *Participation in God*, 306–7
[25] *ST* I.75.6.
[26] *ST* I.75.3, 84.6. Pius XII, *Humani Generis* (1950), §36. For an Evangelical parallel, see P. P. T. Pun, 'Evolution', and H. D. McDonald, 'Mankind, Doctrine of', in Walter A. Elwell (ed.), *Evangelical Dictionary of Theology* (Grand Rapids, MI: Baker, 1984), 415–22, 416 and 730–34, 730.
[27] *Commentary on the De Anima of Aristotle*, book 2, ch. 3, lect. 5, n. 294.

it comes to rationality, the body – and therefore bodily differences – seem to drop out of the picture, and therefore so does the difference between one rational animal and another.

Many theologians today would not agree with Aquinas that reason belongs to the soul operating independently of the brain: that at the apex of rationality, the mind may reason *about* things supplied to it by the body, but not *by means of* anything bodily. Aquinas' point about the non-diversity of rational animals, however, would not necessarily be undone by differences over that point, since it aligns with my suggestion above that rationality has a formal quality, and is therefore underdetermined in its relation to matter. One could make that point without following Aquinas and later Catholic thought on the immateriality of the work of the intellect: one could talk about reason being underdetermined as to its realisation in matter, or emergence from matter, rather than supposing that a soul is created independently and joined to the body as its form, without the body playing a role in the act of the intellect as such.

Although this discussion appears in the *Commentary* as an argument against more than one species of rational animal, it need not be in tension with the prospect of other rational life in the universe. Its force is to minimise the significance of bodily difference in relation to rationality. Again, Aquinas does not so much deny that there could be other rational animals as deny that any such creatures would be fundamentally different from us. Although he approaches the topic from something like an opposite trajectory to the argument in the *SCG*, he is again denying that there could be 'non-human rational' animals only in the sense that they and we would be too similar to count as different species. If that sounds outlandish, we should note that he is speaking about 'species' here in a philosophical rather than biological sense: as a 'kind of thing', here taken in a more fundamental sense ('rational animal') than what we mean biologically by *Homo sapiens*.[28]

---

[28] The Canadian Thomist Charles de Koninck put forward the provocative suggestion in his long essay 'The Cosmos' that the theologian should treat the idea of species

With this in view, we might react with a little more sympathy to a tendency – recurrent, if not exactly common – to describe rational life elsewhere in the universe as 'other humans', especially in older writing.[29] That may sometimes stem from sloppiness and imprecision, or from a failure of imagination; more positively, however, taking Aquinas' writing into view, talk of 'other humans' may represent the considered view of these writers that intelligent, self-conscious material life is sufficiently universal that – with a certain latitude – the word 'human' can be used responsibly for other putative cases. (For my part, I think the dangers and problems associated with doing so ought still to rule it out.)

primarily in a broad philosophical sense, rather than biologically, such that the primary distinctions in being would be between the animate, the vegetal, the animal, and the rational animal ('The Cosmos', in *The Writings of Charles de Koninck*, trans. Ralph McInerny (Notre Dame, IN: University of Notre Dame Press, 2008), 258, elaborated 302–5). (In light of more recent work, that may need to be expanded to include recognition of a wider range of biological kingdoms.) Any biological distinctions within these categories would then be accidental, in philosophical terms. This reduces theological questions about evolution to consideration of transitions between these orders. On de Koninck's view, therefore, we could certainly talk about the rational animal being a single sort of thing (a philosophical 'species'), whether or not it was to be encountered across diverse biological species.

[29] For instance, William of Vaurouillon: 'If it be inquired whether people, existing on that world, have sinned as Adam sinned, I answer, No. They would not have contracted sin just as their humanity [*humanitatis*] is not from Adam' (*Quattuor librorum Sententiarum Compendium: venerabilis patris fratris Guillermi Vorrillonis* (Basel: Adam Petri de Landendorf, 1510), book I, dist. xliv, folio 105, translation from Thomas O'Meara, *Vast Universe*, 75). Campanella wrote of 'humans [*homines*] living on other stars', although he then retracted the term, writing that they would be 'beings there of a different nature who are similar to us but not the same as us [*entis obi esse aterius nature, nostris analoga entibus, non univoca*] no matter what Kepler has said about this in a playful and joking way and as a pure hypothesis in his Dissertatio' (*Defense of Galileo*, 112–13; Latin text *Apologia Pro Galileo, Mathematico Florentino* (Frankfurt: Godefridi Tampachii, 1622); Campanella is citing Galileo, *Letters on Sunspots*, letter 3, and Kepler, *Dissertatio cum Nuncio Sidero*, in Opera II, 500). Henry Moore wrote of 'men and beasts before this Earth … and other beasts and other humane birth' in *Democritus Platonissans, or, An Essay upon the Infinity of Worlds* (Cambridge: Roger Daniel, 1646). Lucretius in the first century BC had

Finally among these three discussions we have the *Disputed Question on Spiritual Creatures* (c. 1267–1268), written around the same time as the *Commentary on the De Anima*. Here Aquinas began by presenting human beings as a boundary case, where 'corporeal nature at its highest point touches the nature of spiritual substances at its lowest point'.[30] He took it to be characteristic of boundaries between orders that they touch, or bridge, at only a single point, not at many.[31] This would again make for there being only a single species in this position of 'rational animal'. In response, of course, we may not agree with the assumption of only a single bridge between orders. Alternatively, as with the two texts above, the import may be more to define all rational animals as being of the same fundamental bridging kind, rather than to deny that there could be multiple biological examples. In any case, Aquinas did not think that this argument based on boundaries between orders of being has absolute force, adding that 'it might be said that there are many species of rational animals, if one were to hold that the heavenly bodies are animate'.[32]

In all three of these discussions, Aquinas averts to the possibility of ensouled heavenly bodies as a kind of parallel to human beings beyond Earth, given that they serve as another possible example of

---

written about *varias hominum gentis* in the cosmos (*De Rerum Natura*, book 2, line 1076). Aquinas mentions the possibility of a humanity different from that coming from Adam in *De Malo*, when he wrote that original sin does not belong to 'human nature' as such (*ad naturam humanam absolute*) but only to human nature as derived from Adam (4.7 *ad* 3).

[30] *Disputed Questions on Spiritual Creatures*, 8 *ad* 10, translation from *On Spiritual Creatures (De Spiritualibus Creaturis)*, trans. Mary C. Fitzpatrick and John J. Wellmuth (Milwaukee, WI: Marquette University Press, 1949).

[31] 'The highest level of any nature, or even the lowest level, is only one' (*On Spiritual Creatures*, 8 *ad* 10). On this principle, see Therese Scarpelli Cory, 'The Distinctive Unity of the Human Being in Aquinas', in *The Oxford Handbook of the Reception of Aquinas*, ed. Matthew Levering and Marcus Plested. (Oxford: Oxford University Press, 2021), 589–92.

[32] *On Spiritual Creatures*, 8 *ad* 10. Aquinas covers similar territory in *SCG* II.68.6.

embodied rationality. In the *SCG* he then set them aside, because he was concerned with bodies mixed from different elements, unlike the heavenly bodies (as he understood them). In the *De Anima* commentary, he also set them aside because he thought heavenly bodies were incorruptible and wished to address only corruptible animals. Only in the *Disputed Questions on Spiritual Substances* did he allow heavenly bodies to stand as a possible counterexample to his argument.[33] His willingness to consider them as examples of material rational beings represents a further concession in his thought to the possibility of other rational, physical life in the universe, although in our case we would be thinking about other evolved animals, rather than living stars or planets.

Moral Awareness

Moral awareness is sometimes invoked as a definitive aspect of the *imago dei*, bearing on both faculty-based interpretations of the image and relational ones.[34] That challenges us to ask whether what we count as moral goodness could transcend our Earthly frame of reference. A particularly forceful treatment of this topic comes from William Hay (1695–1755, barrister and MP), in his extensive, if basically Arian, discussion of theology and exobiology in *Religio Philosophi*.

> [Rules are] either general, and concern all the Universe; or local, which concern only particular Planets. To love God, and adore him; to love their own Species, and assist them; to use other Creatures to the ends for which they were given, and not abuse them; are of the first sort of Rules, which God has prescribed to all rational

---

[33] *SCG* II.90.1 (having discussed the ensouledness of heavenly bodies earlier in II.44.4 and 70.2, 4, 7); *Commentary on the De Anima of Aristotle*, §293; *On Spiritual Creatures*, 8 *ad* 10.

[34] Normal Lamm does so, for instance, in 'Religious Implications', 22.

material beings throughout the Universe; and are eternal Foundations of Religion and Morality. But the particular form and manner
in which these Actions are to be performed in each Globe, must be
as various as the nature and situations of the Globes themselves, as
the rational Creatures that inhabit them, and the Objects with which
such Creatures are surrounded. These external modes of Religion
and Morality which are practiced in any particular Globe cannot
be known in the rest, but are the peculiar concern of that Globe
only. And the only way to judge of their propriety is, to consider,
if they are agreeable to reason, if they are adapted to the nature of
the things on that Globe, and if they tend to promote the great ends
abovementioned.[35]

Others have been less sanguine, supposing that our sense of moral
matters is so shaped by the contingency of our experience on our
planet, and by human forms of life, as to render foolish and arro-
gant any confidence about what applies elsewhere. Michael Ruse,
for instance, has suggested that human moral categories might no
more apply to other civilisations than they do to species of social
bees, which we do not judge as immoral for killing workers at the
onset of winter.[36] On this topic, our underlying convictions about
moral philosophy (or meta-ethics) are likely to influence our perspective profoundly. If one tends towards relativism in thinking
about human ethics, one is likely to see that relativism writ large
across the cosmos; if one tends towards a morality grounded in
metaphysical realism, one is likely to suppose that such a foundation would also operate elsewhere.

That later perspective need not, however, set context aside.
Traditions of virtue ethics, for instance, while standing on the more
realist and objective side of the above spectrum, will likely combine

[35] William Hay, 'Religio Philosophi', in *Work of William Hay*, vol. 1 (London:
J. Nichols, 1794), 197.
[36] Michael Ruse, '"Klaatu Barada Nikto" – or, Do They Really Think like Us?', in *The Impact of Discovering Life Beyond Earth*, ed. Steven J. Dick (Cambridge: Cambridge

the idea that goodness itself is not relative, or merely imputed to an act, with the sense that virtues play out in different situations in different ways. What the virtue of moderation might require in relation to diet will depend on whether one is in good or poor health, is travelling, has arduous labour to undertake, or is responsible for the demanding care of another person.[37] Similarly, while exponents of natural law will ground norms for human conduct in objective foundations, they are also typically aware of the need to translate broad fundamental principles into more specific ones appropriate to the context, not least as they are embodied in human or 'positive' law.[38] For example, the same principles of justice translate differently into local laws and customs in relation to fishing in a coastal community than they do to forestry in a woodland community.

A dynamic of accommodation is at work here, akin to the way that revelation is accommodated to human understanding, as we discussed in Chapter 5. Indeed, historical discussions of accommodation in revelation have often addressed how moral precepts in scripture change in response to changing circumstances. Augustine, for instance, wrote that

> the art of medicine remains the same and quite unchangeable, but it changes its prescriptions for the sick, since the state of their health changes. So the divine providence remains entirely without change, but comes to the aid of mutable creatures in various ways, and commands or forbids different things at different times according to the different stages of their disease.[39]

University Press, 2015), 175–88. John W. Macvey points to the absence of ethics around 'courtships, marriage or family life' for a 'monosexual race (*Alone in the Universe* (New York: MacMillan, 1963), cited by Delano, *Many Worlds, One God*, 116–17). He takes it that principles such as the Golden Rule or being true to one's nature would serve as 'metalaws' across species and cultures (117).

[37] In Aquinas, see *ST* II-I.147.2, for instance.

[38] For instance, *ST* II-I.95–97.

[39] *On True Religion*, XVII, 43, translation from Benin, 98. More generally see Benin, *Footprints of God*, 93–126; Sunshine, 'Accommodation Historically Considered', 243.

Augustine's comments are addressed to divine revelation of the good, but they would also apply to creaturely discernment of the good, along the lines we saw above. Recognising the need for prudential attention to context should be enough for us to imagine that metaphysically realist ethics, such as natural law or virtue, could apply appropriately across many worlds without supposing that to neglect differences of biology or culture.

Conclusion

We have identified several factors to guide our reflections on the degree of similarity and difference we might expect to find among life beyond Earth. Convergence on Earth suggests convergence elsewhere, while the relation of rationality to embodiment and forms of life may point to the possibility of wide-ranging differences in the shape that rationality and sociality might take. On the other hand, there may be grounds for convergence: perhaps because certain bodily forms, or forms of life, turn out to be closely allied with the possibility of rationality. Alternatively, certain capacities, such as memory, intellect, and will, might recur because they can be realised in many different material forms, especially if those capacities have a grounding in fundamental aspects of reality, such as temporality. As we have seen, these questions are not foreign to a thinker like Aquinas, for all he lived many centuries ago, who suggested that regardless of the variety among them, all rational animals are ultimately a single kind of thing. This will have ramifications for how we think about how such creatures might relate to the fallenness and redemption of humans on earth. Alongside rationality, morality is often associated with the *imago dei*, and we have seen that the possibility of applying categories of moral awareness depends on how we understand those concepts here on Earth. Metaphysically realist ethics, such as virtue and natural law, could transcend our earthly frame of reference without neglecting differences of biology or culture.

That brings us into the territory of sin and fallenness. Where some compatible spiritual disaster to be found elsewhere, the dealings of the creature involved would not be ones of pristine goodness. Neither, however, should we expect that creaturely wrongdoing would entirely extinguish either goodness or reason elsewhere. A culture characterised by total animosity would not be a particularly stable one because, as Jesus put it, a house divided against itself cannot stand.[40] Moreover, cooperation, both within and between species, is no less fundamental than competition, emerging naturally and underpinned by mathematics.[41] Studies in game theory show that cooperation confers benefits, and that it can arise spontaneously, propagate, and persist.

With this mention of sin and fallenness, but also the persistence of the good, and the divine purpose to perfect it, we move from considerations of creatures and the *imago dei* to a group of chapters on sin, redemption, and the Incarnation.

---

[40] Mark 3.25.
[41] On this see my 'Christian Doctrine and Biological Mutualism'.

Part IV | Christology, Salvation, and Grace

The two broad themes in this section are the person and work of Christ. Although those themes invite us to consider sin and redemption, the idea of Christ's work as more than a remedy will also be in view, since a theologian might suppose the Incarnation to achieve or bestow a gift beyond that of putting right what has gone wrong. In that way, the Incarnation might be thought capable of bestowing a gift of grace even upon creatures without sin. Although sin, redemption, and Incarnation have featured prominently in theological discussions of other life since the twentieth century, much theological territory still remains unconsidered. In this introductory section I wish to illustrate just how broad the range of options around those topics might be. As an indication of that, consider the diagram below, which maps some of that terrain.

In part, this variety stems from the diversity of Christian thought: some traditions will offer or favour certain elements, while others will reject them, stressing others. Beyond that, however, some of the latitude represented by this diagram will be embraced even within an individual tradition, particularly in as much as it refrains from saying what God must necessarily do.

We might start a survey of our diagram by considering that the putative life we are thinking about could conceivably be either fallen or unfallen. Few theologians will imagine that every other creature is necessarily free from sin, and some will go so far as to take the ubiquity of fallenness for granted. It will be helpful for our exploration to keep both options at least theoretically in play:

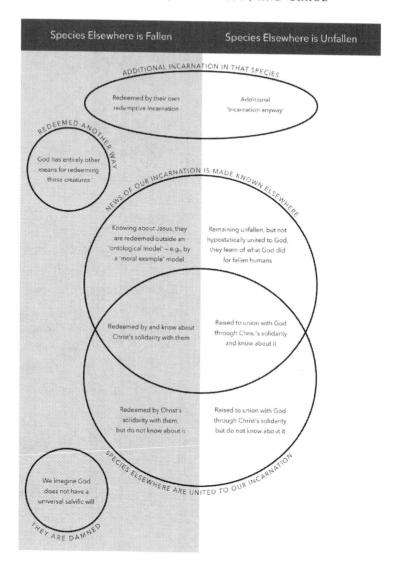

at the very least, if one is going to come down firmly on one side or
the other, one ought to be able to give reasons for it. Our diagram
also reminds us that while some traditions assume a 'universal

salvific will' in God, others do not.[1] Some assume that no sinner is left without an opportunity for redemption, while others find it plausible to suppose that God would leave fallen creatures to a fate of inevitable damnation, the fault for which would lie at their own door.[2,3] From an Anglican perspective, the Thirty-Nine Articles of Religion concur, with their claim that 'predestination to Life is the everlasting purpose of God'.[4] Of course, it is one thing to say that God leaves redemption open as a possibility, and another to say that God ensures that every creature in a state of sin *is* redeemed. The first is a matter of opportunity, the second is one of outcome. I would commend the former as a matter for belief, but the latter as only a matter for hope. To discount the possibility that any creature may respond by rejecting the redeeming offer of God risks presumption: the one creature that might not accept it may be oneself. When asked whether only few would be saved, the Gospels have Jesus placing the emphasis not on theoretical questions, but on the urgency of human decision: 'Strive to enter through the narrow door'.[5]

---

[1] Explicit examples that deny that God has a universal salvific will are less clear in the magisterial reformers than in some later formulations of Protestant theology. An example might be the *Larger Catechism*, qu. 13. Michael J. Lynch offers a thorough historical treatment of whether some were specifically excluded from the benefits of Christ's death in *John Davenant's Hypothetical Universalism: A Defense of Catholic and Reformed Orthodoxy* (Oxford: Oxford University Press, 2021), 23–47.

[2] Aquinas held that God wishes all to be saved 'absolutely' speaking, but that does not extend to saving those who forfeit grace (*ST* I.19.6 *ad* 1), and God's will runs to 'permit[ting] a person to fall into sin' (I.23.3). Nonetheless, as we will see in Chapter 11, he did not think that it would be consistent with the character of God for anyone to be left without the possibility, in history and context, of responding to an offer of redemption (*De Veritate*, 14.11 *ad* 1).

[3] Texts that have been historically important include Heb. 11.6, 1 Tim. 2.4, and 2 Pet. 3.9. On interpretation of 1 Tim. 2.4 across Aquinas' early works, see Franklin T. Harkins, 'The Early Aquinas on the Question of Universal Salvation, or How a Knight May Choose Not to Ride His Horse', *New Blackfriars* 95, no. 1056 (2014): 208–17.

[4] Article 17.

[5] Luke 13.24.

Turning to the region of our diagram on the means of redemption, further alternatives multiply. We might be open to the possibility that the working of grace could proceed according to completely different means from the Christian account of terrestrial redemption: not because that account is inaccurate when it comes to our story, but simply because what happens here – the means of salvation – is different from salvation elsewhere. That may not be palatable for theologians who see the work of redemption presented in the Christian tradition as the only possible means by which God could redeem creatures. Others, however – a significant swathe – would stress that God is not limited in his dealings with creatures, other than by the rule of his own nature. God is not determined to achieve salvation by one route only.[6] If, in particular, the work of God is characterised by fittingness, then different creatures, and different situations, might artfully receive different responses.

For my part, I would argue that any attempt to find a single means of redemption may be mistaken even within our Earthly story. As a commonplace, we recognise that different Christian traditions have emphasised different understandings of redemption. In my view, these 'models' are best seen as overlapping, not as excluding one another. We have many different images of redemption because they refer to something too expansive and remarkable to be captured in one image, be it ransom, healing, sacrifice, victory, or some other way of talking about what Christ did for human beings. We do not need to choose, or even to highlight, only one.

Even with many models in play, the temptation may be to focus on the crucifixion, but the idea that Christ redeems in many overlapping ways, relating to the whole of his life, is attested in various theological and liturgical sources, for instance, in the Litany in the *Book of Common Prayer* (1549, here from 1662):

---

[6] Aquinas discusses this point in *ST* III.1.2 and III.46, especially articles 1 and 2.

By the mystery of thy holy
Incarnation; by thy holy Nativity
and Circumcision; by thy Baptism, Fasting, and Temptation,
Spare us, good Lord.

By thine Agony and Bloody Sweat;
by thy Cross and Passion; by thy precious Death and Burial; by thy
glorious Resurrection and Ascension,
and by the Coming of the Holy Ghost,
Spare us, good Lord.

Similarly, the cycle of the Church year opens a range of vistas onto
the means of salvation. At Christmas we might sing that by Christ's
birth 'God imparts to human hearts/The blessings of his heaven'.[7] A
few weeks later, at the feast of the Baptism of Christ, an ancient office
hymn explores the redemptive quality of his baptism: 'He who sin
had never known/By washing hath our sins undone'.[8] Each season
offers an account of salvation as, in due course, do Passiontide and
Eastertide. The nativity, the temptation, the agony in the garden, the
cross, and the Resurrection – each is perhaps 'enough' for redemption. Indeed, perhaps even Christ's plea from the cross, 'Father, for-
give them, for they know not what they do', would have sufficed. To
see them alongside one another is to see an extravagant superfluity
at play: 'from his fullness have we all received' not simply grace, but
'grace upon grace'.[9] I see no reason to suppose that the extravagant
plurality of redemption set before us on Earth is any less fulsome
elsewhere, perhaps sometimes following the pattern that applies on
Earth, and sometimes not. In what follows, we will think about the
ways in which our story might be echoed elsewhere, or their story
engrafted into ours, while also remembering that the grace of God
could take shapes among other creatures that we could never guess.

[7] Phillips Brooks (1835–1893), 'O Little Town of Bethlehem'.
[8] *Hostis Herodes impie*, Caelius Sedulius (mid-fifth century), trans. Percy Dearmer
(1869–1936).
[9] John 1.16.

I will not speculate about the other possible means of redemption, but they occupy a region in our diagram of options. Sticking with what we know – the Incarnation (and Jesus' death and resurrection) – we find a particularly central bifurcation, with two strikingly different lines of enquiry presenting themselves. According to one, there is a single Incarnation in the history of our universe, the one known to human beings, which can (or does) avail for all: the Incarnation in and as Jesus of Nazareth. The other possibility is multiple Incarnations: that God unites himself hypostatically to other kinds of creaturely natures, as well as to our own.

We find no greater point of divergence in thinking about the theological implications of life elsewhere in the universe than over this idea of multiple Incarnations. For some it appears as blasphemy, or at least a denial of something integral to Christianity, namely the centrality of Christ to the whole cosmos; for others, it seems to be the most natural way to think through Christian principles within the wider exobiological frame. I respect the concerns of the former group, but incline to the second. If we do pursue the route of thinking about a single Incarnation, however, we can then go on to think about different accounts of the work of Christ, and how they would, or would not, readily apply to life elsewhere. In Chapter 11, for instance, I will ask what it might mean for Christ to redeem other creatures after the model of ontological union, moral example, or substitution.

At this point, we can return to the opening question of this introduction to Part IV, and the possibility of unfallen creatures. The possibility of such a state provokes the useful question of whether they too would benefit from the work of the Incarnation, either that of Jesus Christ or of an additional Incarnation in their own nature. It presents us with the question of whether the coming and work of Christ is only redemptive, which is to say remedial, or whether it is not also about the elevation of human beings (and creaturehood, and materiality) to a dignity beyond anything that could belong to it simply by nature, fallen or not.

10 | Sin and Fall

The themes of sin and Fall benefit a good deal from an examination with astrobiology in view. Approached through that lens, this chapter will consider such central topics as what sin might or might not change about the rest of the world, in what sense it might be contagious on a cosmic scale, whether it rests on a fundamental fragility to creatures, and whether it is therefore inevitable, here or elsewhere.

Theological comments on exobiology often discuss a Fall. This is perhaps hasty, in as much as it jumps straight to rational or morally responsible life, overlooking the scientific truism that the vast majority of life elsewhere in the cosmos would lack mental and moral development. The category of the Fall might not apply to such organisms as agents, although questions might remain as to how they might be affected by the consequences of sin, cosmically conceived. Turning to fallenness too hastily also risks overlooking the possibility of unfallen life, and of not asking how the themes we are discussing might apply nonetheless. Just because such creatures would not need remedy for sin does not mean that they could not receive gifts of grace beyond nature, whether in the gift of the Incarnation, as the highest dignity conferred by God and the deepest divine self-revelation, and in theosis.

Understandings of the Fall are contested and complicated enough when it comes to life on Earth, especially with science in view; we can only conjecture about its relation to other life. Nonetheless, conjecture can be useful for theologians, since it provokes us to ask fundamental questions about the nature of sin, its causes, and its transmission, all of which will be valuable when we return to having a terrestrial canvas in mind.

In much traditional Christian theology, the proposed account of the Fall was straightforward: a pair of human beings were created by God in a state of innocence, formed directly from the dust of the ground. They subsequently disregarded the commandment of God and, in turning their back on him, plunged themselves and their descendants into a state of estrangement from God, and from one another. For many writers, death itself is a consequence of that act of rebellion.

As Christians have come to accept an evolutionary account of the origin of species, the Fall story from Genesis 3 has been less frequently taken as straightforward history. We know that *Homo sapiens* evolved from earlier hominid stock (as did other hominid species, now extinct), and – further back – that hominids evolved from an origin common to primates more generally. Death *per se* did not enter the world because of actions taken by a pair of human beings. While scientific findings have influenced how we now read the opening chapters of Genesis, however, the text itself already gives reasons to not see it as a straightforward history, or a scientific textbook: there is its poetic form, for one thing, but also some of the details of the account. For instance, although in the opening trajectory of Genesis Adam and Eve seem to be presented as the sole progenitors of the human race (Eve is given her name as 'the mother of all who live'), we do not need to read much further before we encounter other human beings and communities, not obviously descended from that pair. We might think of the families from which the sons of Adam and Eve take wives, or of the inhabitants of those cities, in fear of which Cain lives after he has murdered his brother.[1]

Among ways to think about the story of Genesis 3 in constructive relation to contemporary science, perhaps the most conservative

---

[1] Gen. 3.20, 4.14–16, 17.

response is to treat that text as an account of a particular hominid pair in which humanity came of age: our arrival on the scene in full moral freedom and accountability. They were the first to stand before God in the way we would recognise and, faced with the possibility of turning to him, or away from him, they chose rebellion. For some who follow Aquinas, the favoured option is to see this couple as the first beings upon which God had conferred human status and dignity.[2]

Other approaches will not place emphasis on an original pair, but will see the story as corresponding to something broader and more gradual. It might recount, under the figure of this pair and their decision, a long history of evolution into moral responsibility, and of using it poorly. In a less historical register still, the story might be taken as a meditation on the sort of moral choice that is recapitulated in every human life, or as a reflection on the nature of rationality and freedom as human faculties, and the direction in which they so typically tend.

What a theologian makes of the supposed state of intelligent life elsewhere in the universe, as fallen or otherwise, will recapitulate in that register what he or she also thinks about the consequences of fallenness for human beings. To a good approximation, we can distinguish two angles. One thinks about the consequences of the fall in terms of an addition. This is usually described as 'original sin'. Aquinas is fairly representative in seeing its consequences as a wound to human nature, defilement (or stain), and a debt of punishment due.[3] More distinctly, however, he also represents the second angle, approaching the condition of fallenness not only

---

[2] For explorations of such a view, see the forthcoming collection of essays on Thomism and evolution produced between the Dominican houses in Oxford and Providence, Rhode Island.

[3] *ST* II-I.85–7. In *ST* II-I.85.3 Aquinas attributed to Bede the idea that sin brings about 'weakness, ignorance, malice and concupiscence'. The citation in Bede is unknown. Elsewhere, he will distinguish between 'temporal' and 'eternal' aspects of punishment due (for instance, *ST* III.86.4).

in terms of addition, but also of subtraction. On his influential account, what has been lost is 'original justice': a grace, previously present as a divine gift, which allowed for the harmonious coordination of human faculties, over and above an otherwise 'natural' constitution. On this view, the problem is not so much that the human being is now less than natural, it is that we have returned to the level of nature.

In writing about original justice, Aquinas' approach resonates with a modern, scientific sense of the fragility of material things.[4] While he would have thought of neither sin nor death as according with God's intention for human beings, if the gift of original justice had not been rejected, he accepted that mortality, and probably also moral fragility, would be inherent in the human constitution naturally as such, if not guarded and strengthened by that additional gift of grace.[5] The effect of sin was the forfeit of original justice – 'the effect of the sin of our first parent was that his nature was left to itself' – with human reason and love towards God no longer able to keep the passions under control: passions that are not sinful in themselves, but which run to sin when not well ordered.[6]

Aquinas was not alone in developing this broad line of thinking. Athanasius wrote in *Contra Gentes* that any human life that 'might not ever either depart from his idea of God, nor recoil from the communion of the holy ones' must, from the start, be aided by grace: 'having the grace of Him that gave it, having also God's own

---

[4] David Brewster saw an inevitability to sin grounded in human fallibility and finitude, such that we can 'but feebly defend [ourselves] against the ferocity of animal life' and our 'high reason does not, in many emergencies, compensate for [our] inferior instinct' (*More Worlds Than One*, 147). Recent discussions include Daniel W. Houck, *Aquinas, Original Sin, and the Challenge of Evolution* (Cambridge: Cambridge University Press, 2020); Paul A. Macdonald, 'In Defense of Aquinas's Adam: Original Justice, the Fall, and Evolution', *Zygon* 56, no. 2 (2021): 454–66. Eric Mascall commented on the transmission of original sin and original justice in *Christian Theology and Natural Science*, 33–34.

[5] *ST* I.95.1.

[6] *ST* I-II.17.9.

power from the Word of the Father', such a human being might 'rejoice and have fellowship with the Deity, living the life of immortality unharmed and truly blessed'.[7]

Sin and the Rest of Creation

For some writers, questions about the effect of human sin on humans are inextricably bound up with questions about its effects upon the wider cosmos. It may be helpful to begin with the distinction between positions that imagine a change purely to human beings, and ones that see the Fall as dislocating the whole of creation. For Aquinas, in the former camp, what is perpetuated now is the guilt associated with belonging to the rebellious human race, and the absence of the gift of original justice. At the other pole, we find accounts of the Fall as affecting and changing the entire terrestrial world, and indeed perhaps the whole cosmos. A theological incentive for that perspective has been the language of Romans 8, where the 'groaning' of all of creation is linked to the fallenness and redemption of human beings. Luther belonged in this group, as did the Calvinist Lambert Daneau, whom we have already encountered attacking the idea of many worlds. In his view, such features of the world as the poison of snakes and herbs were down to a transformation attendant upon human wrongdoing:

> By sinne and for the sinne of man, these so many Plagues, venimes, poysons, hurtful hearbes, and noysom beastes sprang up, as the wordes of the Lorde doe declare in the booke of *Moses, Genesis* the 3. chapter, and 18. verse. For God made nothing at the beginnyng that was unto any thing poyson, deadly, hurtfull, and discommodious.[8]

---

[7] Athanasius, 'Contra Gentes', in *Nicene and post-Nicene Fathers: A Select Library of the Christian Church – Second series*, vol. 4, ed. Archibald Robertson, trans. John Henry Newman and Archibald Robertson (Grand Rapids, MI: Eerdmans, 1980), 1–30, I.2, p. 5.

[8] Daneau, *Wonderful Worksmanship*, 83.

In contrast Augustine, who has been so influential on Western thought about the Fall, was rather restrictive when it came to the effect of sin on other creatures. In *On Genesis against the Manichees*, he wrote that 'They [the Manichees] say that God's nature is injured by the sins of others; we deny this, but say instead that no nature is harmed by any sins except its own'.[9] Although there is much in creation for which he cannot attribute a purpose ('frogs … and flies and worms'), nonetheless,

> there is not a single creature, after all, in whose body I cannot find, when I reflect upon it, that its measures and numbers and order are geared to a harmonious unity … and since none of these things is offensive to reason [in itself], then whenever our carnal senses are offended, they [the right-thinking person] would put it down to what is due to our mortality, not to anything wrong with the things themselves.[10]

In the *Literal Meaning of Genesis*, he wrote that poisonous creatures were poisonous from the start, and not as a change or addition due to the human Fall. It is integral to nature and the identity of these creatures that 'beasts injure one another', since 'some are the proper diet of others'.[11] The beauty of the temporal world is an inherently temporal beauty, characterised by change and passing.

> [All things] have their own proper measures, numbers and destinies. So all things, properly considered, are worthy of acclaim; nor is it without some contribution in its own way to the temporal beauty of the world that they undergo change by passing from one thing to

---

[9] Augustine, *On Genesis: A Refutation of the Manichees*, II.29.43, translation from 'On Genesis: A Refutation of the Manichees', in *On Genesis*, trans. Edmund Hill (Hyde Park, NY: New City Press, 2002), 96.

[10] Augustine, *On Genesis: A Refutation of the Manichees*, I.16.26, translation from 'Refutation of the Manichees', 40. Aquinas quotes a preceding paragraph, I.16.25, discussing this topic in *ST* I.72.1 *ad* 6.

[11] Augustine, 'Literal Meaning of Genesis', III.16.25, 247.

another. This may escape fools; those making progress have some glimmering of it; to the perfect it is as clear as daylight.[12]

Similarly, thorns and thistles had a proper part in the natural order from the beginning, since they are food to some animals, and can be useful to us for purposes beyond food.[13] Thus, Augustine does not interpret Gen. 3.18 ('thorns and thistles it shall bring forth for you') as meaning that the earth did not previously produce them. It is simply that before they were no impediment to human beings (not being agriculturalists), and only once we began to till the land was the bringing forth of thorns and thistles a matter 'for you'.[14] The picture that emerges from Augustine is of a wider world not changed by sin as to its nature: what changes is the human being, and therefore his or her interactions with it, not least with an emotional response now overlaid with foolishness and a fear of death. This is significant for thinking about how human sin might affect life elsewhere: it would not. Neither, therefore, would there seem justification, on this view, for suggesting that a human propensity or provocation to sin rests on the Fall of any other physical species somewhere else.[15]

---

[12] Ibid., III.16.25, 247.

[13] Ibid., III.18.27, 248–49.

[14] Ibid., III.18.28, 248–49.

[15] The language of a fallenness derived by descent from Adam is central to many discussions of the antipodes, and is found in the passages from William of Vaurouillon and Campanella discussed elsewhere in this book. More recently, such questions surfaced in disputes between monogenic (one common descent) and polygenic (descent from distinct origins) accounts of human origins, the latter not infrequently with racist import (and notably condemned as incompatible with Catholic teaching by Pius XII in *Humanae Generis*, §37). Among recent discussions of monogenesis in relation to extraterrestrial life, see Simon Francis Gaine, 'Did Christ Die for Neanderthals?', *New Blackfriars* 102, no. 1098 (March 2021): 225–38. R. J. Pendergast advanced a position of intense monogenism in suggesting that the Adam of the Book of Genesis is the first rational being in the cosmos and, in that, the progenitor of all other examples of rational life (R. J. Pendergast, 'Terrestrial and Cosmic Polygenism', *Downside Review* 82, no. 268 (July 1964): 189–98).

The Root of Sin Elsewhere

For those of us who follow Augustine's understanding that human sin does not change the natural world more widely, the grounds for the possibility of sin must lie not in the effect that one species has on the cosmos, but within each species. We can usefully enumerate four broad perspectives on the origin of sin, with the suggestion that they would apply not only to humans, but also among other rational, material creatures, if any such exist: (1) a refusal or reluctance to give a reply, based on the incomprehensibility of sin and evil; (2) a reply based on a sense of the fragility of our constitution, which might be approached in terms of the consequences of an evolutionary process; (3) a gesture towards the notion of a prior, immaterial fall; and (4) the sense of fallenness as springing from divine intention.

The first response, or non-response, has a long and distinguished pedigree. It arises not out of a failure to think the question through, but from a careful consideration of the nature of the topic at hand. Sin, on this view, resists rational analysis, having at root a character close to insensibility. We might follow the track of virtue ethics here: right action accords with the realisation of human excellence, so why would anyone, acting from a position of supposed equilibrium, choose the less excellent over the more excellent? Similarly, from the perspective of natural law, the witness of the nature of things – of the world around us, and of the human being, and of human society – would similarly indicate the path of right action. That is the rational path, and one could turn from it only irrationally.[16] The most we can say about sin may be that it is grounded in ignorance, but it may be even more irrational than that. This position applies especially if one sees the first human beings properly-so-called as fortified by a gift of original justice. Why would such a creature sin? Without this gift, however, it is not clear that human

---

[16] For a discussion of the irrationality of evil, see my *Participation in God*, 245–48.

beings in a purely natural state would ever have honed the faculties to let knowledge of what is right set the running, alongside a properly enlightened self-interest that is invested in the common good.

This brings us to the second approach, where science may now suggest to us that no human being, however far back we go, ever acted from a position of pure moral equilibrium or innocence. Setting ideas of original justice aside here, human beings would never have been unclouded agents, who might be expected simply to follow the rational road to morally right action. This is an important part of the message of evolution: the earliest hominids came with a fully animal inheritance, with its urges to violence, greed, and unbounded sexual pursuit. Those urges evolved as responses to threat, scarcity, and the evolutionary pressure towards reproduction. In other animals, they have no moral register. Moral responsibility comes with the development of certain faculties, including self-awareness, the capacity for thought, and the ability to relate as a person to other persons. When these features dawned upon the planet, they came to creatures already possessed of animal tendencies which, now expressed under conditions of culpability, conduce to sin. On this view, to have evolved – for a species to have arrived where it is by means of a competitive process – is inevitably for it to be constituted in a way that will cut against living by the divine standard of perfect goodness.

Turning to our penultimate category, Christian theology has not infrequently asked whether human sin might in some way rest upon a prior fall, namely that of the angels. Here, the accusation of a certain circularity might be levelled: this would be to approach the mystery of one Fall by deferring it to another. Moreover, I have heard attempts to understand human fallenness in terms of an angelic fall described as a venture to understand a difficult thing in terms of something yet more obscure. Indeed, we might even think that an angelic fall requires *more* explanation than a material one. Matter, perhaps, has a certain fragility to it. It has a complexity not found among the angels, and complex things are prone to come apart. Is it not more difficult to see why a spirit would rebel than an animal? In response, it may be that the theological tradition has found a certain *satisfaction* in tracing the provocation to human sin (rather than a sufficient condition for it) back to a more radically unprovoked angelic fall, precisely because, with the angels, the state of sin is led back to the *mysterium iniquitatis* at its most stark: to the choice against God of those without the weight of materiality, who could contemplate the good as pure intelligences, but forfeited it. Augustine, and many who follow him, associated this with pride: 'the devil fell by pride from the beginning of time, and ... there was no time before that in which he lived at peace and in bliss with the holy angels. On the contrary, from the very starting point of creation he apostatized from his creator'.[17] Here, the tradition has been guided by Sirach, 'For the beginning of pride is sin', and it is the character of pride 'to forsake the Lord', whereby 'the heart has withdrawn from its Maker'.[18] Exponents of the angelic fall may go so far as to suggest that this prior fall set askew the fundamental nature of the cosmos, allowing for the development of an entire cosmos with sin, death, and suffering.

Among the different traditions within Christian theology, then, we will find various emphases regarding how sin could be possible. They are not inherently incompatible. One could maintain that the possibility of sin rests on the fragility of the human constitution, as a result of our evolutionary inheritance, which has the form it does because of the effect of some prior angelic fall, returning again to the sheer inexplicability of evil. This leaves one final angle to explore concerning the origins of sin, which is where many theologians will feel that they must tread most carefully: placing the origin of sin within the foreordained purposes of God. For swathes of the tradition, this is terrain to avoid altogether. It would be axiomatic for many theologians that God is simply not the origin of evil at all.

[17] Augustine, 'Literal Commentary on Genesis', 11.16.21, 440.
[18] Sirach 10.12.

Evil, they would say, simply and completely falls outside the direct intention of God: there is no evil in God, so no evil can spring from God.[19] Where God does act in some sense to bring about 'evil' – the classic example being the punishment of the wicked – that is enfolded, more broadly, within the achievement of a wider *good*: for instance, in the establishment of justice. In that case, the wellspring of the evil endured would rest with the one who provoked it by wrongdoing.[20]

Relatively few theologians until recent centuries would conclude that there is sin because God wants there to be sin. Calvin, for instance, recognised a tension in his own work on this front. On the one hand, he could write that 'the proper and genuine cause of sin is not God's hidden counsel but the evident will of man'; on the other, he also thought it necessary to say that sin, and indeed the fall of Adam, was not simply foreknown by God but also even divinely ordained.[21] Here, he thought, we touch upon something that surpasses human understanding: 'But how it was ordained by the foreknowledge and decree of God what man's future was without God being implicated as associate in the fault as the author and approver of transgression, is clearly a secret so much excelling the insight of the human mind, that I am not ashamed to confess ignorance'.[22] In the *Institutes* he summarizes the situation in this way:

the Lord had declared that 'everything that he had made ... was exceedingly good' (Gen. 1.31). Whence, then comes this wickedness to man, that he should fall away from his God? Lest we should think it comes from creation, God had put His stamp of approval on what had come forth from himself. By his own evil intention, then, man

[19] This would be the import not only to the opening of Genesis (Gen. 1.31) but also of various New Testament discussions, among them 1 Cor. 14.33, James 1.13, and 1 John 1.5.
[20] *ST* I.49.2.
[21] John Calvin, *Concerning the Eternal Predestination of God* (London: James Clarke, 1961), 121–22 (first published in 1552).
[22] Ibid., 124.

corrupted the pure nature he had received from the Lord; and by his fall drew all his posterity with him into destruction. Accordingly, we should contemplate the evident cause of condemnation in the corrupt nature of humanity – which is closer to us – rather than seek a hidden and utterly incomprehensible cause in God's predestination.[23]

The positive association of sin with the divine purposes that stands out in the liturgy of the Western Church is the *felix culpa*: the 'happy fault' in the *Exultet* (or *Pascal Praeconium*), a liturgical text in praise of the Resurrection sung at the Vigil of Easter, dating from the seventh or eighth century.[24] Famously, or notoriously, the *Exultet* contains the lines 'O truly needful sin of Adam [*certe necessarium Adae peccatum*], which was blotted out by the death of Christ! O happy guilt [*felix culpa*], the desert of which was to gain such and so great a redeemer!'[25] While it does not have the authority of scripture, few texts outside the Bible have quite the prominence of one authorised for almost 1,500 years to lie at the heart of the most solemn celebration of the year. The text leaves the question of causation open, since it is one thing retrospectively to glory in the good that has come from evil, and another to suppose that the evil was caused and intended so that the good could come from it. On similar ground, in the fifteenth century Julian of Norwich would introduce the most famous line in her *Revelations of Divine Love*, that 'but all will be well, and all will be well, and every kind of thing will be well', with the statement 'Sin is necessary'.[26] That brings us back to the theme of the 'suitable', so often in view in this book, since her word is that sin is 'behovely', or

[23] *Institutes*, III.23.8.
[24] 'Exultet' in F. L. Cross and E. A. Livingstone, eds., *The Oxford Dictionary of the Christian Church*, 3rd rev. ed. (Oxford: Oxford University Press, 2005), 593–94.
[25] *The Sarum Missal in English*, ed. and trans. Albert H. Pearson (London: Church Press, 1868), 161. Compare Milton, *Paradise Lost*, book XII, lines 469–478.
[26] *Showings*, trans. Edmund Colledge and James Walsh (Mahwah, NJ: Paulist Press, 1978), ch. 27, showing 13, p. 255

fitting.[27] For his part, God for Aquinas is not the origin of evil or sin, most ultimately considered, although he accepts that the presence of sin illustrates the principle that 'God allows evils to happen in order to bring a greater good therefrom', quoting Rom. 5.20: 'where sin increased, grace abounded all the more'.[28]

The Inevitability of the Fall

All of that bears upon questions about the inevitability, or not, of a Fall, here or elsewhere. It is difficult to discern trends here, except perhaps to say that Protestant writers rarely entertain the possibility of sinlessness, whereas Catholic writers are more divided on the matter, and more apt to list a range of possibilities or trajectories for thought.[29]

---

[27] '"Behovely" means to Julian much the same as what *conveniens* means to Thomas Aquinas and Bonaventure. So, when Julian says that "sin is behovely" what she means is that sin is *conveniens* …: that it "fits", it is "just so" and that there is something it fits with' (Denys Turner, '"Sin Is Behovely"', in Julian of Norwich's Revelations of Divine Love', *Modern Theology* 20, no. 3 (2004): 409).

[28] *ST* III.1.3 *ad* 3.

[29] Among Catholic writing on exobiology, consider that Joseph Pohle thought sinlessness possible (*Die Sternenwelten und ihre Bewohner*, 2nd ed. (Köln: Bachem, 1899), 457–58)), as does Thomas O'Meara (*Vast Universe*, 25), whereas Pierre Teilhard de Chardin thought sin universal, characterising it gloomily as 'the essential reaction of the finite to the creative act' ('Fall, Redemption, and Geocentrism', in *Christianity and Evolution*, trans. René Hague (New York: Harcourt, 1971), 40). Kenneth Delano cites two Catholic writers (Francis Connell and Domenico Grasso) as each laying out a variety of options on sin and redemption, fallenness, and unfallenness (*Many Worlds, One God*, 112–14), as does Roch A. Kereszty in *Jesus Christ: Fundamentals of Christology*, 2nd ed. (New York: Alba House, 2002), 447–48. David Brewster saw a theological inevitability to sin in the idea that the Incarnation was planned from before the beginning of creation (*More Worlds Than One*, 143–46, quoting Hugh Miller, *The Foot-Prints of the Creator: Or, The Asterolepis of Stromness* (Boston: Gould and Lincoln, 1868), 325–27). Robert Russell has proposed that all rational life experiences a moral ambivalence or 'dilemma' similar to that of human beings, and is unlikely to 'outgrow' temptation ('Life in the Universe: Philosophical

Keith Ward, an Anglican, aligns here with a more Catholic out-look, holding to a strict non-necessity of sin:

> God did not have to create humans, humans did not have to become prey to hatred and greed, and God did not have to deliver humans by death on a cross ... these are all contingent occurrences. They did not have to happen. God might well have created other kinds of intelligent life, there could have been intelligent life that did not fall into evil, and God might have chosen another way of reuniting the human species to the divine.[30]

Ward takes this to be 'part of most traditional Christian beliefs', citing Aquinas as an example for each of these positions.[31] Ward bases this possibility of sinlessness on freedom: 'though some theologians postulate that such estrangement is a necessary part of the process of the creation of those who are genuinely other than God, a strong view of moral freedom would suggest that sin is not necessary to finite personal beings as such'.[32] C. S. Lewis explored fallenness as a central theme in his novel *Perelandra,*where he also presents both outcomes as plausible.[33]

A theologian's attitude towards the inevitability of sin is likely to rest strongly upon assumptions about the differences between our present situation and one where sin could fail to appear. With the exception of Pelagians, no one is likely to suppose that human beings – for the moment setting aside the effects of baptism and redemption – are now able to avoid sin. We are 'set in the midst

---

and Theological Issues', in *First Steps in the Origin of Life in the Universe: Proceedings of the Sixth Trieste Conference on Chemical Evolution*, ed. Julián Chela Flores, Tobias C. Owen, and F. Raulin (Dordrecht: Kluwer Academic, 2001), 370). O'Meara also points to those traditions of thought that associate creaturely finitude with evil on a deep metaphysical level, citing Friedrich Schelling and Paul Tillich (*Vast Universe*, 26).

[30] Ward, *Christ and the Cosmos*, 249–50.
[31] Ibid., 251.
[32] Ibid., 253.
[33] C. S. Lewis, *Perelandra: A Novel* (London: Bodley Head, 1943).

of so many and great dangers, that by reason of the frailty of our nature we cannot always stand upright', as an ancient collect has it, still in liturgical use.[34] For Catholic Christianity, the possibility of not sinning is restored with baptism. While the Christian in this life is not yet in a state of not being able to sin (*non posse peccare*), she is now able not to sin (*posse non peccare*). Reformation traditions are generally less optimistic about the effects of the work of the Holy Spirit in this life, although we find dissenting voices, associated particularly with Wesleyanism and traditions emerging from it such as the Holiness Movement, according to which a 'second work of grace' leads to 'entire sanctification'.[35]

Taken simply on its own terms, the pressures of nature – of matter and its frailty, and of evolution, and the propensities it bakes in – seem to push inexorably in the direction of selfishness and sin. On the other hand, if we have an idea of original justice in play, we can imagine other creatures for which the fatal turn to self and minor pleasures, and away from God and grace, is by no means determined, thus preserving sinlessness as an option. It should be noted here that a choice for or against God has usually been seen as then 'confirmed', or fixed, for good or ill. That is to say, we are not dealing with what a mathematician might call an open-ended 'stochastic' process, whereby a fall might not be inevitable at any one moment, but would become more and more likely if considered over a lengthening timeframe. As Augustine saw it, for instance, the human being, having made the choice for God, would have been elevated to a state more akin to the resurrected body.[36]

---

[34] Collect for the Fourth Sunday after Epiphany, *Book of Common Prayer* (Cambridge: Cambridge University Press, 2004).

[35] John Wesley, *A Plain Account of Christian Perfection* (Bristol: William Pine, 1766); Abraham Worsnop, *Entire Sanctification Distinct from Justification, and Attainable before Death* (London: R. Davies, 1859); Anthony D. Baker, *Diagonal Advance: Perfection in Christian Theology* (Eugene, OR: Cascade, 2011); Harold G. Coward, *The Perfectibility of Human Nature in Eastern and Western Thought* (Albany: State University of New York Press, 2008).

[36] Augustine, *City of God*, book 13, ch. 1.

Pure Nature

We can conclude this survey by noting that for some Roman Catholic writers on this topic a further option has been to imagine creatures created, and remaining, in a state of pure nature (*natura pura*).[37] These would be creatures whom God had not destined for a life beyond that of nature as such, and which would not be aware or desirous of a destiny beyond a purely natural one. Nonetheless, within the limits of a 'purely natural' state of life, they would live out that state to its fullest. Their lives would have a telos without the vision of God, whether we think of their existence as ending with death, or in a future life of natural rather than supernaturally beatific happiness.

In raising the possibility of a purely natural existence, these writers place themselves in some of the most contested territory in theological writing of the past century or so, at least in the Catholic sphere. Writers such as Henri de Lubac and, following him, John Milbank, have denied that this sort of state of pure nature is possible. As de Lubac put it,

> There can never be any reference to a 'natural beatitude', that is, some kind of final end for a rational creature which would not be the vision of God, and in relation to which, in another order of things, in another 'hypothesis', this creature would be impeccable.

---

[37] Kenneth Delano points to two writers who offered a purely natural existence as one possibility among others (*Many Worlds, One God*, 112–14). One is Francis J. Connell: 'They might have been created as pure creatures of nature, enjoying none of the preternatural or supernatural gifts which our first parents had, but able to enjoy a very natural happiness, continuing after their death, though they would never see God' (no citation given). The other is Domenico Grasso, who wrote about 'Beings who were created by God without the gift of supernatural destiny. They could be among the most intelligent of animals, perhaps equalling Homo sapiens in intelligence, but they would be lacking man's knowledge of God and all hope of ever participating in the divine life' (no source is given, but it would seem to be an edition of *Newsweek* from 1960, vol. 55).

[The rational creature is] always created not in relation to some object 'proportioned to its nature' but in relation to God 'as he is in himself.'[38]

Augustine's contention that God has made us for himself, such that our hearts are restless until they find their rest in him (so widely quoted today, but quite a bone of contention on this front in the mid-twentieth century) would apply to any self-aware creature, simply as such.[39] Other writers have suggested that that idea of a purely natural state is a useful tool for thought, as a sort of 'limit case', even if it could not be brought about in reality.[40] For other Catholic writers, the idea of 'purely natural' intelligent life – such as that of the pre-humans envisaged by Pius XII in *Humani Generis* – lies at hand as a possible reality.[41]

Conclusion

Soteriological discussions of life elsewhere need not follow only from thought of sin and fallenness, since we should at least consider

[38] Henri de Lubac, *Surnaturel: Études historiques* (Paris: Aubier, 1946), 255, 256–57, translation from Adam Cooper, 'The Reception of Aquinas in Nouvelle Théologie', in *The Oxford Handbook of the Reception of Aquinas*, ed. Matthew Levering and Marcus Plested (Oxford: Oxford University Press, 2021), 438. For my part, I would be concerned that any attempt to speak of nature that brackets grace does not sufficiently reflect the gratuity, and therefore graced nature, of creation as an undeserved gift.

[39] Augustine, *Confessions*, I.1.1.

[40] Oakes writes that '*natura pura* does not actually obtain in the world as it was actually created by God. As Reginald Garrigou-Lagrange rightly points out: "All theologians agree that the state of pure nature never existed" (Edward T. Oakes, *A Theology of Grace in Six Controversies* (Grand Rapids, MI: Eerdmans, 2016), 18, n. 25, quoting Réginald Garrigou-Lagrange, *Grace: Commentary on the Summa Theologica of St. Thomas, Ia IIae q. 109–114*, trans. Nuns of Corpus Christi monastery (Saint Louis, MO: B. Herder, 1957), 23).

[41] Pope Pius XII, *Humani Generis* (Vatican City: Libreria Editrice Vaticana, 1950). For discussions of the non-necessity of sin along these lines, and that sin might take different forms from that on Earth, see Thomas O'Meara, *Vast Universe*, 25–27; Mascall, *Christian Theology and Natural Science*, 43.

the possibility of unfallen creatures, and recognise that grace confers gifts beyond restoration. With sin in view, however, astrobiology provides us with an impetus to consider afresh its nature, causes, and transmission. As we have seen, among the questions which impact what we might say about the state of intelligent life elsewhere is whether we consider the consequence of the fall as an addition (such as a stain of sin) or a subtraction (such as a loss of original justice), or both. Another question is whether sin affects humans alone or the wider cosmos. For those who take the former approach, the root of sin would lie within each species, rather than stemming from a broader fallen condition within creation. This leads naturally to the question of how sin arises, and whether or not it is inevitable for rational creatures.

I have advocated an approach that holds open the possibility of unfallen life elsewhere. However, even if we imagine the existence of an unfallen species, that does not preclude questions of whether and how they might benefit from the Incarnation of the Son, be that on Earth as Jesus Christ (with them sharing in his nature as other 'rational animals'), or on their own planet (in that case with God taking up their species-specific nature). We will turn to these questions in Chapter 17. Of course, even with sin in mind, God – for the Christian theologian – does not leave the story there. In the next chapter, therefore, we turn to themes of remedy, and indeed of why the Incarnation might be thought to be more than even that.

11 | Responses to Sin

One Incarnation

For most of theological history, when life elsewhere has been considered, it has been within the fame of a single Incarnation, on Earth. That is where we also start, before turning to the possibility of multiple Incarnations, and what might or might not commend that as a theological option. The questions surrounding the idea of one Incarnation in a universe containing other life turn out to run in close parallel to previous theological questions about how the life, death, and Resurrection of Christ might apply to those on Earth who do not know about him, or who are separated from him in space or time.

The Fate of the Unevangelised

The prospect of life elsewhere in the universe raises questions that theologians are only just beginning to consider in the detail they deserve. Nonetheless, our themes relate to the long history of Christian thinking on a wide range of doctrinal topics, sometimes offering quite direct parallels. The contention of this book has been that rather than limiting our historical retrieval to explicit theological discussions of exobiology, we do better to consider the broader twists and turns of systematic theology, although neither originally posed nor worked through in terms of exobiology. Among these parallels, the 'fate of the unevangelised' is significant.[1] Just as our

---

[1] On this question, my own thinking was shaped some decades ago by John Sanders, *No Other Name: Can Only Christian Be Saved?* (London: SPCK, 1992), and more recently

understanding of the cosmos in the West was being transformed by the work of Copernicus and those who followed him, European Christians were beginning to appreciate the expansiveness of this planet, and the fact that it is full of people with previously unknown cultures and religions.[2] There are differences, of course, between extending our thinking to take in other rational species and becoming aware of new populations of our own species with no prior knowledge of Abrahamic faiths.[3] However, the challenges posed to the theology of salvation, in particular, are at least somewhat comparable to those posed by thought of other habited planets.[4]

Aquinas held that Christ's work could avail for any who lived outside the known world, as he understood it, although he thought

---

by Francis Aloysius Sullivan, *Salvation outside the Church? A History of Christian Thought about Salvation for Those 'Outside'* (London: Geoffrey Chapman, 1992).

[2] While we might expect exposure to human life elsewhere on the planet to have provoked thought about the rest of the cosmos, the earliest discussions begin in the fifteenth century. Before that, expansion of terrestrial awareness had begun to take place. In talking about the impact on European theologians here, I am not suggesting that theology is inherently European, only that the recorded challenges to European traditions of thought presented by a new awareness of other human life offer a direct parallel for Christian theologians thinking about life elsewhere in the universe.

[3] That commonality of humanity, deplorably, was not uniformly recognised.

[4] Approaching this in terms of historiography rather than metaphysics, Steven J. Dick has written about the value of drawing an analogy between putative extraterrestrial contact (not a topic in this book) and the 'New World'/'Old World' encounter (*Astrobiology, Discovery, and Societal Impact* (Cambridge: Cambridge University Press, 2020), 65–96). For a discussion of Huldrych Zwingli on the possibility of salvation outside of Christendom, including his belief in elect righteous pagans, see J. Samuel Preus, 'Zwingli, Calvin and the Origin of Religion', *Church History* 46, no. 2 (June 1977): 186–202, particularly the discussion of Zwingli's treatise *De peccato originali* (194, n. 37). In contrast, Calvin tended more forcefully to associate salvation with being within the bounds of the church (*Institutes*, IV.1.4), and seems to indicate that not having had access to the message of the Gospel is a sign of reprobation (III.24.12). On this topic more widely, see George Huntston Williams, 'Erasmus and the Reformers on Non-Christian Religions and Salus Extra Ecclesiam', in *Action and Conviction in Early Modern Europe: Essays in Memory of E. H. Harbison*, ed. Theodore K. Rabb and Jerrold Seigel, 319–70 (Princeton: Princeton University Press, 1969), and Sullivan, *Salvation outside the Church*, 63–81.

that a lack of exposure to the tenets of Christianity would be so rare that God would mop up any incongruous situations by miraculous inspiration, or by sending a messenger.[5] Someone 'brought up in the forest or among wolves' could not have 'explicit knowledge of any matter of faith' and yet it would be 'untenable' (or inappropriate – *inconveniens*) that anyone should 'inevitably be damned [*de neces-sitate damnabitur*]'.[6] On that basis he wrote that

> it pertains to divine providence to furnish everyone with what is necessary for salvation, provided that on his part there is no hindrance. Thus, if someone so brought up followed the direction of natural reason in seeking good and avoiding evil, we must most certainly hold that God would either reveal to him through internal inspiration what had to be believed, or would send some preacher of the faith to him as he sent Peter to Cornelius.[7]

For Aquinas and other European Christians, writing before the age of Christopher Columbus or Ferdinand Magellan, the number of people thought to be living beyond knowledge of the rudiments of the Christian faith was so small that they could imagine such *ad hoc* arrangements could be made for them, whether by visions, angels, or specially directed missionaries. By the sixteenth century, European theologians were beginning to have to consider the fate of a vastly expanded range of people. The deliberations that have

---

[5] Aquinas quotes Heb. 11.6: 'without faith it is impossible to please God, for whoever would approach him must believe that he exists and that he rewards those who seek him', the first part in *De Veritate*, 14.10, and the second part in 14.11. There are parallel discussions in the *Commentary on the Sentences*: 'If a man born among barbarian nations does what he can, God Himself will show him what is necessary for salvation, either by inspiration or sending a teacher to him' (*Commentary on the Sentences*, book 2, dist. 28, q. 1, a. 4, *ad* 4, translation from Anthony Carty and Janne Nijman, *Morality and Responsibility of Rulers: European and Chinese Origins of a Rule of Law as Justice for World Order* (Oxford: Oxford University Press, 2018), 134. See also *Commentary on the Sentences*, book III, dist. 25, q. 2, a. 2, sol. 2).

[6] *De Veritate*, 14.11 *obj.* 1.

[7] Ibid., 14.11 *ad* 1.

continued along those lines offer important resources for thinking about intelligent extraterrestrial life: for instance, the approaches sometimes classed as 'pluralism' (redemption outside of the work of Christ – popular at the end of the twentieth century), 'exclusivism' (that only those who know about Christ and confess him are redeemed – a position that risks turning faith into a work), and 'inclusivism' (that the work of Christ can apply more widely than it is understood). These all apply as angles for thinking about exobiology, and to them a discussion of multiple Incarnations can also be added.

The Effects of a Single Incarnation

In what follows in this chapter, we will consider ways in which a single Incarnation could be salvific for creatures elsewhere. In later chapters, we will turn to the alternative possibility of multiple Incarnations.

By way of introduction, it will be useful to consider some of the principal accounts of redemption put forward within the Christian tradition. Gustav Aulen's threefold distinction, of atonement as substitution, victory, or moral example, is particularly well known, although it tends to elide important differences.[8] There are many different accounts of substitution, for instance, and his 'victory' model includes at least two distinguishable approaches: one where the emphasis is on Christ overcoming an enemy power, the other where the assumption of human nature is itself already salvific. For our purposes, I will distinguish between moral example, ontological models, and substitution.

Today, approaches to Christ's redemptive work that rest solely, or principally, on offering a moral example typically do not command

[8] Gustaf Aulén, *Christus Victor: An Historical Study of the Three Main Types of the Idea of the Atonement*, trans. A. G. Herbert (London: SPCK, 1931).

a great deal of favour. As a complete notion of redemption, it is hardly satisfactory: indeed, it is inherently Pelagian to suppose that human beings need only inspiration in order to sort out their own moral and spiritual trouble by their own strength. Moreover, it offers a moralistic and truncated view of what God offers as redeemed human destiny, which is not a life of good behaviour, but participation in the divine nature: a gift so far beyond what is possible to even a perfect creature by nature as to render Pelagianism a sort of category mistake as an account of salvation.[9]

> The human being can acquire, by natural powers, the imperfect happiness that can be had, in the same way as virtue, in whose operation it consists ... Our perfect happiness, however, ... consists in the vision of the Divine Essence. Now the vision of God's Essence surpasses the nature not only of the human being, but also of every creature ... Consequently neither the human being, nor any creature, can attain final happiness by his natural powers.[10]

Approaches to redemption do not need to stand alone, however, and few theologians would wish entirely to discard the sense that part of what Christ does is to show us how to live. Applied to creatures elsewhere, nonetheless, even if only as part of how to think of the life and work of Christ, the moral example theme may have little to offer. One could imagine, certainly, that the life, death, Resurrection, and teaching of Jesus could be revealed elsewhere, but given the likely range of any exobiology, and its cultures and ways of life, we come up against the question of how comprehensible to them the life story of a possibly very alien life-form indeed – a human being – would be. If communication and example are the essence of this angle on God's saving work, the idea of multiple Incarnations should, at the very least, be thought through as an alternative.

---

[9] 2 Peter 1.4.
[10] *ST* II-I.5.5.

A second set of approaches to redemption emphasise not epistemology, that is, moral instruction, but ontology. They are about *being*: redemption through God-being-human. This ontological model of the atonement is sometimes called 'Greek', on account of its association with the Greek fathers, although it has also been powerfully explored in the West.[11] On this view, humanity is elevated, and freed from sin and death, by the Son's 'taking up' of human nature. This is rarely explored in strictly analytic terms, but rather in a more poetic or narrative style: the Son vivifies human nature, dead in its sin, by infusing it with his divine life; the Wisdom that created all things in the beginning refashions what has been broken; God endures all that the journey of human life and death offers, and, through death and resurrection, takes that life on to new life beyond sin and death; and so on. As I mentioned above, following Aulen's taxonomy of approaches to the atonement, this angle is sometimes associated with themes of victory: in Christ, God faced down sin and death, and triumphed over them. Significantly, in Christ God did this not instead of humanity, but as a human being.

If ontological accounts of redemption are to be extended to life elsewhere in the universe, by means of a single Incarnation, we would be seeing that Incarnation as a divine act that embraces the whole cosmos.[12] The role of humanity in God's sharing of creaturely life, and humanity's consequent sharing in divine life, would be representative

---

[11] See, for instance, A. N. Williams, *The Ground of Union: Deification in Aquinas and Palamas* (Oxford: Oxford University Press, 1999); Pavel L. Gavriljuk, 'The Retrieval of Deification: How a Once-Despised Archaism Became an Ecumenical Desideratum', *Modern Theology* 25, no. 4 (2009): 647–59; Veli-Matti Kärkkäinen, *One with God: Salvation as Deification and Justification* (Collegeville, MN: Liturgical Press, 2004); Daria Spezzano, *The Glory of God's Grace: Deification According to St. Thomas Aquinas* (Ave Maria, FL: Sapientia Press of Ave Maria University, 2015); S. T. Kimbrough Jr, *Partakers of the Life Divine: Participation in the Divine Nature in the Writings of Charles Wesley* (Eugene, OR: Cascade, 2016). See also the forthcoming *Oxford Handbook on Deification*, to which I have contributed a chapter on deification and the metaphysics of participation.

[12] So, for instance, the American Catholic writer Januarius De Concilio (1836–1898) stressed that one Incarnation could effect 'the divinization of the universe' in as

of life more generally. The principal question for this model, in expanding it to other life, is therefore to ask what is shared between human beings and those other beings. If we were to stress that the human nature God took up was assumed *in contrast to* other forms of creaturely existence, we may have difficulty seeing how what God did for human beings in Christ could be extended to other creatures. Such a restrictive line, however, does not necessarily need to be drawn. Broadly, two approaches might be considered. The first stresses God's identification in Jesus as reaching down to embrace that which is most common: that Christ took on not just humanity but also animality, not just animality but materiality, not just materiality but creature-hood. Just such an approach has been explored in recent years by advocates of the idea of 'Deep Incarnation', including Niels Gregersen and Elizabeth A. Johnson.[13] A second approach seeks to broaden that which God has taken up in Christ without pushing the identification as far 'down' as the first. If we were able to take a category such as 'rational life' or 'personhood' as universal, it would be possible to say that in assuming one such nature – a nature characterised by 'rational life' or 'personhood' – God assumed rational life as such, or person-hood as such, thereby embracing every nature characterised that way. To put this in Thomist terms, in Jesus Christ God is united to the nature of a rational animal, redeeming rational animals everywhere.

While we might struggle to imagine how Christ's moral example could bear upon other creatures without them being made aware

much as human nature is of a sort that 'abridges in itself all created species … inorganic species, living species, sensitive species, spiritual species of any degree, united to any kind of material body, and pure intellectual species like the angels' (*Harmony between Science and Revelation*, 229–30).

[13] Elizabeth A. Johnson, 'Deep Christology', in *From Logos to Christos: Essays on Christology in Honour of Joanne McWilliam*, ed. Kate Leonard and Ellen M. Merriman (Waterloo: Wilfrid Laurier University Press, 2009); Elizabeth A. Johnson, 'Jesus and the Cosmos: Soundings in Deep Christology', in *Incarnation: On the Scope and Depth of Christology*, ed. Niels Henrik Gregersen (Minneapolis, MN: Fortress Press, 2015), 133–56; Niels Henrik Gregersen, ed., *Incarnation: On the Scope and Depth of Christology* (Minneapolis, MN: Fortress Press, 2015).

of it, ontological models of redemption allow us more readily to conceive of Jesus' Incarnation having a widespread effect without widespread knowledge of it. Other creatures, indeed the whole of creation, might be redeemed in Christ, despite being ignorant of the fact, or at least being aware of the effect but not of the cause. This brings us back to the discussions of the fate of the unevangelised, and the inclusivist view introduced above. From a strictly ontological perspective, what matters is what Christ does for humanity, not our knowledge of it, not even our response. We may have reasons for supposing that in his act of redemption, God achieves not simply a widespread effect, but also widespread knowledge of that effect – not least based on the association of God with truth – but this might be secondary for an ontological model. This model can easily be 'objective' rather than 'subjective', placing a higher premium on the redemption of creatures than on their subjective understanding, or assent to it. This is why it can easily be seen as universalistic, not out of a low or weak Christology, but from a form of elevated Christological maximalism.

Contrasts between ontological models of the atonement and ones set out in terms of substitution are easy to make. The former is about sharing, while substitution looks close to the opposite: not about this *through* that, but this *instead of* that. With a little scrutiny, however, a simple division between these approaches to redemption – solidarity and substitution – is harder to sustain. This is most evident if we ask whether it matters *what* substitutes for whom. If a theologian thinks it matters that the one who stood in for the rest of humanity was a human being, she is assuming that substitutionary atonement rests on an element of sharing, or a unity in nature, which is the territory of the ontological approach.[14] In other words, the atonement does not involve God doing something, or suffering something *instead of* humanity, after all, but rather doing something *as* a human being.

---

[14] On this, see my *Participation in God*, 263–65.

To write of what Christ 'did … or suffered', as I just did, flags the diversity of accounts that might be gathered under a substitutionary banner. The most common substitutionary understanding today would be one of punishment: that Jesus endured something so that other human beings would not have to. That, however, is only one among several substitutionary perspectives, and a latecomer in terms of being asked to do all the heavy lifting. Anselm, for instance, is rightly understood as offering a substitutionary model of the atonement in *Cur Deus Homo*, but his treatment breathes different air from the substitution of punishment advanced by the Reformers. For Anselm, Christ's substitution is one of honour. The divine human Jesus Christ is able to fulfil the debt of honour due to God from humanity, which humanity, in its sin, is unable to provide. Other substitutionary perspectives include a substitution of penance, where Christ offers penitence to the Father – on the cross, for instance, but also in his baptism – which avails for the whole of humanity, who by sin are prevented from being perfectly penitent. Among these interpretations, it is worth noting that while a substation of punishment ('penal substitution') involves a descent from the Father to the Son (the Father metes punishment upon Christ), the forms of substitution that dominated earlier are different. They concern an ascent rather than a descent: an ascent of honour or penance from the Son to the Father.

Substitutionary models of the atonement, like others discussed here, can be extended to other creatures. Jesus stands in for, and represents, his fellow human beings (whether rendering honour or penance, or receiving punishment), and he could stand in for and represent a wider cohort of creatures. Here, the connection between ontological and substitutionary models of the atonement again comes to the surface. It would seem important, if one were to embrace a vision of cosmos-wide substitution by Christ, to stress some wider bond of solidarity between Christ as human and those other creatures, as rational beings, for instance, or as persons.

Timing

In thinking about the universal benefits of a single Incarnation, whether redemption from sin is in view or theosis, temporal questions emerge about how the fruits of Christ's works relate to those who benefit from them. If the evolution of life is reasonably common, such that the universe contains other life now, then the universe has likely contained other life for a long time. The sun is a 'population I' star, which means that it falls in the third generation of stars. (In this nomenclature, population III stars are the oldest, and population I the youngest.) The first stars ('population III') were composed of helium and hydrogen, with heavier elements, such as metals, being so rare as to preclude life. However, those stars that ended their lives in supernovae produced and dispersed metallic elements, bequeathing them to the second generation of stars ('population II'). Our solar system, which itself contains the remnants of the further explosions of population II stars, is even richer in complex, metallic elements by a wide margin. Our sun is 4.5 billion years old (it dates from around 9.3 billion years after the big bang), and for around 3.5 billion years at least one of its planets, Earth, has harboured life. The first population I stars (those with the best capacity for planets with life, on account of their enriched levels of heavy elements) go back at least twice as far as the sun. If life also evolved on planets around those earlier stars within around a billion years of the formation of their stars, it could have been present in the solar systems of population I stars as long as 8 billion years ago, compared to 3.5 billion years on Earth. That would be extended further still if we take rocky planets or moons around population II stars into account, which go back at least 13 billion years.[15]

The upshot is that there has been plenty of time for a good deal of life already to have come and gone elsewhere in the universe.

[15] Safonova, Murthy, and Shchekinov, 'Age Aspects of Habitability'.

We should therefore ask whether it would make sense to say that a species elsewhere, several billion years *before* Christ, could benefit from his work.[16] The idea of a moral example would offer few problems, at least if we think about some form of supernatural revelation.[17] Forms of substitution may also not prove difficult, either, if they involve God, who is outside time, accepting one life or offering in place of others. I cannot see a problem with the honour or penance that Christ offers being of consequence for those born long before him, nor with a substitution of punishment *per se*, although the latter would not feature prominently in my own thinking. Nor do I necessarily find it difficult to suppose that incorporative, ontological models of salvation through sharing in Christ could apply before his birth.[18] In the words of David Brewster in the mid-nineteenth century, 'When our Saviour died, the influence of His death extended backwards, in the past, to millions who had never heard His name, and forwards, in the future, to millions who will never hear it'.[19] Or, as Aubrey de Vere had it,

---

[16] I will turn to Oakes' *Theology of Grace* below. Here, however, it is worth noting that he frames his discussion of exobiology and Incarnation with what he takes to be a common assumption, or at least assertion, not only 'that if extraterrestrial intelligence should ever be discovered, this would prove to be a body-blow to Christocentrism' but also that 'this dilemma would become even more exigent if some future human astronauts were to discover an exo-civilization on another planet that had long died out' (Oakes, *Grace*, 240). The reader will appreciate by now that I disagree.

[17] I suppose there are questions about information getting 'back' to Earth about something that has yet to happen, but the distances involved, and the difficulty of communication, seem to make that practically irrelevant as a consideration.

[18] De Concilio set this out for creatures living before the birth of Christ both for any who needed redeeming, and for any who did not fall: 'if they enjoyed ... this union in anticipation before Christ and were faithful to it [rather than falling] they owe this constancy and fidelity to the grace of Christ. If they fell, they were included in our redemption, and were made partakers by God of Christ through any means which in His infinite wisdom He may have seen fit to adopt' (*Harmony between Science and Revelation*, 233).

[19] Brewster, *More Worlds Than One*, 149.

> Judaea was one country, one alone:
> Not less Who died there for all. The Cross
> Brought help to vanished nations: Time opposed
> No bar to Love: why then should Space oppose one?
> We know not what Time is nor what is Space;
> Why dream that bonds like theirs constrain the unbounded?[20]

Christian theology offers precedents when it comes to proleptic efficacy. One relates to the effectiveness of the rites of ancient Judaism, which has often been attributed ultimately to the work of Jesus. On that topic, theologians are certainly not of one mind, as Aquinas indeed makes clear in setting out a series of perspectives about whether circumcision bestowed sanctifying grace.[21] Thomas, for his part, ascribed to the most fulsome of the versions he discusses regarding the efficacy of circumcision: that 'grace was bestowed in circumcision as to all the effects of grace, but not [in the same manner] as in Baptism'.[22] A further example of a transformation effected by what would come later in time – of an effect that temporally proceeds its cause – is the sanctification of the Virgin Mary, described in Catholic theology as her Immaculate Conception. Typically, where her sinless state is accepted, the idea is that the fruits of her son's death and Resurrection were proleptically applied by God to his mother. As Aaron Riches has put it, 'every honour attributed to Mary thus lies in a prior grace divinely given and mysteriously rooted in the merits of her Son's Cross'.[23]

---

[20] Aubrey de Vere, 'The Death of Copernicus', in *Poems*, 171–72.

[21] *ST* III.70.4.

[22] *ST* III.70.4.

[23] Aaron Riches, *Ecce Homo: On the Divine Unity of Christ* (Grand Rapids, MI: Eerdmans, 2016), 228. Riches quotes the Collect for the Feast of the Immaculate Conception in the Modern Roman Rite: 'as you preserved her from every stain by virtue of the Death of your Son, which you foresaw' [*qui ex morte eiusdem Filii tui praevisa, eam ab omni labe praeservasti*]. Aquinas rejected the idea that Mary never inherited original sin, supposing her to have been born in it, but redeemed in the womb (*ST* III.27.2). He still holds, however, that what pertained to Mary came

Conclusion

The question of whether Christ's work on earth could avail for those who do not know of it is not new to Christian theology, though astrobiological questions extend the range of that question. Of the three broad categories of thinking about the atonement set out here, models centred on moral example pose the greatest challenges. If Christ's example is the essence of his saving work, then multiple Incarnations may provide a better alternative. Ontological and substitutionary approaches have more to draw on. To consider the possibility of the Incarnation as embracing the whole cosmos, we might emphasize Christ's assumption of what is common: not just humanity, but rationality, animality, materiality, even creaturehood. In this way, the objective aspect of the atonement poses few problems, though questions remain regarding the nature of the communication or revelation necessary for creaturely response to Christ's saving work. Christian theology also has significant resources for thinking about the proleptic efficacy of the atonement, though this may have to be expanded to encompass not thousands, but billions, of years.

In summary, I would stress that the theology of a single Incarnation in the entire cosmos could generally quite easily stretch to take in and affect species elsewhere. As we have seen, that proves to be a parallel with trends in theology to see the life,

---

from Christ ('without whose power no one had been freed from the first sentence of condemnation') but, because he wished to mark more of a distinction between Mary's state of innocence and that of Christ than later Catholic thought did, he saw what is applied to her proleptically as partial, with her further sanctification coming only with the Incarnation of Christ in her womb, 'in which for the first time immunity from sin was to be conspicuous … [such] that entire freedom [from the disordering effects of sin] redounded from the Child to the Mother' (III.27.3). Aquinas, then, does not offer quite as fully proleptic a picture of the mother benefiting, from her own beginning, from the work of her Son as we find in later Catholic writing.

death, and Resurrection of Christ as applying broadly in time and space upon Earth. The emphasis in this chapter has been on redemption, but we can also ask about the relation of unfallen species to a single, human Incarnation, and we will turn to that in Chapter 17. First, however, I will consider the alternative view, of many Incarnations.

12 | Multiple Incarnations

Introduction

Among the theological topics raised by the prospect of other life in the universe, discussion of multiple Incarnations appears to be the most highly contested among Christians today. Since Christianity is centred on the Incarnation, it is perhaps no surprise that theologians should be so invested in whether God is Incarnate in Jesus Christ alone, or whether our experience here is representative of God's dealings with creation more widely. To my mind, theologians can argue the matter in good faith either way.

In subsequent chapters, we will go on to look more systematically at some of the major themes that are raised, seeking to do so in terms of the ideas and categories set out in centuries of discussion of Christology. As we will see, much writing on exobiology has been worked out in terms markedly different from those of traditional 'Conciliar' Christology.

In this chapter, I start with an overview of the idea of multiple Incarnations, with history particularly in view. I will also take a step back, to think about the terms in which we are assessing the proposal of multiple Incarnations: whether that is in terms of necessity, of possibility, or – as I would favour – of their suitability or fittingness.

Discussions of Multiple Incarnations in Christian History

Multiple Incarnations have been entertained seriously in Christian discussions of exobiology only recently. Indeed, although the prospect of life elsewhere in the universe has been a topic of discussion by Christian theologians since the fifteenth century, little attention was given to Incarnation or salvation at first. Consideration of revelation set the running, alongside topics related to the doctrine of creation. Neither Nicholas of Cusa, John Wilkins, nor John Ray, for example, seem to have been interested in Incarnation. Guillaume de Vaurouillon and Tommaso Campanella turned to it briefly – so briefly, indeed, that we cannot be clear what they are denying when they disallow additional Incarnations, although it is almost certainly something quite different from what I discuss below. In any case, for all they affirmed the possibility of life elsewhere, they mentioned other Incarnations only to discount them. Philip Melanchthon was similarly brief. While he also denied other Incarnations, he went so far as taking that denial as the basis for rejecting the possibility of life elsewhere.

The longest pre–twentieth century discussion of other Incarnations I know that accepted the idea turns out to be an exception that proves the rule. It is William Hay's treatment in *Religio Philosophi* (which we encountered above in relation to ethics), which proves to be more or less Arian.[1] As such, while he entirely accepts the idea of multiple 'Incarnations', once again what he has in mind is far from the idea of Incarnation in the classical Christian theological sense. His Christology is adoptionist, and the 'Son' who is Incarnate, along with the Spirit, is understood to be strictly secondary and subordinate to the Father (as truest God). Even if he is begotten before time, that 'begetting' is something close to creation, and God is not intrinsically Trinity, nor are the Persons equal or co-constituting. As such, he does not represent an embrace of multiple Incarnations, in a Nicene sense, at all.

The history of theological writing on exobiology is extensive, and a writer should hesitate to make claims about what was and was not said before a certain point. With that caveat in mind, however,

[1] Hay, 'Religio Philosophi', 241–49.

it seems safe to say discussions that embraced the possibility of multiple Incarnations take off only in the twentieth century.[2] The 1911 poem 'Christ in the Universe' by Alice Meynell (1847–1922), reproduced at the opening of this book, is an example.[3] Another is the Scots poem 'The Innumerable Christ' by Hugh MacDiarmid (1892–1978) writing as Christopher Murray Grieve, which was published in 1925.[4] It contains the lines

> An' when the earth's as cauld's [cold as] the mune [moon]
> An' a' its folk are lang syne [long since] deid [dead]
> On coontless [countless] stars the Babe maun [must] cry
> An' the Crucified maun [must] bleed.

Although explorations such these in the early twentieth century had begun to open people's imaginations to the possibility of multiple Incarnations, rejections were still common, as they are today. In 1952, the mathematician and astrophysicist Edward Milne reacted negatively to the suggestion, in an influential chapter on exobiology and theology in his *Modern Cosmology and the Christian Idea of God*:

---

[2] David Brewster stands as a pivotal case. In *More Worlds Than One*, he argued for the universal efficacy of the Easter events in 'the Holy City'. However, he was willing at least to raise the idea of multiple Incarnations, although he explains that 'we ourselves may not admit it into our creed': 'May not the Divine nature, which can neither suffer nor die, and which in our planet, *once* only, clothed itself in humanity, resume elsewhere a physical form, and expiate the guilt of unnumbered worlds?' (*More Worlds Than One*, 148–51).

[3] It was first published in *The Fortnightly Review* in October 1911 (date from *The Selected Letters of Alice Meynell, Poet and Essayist*, ed. Damian Atkinson (Newcastle upon Tyne: Cambridge Scholars Publishing, 2013), 302, n. 321). It was collected in Alice Meynell, *Collected Poems* (London: Burns & Oates, 1913), 114–15.

[4] Hugh MacDiarmid, *Sangschaw* (Edinburgh: William Blackwood, 1925), 33. The poem was set to music by Francis George Scott (1880–1958) and has been recorded by Signum Records (SIGCD096). The poem bears the epigraph 'Other stars may have their Bethlehem and the Calvary too | Professor JY Simpson'. This is almost certainly a quotation from James Young Simpson (1873–1934), a Scottish scientist who wrote on theological topics.

God's most notable intervention in the actual historical process, according to the Christian outlook, was the Incarnation. Was this a unique event, or has it been re-enacted on each of a countless number of planets? The Christian would recoil in horror from such a conclusion. We cannot imagine the Son of God suffering vicariously on each of a myriad of planets.[5]

C. S. Lewis also rejected the idea of multiple Incarnations, explicitly commenting on Meynell's poem in *Miracles* (1947):

> I do not think it at all likely that there have been (as Alice Meynell suggested in an interesting poem) many Incarnations to redeem many different kinds of creature. One's sense of style – of the divine idiom – rejects it. The suggestion of mass-production and of waiting queues comes from a level of thought which is here hopelessly inadequate.[6]

The irony here is that, for a wide readership, Lewis' own figure of Aslan opened up, in perhaps an unprecedented way, an imaginative sense of what it might mean for the Son to be Incarnated in a different world, albeit, of course, in a fictional one in that case. In Lewis's own words,

> Aslan … is an invention giving an imaginary answer to the question, 'What might Christ become like if there really were a world like Narnia and *He* chose to be Incarnate and die and rise again in that world as *He* actually has done in ours?' This is not allegory at all … The Incarnation of Christ in another world is mere supposal: but granted the supposition, he would really have been a physical object in that world as he was in Palestine and his death on the stone table would have been a physical event no less than his death on Calvary.[7]

[5] Milne, *Modern Cosmology*, 154.

[6] C. S. Lewis, *Miracles: A Preliminary Study* (London: Geoffrey Bles, 1947), 150. On this, see P. H. Brazier, 'C. S. Lewis: The Question of Multiple Incarnations', *Heythrop Journal* 55, no. 3 (2014): 397.

[7] Letter to Mrs Hook, 29 December 1958, in C. S. Lewis, *The Collected Letters of C. S. Lewis*, ed. Walter Hooper, vol. 3 (San Francisco: HarperSanFrancisco, 2004), 1004–5, quoted by Brazier, 'Question of Multiple Incarnations', 393.

Among more recent theologians, Paul Tillich assented to the idea of multiple Incarnations, although again what he meant by Incarnation may lie somewhat outside the historical trend. The appearance of Christ 'in existence', he wrote,

> represents human history; more precisely, as its central event, he creates the meaning of human history. It is the eternal relation of God to man which is manifest in the Christ. At the same time, our basic answer leaves the universe open for possible divine manifestations in other areas or periods of being. Such possibilities cannot be denied. But they cannot be proved or disproved. Incarnation is unique for the special group in which it happens, but it is not unique in the sense that other singular incarnations for other unique worlds are excluded. Man cannot claim that the infinite has entered the finite to overcome its existential estrangement in mankind alone. Man cannot claim to occupy the only possible place for Incarnation.[8]

In contrast, Wolfhart Pannenberg (1928–2014) rejected the idea,[9] while a snapshot of theological life from around Cambridge at the turn of the twenty-first century again shows a breadth of opinion, even between three Anglican theologians of a similar generation. Both Arthur Peacocke (1924–2006) and Brian Hebblethwaite (born 1939) thought multiple Incarnations to be theologically problematic, yet also expected them were there to be life elsewhere. From Peacocke's more liberal perspective, that would call for a wholesale revision of Christian doctrine.[10] From

---

[8] Paul Tillich, *Systematic Theology*, vol. 2 (Chicago: University of Chicago Press, 1957), 110–11, 96; on his ambivalence to the term 'Incarnation', see 108–10.

[9] Wolfhart Pannenberg, *Systematic Theology*, trans. Geoffrey W. Bromiley, vol. 2 (Edinburgh: T&T Clark, 1994), 76.

[10] 'Does not the possibility of extraterrestrial life render nonsensical all superlative claims made by the Church about the significance of Jesus?' (Arthur Peacocke, 'The Challenge and Stimulus of the Epic of Evolution to Theology', in *Many Worlds: The New Universe, Extraterrestrial Life, and the Theological Implications*, ed. Stephen Dick (Philadelphia: Templeton Foundation Press, 2000), 89). Norman Pittenger had expressed a similar view in *The Word Incarnate* (London: Nisbet, 1959), 248.

a less revisionist position, Hebblethwaite hoped that no other intelligent life would exist, writing that 'an implication of the Christian Incarnation' is 'that there are no other intelligent, personal creatures in God's creation than human beings on earth'.[11] This 2001 essay would prove to be a significant provocation for later discussion of the topic, with notable responses particularly from writers in the school of analytic theology, including Tim Pawl and Oliver Crisp.[12] We will return to the detail of some of these discussions below. In contrast, John Polkinghorne (1930–2021), wrote that 'if little green men on Mars need saving, then God will take little green flesh': a positive assessment that would align him with a fourth Anglican, of distinctly Thomist stripe, Eric Mascall.[13]

In recent years, the theme of multiple Incarnations has been taken up by writers associated with the 'Polydoxy' movement, drawing on feminist, womanist, and queer theological perspectives. There, the idea is aligned with a broader stress on variety and openness in preference to settled or singular outlooks, as a perspective where 'multiplicity abounds', even a 'full on embrace of multiplicity – of multiplicity wherever it is found – in the divine and temporal

---

[11] Brian Hebblethwaite, 'The Impossibility of Multiple Incarnations', *Theology* 104, no. 821 (1 September 2001): 323–34. Hebblethwaite discusses what provoked him to think about this topic, coming out of the 'Myth of God Incarnate' and subsequent material, on pp. 323–25.

[12] Peter Kevern, 'Limping Principles: A Reply to Brian Hebblethwaite on "The Impossibility of Multiple Incarnations"', *Theology* 105, no. 827 (September 2002): 342–47; Oliver Crisp, *God Incarnate: Explorations in Christology* (London: T & T Clark, 2009), 157–64; Robin Le Poidevin, 'Multiple Incarnations and Distributed Persons', in *The Metaphysics of the Incarnation*, ed. Anna Marmodoro and Jonathan Hill (Oxford: Oxford University Press, 2011), 228–41; Timothy Pawl, 'Brian Hebblethwaite's Arguments against Multiple Incarnations', *Religious Studies* 52, no. 1 (March 2016): 117–30. Thomas Morris responded to earlier versions of Hebblethwaite's argument in *Logic of God Incarnate*, 181–86.

[13] John Polkinghorne, *Observer*, 11 August 1996; Mascall, *Christian Theology and Natural Science*, 36–45. As on many other topics, I am in debt to Mascall in writing this book.

world'.[14] In a soteriological register, that involves a vision of 'the intersections of multiple religious traditions, multiple divine forces, multiple Incarnations, and multiple Saviors'.[15] In characteristically rhapsodic language, Catherine Keller and Laurel C. Schneider refer to 'Our own multiplicities, enfolded here in the structure and personalities of this volume, [which] unfold within the body of Christ, itself multiply Incarnate in a logos-invoked cosmos'.[16] Schneider returns to this theme in her essay, 'Promiscuous Incarnation'. In her view, questions about additional Incarnations were not taken up in the Early Church, or were even suppressed, as a matter of political expediency: it suited Constantine to claim 'exclusive status as sole ruler', and that was reflected in Christological settlements.[17] What Schneider means by Incarnation, however, soon turns out to be something very different from a permanent hypostatic union. For her, it is any 'coming' of God that is mediated through the flesh: 'Christians can claim that God always becomes flesh for a purpose and so can be found wherever that purpose is being pursued ... the suffering of any person, any body, is a wound in God's flesh, a diminishment of God's own beloved, a gravitational pull on God to come, again. And again'.[18] 'Multiple Incarnations', from that perspective, rests on a meaning of 'Incarnation' quite different from one set out in terms of a hypostatic union of two natures in one

---

[14] Monica A. Coleman, 'Invoking Oya', in *Polydoxy: Theology of Multiplicity and Relation*, ed. Catherine Keller and Laurel C. Schneider (London: Routledge, 2011), 186–87. A significant provocation for polydoxy was Laurel C. Schneider, *Beyond Monotheism: A Theology of Multiplicity* (London: Routledge, 2008).

[15] Coleman, 'Invokng Oya', 186. There is a similar list on p. 198, without further elaboration of detail.

[16] Catherine Keller and Laurel C. Schneider, 'Introduction', in *Polydoxy: Theology of Multiplicity and Relation*, ed. Catherine Keller and Laurel C. Schneider (London: Routledge, 2011), 13.

[17] Laurel C. Schneider, 'Promiscuous Incarnation', in *The Embrace of Eros: Bodies, Desir es, and Sexuality in Christianity*, ed. Margaret D. Kamitsuka (Minneapolis, MN: Fortress Press, 2010), 240–41.

[18] Ibid., 245.

Person. As such, those perspectives will not have a great deal of purchase on what follows, or vice versa.

Historically speaking, the most influential analysis of the possibility of multiple Incarnations in Christian theological history was presented in relation to our Earthly story, rather than in relation to life elsewhere in the universe, coming towards the beginning of the third part of Aquinas' *Summa Theologiae*.[19] One of the principal aims behind this book has been to move the discussion of theology and astrobiology beyond the relatively restricted number of standard historical texts deployed in writing on the subject, to others that were not directly addressed to, or occasioned by, thoughts of life elsewhere in the universe, but which nevertheless could bear directly upon the topic. Aquinas' text cannot count as untilled soil in that way, but it repays consideration, nonetheless.

Aquinas did not have non-human creatures in mind, but asked instead whether the Son could have assumed human nature more than once: 'it seems that after the Incarnation the Son can assume another human nature [*aliam humanam naturam*] distinct from the one He has assumed'.[20] His arguments, however, bear just as readily on the assumption of a second (or third) nature *different in kind* from humanity.[21] Perhaps, indeed, the phrase 'another human nature' (*aliam humanam naturam*) is infelicitous in itself. For Aquinas, there is one human nature, shared by all human beings, and rendered individual in each. In the case of the divine human being Jesus Christ, it is individuated by its assumption by the Second Person. Thomas' question is therefore not so much about the Word assuming 'another human nature' – if there is only one – as about the Word assuming human nature an additional time. Significantly, moreover, we can remember that Aquinas was inclined to think of

[19] *ST* III.3, especially q. 7.
[20] *ST* III.3.7 *resp.*
[21] Something more expansive is also suggested by the way the topic is set out at the beginning of the question: 'Whether one Person can assume two individual natures [*duas naturas numero*]?'

the category of 'rational animal' as a single thing, as we discussed in Chapter 9. Talk of 'another human nature' may therefore translate more readily than it first appears to into precisely the terms we have in mind here: whether God could be Incarnate as more than one form of 'rational animal'.

Putting Aquinas' article to work in relation to exobiology, Eric Mascall found fault with the idea of more than one human Incarnation, but endorsed the idea of various single Incarnations into different biological species. My inclination would be to follow the same path: multiple Incarnations into the same biological nature may or may not make sense (a question of possibility), but I am inclined to see them as unnecessary, superfluous, and unfitting.[22] Multiple Incarnations across different biological species, however, may be particularly fitting, replicating the intimacy of God's relation to human beings with other species, as I will discuss in Chapter 16. We will return to Aquinas in *ST* III.3 later, not least in Chapter 14. First, a comment on method or outlook in writing on multiple Incarnations is due.

Possibility, Necessity, and Suitability

I have just introduced ideas of possibility, necessity, and fittingness, and this is a good point to take a step back and consider these modes of talking about theology. When it comes to Christ and Incarnation, the central questions raised by the idea of extraterrestrial life have typically been the *plausibility* and *likelihood* of

---

[22] Pawl also thinks that 'idea that there could be two Incarnations of the Son in the same nature at the same time is highly dubious. What would it be for the divine and human natures to be doubly united together in the same Person, but by different hypostatic unions?' (Timothy Pawl, 'Thomistic Multiple Incarnations', *The Heythrop Journal* 57, no. 2 (March 2016): 360). Aquinas' discussion as to why the Son has not 'assumed human nature in all individuals' also seems to argue against multiple Incarnations in the same species (*ST* III.4.5). Polkinghorne agreed. See the discussion of *Theology in the Context of Science*, 53, below.

multiple Incarnations. Those approaches have often been discussed quite distinctly in the literature to date. Typically, matters of plausibility are set out in the language of possibility, while matters of likelihood are set out in terms of necessity. A former set of questions asks what might be thought to be possible, Christologically speaking, in the Word's taking up of creaturely flesh. Then, as to the purpose and impact of the Incarnation, comes a set of questions to do with necessity: given the plight of creatures (or to achieve a more than natural existence), what must God have done to save, reconcile, redeem, and or elevate them? Or are there no bounds, as to either what God might bring about or how that might be achieved?

As we have seen, John Polkinghorne expressed certainty that 'If little green men on Mars need saving, then God will have taken little green flesh ... He will do what is necessary'.[23] Here is necessity. Five years later, as we have also seen, another Cambridge cleric, Brian Hebblethwaite, published his widely discussed article in *Theology*, entitled simply 'The Impossibility of Multiple Incarnations'.[24] Here is possibility or impossibility. These are representative examples of the two modalities in which this subject has typically been explored: necessity and possibility.

In speaking about the coming of God in the flesh, the words 'Incarnation' and 'Christology' are sometimes treated as more or less synonymous. Nonetheless, a distinction between them holds water: Christology is the narrower term, covering a set of technical questions over how to speak about Christ, particularly over how to speak about him as both human and divine. A theology of the Incarnation would bear upon all of that, but would also place it in the wider context of why God became flesh, and what this achieved. Christology focuses on the 'Person of Christ'; Incarnation concerns both the Person and the 'work of Christ' (although no Christology worthy of the name could be explored entirely in isolation from that work).

---

[23] John Polkinghorne, *Observer*, 11 August 1996.
[24] Hebblethwaite, 'The Impossibility of Multiple Incarnations'.

Christological discussions therefore tend towards *what* we can say about how the Son of God came also to be human; discussion of the Incarnation broadens that out to consider *why* God so acted: what it was to achieve.

Within the corpus of writing on multiple Incarnations, our two quite different sorts of discussions – one over possibility and one over necessity – align with Christology and Incarnation, respectively. Attention to Christology, with its language of person and nature, of *supposita* and *hypostases*, and so on, has characterised discussions about whether multiple Incarnations are *possible*. Its material is the nuts and bolts of technical Christological mechanics concerning the *Person* of Christ. In contrast, discussions of the more expansive 'what for?' questions of the doctrine of the Incarnation have often not been concerned so much with the technical details of Christology, but rather with the broader picture of how the Incarnation integrates with themes of salvation, theological anthropology, and the doctrine of God.[25]

We can see this distinction at work, for example, in Polkinghorne's later discussion in *Theology in the Context of Science* (first published in 2008). It is generally laid out in terms of the economy of salvation, and therefore of necessity. The argument he considers against multiple Incarnations is that the death of Jesus Christ would be sufficient (rendering other Incarnations *unnecessary*). His argument in favour is that if the way to meet a 'need' elsewhere were to be by Incarnation, then the Word 'would' have taken flesh elsewhere (again, this is the territory of necessity: God would do what is required). Notably, it is only when Polkinghorne moves closest to more technical questions of Christology (whether the Word could be Incarnate, for instance, more than once as a human being) that his register shifts from necessity to possibility: multiple Incarnations in

---

[25] I set this out in my article 'Christian Systematic Theology and Life Elsewhere in the Universe: A Study in Suitability', *Theology and Science* 16, no. 4 (2 October 2018): 447–61.

the same species may be an 'incoherent notion' (that is, *impossible*), while multiple Incarnations in different rational species are not.[26]

We have already noted Tillich's discussion in *Systematic Theology*. Operating on Christological territory, he considers the matter of possibility: 'our basic answer leaves the universe open for possible divine manifestations in other areas or periods of being. Such possibilities cannot be denied. But they cannot be proved or disproved'.[27] In the next paragraph, however, he asks what can be inferred from consideration of a larger picture, including salvation. The 'participation of nature in history' and of 'the whole universe in salvation' suggest that 'such [extraterrestrial] worlds cannot be without the operation of saving power within them'. To write 'cannot be without' is to argue in terms of necessity, as when he writes that our Earthly story 'implies' and 'presupposes' the dynamics of Incarnation elsewhere.[28]

We might also consider Frank Weston. In his *Revelation of Eternal Love* (1920), he framed discussion of the logic of the Incarnation in terms of necessity: 'Eternal Love holds all things that exist in close relation with Himself. He reveals Himself to all rational beings on a level at which they can respond. And each activity these loving relations makes *necessary* is included within the one divine act we call eternal Love'.[29] In contrast, he approached the mechanisms of Christology according to possibility: 'The Incarnation, as it is revealed to us, is one activity of the Response of Love. *Why may He not* exhibit, on another planet, another activity of like kind? He Who upholds the universe while lying a babe on Mary's knee *can*, surely, be revealed in another planet in some form appropriate thereto'.[30]

---

[26] Polkinghorne, *Theology in the Context of Science*, 53.
[27] Tillich, *Systematic Theology*, 2:111.
[28] Tillich, *Systematic Theology*, 2:111.
[29] Weston, *The Revelation of Eternal Love*, 130, emphasis added.
[30] Ibid., 129, emphasis added.

A final example comes from Thomas Morris' *The Logic of God Incarnate*, addressing arguments against the coherence of belief in the Incarnation.[31] In the chapter on extraterrestrial life and multiple Incarnations, he addresses a discussion from Paul and Linda Badham in *Immortality or Extinction*,[32] which again unfolds precisely along the terms that I see bisecting this literature. Faced with the prospect of extraterrestrial intelligent life, they write that Christian doctrine requires that multiple Incarnations should be considered both *necessary* and *impossible*. Morris' reply proceeds first according to the economy of salvation, and what is, or is not, necessary, before turning to technical questions of Christology, and whether multiple Incarnations are possible.[33] The conclusion of the chapter sums up this distinction:

> If a reasonable consideration … would not result in the conclusion that multiple Incarnations *must be* postulated throughout the universe in order for most traditional Christian assumptions about salvation and revelation to be squared with any reasonable beliefs we have about the nature of the cosmos, then no challenge for Christian orthodoxy results from this quarter. On the other hand, if multiple Incarnations were to be *required*, any challenge *could* be met by the two-minds view I have developed. So I am concerned in this chapter only to argue that distinctively cosmological challenges do not successfully show Christian theology concerning the Incarnation to be in any way incongruous or absurd.[34]

As these quotations indicate, these groupings – of the economy of Incarnation with necessity, and of technical Christology with possibility – can proceed in terms of both affirmation and denial: they can be about both possibility and impossibility, and about

---

[31] Morris, *Logic of God Incarnate*.
[32] Paul Badham and Linda Badham, *Immortality or Extinction?* (London: SPCK, 1984).
[33] Morris, *Logic of God Incarnate*, 173–81.
[34] Ibid., 186, emphasis added.

both what is necessary and what is unnecessary. The Badhams considered multiple Incarnations to be soteriologically *necessary*, but Christologically *impossible*. Morris argues that they may be either *necessary* or *unnecessary*, but are in any case *possible*.

The combination of possibility and necessity therefore offers us various options. Some writers take a definitive view, saying, for instance, that multiple Incarnations are simply not possible, or are simply necessary. The former is Hebblethwaite's position, while the latter looks close to Tillich's. A more reserved position would involve saying that multiple Incarnations are possible, without commenting on whether they are actual, even given life elsewhere (for which Tim Pawl would be an advocate, as would I).[35] The Badhams, as I have mentioned, try to push Christian theology to a *reduction ad absurdum* by suggesting that multiple Incarnations would be both necessary and impossible.

The distinction, between possibility/Christology/Person and necessity/Incarnation/work was first suggested to me by reflection on arguments put forward in rejection of the idea of multiple Incarnations. While some writers are willing to consider it as a serious topic for theological attention, and will devote considerable time or space to it, even if they come down against the idea (Hebblethwaite provides an example), others seem instead to evade or diffuse the need to talk about multiple Incarnations in the first place, at least in any detail. They do so not by arguing that it is impossible, but by arguing that it is unnecessary, and leaving it at that. To this, of course, the charge could be laid that a lack of necessity hardly settles the question of actuality, and especially in relation to God's supremely free action, as I will suggest below.[36]

---

[35] Pawl, 'Thomistic Multiple Incarnations'; Pawl, 'Brian Hebblethwaite's Arguments against Multiple Incarnations'.

[36] Parallel to this we might list Stanley Jaki's attempt to list reasons for why other planets like Earth are vanishingly unlikely elsewhere in the universe, foreclosing the need for any squaring of theology with the idea of other life (*Maybe Alone in the Universe, After All* (Pinckney, MI: Real View Books, 2000). Many of his arguments

Milne provides a striking example of managing to set the whole question of other Incarnations aside. As we have seen, he maintains that the notion of multiple Incarnations is one from which the Christian should 'recoil in horror', but adds that we can be delivered from having to entertain it any further by the prospect of broadcasting the Christian gospel by radio waves.[37] (The problems associated with broadcasting, however, are manifold, both in terms of theology and of science. What, for instance, of the possibly enormous number of civilizations that may have flourished and died out before human beings ever came onto the cosmic scene? What of galaxies 12 billion light years away? What of whether another creature would find our story communicative, a question to which I return in Chapter 16?)

David Wilkinson also shows distinct wariness about the idea of multiple Incarnations.[38] One of his several angles on the theme concerns Christology, and a worry that speaking of other Incarnations 'opens the door' to poor Christology: to saying that Jesus is 'just a good man used by God'. His other angles concern Incarnation, and the economy of salvation, and are set out, as we have come to expect, in terms of necessity: that more than one Incarnation in the universe may suggest that we need more than one Incarnation on Earth, which is to be denied; that further Incarnations on other planets are not necessary because God can reveal the story of Christ elsewhere without becoming Incarnate again; and that if intelligent

---

are now discredited, and some looked stretched even at the time he was writing. After the discovery of exoplanets, he continued to plough this furrow, for instance, arguing that theological consideration of exobiology was a demonic deception ('Christ, Extraterrestrials and the Devil', in *A Late Awakening; and Other Essays* (Port Huron, MI: Real View Books, 2006), 93–106).

[37] 'We cannot imagine the Son of God suffering vicariously on each of a myriad of planets. The Christian would avoid this conclusion by the definite supposition that our planet is in fact unique … [Radio communication would be possible] to other planets and the re-enactment of the tragedy of the crucifixion in other planets would be *unnecessary*' (Milne, *Modern Cosmology*, 153–54, emphasis added).

[38] Wilkinson, *Search for Extraterrestrial Intelligence*, 158.

extraterrestrial beings have not sinned, then another Incarnation would not be necessary.[39]

In his first argument, Wilkinson worries that the suggestion of more than one Incarnation could possibly lead to poor Christology, although that does not seem to be a strong argument to advance among theologians. Almost anything can be argued poorly; the task is to do it well: *abusus non tollit usum*. It is possible to consider the theological cogency, or not, of multiple Incarnations from within a robustly Chalcedonian framework, for instance: I have sought to do that here. The second argument remains in the broad realm of the economy of salvation, and again takes the unsatisfying form on an invocation of a slippery slope. There is indeed a question to be faced as to whether multiple Incarnations in the universe go hand in hand with multiple Incarnations on Earth.[40] (I think not.) The theologian should look such questions in the face.

The final two of those discussions from Wilkinson get to the heart of why an analysis of the literature in terms of possibility and necessity is so useful. In his third point, Wilkinson proposes that a further Incarnation may not be necessary because God has other ways to reveal himself: 'We do well to remember that the Incarnation is central, but not the only form of relational communication'.[41] Since Wilkinson clearly operates with a more than simply educational

---

[39] Ibid., 158–59.

[40] John Hick, Maurice Wiles, and Paul Badham and Linda Badham all proposed that arguments from the Christian doctrine of the economy would suggest the necessity of multiple human Incarnations, in all three cases taking this to be an argument against traditional Christian theology (John Hick, 'A Response to Hebblethwaite', in *Incarnation and Myth: The Debate Continued*, ed. M. D. Goulder (London: SCM Press, 1979), 192; Maurice Wiles, 'A Survey of Isses in the Myth Debate', in *Incarnation and Myth: The Debate Continued*, ed. M. D. Goulder (London: SCM Press, 1979), 7–8; Badham and Badham, *Immortality or Extinction?*, 51–58). (This interpretation of Wiles follows Morris, *Logic of God Incarnate*, 184–86.) These are unusual positions in the history of Christian thought, and are ably criticised by Morris (ibid., 172–86).

[41] Wilkinson, *Search for Extraterrestrial Intelligence*, 158.

model of redemption, his point must either be that intelligent life elsewhere is not fallen, in which case perhaps communication would be enough, or that the redeeming work of the divine human being Jesus Christ can apply universally to sinful creatures, about which they are then informed. While, Wilkinson writes, it is not necessary to know about Christ for his death to set one right, God would nonetheless communicate the good news, and, for that, revelation without further Incarnation would suffice.[42] Morris makes a similar point: 'If saving knowledge of a divine Incarnation can be offered to a created being directly by God', by a means other than Incarnation in that species, 'it would not be necessary in any sense for God to engage in local planetary Incarnations in order to save creatures in widely disparate places and times'.[43] We have seen Milne invoke communication rather than additional Incarnations.[44] I will return to these proposals in Chapter 16, in thinking about the importance, or otherwise, of encountering God face to face, in recognisable flesh. Each of them ought to be faced with the question of whether God does only what is strictly necessary. I will argue below that this is not the best way to approach God's works.[45]

Wilkinson's fourth and final proposal is that life elsewhere may be without sin, and that this would make redemption, and therefore further Incarnation, again unnecessary. This touches in another way on the heart of the question as to *why* there was an Incarnation: it address the fault line, running down theological history, as to whether the Incarnation is contingent upon sin, or whether it was

[42] Ibid., 165.
[43] Morris, *Logic of God Incarnate*, 177.
[44] Milne, *Modern Cosmology*, 153–54.
[45] These discussions also raise as many questions as they settle, especially about how redemption might be considered to apply across species (the Incarnation in one species redeeming organisms in others), and about whether treating revelation as the communication of propositions (such as 'Jesus the human being redeemed you') really measures up to what Christians have thought divine self-communication has meant for us in Christ.

destined to be the culmination of human (and other creaturely) life, sin or no sin. A significant swathe of Christian thought has proposed that sinlessness closes down nothing when it comes to the plan, glory, and benefit of the Incarnation. If the Incarnation is about more than remedy or repair, then the fact that some putatively unfallen species would not require redemption from sin does not settle the question of another Incarnation. We will return to this in Chapter 17.

Suitability

The distinction between possibility and necessity, between Christology and Incarnation, between the Person of Christ and Christ's work, criss-crosses the literature on multiple Incarnations in relation to exobiology. Possibility and necessity are obviously alternatives. Some writers focus on possibility, others on necessity; some address both, sequentially or episodically. In one sense they contrast as modes of thinking; in another sense, possibility and necessity are not so contrastive at all. As logical modes, they are convertible. To think that something is necessary is to think that it could not possibly be otherwise; to think that something is impossible is to think that it necessarily cannot be so. These two logical 'modes' are also generally binary: a proposition is thought to be possible or impossible, necessary or unnecessary. There is little room for gradations.

Consider, however, the alternative category of *suitability*. Unlike necessity or possibility, it is not a binary category. We can talk about something as simply suitable or unsuitable, but also about gradations of suitability. Approached this way, possibility and necessity, taken together, can be contrasted with the category of the suitable, fitting, or appropriate, which will come to be one of the most prominent concepts within this book.

As a theological outlook, the difference of suitability from possibility and necessity is striking. Both the theologian of possibility and the theologian of necessity make categorical claims. They make claims about knowledge of God and the divine economy, which are strong enough to rule on what is or is not possible, what is or is not necessary. Sometimes, they will go so far as to put themselves in God's position, to work out what God could or could not do, or what God must or must not do. We find that, for instance, in Anselm's *Cur Deus Homo*, and in a good deal of theological writing influenced by analytic philosophy. In contrast, theology carried out in terms of suitability looks rather different. Its approach is not one of working out what had to be, or what might or might not have been, but of exploring the concrete case of the divine work before us. It is not primarily a reflection on whether things could have been otherwise, but an exploration of the fittingness of what God has done: to use a Barthian phrase, it is *Nackdenken* – thinking that follows after, and meditates upon, the works of God.[46] One is not arguing a case in abstract terms – 'why any sensible God would do this' or 'why the workings of the hypostatic union are obvious' – but rather thinking through what God has done but could not be expected. In a way rather similar to Barth on this point, Aquinas wrote that

> if one earnestly and devoutly weighs the mysteries of the Incarnation, he will find so great a depth of wisdom that it exceeds human knowledge. In the Apostle's words: 'The foolishness of God is wiser then men' (1 Cor. 1.25). Hence it happens that to him who devoutly considers it, more and more wondrous aspects of this mystery are made manifest.[47]

In this way, while a logic of suitability might look close to one of necessity, in that both are more pan-optic, or big-picture, in approach than discussions of possibility, a theology explored in

---

[46] David Ford, 'Barth's Interpretation of the Bible', in *Karl Barth: Studies of His Theological Method*, ed. S. Sykes (Oxford: Clarendon Press, 1979), 81–86.

[47] *SCG* IV.54.1.

terms of suitability will be more cautious than one that invokes necessity, not least when it comes to what God might or might not have done. God's freedom will be respected, but while the suitability of one or more actions is considered, other possibilities are left within the counsel of God. Characteristically, the theologian of suitability will not wish to place herself in the position of God; she will remain in the position of the creature and exhibit the creature's proper response to divine action, which is praise, seeking to respond in informed wonder to what it is that God has done.

Conclusion

It seems safe to say that it was only in the previous century that the idea of multiple Incarnations began to be entertained among theologians. Among more advocates of classical Christology, Aquinas' arguments have loomed large, since he maintained that the Word could assume a human nature in addition to its assumption in Jesus. In my view, multiple Incarnations across different biological species would not only be possible, but – as I will lay out in Chapter 17 – might be fitting in a way that multiple Incarnations in the same nature might not be. While a good deal of writing on the subject has been cast in terms of possibility and necessity, I have suggested that fittingness is a preferable mode of theological enquiry on this score. By taking us beyond the strong categorical claims of what God can or must do, suitability opens a new vista on the nature of the questions at play.

We will consider suitability in more detail in Chapter 16. First, however, we turn to themes of possibility when it comes to thinking about multiple Incarnations. As we will see, that lends itself to discussions of Christological detail, or precision.

13 | Distinct Incarnations

Possibility and Christological Detail

As we saw in the previous chapter, when theological considerations of exobiology turn to discussion of Christology, it is typically framed in terms of possibility. Those discussions, however, are quite often unclear about their theological framework: whether are they Chalcedonian, for instance. Much could therefore be added to these conversations by a more detailed engagement with the history of writing about the doctrine of Christ: what, in the title of this chapter, I am calling 'Christological detail', with its language of Person, hypostasis, natures, and so on.[1] That is the task of this chapter.

I will begin by suggesting that when historical authors have written about multiple Incarnations, and dismissed it, what they have in view does not really count as multiple Incarnations in the 'conciliar' terms in which the ancient churches have typically expressed their Christology.[2] In the second half of the chapter, I will consider

---

[1] Alice Meynell's poem provides a counterexample. In terms of technical, conciliar Christology, she never puts a foot wrong, always attributing to the Person – through capitalised pronouns, for instance – that which would underlie many Incarnations, and speaking in terms of distinct and creaturely natures (with lowercase pronouns) for what would be varied and multiple.

[2] I am taking 'conciliar' Christology to refer to the first seven ecumenical councils, and in particular for it to be Chalcedonian. I should add that I welcome the results of recent dialogues that suggest considerable common ground between Chalcedonian Christians and other traditions, such as the Oriental Orthodox Churches, leading even in some cases to agreed statements. In my attachment to all seven of those councils, I do not wish to denigrate venerable but divergent traditions, which the Chalcedonian churches are increasingly coming to see as sharing common convictions although I am a convinced Chalcedonian myself. I also note that what I describe as 'conciliar' Christology was not necessarily always formed by direct knowledge of the

some of the questions around whether multiple Incarnations make theological sense by looking at an influential objection from Brian Hebblethwaite.

Those questions are part of the business of asking whether multiple Incarnations are possible. We have reasons to be uncomfortable about arriving too easily at an account of what God could or could not do, whether out of a respect for divine power and freedom, or from a recognition that we cannot hope to comprehend God or his ways. Nonetheless, the theologian may feel that she pays God no particular complement by ascribing intrinsically impossible actions to divine agency. God, who is order and truth, is not glorified by association with intrinsically disordered or untrue notions, such as the production of a square circle. A meaningless phrase is not transformed into something meaningful simply by placing the phrase 'God can' or 'God did' in front of it. Furthermore, what might or might not be possible in relation to a creature as a creature is a reasonable object of study in theology, and that may too have bearing on multiple Incarnations.

Moreover, attention to Christological detail is useful for developing our sense of what the concept of multiple Incarnations does and does not mean in the first place. Before we can ask whether it is consequential or theologically palatable, we first need some clarity about what it is that we are discussing. Our conversations may otherwise be at cross purposes.

Not everyone who writes about multiple Incarnations – whether to commend the idea or reject it – will be doing so from the theological perspective adopted in this book. I have already noted that when Tillich advanced the idea that what we have known on Earth is relative only to Earth-dwellers, and would be repeated elsewhere, he was not necessarily thinking about Incarnation as Christian theologians had previously understood it, for instance, in patristic, mediaeval,

councils, and their acts and canons. Indeed, it is striking how little of the formulations of the councils was known for much of later Christian history, beyond florilegia, until the work of figures such as Giovanni Domenico Mansi (1692–1769).

or Reformation traditions. The misgivings he avows over the word 'Incarnation' itself may alert us to that. Similarly, the sense of multiple Incarnations envisaged by the 'Polydoxy' writers, discussed in the previous chapter, is clearly quite different from that in view in this book.

For example, a recurrent concern in writing that is critical of multiple Incarnations is that they would involve Jesus Christ, the divine *human being*, suffering again. In the terms of classical Christology, however, in relation to life elsewhere in the universe, we are instead considering an additional Incarnation, in a different nature from the human nature of Christ. That is a long way from talking about Jesus or Christ being elsewhere in the universe. We find that language in Guillaume de Vaurouillon (in, as I have mentioned, what seems to be the earliest discussion in Christian theology of Incarnation, sin, and redemption in relation to life on another world, written around the middle of the fifteenth century):[3]

> As to the question whether Christ by dying on this earth [*Christus moriendo in isto mundo*] could redeem the inhabitants of another world [*illos redemisset*], I answer that he was able to do this not only for our world but for infinite worlds [*potuit non solum pro isto mundo sed pro infinitis si essent*]. But it would not be fitting for him to go to another world to die again [*nec oportuisset eius in alium ire mundum ut de novo moreretur*].[4]

That *Christ* ('him') should travel to another place is not, however, what I take a discussion of multiple Incarnations to have in

---

[3] Michael J. Crowe, 'A History of the Extraterrestrial Life Debate', *Zygon* 32, no. 2 (1997): 149. Origen's imagined situation of eternal repetition, discussed below, seems sufficiently different not to be directly comparable with later discussions of life on other planets.

[4] Guillaume de Vaurouillon, *Quattuor librorum Sententiarum Compendium: venerabilis patris fratris Guillermi Vorrillonis* (Basel: Adam Petri de Landendorf, 1510), book I, dist. 44, fol. 104v, translation from O'Meara, 'Christian Theology and Extraterrestrial Intelligent Life', 15. Conceivably, the Latin might leave it ambiguous as to whether *Christus* should be translated more as 'the Christ' or as 'a Christ', but here it is clear that the particularity of Jesus the Christ is in view, as with Melanchthon below.

mind, when set out in Chalcedonian terms. Melanchthon uses a similar construction in his forthright denial not only of multiple Incarnations, but also the existence of any other worlds in the cosmos:

> The Son of God is one: our master Jesus Christ, coming forth in this world, died and was resurrected only once [*tantum semel mortuus est, et recuscitatus*]. Nor did he manifest himself elsewhere [*Nec alibi se ostendit*], nor has he died or been resurrected elsewhere [*nec alibi mortuus aut resuscitatus est*]. We should not imagine many worlds because we ought not imagine that Christ died and was risen often [*saepius Christum mortuum et resuscitatum esse*]; nor should it be thought that in any other world without the knowledge of the Son of God [*sine aguitione filii Dei*] that people [*hominibus*] would be restored to eternal life.[5]

Similarly, in defending Galileo, Campanella dismissed as false any association of Galileo's system with the implication that 'Christ also died on other stars to save those inhabitants'.[6]

Much further back, Origen offered an intriguing discussion in *On First Principles*, set out not in terms of one world alongside another, but of a cyclic repetition of time and history. Origen denied any such succession of previous ages, and that Christ could suffer more than once.[7] He wrote that 'the holy apostle' (Paul, taken as the author of the Letter to the Hebrews), teaches that

[5] Philipp Melanchthon, *Initia Doctrinae Physicae: Dictata In Academia Witebergensi* (Vitebergae: Crato, 1565), 42–43; reprinted in Philipp Melanchthon, *Corpus Reformatorum – Series 1: Melanthonis Opera Quae Supersunt Omnia*, ed. Carolus Gottlieb Bretschneider, vol. 13, 28 vols (Halis Saxonum: C. A. Schwetschke et Filium, 1846), column 221, translation from Thomas O'Meara, *Vast Universe*, 81–82.
[6] That, he writes, would be 'to revive the heresy, which some have maintained, that at one time Christ was crucified a second time in the other hemisphere of the earth to save the humans living there as he has to save our part of the world'. *Arguments against Galileo*, number 9, p. 45.
[7] Origen, *On First Principles*, II.3.1, 4, English, translation in *On First Principles*, trans. John Behr (Oxford: Oxford University Press, 2019), 79, 83.

In that age which was before this Christ did not suffer before, not even in the age which was before that; and I know that I am not able to enumerate the number of anterior ages in which he did not suffer ... He [the author of Hebrews] says, 'But now he has appeared, once for all, at the consummation of the ages to take away sin by the sacrifice of himself'.[8]

This passage seems again to rule out multiple Incarnations, but it does not actually have the same question in mind as ours in this book. Origen is not considering Incarnations *in other natures*, at a different time and place in the cosmos, but the recurrence of the Incarnation in Christ. Therefore, when Origen writes about *Christ* suffering again, that is exactly what he means: the divine human being Jesus Christ. The scenario he is refuting is one in which the whole history of Earth is repeated:

a world similar in all respects to this world ... [in which] Adam and Eve will do the same things as they did before, again the same flood, the same Moses would again lead a people numbering six hundred thousand out of Egypt, Judas will also betray the Lord twice, Paul will a second time keep the clothes of those who stoned Stephen, and everything which has been done in this life will be said to be repeated.[9]

Although ostensibly each of the above texts is about multiple Incarnations, in an important sense none of them really is: they do not concern additional Incarnations beyond Jesus Christ; they have some other odd, largely undefined, notions in play, involving the replication or transport of Christ.

Ironically, perhaps, Thomas Paine (1737–1809) comes closer to a more precise account of what the Incarnation has been said to entail (with precision in 'Christological detail') in his polemic

---

[8] Origen, *On First Principles*, II.3.5, 83–84, with a small change to formatting, quoting Heb. 9.26.

[9] Origen, *On First Principles*, II.3.4, 83.

against Christianity in *The Age of Reason* (1794), in that he identifies the person or agent acting multiply not as Christ but as 'the Son of God' (a term he does not like), although perhaps more by luck than by good judgement:

> Are we to suppose that every world in the boundless creation had an Eve, an apple, a serpent, and a redeemer? In this case, the person who is irreverently called the Son of God, and sometimes God himself, would have nothing else to do than to travel from world to world, in an endless succession of deaths, with scarcely a momentary interval of life.[10]

This, he thinks, would be a 'wild and whimsical system of faith and of religion'.[11] At this point, however, Paine's grasp of traditional Christology already shows its limits, with this language of 'travel', as also when we read, only a little earlier, that the Incarnation means 'the solitary and strange conceit that the Almighty, who had millions of worlds equally dependent on his protection, should quit the care of all the rest, and come to die in our world'.[12] Only an exaggerated and untenable kenoticism could make any such claim.

Paine's 'succession' of Incarnations introduces us to a set of authors who suppose that in order for the Son to be multiply Incarnate those Incarnations have to be sequential, in one nature at a time, each taken up for a period and then laid down. On these terms, so at variance with traditional Christology, if there were a sufficiently large number of intelligent species in different places simultaneously, time may not allow for successive Incarnations to thread their way between them.[13] Such an approach stands in stark

---

[10] Thomas Paine, 'Age of Reason', in *The Thomas Paine Reader*, ed. Michael Foot and Isaac Kramnick (London: Penguin Classics, 1987), 442.

[11] Ibid.

[12] Ibid.

[13] For instance, Robin Collins, 'Extraterrestrial Intelligence and the Incarnation', in *God and the Multiverse: Scientific, Philosophical, and Theological Perspectives*, ed. Klaas J. Kraay (London: Routledge, 2014), 223–24. Roland Puccetti also sees an

contrast to a cardinal contention in classical Christology that the created nature, once taken up, is never laid down.

Our short survey of representative figures – Origen, Vaurouillon, Melanchthon, Campanella, and Paine – has demonstrated that the idea of genuinely multiple Incarnations has not been in view as often as might at first appear. To these we might add Hay's Arian account in Chapter 12. The accounts of Incarnation we find there, whether single or multiple, whether accepted (Hay) or rejected (the others), stand outside of the Christology of the conciliar sources that are foundational for Roman Catholics, Anglicans, the Eastern Orthodox Churches, and many Protestants.

To talk about a second Incarnation on Chalcedonian terms would not be to suggest that this person, Jesus Christ, was to be found on another planet, as well as on Earth; it would not be to say that Jesus Christ was killed and rose again a second time (indeed, perhaps death and resurrection would not be the mode of redemption elsewhere); nor would it say that the Son was Incarnate as Jesus Christ for a while, then ceased to be, and became Incarnate in some different way. Rather, we would be saying that the Eternal Son separately assumed a different creaturely nature in addition to his human nature in Christ. Jesus Christ is the human being constituted by the individuation of human nature by its assumption by the Second Person of the Trinity: in Jesus we find the Person of the Word with two natures, human and divine, one intrinsically his as eternally Divine, the other assumed 'for us and for our salvation'. Another Incarnation would parallel that, in a different creaturely nature. How distinct those Incarnations would be is a topic to which I turn below.

We would not be talking about Jesus Christ being somewhere else, or of there being more than one Jesus Christ at all. We would be talking about Jesus Christ *and* another Incarnate being: one whose

obstacle to multiple Incarnations in terms of temporal overlaps (*Persons: A Study of Possible Moral Agents in the Universe* (London: Macmillan, 1968)).

existence also rests on the individuation of that nature, different from our own, by being taken up by the Son. Talk, therefore, of a 'planet-hopping Christ' would not present us with a Chalcedonian view of things.[14] Similarly, when the Jesuit George Coyne asked, 'Could Jesus Christ, fully a human being, exist on more than one planet at more than one time?' I would rather not reply, as he did, that 'We are obviously very limited today in our ability to answer such questions' – as this seems like an unfortunate way to pose the question at all.[15]

When it comes to multiple Incarnations, the issues earlier discussions considered and found objectionable seem, indeed, implausible or objectionable, but they are simply not what multiple Incarnations would mean, as explored according to conciliar Christology. Any suggestion, for instance, that Jesus was born a second time, or that he suffered and was raised a second time, would be unsuitable, impossible, or simply nonsensical. Jesus was a human being. While human beings can be 'born again' in the important spiritual sense of that term, they cannot be born a second time in the natural sense. Recognition of that, after all, undergirds the logic of Jesus' conversation with Nicodemus.[16] Similarly, the risen Jesus is immortal, in his humanity as well as his divinity: 'We know that Christ, being raised from the dead, will never die again; death no longer has dominion over him'.[17] It would be nonsense, or blasphemy, to suggest that Jesus, risen from the dead, subsequently

---

[14] The phrase appears in four chapters in Peters et al., *Astrotheology: Science and Theology Meet Extraterrestrial Life*, and particularly in Peters, 'One Incarnation or Many?', in *Astrotheology: Science and Theology Meet Extraterrestrial Life*, ed. Ted Peters et al. (Eugene, OR: Cascade, 2018), 272, 273, 275, 277, 292.

[15] George V. Coyne, 'The Evolution of Intelligent Life on the Earth and Possibly Elsewhere: Reflections from a Religious Tradition', in *Many Worlds: The New Universe, Extraterrestrial Life, and the Theological Implications*, ed. Stephen Dick (Philadelphia: Templeton Foundation Press, 2000), 187.

[16] John 3.1–21.

[17] Rom. 6.9.

suffered and died elsewhere. Nothing of the sort, however, need be in mind when the idea of multiple Incarnations is expressed within the terms of traditional Christology. Other Incarnations would be complete beings, distinct from Jesus as to their creaturehood, with their own life stories, embedded in their own cultures, which might or might not involve death and resurrection. To pick up the language of the Council of Chalcedon, they would have their own rational soul and body, of a different kind from Jesus.

Hebblethwaite's Argument for the Impossibility of Multiple Incarnations

Leading the way among recent discussions of the possibility of multiple Incarnations (or, in his case, impossibility) is a paper by Brian Hebblethwaite mentioned in the previous chapter. He begins by quoting Keith Ward (who would go on to write about Christology and astrobiology at much greater length in 2015 in *Christ and the Cosmos*),[18] that 'God could in theory take many minds and bodies to be finite forms of the divine nature. There is nothing to prevent the infinite God from taking any number of finite forms'.[19] At the time, Ward thought that multiple Incarnations were possible but not actual.[20] In contrast, for Hebblethwaite, 'multiple Incarnations, in the sense of Incarnation outlined by Ward, are logically impossible'.[21] Recognising that earlier discussions of multiple Incarnations were carried out in terms of multiple human Incarnations, Hebblethwaite wished to expand the discussions to consideration of God's dealings with creatures on other planets:

---

[18] Ward, *Christ and the Cosmos*.

[19] Keith Ward, *God, Faith and the New Millennium* (Oxford: Oneworld, 1998), 162–64.

[20] Hebblethwaite, 'Impossibility of Multiple Incarnations', 323. Today, Ward considers life elsewhere, and multiple Incarnations, to be much more likely.

[21] Ibid.

The more controversial point concerned the implications of a necessarily unique Incarnation for possible extraterrestrial intelligent life. I suggested that if, logically, there can be only one Incarnation of the divine Son in a finite personal form, it would make more sense to suppose that humanity is the sole instantiation of finite personal life in the universe.[22]

Hebblethwaite sought to base his argument on a solid point of traditional Christology. The being of the Son as God is prior in every way to the coming to be of the (divine) human being Jesus Christ. There is no prior human person, Jesus Christ; the whole personhood of Christ is constituted by the personhood of the Word, who causes there to be a distinct human being, Jesus Christ, *at all*, by taking up human nature. There is one Person in Christ, in two natures, and that Person is the divine Person of the Son. As Hebblethwaite puts it, there is 'one metaphysical *subject* of the Incarnate life', and that, he thinks, 'precludes there being a plurality of human vehicles of that one life', since we cannot imagine there being many human beings who are, nonetheless, the same subject: 'to assume more than one human nature (which is in view for now) would entail having more than one human subject as vehicles of the divine subject, entailing that, ultimately speaking, each would be identical with the others'.[23]

Hebblethwaite notes that 'the tradition has shunned talk of a human person as well as a divine person: two wills, yes; two minds, perhaps; but two persons, no … Classically, there is only one person – the divine Son – who is the subject of the Incarnate life'.[24] The rest of his argument follows from that point:

---

[22] Ibid., 324.

[23] Ibid., 325–26. Hebblethwaite criticizes Aquinas, and other 'classical talk of the divine Son assuming impersonal human nature', on the basis that 'justice is simply not done to the individual subjectivity and personality of the one who is the human form of the divine life' (326). Nonetheless, his argument in the paper overall rests on there being one Person in Christ, as we will see.

[24] Ibid., 326

If Jesus was the same person as God the Son, so would other Incarnations be. They would all have to be the same person. That makes no sense, least of all if they exist simultaneously in the eschaton ... we do not, in the eschaton, expect to be encountered by a group of divine Incarnations, themselves in theory capable of interpersonal relation.[25]

Here, Hebblethwaite turns to Eric Mascall, and his discussion of Aquinas on multiple Incarnations.[26] As mentioned in the previous chapter, Mascall rejected Aquinas' proposal that there could be multiple Incarnations in the same species – as more than one human being, for instance – for two reasons. The first is that 'if *per impossibile* he assumed, and conferred his personal individuality upon human nature twice over, there would not after all be two individuals but only one'.[27] That, as Hebblethwaite notes, chimes with his own rejection. Mascall's second argument is one of redundancy: a second Incarnation would add nothing. 'There is nothing that a second Incarnation in human nature could achieve that has not been achieved by the first'.[28] Mascall thought that there could be Incarnations into multiple distinct natures, but not into one nature, such as human nature.[29] For Hebblethwaite, however, Mascall's first objection applies even to multiple Incarnations in different natures, ruling them out as well:

God would be conferring his personal individuality upon another finite, rational, personal, nature, and, again, one and the same

[25] Ibid., 327. He had explored this avenue in 'The Resurrection and the Incarnation', in *The Resurrection of Jesus Christ*, ed. Paul D. L. Avis (London: Darton, Longman and Todd, 1993), 155–70.
[26] Hebblethwaite, 'Impossibility of Multiple Incarnations', 329.
[27] Mascall, *Christian Theology and Natural Science*, 41, discussed by Hebblethwaite on p. 330.
[28] Ibid., 42. Discussed by Hebblethwaite on p. 330. The first argument concerns Christological detail, we might note, and is about possibility; the second is about the wider purpose of the Incarnation, and it is about necessity.
[29] Recalling the breadth of what Aquinas might mean here by 'human nature'.

individual would result. God Incarnate would now have three natures, not two. But the two different finite natures would be individualized by the same metaphysical subject, and would have to be thought of as the same person. Again, there would not, after all, be two individuals but only one. The same point, of course, can be made about this speculation being ruled out by eschatological considerations.[30]

We will consider the force of this argument below, but first it is useful to note just how significant this point is for Hebblethwaite. He maintains that other sentient creatures would necessitate further Incarnation, and yet he also holds that to be Christologically impossible.[31] That other Incarnations follow necessarily for other life comes from his contention, shared again with Mascall, that 'it is indeed difficult to see how what God has done for humankind in Christ could affect unknown extraterrestrials in unknown galaxies', and that 'attempts to extend the significance of the cross and resurrection of Christ to other worlds are all pretty bizarre'.[32] (There are ways to conceive of such an 'extension', whether they are plausible or not, as we saw in Chapter 11.) On that basis – with the contradiction of necessity and impossibility in mind – Hebblethwaite argues that it behooves the Christian to hope that there simply is no life elsewhere.

> Since multiple Incarnations are not possible, it is perhaps an implication of Christian soteriology, bound up as it is with a strong doctrine of the Incarnation and resurrection of Jesus Christ, that there are no other rational natures in the universe apart from the humankind whom Jesus, God Incarnate, came to save.[33]

---

[30] Hebblethwaite, 'Impossibility of Multiple Incarnations', 330.
[31] Note, again, the association of possibility with Christology, and the purpose of the Incarnation with necessity.
[32] Hebblethwaite, 'Impossibility of Multiple Incarnations', 330, 334, n. 24.
[33] Ibid., 330.

Proposing the universe beyond earth to be devoid of life was already becoming less and less tenable when Hebblethwaite's paper was published in 2001, and since then it has become more precarious still.

Christ's Person

At the heart of Hebblethwaite's objection to multiple Incarnations is the idea that it would result in the repetition of the same 'individual' or 'person', which he takes to be impossible. He addresses this both in abstract, logical terms, and in a more pictorial fashion with an eschatological thought experiment *reductio ad absurdum*: the prospect of two Incarnations meeting each other, and that being a meeting of a particular individual, or person, with itself.[34]

In response, I suggest that we should be wary of treating 'person' univocally here, supposing its various meanings to be directly equivalent, as if we meant precisely the same thing by the Personhood of the Word, and by my human personhood, or the personhood of an angel, or of Sherlock Holmes, or the legal 'personhood' of a corporation. These are not simply and entirely different: in various ways and to various degrees, each of the other others is a likeness to the first (although we might think that the personhood of a corporation bears a very attenuated resemblance).

In Christological discussions, the Greek word that set the running was *hypostasis*. It originally meant something similar to *ousia* (being), but by the time it was used in the decisive Christological and

---

[34] Although this is not Hebblethwaite's point, there is also the question of what a 'meeting' would be like between two Incarnations who, on account of the hypostatic union, already enjoyed more-than-creaturely knowledge (or access to it). That might problematise the word 'meet', as if it implied ignorance before. However, that is not unique to the question of multiple Incarnations: Jesus knew all things, but that perfected rather than abolished his meetings, for instance, with the Samaritan woman by the well.

Trinitarian discussions, it had morphed to mean something closer to 'entity' or 'individual reality'.[35] Nevertheless, in Christological writing, as in Trinitarian thought, 'person' does not mean 'person' as we use it of a human being today: a bundle of memories, emotions, desires, thoughts, and so on. A *hypostasis* is an individual or 'distinct manner of existing'.[36] It functions as a metaphysical term, not a psychological one, as Hebblethwaite himself acknowledges: the Son is the 'one metaphysical subject of the Incarnate life'.[37]

There is only one *hypostasis* in Christ, which is the *hypostasis* of the Word. That is why the tradition has said that there is no distinct human person in Christ. However, as Mascall put it, 'nothing human is missing in Christ except a human person or *hypostasis*', such that 'the absence of a human person does not mutilate the nature, for "person" is not the name of a constituent of human nature, it is a purely metaphysical term'.[38] As a result, our Christological claim 'does not mean that the manhood lacks a human soul, or a human will, or any other component of human nature; the "person" which it declares to be absent is not a psychological or physical entity, but a metaphysical one'.[39]

Mention of the soul and will of Christ reminds us of another doctrinal path considered by the Early Church but set aside by the Fathers and Councils, in the broad trend we can gather under the

[35] See my *The Love of Wisdom: An Introduction to Philosophy for Theologians* (London: SCM Press, 2013), 80–82.

[36] Austin Stevenson, 'The Unity of Christ and the Historical Jesus: Aquinas and Locke on Personal Identity', *Modern Theology* 37, no. 4 (2021): 851–64.

[37] Hebblethwaite, 'Impossibility of Multiple Incarnations', 325.

[38] E. L. Mascall, *Via Media: An Essay in Theological Synthesis* (London: Longmans, Green, 1956), 101–2.

[39] Ibid., 103. Mascall quotes R. V. Sellars: 'Certainly, "an impersonal manhood" is an unfortunate phrase, which, anti-Nestorian in purpose, means no more than that the manhood had no independent existence; it does not mean that the manhood was deprived of its properties in its union with Godhead, but, as it implies, that these were exercised not separately but in the *hypostasis* of the Logos' (*The Council of Chalcedon*, 345, quoted in *Via Media*, 102). The phrase 'impersonal manhood', as Mascall notes, does not occur in Chalcedon (ibid., 102–3).

name of *Apollinarianism*, after the bishop Apollinaris of Laodicea (died 390). He had proposed a too-simple solution to the task of speaking about Christ: that, in Jesus, the Word took the place of the human soul. This is sometimes described as *Logos-sarx* Christology, on the basis that instead of the usual conjunction in a human being of *pneuma* (soul) *and sarx* (body), in Jesus the Logos substituted for a soul, giving the combination of *Logos-sarx*. Rejection of this proposal drew from Gregory of Nazianzus one of the great theological maxims of antiquity: what he did not assume, he did not heal.[40] Exemplifying here the ontological model of redemption discussed in Chapter 11, Gregory held that God restored humanity by uniting it to himself. Were, then, anything to be missing in Christ – a human soul, for instance – something definitively human would remain un-united with God, and therefore unrestored and unredeemed. In later councils of the Early Church, what we might call the anti-Apollinarian conviction found additional purchase, beyond discussion of the presence of a human soul, in the insistence that Christ had a human will (not in conflict with the divine will, but metaphysically distinct from it) and a human 'energy' or principle of operation (again, not in conflict with the divine energy, but existing in a properly human fashion all the same).[41]

The anti-Apollinarian stance reminds us that no constitutive part of humanity was missing from Christ. He has a human body and soul; a human will and a human principle of action or operation; and also, on this basis, human memory and intellect. To say that the *hypostasis* of the Word is the *hypostasis* of Christ is not to suggest any lack in Christ. He is fully and distinctly human. Our hypothetical meeting between two Incarnations of the Word would involve two beings complete – and therefore distinct – in all that makes for

[40] 'The unassumed is the unhealed, but what is united with God is also being saved' (Gregory of Nazianzus, *Epistle* 101.5, translation from *On God and Christ: The Five Theological Orations and Two Letters to Cledonius*, trans. Frederick Williams and Lionel R. Wickham (Crestwood, NY: St. Vladimir's Seminary Press, 2002), 158).
[41] Discussed in *ST* III.18 and 19.

their creaturehood. In each, their natures would be realised in a particular way, and would be complete and characterfully distinct from other individuals, not least as to metaphysical accidents, history, and narrative. On that basis, I think we see no *reductio ad absurdum* after all, in one Incarnation, complete in creaturehood of a particular kind and distinct from all other individuals within that kind, meeting another Incarnation, equally complete in a different kind of creaturehood and equally distinct from other individuals in that species and culture.

In response, it could be said that what I have written here works on the level of nature, but that Hebblethwaite is arguing at the level of personhood or hypostasis. He claims that the meeting he envisages would be nonsensical because it would involve the meeting of a Person with himself. In affirming the anhypostatic union (that there neither is, nor ever was, any non-divine personhood to Christ), I recognise the point that Hebblethwaite is making. My reply is that theologians should limit their thinking to what falls within our capacity as created minds to think about created natures. Within those bounds, I do not see a problem with Hebblethwaite's imagined meeting. As, however, for what such a meeting might 'mean for God', that is beyond my powers of consideration, and yet that seems to be at the heart of Hebblethwaite's concern: that it is difficult (or absurd) to imagine what it would be like for the God as Christ's hypostasis to encounter himself as God as the hypostasis of some other Incarnation. For my part, rather than finding it difficult or absurd to imagine what it means for God to encounter God in that way, I would rather say that it is difficult – absurd even – to seek to imagine what it would be like to be God *at all*. I do not know what it means for God to experience anything. God is not Christ's 'person' in any sense that would have sprung to mind for Locke or Freud.[42] God is Christ's act of being, and principle of individual

---

[42] Stevenson, 'Unity of Christ'.

subsistence, and that is not something I can attempt psychologically to explore.[43]

I can, however, seek to think matters through on the creaturely side of things, and on that score it is important to say that Christ, and any other Incarnation, is complete and characterfully distinct in his humanity (or in whatever other creaturely nature we are talking about). A meeting between two Incarnations would not be between two identical consciousnesses or sets of memories. There would be two created natures (as two finite instantiations of the infinite act of being of the Word of God), with different creaturely histories and memories: with all, indeed, that pertains to having a body, soul, intellect, mind, and will (assuming that we can use those terms of that other nature).[44] An encounter here is not a meeting between two identical repetitions.

The completeness of the humanity of the Incarnate Word is underlined by Aquinas's discussion of a conundrum posed by many mediaeval scholastics: the 'medieval debate about the ontological status Christ's human nature would have if God dissolved the hypostatic union at some time after uniting the human nature to the Divine nature'.[45] Considering the idea that 'through some impossibility... the Word of God set aside the human nature', Aquinas replied that

[43] *ST* III.17.2.
[44] *ST* III.5 and 18. While III.16.8 and 10 are cautious about how creaturehood is to be predicated of Christ, Aquinas is insistent that Christ has in full what belongs to human creaturehood. In this section I am particularly indebted to Rowan Williams for a conversation on this topic, and for his 2016 Hulsean Lectures (on Christ and the Logic of Creation), published as *Christ the Heart of Creation* (London: Bloomsbury Continuum, 2018), here especially 12–35.
[45] Jason Lewis Andrew West's translator's note on *Disputed Question on the Union of the Word Incarnate*, a. 2, *obj.* 2. In *The Metaphysics of the Incarnation: Thomas Aquinas to Duns Scotus* (Oxford: Oxford University Press, 2002), Richard Cross discusses perspectives on this question from Aquinas, Duns Scotus, Giles of Rome, Olivi, Raymund of Guilha, Richard of Middleton, and William of Ware.

As long as the human nature is united to the Word of God, it does not have its own suppositum or hypostasis beyond the person of the Word, because it does not exist in itself. But if it were separated from the Word, it would have, not only its own hypostasis or suppositum, but also its own person; because it would now exist per se.[46]

That speaks powerfully to the completeness of Christ's humanity and, assuming that would also be true of any other Incarnation, there would be nothing different, on a creaturely level, between the meeting of one Incarnation with another than a meeting between two creatures whose hypostasis was not that of the eternal Word. Yes, God would 'meet' God, but since God can be said to *be* knowledge of himself, perhaps that is not a problem.

Conclusion

Questions around the possibility of multiple Incarnations belong to the theological territory of Christology, as we have seen, although historical discussions have been notably imprecise about the sorts of Christological claims being made. Broadly sketched, the picture they offer often stands some way from the Chalcedonian view I am advancing in this book: of additional hypostatic unions, by which the Word takes up a creaturely nature, and constitutes the hypostasis and grounding-in-being of the divinely creaturely individual realised in that way. Hebblethwaite has provided us with something of a counterargument, in his case working with

---

[46] *Concerning the Union of the Word Incarnate*, q. 2, *ad* 2. The same point is made in *Quodlibetal Questions*, IX, q. 2, a. 3, *responsio*. In *ST* III.4.2 *ad* 3, he considers this from a different counterfactual perspective, namely whether the humanity of Christ would have existed as a distinct human person were it to have come into existence without having been assumed by the Word. He replies that it would. These references come from Alfred J. Freddoso, 'Human Nature, Potency and the Incarnation', *Faith and Philosophy* 3, no. 1 (1986): 27–53.

Christological detail in a traditional sense, although I do not find his objections convincing. In the next two chapters, we continue our discussion of Christological detail, in terms both of the Person assuming and of the sort of nature, or natures, that might be assumed.

14 | The Word Unchanging and Unchanged

In this chapter and the next, my aim is to approach multiple Incarnations in terms of the nature of the One who assumes a created nature, and of natures that are assumed. In this chapter, I start with the contention that the Incarnation changes neither the Person assuming nor the nature assumed. This is relevant for being able to say that more than one Incarnation does not preclude another.

In terms of the One assuming, multiple Incarnations seem to be allowed on the basis of divine plenitude and immutability. We might begin from the theological conviction that the Incarnation does not change the Word in any way (or any other Person, or the divine nature). To say that 'the Word became flesh' is not to say that the Word was changed into flesh, nor that there was some sort of 'becoming' for the Word. Christ is human and divine 'not by conversion of Godhead into flesh: but by taking manhood into God', as the *Quicunque Vult has it*.[1] What changes is that human nature has now been taken up by the unchanging Word. As a result, there is now a case of human nature rendered particular and personal by the hypostasis of the Word.[2] If Incarnation does not change God, then it does not change God's capacity to assume any other created nature. Approached in this way, in relation to divine immutability, nothing about one Incarnation precludes another.

---

[1] *Book of Common Prayer.*
[2] On this, see Thomas Weinandy, *Does God Change?: The Word's Becoming in the Incarnation* (Still River, MA: St Bede's Publications, 2002). The discussion of Cyril of Alexandria is particularly central to the argument (46–63).

To put this a different way, Incarnation, as with creation, is an asymmetrical relation. Incarnation, like creation, provides the entire basis for the being and actuality of the nature that now exists concretely in this way, and on that account, yet it does not in any way change the one who is Incarnate, any more than the act of creation changes the creator. In the words of Kathryn Tanner, 'the mission in which the one Jesus calls Father sends the Son and Spirit' involves 'no new movements of the trinity': 'the usual movements among the persons of the trinity continue; it is just their relations with humanity that are now different'.[3] The outworking of the divine missions in time, in the Incarnation, do not change the processions in God. On this basis, again, one Incarnation does not preclude others.

This first approach is somewhat blunt, based simply on divine immutability: no Incarnation changes God, and I take that to mean that no Incarnation changes God's capacity to take up another nature. We can, however, explore the idea further that no Incarnation empties or curtails what it would mean for God to take up another creaturely nature.[4] Christ is the perfect embodiment of God as human, but no Incarnation exhausts God: no finite embodiment of God exhausts divine plenitude. We might approach that in at least two ways: ontologically and narratively.[5] In the first way, the Son fittingly took up human perfections, and indeed certain defects, which served his saving mission.[6] Those human

---

[3] Kathryn Tanner, *Christ the Key* (Cambridge: Cambridge University Press, 2010), 145.

[4] Caution is called for in how we express this. We might find ourselves talking about 'God's potential for Incarnation', as something unchanged by any particular Incarnation. There are, however, good theological arguments for not talking about potentiality in God. That, however, is precisely the point. The 'capacity' here is not one of a potential to be realised, but of a freedom that can be exercised, a kindness that can be shown, an action that goes on acting, but can be expressed in various ways externally.

[5] While grateful to Austin Stevenson for comments on the entire manuscript, I am particularly indebted to him for formulations in this paragraph and the next.

[6] *ST* III.14–15.

perfections express God fully in the sense that they express the perfection of God as fully as humanly could be, but they do not comprehend or exhaust God. We can also say that what God assumed of human defects, such as Christ's ability to be wounded or to die, also reveals God to us: not because God-as-God has defects (God, for instance, cannot be hurt), but because they too allow the character of God to shine out according to our human mode. They reveal the love of God, for instance, or the artfulness of God, in 'trampling down death by death', or the compassion of God, in dignifying even our weaknesses, by making them a part of the means of salvation. An Incarnation in a different nature would see God revealed in that different nature, with a different mixture of perfections (and defects), such as belonged to that nature, in their own way serving that saving or deifying mission.

Speaking in terms of narrative, the words and actions of Jesus, the unfolding story of his life and encounters, show God to us, since his Person is the Person of the Word, and they do so in a definitively human mode. Again, they express God fully – as fully as God can be expressed humanly – but not comprehensively, in that they show the infinite God in finite ways. We should suppose that an Incarnation in a different nature would offer another full and perfect expression of the Person of the Word: perfect as worked out in that likely very different mode and context.[7]

Jesus is God-as-human, and there is nothing to Jesus that is not God-as-human. That, however, does not stand against saying that God could be Incarnate in some other species. That Incarnation would be the outcome of God realising that nature by taking it up as its substantiation and hypostasis. This would be a different presence of the archetype in and as the image. It would be what it means for God to be Incarnate and expressed according to that form of creaturely being. Such Incarnations would be different as to the nature

---

[7] In scholastic terms, one could describe the ontological angle here as 'first act', and the narrative one as 'second act', with the second flowing ineluctably from the former.

assumed, and each would be fully and perfectly what each species could be.

In his paper, Hebblethwaite is critical of what he calls an 'adjectival' approach to Christology, by which I take him to mean something like what I am saying here: that Jesus is God divinely human.[8] In contrast to him, I find the idea to have promise. Criticising Aquinas on the possibility of multiple Incarnations, Hebblethwaite wrote that

> One cannot treat the human nature in a purely adjectival way, as a theoretically multipliable garment. Granted that there is only one ultimate metaphysical subject, namely God the Son, nevertheless, the human being God became is a human being, a personality, a subject, and a life that actually constitutes the human form of the divine life. One could even say that the human person is the divine person Incarnate, though not, of course, an independent human person related to the divine person. Sadly, it is this generic, adjectival talk of human nature being assumed that permits Thomas to envisage the possibility of multiple Incarnations. Even he does not take seriously enough the fact that a series of divine Incarnations would have to be the same person, human as well as divine.[9]

The supposed problem here strikes me as lacking force. Jesus is the human form or expression of the divine life by hypostatic union. He is what it means for God to have united human nature to himself, and to have rendered it particular with his own particularity. I find that a useful way to proceed in thinking about other Incarnations: a Martian Christ would be what it means for God to have united a Martian nature to himself and to have rendered it particular with his own particularity.

---

[8] Fred Pratt Green (1903–2000) in the carol 'Long ago, prophets knew'.

[9] Hebblethwaite, 'Impossibility of Multiple Incarnations', 326. The opening allusion is to *ST* III.3.7 *ad* 2. Here, Hebblethwaite has multiple human Incarnations in mind (the humanity is 'a theoretically multipliable garment'), which I also find at best unfitting.

Hebblethwaite objects to this, as suggesting that the creaturely nature in an Incarnation is being treated as no more than a 'garment', perhaps suggesting that Christ is a divine Person with merely the appearance of humanity. For Aquinas' part, he explicitly rejects 'garment' language in his discussions of approaches to the metaphysics of the Incarnation, since it is not an 'accidental' union.[10] He goes on to say that in as much as one allows for garment language – for instance, because it has been used by John of Damascus – it must be interpreted carefully, not as serving as a core elucidation of the metaphysics of the Incarnation, but as pointing to certain significant elements, both of which are relevant for our discussion.[11] First, the creaturely nature is visible, as a garment is (largely) what we see of a person; second, because a garment is shaped by the one who wears it, without shaping the person in return, and the creaturely nature in the Incarnation is shaped by the Person assuming it (it shows a God-shaped human life, for instance), while the Person is unchanged. That, however, is only to make some secondary points about the Incarnation using this image, rather than supposing that the language of garment offers a fundamental description of the union.[12]

Meanwhile, Aquinas also endorsed the idea of multiple Incarnations on the basis that no Incarnation exhausts what God can be or do.

> What has power for one thing, and no more, has a power limited to one. Now the power of a Divine Person is infinite, nor can it be limited by any created thing. Hence it may not be said that a Divine

---

[10] *ST* III.2.6.

[11] *ST* III.2.6 *ad* 1.

[12] We should also note that what is taken up bears the full metaphysical heft of humanity-as-such, made individual by the Word in the fullness of all that pertains to humanity: soul, body, will, mind, memories, and so on. It seems to me to be Hebblethwaite, rather than Aquinas, who does not make enough of how differences of creaturehood and particularity would render one Incarnation distinct from another.

Person so assumed one human nature as to be unable to assume another. For it would seem to follow from this that the Personality of the Divine Nature was so comprehended by one human nature as to be unable to assume another to its Personality; and this is impossible, for the Uncreated cannot be comprehended by any creature.[13]

On first appearance this might look like rather a blunt invocation of divine power, but in interpreting it we should remember that Aquinas did not hold that God can do impossible things: things nonsensical or meaningless.[14] The argument is not, therefore, simply that multiple Incarnations are a thing, and God can do anything, so God can become Incarnate more than once. His argument is about the meaningfulness of talking about more than one Incarnation, here set out in terms of the inexhaustible plenitude of God, and the disjunction between the creaturely finite and the divine infinite.

While I hold that Incarnation does not exhaust the Word, and that one finite embodiment of God does not embody all that could be embodied, such that other Incarnations are possible, I would not necessarily align myself with everything that has been written to that effect. An example comes from Thomas F. O'Meara, in his 1999 paper in *Theological Studies*, later expanded as his otherwise often admirable book *Vast Universe: Extraterrestrials and Christian Revelation* in 2012.[15] There he writes that 'Incarnation is one aspect of boundless divine power',[16] and that 'while the Word and Jesus are one, the life of a Jewish prophet on Earth hardly curtails the divine Word's life'.[17] Indeed, it does not curtail it at all. More questionable

---

[13] *ST* III.3.7.

[14] *ST* I.25.3.

[15] Thomas F. O'Meara, 'Christian Theology and Extraterrestrial Intelligent Life', *Theological Studies* 60, no. 1 (1 February 1999): 3–30; *Vast Universe*.

[16] Thomas O'Meara, *Vast Universe*, 47.

[17] Ibid., 48.

is his statement that 'the man Jesus of Nazareth remains minute compared to the Word of God; the reality of a divine person is always open to further realization'.[18] Quantitative comparisons between God and creatures are rarely helpful, not least because they assume – despite their appearance – too great a continuity between God and creatures: the continuity of being in some way on the same scale.[19] Nor, for that matter, can the language of 'realization' be comfortably applied to God. Most unfortunate of all is the statement that 'In each Incarnation, the divine being communicates something from its divine life – but not very much'.[20] I would rather say that in the Incarnation God communicates his whole self in the Second Person.

Keith Ward has explored similar territory, but without the quantitative angle. The human Incarnation of the Word, he writes,

> will not be the completeness of his eternal and divine reality. It therefore becomes reasonable to think that the Word of God could also unite many other finite forms to itself. If there are persons on other planets, we might even expect that this would be so. In other words, the cosmic Word, which is presumably unlimited in nature, can have many finite forms, of which Jesus may only be one.[21]

This seems to me at once both correct and, in another sense, again liable to underplay the completeness of God in Christ. Christ is God in all the divine fullness, although his humanity is incommensurate with the divine nature: it is finite and circumscribed, while God, as

---

[18] Ibid.

[19] On this see my *Participation in God*, 136–37. I will develop this further in my forthcoming book on theology and finitude.

[20] Thomas O'Meara, *Vast Universe*, 48. Quantitative language returns on the next page: 'each Incarnation has its own identity, even as it is sustained by an infinitely removed divine ground'. Here O'Meara cites *ST* III.8.3, but that is certainly incorrect. The most likely intended passage is *ST* III.1.3 *obj.* 2 and *ad* 2. The point in Aquinas' objection, however, is that what would otherwise be at an 'infinite distance' is in fact united in Christ. That is not overturned by the reply.

[21] Ward, *Christ and the Cosmos*, 140.

God, is not. Nonetheless, this is the whole of God as Son in the flesh. I would go beyond Ward, then, and stress that Jesus is fully divine, such that nothing of divinity is absent: as to his Person, in that his Person just is the Person of the Son, and as to his human nature in that it shows forth the character of his Person to the fullest extent that a human nature could do so.

Christ is fully divine, and in an absolute sense, because his hypostasis is the hypostasis of the Word. On account of that, he is then also divine and full in the manner of his humanity: this is what it means for a human nature fully to be animated and rendered actual by divine life and personhood. Christ's humanity is fully and perfectly expressive of God in this sense: Christ's humanity is as fully expressive of divine life and personhood as it is possible for humanity and a human life to be, although its expression of God – whose human nature it is – is properly limited by what pertains to human nature. That, indeed, is its commensurate strength and glory, not its weakness.

The Extra Calvinisticum: Definition and Introduction

At the heart of the implications of Christology for thinking about plural Incarnations is the question of what the union of the Son with human nature means for possible union with other created natures and, at the most basic level, whether it allows for that, or rules it out. Conveniently, we have a dispute in theological history that maps directly onto this question, although its protagonists were far from having the question of multiple Incarnations in mind. This debate was over the *extra calvinisticum*: which is to say, whether it is legitimate to talk about the Son as present and acting beyond the humanity of Jesus. We find a classic formulation from the French Protestant theologian Samuel Maresius (1599–1673): 'Thus the Logos has united the human nature to itself so as at the same time wholly to inhabit it and wholly to be outside it as being transcendent and infinite'.[22] To speak of an *extra calvinisticum* is to talk of the Word active and present 'beyond the flesh' (*etiam extra carnem*). We find it put to work in one of Aquinas' Eucharistic hymns, *Verbum Supernum prodiens*:

> The heavenly Word proceeding forth,
> yet leaving not the Father's side,
> accomplishing his work on earth
> and reached at length life's eventide.[23]

As the name *extra calvinisticum* suggests, the Genevan reformer was a particularly staunched defender of this position, teaching that the Word was united to Christ's human nature without being confined to it:

> For even if the Word in his immeasurable essence united with the nature of man into one person, we do not imagine that he was confined therein. Here is something marvellous: the Son of God descended from heaven in such a way that, without leaving heaven, he willed to be borne in the virgin's womb, to go about the earth, and to hang upon the cross; yet he continuously filled the world, even as He had done from the beginning.[24]

---

[22] Samuelus Maresius, *Collegium theologicum sive Systema breve universæ theologiæ* (Geneva: Sumpt. Ioannis Antonii and Samuelis De Tournes, 1662), 118, IX.30, translation from Heinrich Heppe, *Reformed Dogmatics*, ed. Ernst Bizer, trans. G. T. Thompson (London: Allen and Unwin, 1950), 418. Maresius was also known as Samuel Des Marets, or Desmarets. In more recent philosophical terms, we are talking about 'a Lutheran name for Calvin's doctrine that the Son in his complete transcendence became man, and remains transcendently the Son of God, while also man in the form of a servant' (Thomas F. Torrance, *Incarnation: The Person and Life of Christ* (Milton Keynes: Paternoster, 2008), 216).

[23] Thomas Aquinas, *Verbum Supernum prodiens*, trans. John Mason. Neale and the compilers of *Hymns Ancient and Modern*, emphasis added. Aquinas addresses this in *ST* III.5.2 *ad* 1. Consider also the hymn by St Germanus (c. 634–734), *Méga kai parádoxon thaûma*, translated by Neale as 'A great and mighty wonder', with the line 'The Word becomes Incarnate, | and yet remains on high'.

[24] John Calvin, *Institutes*, II.13.4, translation from *Institutes of Christian Religion*, ed. John T. McNeill, trans. Ford Lewis Battles, vol. 1 (Philadelphia: Westminster Press, 1960), 481.

Were the Word 'confined' to the humanity of Christ, union with a second created nature might be difficult to imagine. If, on the other hand, the hypostatic union leaves the Word 'continuously fill[ing] the world, as he had done from the beginning', we seem to be in a stronger position to talk about subsequent unions. As the Reformed Heidelberg Catechism puts it, 'for since the Godhead is incomprehensible and everywhere present, it must follow that it is indeed beyond the bounds of the Manhood which it has assumed, but is yet none the less in the same also, and remains personally united to it'.[25]

The name *extra calvinisticum* would mislead us if we took it to mean that Calvin's position was a deviation from the tradition, deserving a distinctive name. In fact, the opposite is true, as the quotation from Aquinas illustrates. On this point, as on many others, Calvin's theology reflects the mind of the historical Christian tradition, of both East and West. His particular formulation of this point of doctrine, for instance, as many have pointed out, follows that of John of Damascus.[26] Calvin's belief that the Word is present

---

[25] *Heidelberg Catechism: Text of Tercentenary Edition.* (Cleveland, OH: Publishing House of the Reformed Church, 1877), q. 48, p. 30. This is in answer to the question 'But are not ... the two natures in Christ separated from each other, if the Manhood be not wherever the Godhead is?'

[26] Barth quotes the following as examples of an *extra calvinisticum* position: Athanasius, *On the Incarnation of the Word*, 17; Gregory of Nyssa, *Catechetical Sermon* 10; Augustine, *City of God*, IX.15.2 and *Letter*, 137.2, '*ad Volusianum*'; John of Damascus, *Ekdos*, 3.7; Thomas Aquinas, *ST* III.5.2 *ad* 1 and 10.1 *ad* 2; and 'even Luther himself', *On the Bondage of the Will*, WA 18, 685, 23 (*Church Dogmatics: The Doctrine of the Word of God (I/2)*, trans. G. T. Thomson and Harold Knight (Edinburgh: T&T Clark, 1956), 169). E. David Willis has surveyed the historical continuity of Calvin's position on this point with earlier theology, especially that of the Fathers, in *Calvin's Catholic Christology: The Function of the So-Called Extra Calvinisticum in Calvin's Theology* (Leiden: E. J. Brill, 1967). In addition to some of the texts quoted by Barth, Willis cites Cyril of Alexandria, *Letter*, 17, and Peter Lombard, *Sentences*, III, d. 22, 3 ('Extra Calvinisticum', in *The Westminster Handbook to Reformed Theology*, ed. Donald K. McKim, *The Westminster Handbooks to Christian Theology* (Louisville: Westminster John Knox Press, 2001), 78).

'beyond the flesh' of Jesus picks up the long historical pedigree of talking about the *Logos asarkos* (the fleshless Word, or the Word beyond the Incarnate Christ). That is what Luther denied: for him, there can be no talk of the *Logos asarkos* 'after' the Incarnation.[27]

The countermanding position is associated with Luther, and with many Lutherans since. Karl Barth went so far as to describe it as the 'the crowning assertion of Luther and the Lutherans about the existence of the Word solely in the human existence of Christ'.[28] Significantly, Luther's move was not so much to sequester the Word into a human body as we know it, as to vary the nature of Christ's humanity to make his body 'ubiquitous' and coextensive with the Word. Luther and Calvin were in complete agreement that the Word fills all of creation, being everywhere present in the completeness of his divinity. Luther's innovation was not to limit the ubiquitous presence of the divine Word as divine, but rather to *expand* the presence of Christ's humanity as human: 'since he is a man who is supernaturally one person with God, and apart from this man there is no God, it must follow that ... he is and can be wherever God is and that everything is full of Christ through and through, even according to his humanity'.[29]

That attribution of ubiquity to Christ's humanity arose as part of Luther's distinctive position on the Eucharist: that Christ was

---

[27] Karl-Heinz zur Mühlen, 'Christology', in *Oxford Encyclopaedia of the Reformation*, ed. Hans J. Hillebrand, trans. Robert E. Shillenn, vol. 1 (Oxford: Oxford University Press, 1996), 316. I place 'after' in inverted commas since, on a traditional view, if the Incarnation does not change the Word, 'after' may be an infelicitous term. On what sense might be made of the language of 'after the Incarnation' in relation to God, see Herbert McCabe, *God Matters* (London: Chapman, 1987), 50.

[28] Barth, *CD I/1*, 168.

[29] Martin Luther, 'Confession Concerning Christ's Supper', in *Luther's Works – Volume 37: Word and Sacrament III*, ed. Helmut T. Lehmann, trans. Robert H. Fischer, vol. 37 (Philadelphia: Concordia, 1961), 218. Sections from this text, on the ubiquity of Christ's human presence, were reproduced in the later confessional 'Solid Declaration', VII.98–103, with only one small change of wording at the beginning. The doctrine of the ubiquity of Christ's humanity, as a matter of Christology, is covered in VIII ('The Person of Christ'), §64–65.

present in both his divinity and humanity in the elements of bread and wine, wherever they may be found. This is his doctrine of consubstantiation: that Christ comes to be really present, in his physical humanity, although not so as to replace the reality of the bread and wine (on that latter point, in contrast with Catholic transubstantiation). Luther wrote about this in 1528, echoing a comment from the year before where, he says, 'I proved that Christ's body is everywhere because the right hand of God is everywhere ... to show at least in one way how God could bring it about that Christ is in heaven and his body in the Supper at the same time'.[30]

Luther's dispute was principally against the Eucharistic theology of Zwingli (which was further from the pre-Reformation perspective than either Luther's or Calvin's). Soon, however, Luther's position on the ubiquity of the body of Christ was to provoke a highly critical reaction from Calvin:

> Obstinately to defend an error once rashly conceived, some of them do not hesitate to boast that they only dimensions Christ's flesh ever had, extended as far and wide as heaven and earth. That he was born as a child from the womb, that he grew, that he was stretched upon the cross, enclosed in the tomb – this came to pass by a certain dispensation, in order that he might discharge the office of birth, of death, and the other offices of men ... What is this but to raise Marcion from hell? For no one will doubt that if Christ's body existed in this state, it was a phantasm or apparition.[31]

Later in the same section, Calvin refers to the 'monstrous notion of ubiquity'.[32]

---

[30] Ibid., 207 citing 'That These Words of Christ, "This Is My Body" Etc. Still Stand Firm against the Fanatics', in *Luther's Works – Volume 37: Word and Sacrament III*, ed. Helmut T. Lehmann, trans. Robert H. Fischer, vol. 37 (Philadelphia: Concordia, 1961), 3–150, 47ff, 55ff.

[31] *Institutes*, IV.17.17, translation from Calvin, *Institutes*, vol. 2, 1379–80.

[32] *Institutes*, IV.17.30, translation from ibid., vol. 2, 1401.

Relation to the Wider Theological Picture of These Reformers

Scholars of theological history are in broad agreement that Luther and his followers placed the emphasis on the union of Christ's two natures, while Calvin and his subsequent tradition placed it on their integrity. As Thomas Torrance put it, 'Roughly speaking … the Lutherans tended to stress in the doctrine of Christ the union of the divine and human natures, with a tendency that appeared to the Reformed to be suspect of Eutychianism; whereas the Reformed tended to lay the stress upon the person of the Son of God as God and man, with a tendency that appeared to the Lutherans to be suspect of Nestorianism'.[33] According to Luther,

> wherever you place God for me, you must also place the humanity for me. They simply will not let themselves be separated and divided from each other. He has become one person and does not separate the humanity from himself as Master Jack takes off his coat and lays it aside when he goes to bed.[34]

In contrast, Calvin wrote, 'For we affirm his divinity so joined and united with his humanity that each retains its distinctive nature unimpaired, and yet these two natures constitute one Christ'.[35]

Rowan Williams ably presented the theological concerns animating the distinctive pieties of the Lutheran and Reformed communities, which illustrates the capacity of the two respective approaches to Christology to belong to consistent overall systems:

> Calvin believed that the relation between the divine Word and the human individuality of Jesus was a relation between conceptually distinct agents (even though their action is inseparable in fact), so that the life of God the Word was not exhausted by the identity

---

[33] Torrance, *Incarnation*, 215.

[34] Luther, 'Confession Concerning Christ's Supper, 1528', 218–19. The Reformed tradition would surely deny strenuously that their perspective involves the sort of 'accidental union' implied here, to use Thomas' language.

[35] *Institutes*, II.14.1, translation from Calvin, *Institutes*, vol. 1, 482.

of Jesus (this is the doctrine of the so-called *extra calvinisticum*); and this allows him to give a creative role to the free human decision of Jesus that is commonly absent in Luther, who made strong claims for the practical identity of Jesus and the divine Word. Thus it would not be possible for Calvin to say, with Luther, that Christ's holiness is simply "timeless", not achieved through his actions. Certainly, Jesus did not become divine as a result of or as a reward for his actions; but this holiness must be (as we might say) constructed in the course of a biography.[36]

The Origin of the Term *Extra Calvinisticum*

Although Luther, Zwingli, and Calvin were all writing in the sixteenth century, it seems that the term *extra calvinisticum* was invented by Balthasar Mentzer in 1621.[37] The phrase rose to prominence through an intra-Lutheran dispute about the exercise of divine qualities as possessed by Christ in his humanity. They believed in common that the humanity of Christ attained divine qualities such as ubiquity, although Christ appeared to his disciples as being in one place, and his humanity suffered in a way that, as divine humanity, it need not have (from that Lutheran perspective). For theologians of the Tübingen Lutheran school, Christ's humanity possessed these divine properties, but they were hidden during his earthly life. He remained ubiquitous but did not demonstrate

---

[36] Rowan Williams, 'Religious Experience in the Era of Reform', in *Companion Encyclopedia of Theology*, ed. Peter Byrne and Leslie Houlden (London: Routledge, 1995), 580. Williams cites Thomas F. Torrance, 'Justification: Its Radical Nature and Place in Reformed Doctrine and Life', in *Theology in Reconstruction* (London: SCM Press, 1965), 150–68. Immediately after the passage quoted here, Williams' discussion of the distinction between Luther's position and Calvin's bears upon the theme of God drawing humanity into the work of redemption, which I take to be central to what is eminently 'suitable' about the terrestrial story of the economy of salvation. See Chapter 16.

[37] Albeit spelt there as *extra calvinianum* (Willis, *Calvin's Catholic Christology*, 21–23).

his ubiquity. In contrast, Lutheran theologians at Giessen held that while Christ's humanity was invested with divine attributes on account of the Incarnation, for the span of his earthly life he abandoned, or emptied himself of, those characteristics.[38]

The contention of the Giessen theologians that the humanity of Christ might suspend its ubiquity was criticised as introducing an incompatible notion into Lutheran theology: an *extra calvinisticum*. However, when a gathering of theologians met from across Saxony to decide the matter in 1624 (the *Decisio saxonica*), they sided with the Giessen position ('in the main issue', as Barth puts it). An *extra calvinisticum* was accepted for the course of Christ's earthly life. This was followed, as Barth puts it, 'by later Lutheran orthodoxy', but not without dispute.[39]

We can note that the story did not stop there. The Giessen proposal introduced a form of kenoticism: the divine humanity of Christ temporarily set its divine properties aside. Nineteenth-century Lutheran theologians, such as Ernst Sartorius and Gottfried Thomasius, went on to apply that not to the proposed divine attributes of the humanity but to the divinity itself, giving us the form of kenoticism we are more familiar with today.[40] Barth is unsparing in his criticism:

> The knot which the earlier Lutheran Christology had arbitrarily tied rather too tightly was certainly loosed. But it was loosed at too great a cost when it meant the open abandonment of the presupposition common to all earlier theology, including Calvinists and Lutherans,

---

[38] On this, see Karl Barth, *Church Dogmatics: The Doctrine of Reconciliation (IV/1)*, trans. G. W. Bromiley (Edinburgh: T. & T. Clark, 1956), 182.

[39] Ibid., 181. J. Gerhard rebelled against the decision, and Barth, for his part, wonders whether the Geissen position ('the impossible theory of Giessen') really made sense from an internal Lutheran perspective (182).

[40] Barth (*IV/2*, 182) cites Ernst Sartorius, *Die Lehre von Der Heiligen Liebe* (Stuttgart: Liesching, 1851); Wolfgang Friedrich Gess, *Das Dogma von Christi Person und Werk* (Basel: Detloff, 1887).

Giessen and Tübingen, that the Godhead of the man Jesus remains intact and unaltered ... If in Christ – even in the humiliated Christ born in a manger at Bethlehem and crucified on the cross at Golgotha – God is not unchanged and wholly God, then everything that we may say about the reconciliation of the world made by God in this humiliated one is left hanging in the air.[41]

Assessment

The time has come to put this to work in relation to multiple Incarnations: a possibility for which the Lutheran position of ubiquity does not seem hospitable. We might express this in two different ways. The first, in less technical language, considers the absolute centrality, in Luther's writings, of the human person of Christ to any consideration of the Son. The Son is so completely identified with the man Jesus Christ that no conceptual room seems to be left for talking about another Incarnation.

> If he is present naturally and personally wherever he is, then he must be man there too, since he is not two separate persons but a single person. Wherever this person is, it is the single, indivisible person, and if you can say, 'Here is God', then you must also say, 'Christ the man is present too' .... wherever you place God for me, you must also place the humanity for me. They simply will not let themselves be separated and divided from each other.[42]

A second angle might set the question out in terms of the metaphysics of natural substances. If Incarnation means 'wherever you place God for me, you must also place the humanity for me', then multiple Incarnations would mean that wherever God is, so is both the humanity of Christ, *and* also any number of other extraterrestrial natures.

---

[41] Barth, *CD IV/1*, 182–83.
[42] Luther, 'Confession Concerning Christ's Supper, 1528', 218–19.

At the heart of the Christian claim about Christ is the denial of a principle of exclusion between a divine nature and a human one: not because they are alike but precisely because they are so entirely unlike.[43] On the other hand it would seem, by definition, that two creaturely natures cannot overlap. Entailed in being an apple is not being an orange. So, while I am happy to entertain the proposition that the divine Person could take up two creaturely natures, it seems that it would do violence to the character of a created nature for one to overlap ('ubiquitously') with another.

That very question of creaturely overlap, however, lies at the heart of Luther's Eucharistic theology, on which his whole doctrine of ubiquity stands: in the doctrine of consubstantiality. On this point, precisely, it differs from transubstantiation. Luther held that the Eucharistic elements were simultaneously bread and wine, *and* the body and blood of Christ. The Catholic position denies that simultaneity, not least on the grounds discussed here: that a creaturely nature does not exclude the divine nature, but it does exclude another created nature. The body and soul of Christ can be united to the Person of the Son; they cannot be united to bread and wine. If Christ is present in the Eucharist in 'body, blood and soul', then the substance of bread and wine cannot be present.

Lutheran theology, then, seems to entertain strands of metaphysics that others reject, and that might ultimately (and somewhat paradoxically) make their position more open to multiple Incarnations than we had at first thought. If a fully committed Lutheran can say that Christ's humanity could be co-present physically with another creaturely nature (that of bread or wine), perhaps she could then say not only 'if he [the Word] is present naturally and personally wherever he is, then he must be man there too', but also, 'then he can be Martian there too, and Titan, and so on'. For my part, the overlap of creaturely natures, which is precisely what consubstantiality

[43] Herbert McCabe, 'The Myth of God Incarnate', *New Blackfriars* 58, no. 687 (1977): 350–57.

affirms, seems to do violence to the nature of creatures, and preclude any multiple Incarnations set out in parallel terms. Moreover, this 'ubiquity' seems to deny the Chalcedonian stricture that the hypostatic union does not change either the divine or the human nature. Christ's human nature here looks unlike any other human nature.[44] Nonetheless, if one is prepared to suspend some of that, and go down the Lutheran line, perhaps what one means by a creaturely 'nature', and how it features in Christology, would be so transformed as not to disqualify the prospect of multiple Incarnations after all, even though denying the *extra calvinisticum*. A fulsome espousal of Luther's position might be open to multiple Incarnations, after all, on the basis of its own distinctive metaphysics.

Reformed theology, nonetheless, with its *extra calvinisticum*, seems even more straightforwardly open to multiple Incarnations, holding that the Word is not only *in* Christ but also *beyond* Christ, as we saw in the quotation from the Heidelberg Catechism above. That 'beyond' opens up the possibility for additional Incarnations, as part of what might belong to this 'beyond'.

A caveat is due here, however. A Reformed theologian might hold to the *extra calvinisticum* while also being sympathetic to some of the Lutheran concerns about what it should not mean. This raises an intriguing possibility: namely, that within an implicit Lutheran metaphysics a thoroughgoing Lutheran might find the resources to affirm multiple Incarnations after all, while a Reformed theologian would reject the ubiquity of Christ's humanity along the lines of the *extra calvinisticum* but still be sufficiently open to the Lutheran concerns to foreclose the possibility of multiple Incarnations. Thomas Torrance stands as an example. He

---

[44] In a sense, it does not matter that Christ's humanity looks different from that of others. He has been held to have enjoyed the beatific vision, for instance, but that does not undo humanity, any more than the vision of God that a human being may have after this life undoes her humanity. The problem would be if the hypostatic union changed Christ's creaturely nature so as to make it no longer human. To me, ubiquity would be an example of that.

upheld the *extra calvinisticum,* in as much as it stands against any doctrine of a ubiquity to Christ's humanity, but followed the Lutherans in rejecting some of the *extra*'s possible implications. He upheld the Reformed contention that

> we cannot think of the Incarnation of the Son in such a way as to deny his eternal transcendence to the creature, by making him a prisoner of time or the time series. The Word cannot be subordinated to the flesh it assumes nor can it be limited by the creaturely reality with which it is united, and so be altered in its transcendent and divine nature'.[45]

Simultaneously, however, he commended Lutherans for wanting to uphold that

> with the Incarnation of the Word, we must never think of the Word apart from the man Jesus, with whom the Word is for ever united, and from whom the Word is never apart. Now that the Incarnation has taken place, we must say that the Son is none other than Jesus, and is identical with him.[46]

In the Reformed tradition, an emphasis on the association of the Word with the humanity of Christ might render talk of additional

---

[45] Torrance, *Incarnation*, 220.

[46] Ibid. As Barth put it, the Reformed position is to deny what the Lutherans negate, namely a '*numquam et nuspiam extra carnem*' [that the Word is never and in no way outside the flesh], rather than to deny what the Lutherans want positively to affirm, namely the '*totus totus intra carnem*' [that the whole of the Word is to be found completely within the flesh] (*CD* I/1, 169, with a reference to *Col.* 2.9). As we might perhaps expect, Barth offers criticisms of both sides: 'But as the Lutherans failed to show how far, by their elimination of the extra, the *vere Deus* is, as they allege, preserved to the same extent as the *vere homo*, so now the Reformed too failed to show convincingly how far the *extra* does not involve the assumption of a twofold Christ, of a *logos ensarkos* alongside a *logos asarkos*, and therefore a dissolution of the unity of natures and hypostatic union, and therefore a destruction of the unequivocal Emmanuel and the certainty of faith and salvation based thereon. In short it cannot be denied that the Reformed *totus intra et extra* offers at least as many difficulties as the Lutheran *totus intra*' (ibid., 170).

Incarnations unpalatable, even if not impossible. From my own perspective, however, neither Reformed nor Lutheran, although certainly closer to the former than the latter, the topics discussed in this chapter form an important basis for supposing that multiple Incarnations make theological sense. That is not – at least not yet – to say that they might be thought suitable or fitting, but it does go so far as to suggest to me that the idea is not theologically nonsensical.

In this chapter, I have considered Incarnation from the angle of the one assuming and the nature assumed, with an emphasis on the unchanged integrity of both. The next chapter continues our attention to the divine and creaturely natures, there approached in terms of whether Incarnation is limited to the Son, or particularly suitable for the Son, among the Persons and, alongside that, whether any creaturely nature is any more suitably assumed than another.

15 | Person Assuming and Natures Assumed

As I have frequently noted already, attention to questions posed by astrobiology can help us return to familiar topics with new eyes. Imagining different trajectories elsewhere, however, need not imply that what happened on Earth might just as well have turned out differently. It may instead help us to appreciate the particular suitability of the story of God's dealings here, with human beings. It is in that spirit that I turn in this short chapter to consider some of the most speculative questions I will address in this book, as to what sort of nature might be assumed by God by way of Incarnation, and the related question, at the limits of theological speculation, as to whether another Person of the Trinity may be Incarnate.[1] An answer to the second question makes no substantial difference to our discussion here, expect perhaps to add precision: when we talk about 'God taking up another nature', it may be good to have thought through in Trinitarian terms what we mean by 'God'. Part of Aquinas' rather radical exploration of the Incarnational landscape in the third part of the *Summa Theologiae* is his proposal that all three Persons of the Trinity could take up a creaturely nature. His argument is considered in terms of possibility and an invocation of divine power. As I noted above, that may appear as something of blunt instrument, and it is uncharacteristic of Aquinas, for whom voluntaristic invocations of divine power are unusual.[2] However,

---

[1] Timothy Pawl discusses these two topics (as 'the Natural Question' and 'the Personal Question') alongside a couple of others in 'Thomistic Multiple Incarnations'.

[2] *ST* III.3.5.

nuance comes when he moves from possibility to suitability: from what could be, to what is most appropriately so.[3]

Remaining for now with the question of other Persons being Incarnate, Thomas argues that possibility relates to the power to do something and that, in turn, pertains to nature. Divine power, therefore, belongs alike to all the Persons. Furthermore, in its fundamental character, the Incarnation is a hypostatic or personal union, and personhood also applies to the three divine hypostases alike: 'the Divine power is indifferently and commonly in all the Persons. Moreover, the nature of Personality is common to all the Persons, although the personal properties are different'.[4]

The objections in this article of the *Summa* offer a variety of arguments that Incarnation is the unique domain of the Son, revolving around the relation of the human story of salvation to eternal dynamics of the Trinity: Jesus is the Son of Man, in reflection of the eternal sonship of the Word; his work is to draw his fellow human beings into that sonship; the temporal begetting of Christ from Mary reflects his eternal generation from the Father.[5] In response, Aquinas provided what he takes to be plausible arguments against excluding Incarnation of the other Persons on these grounds. Nonetheless, while at this stage he wished not to rule out the possibility of Incarnation by the other Persons, a few articles later he turns from possibility to suitability, and defends the suitability of the Incarnation of the Son, rather than of the Father or Spirit.[6] At that point what stood, there unsuccessfully, as arguments for the *impossibility* of Incarnation by the other Persons, come back as forceful arguments *for* the particular *suitability* of Incarnation by the Son. Notably, Aquinas so naturally thinks in terms of suitability,

---

[3] *ST* III.3.8.

[4] ST III.3.5.

[5] John of Damascus, *On the Orthodox Faith*, 4.14; *ST* III.3.5, *obj.* 1, 2, and 3.

[6] *ST* III.3.8.

or fittingness, he writes there in a natural and lyrical style, in contrast to his earlier discussion – about what might be counterfactually possible for God – which feels rather strained in comparison.

One consideration when it comes to suitability picks up the theme of the Son drawing human beings into sonship: 'it was fitting that by Him Who is the natural Son, human beings should share this likeness of sonship by adoption'. To be a child of God, Aquinas writes, is to be conformed to the image of God's Son, citing Rom. 8.29: 'For those whom he foreknew he also predestined to be conformed to the image of his Son, in order that he might be the first-born within a large family'. That is most fittingly accomplished by the Son, and so is redemption if it is seen as refashioning. As the Father's 'word' or 'concept', the Son is the 'exemplar' of all things that spring creatively from God: 'the Person of the Son, Who is the Word of God, has a certain common agreement with all creatures, because the word of the craftsman, i.e. his concept, is an exemplar likeness of whatever is made by him'.[7] For creatures to be made 'through' the Word is for them to be patterned after the Word; fallen creation would then best be restored and reshaped by being united to that Word hypostatically: it was 'fitting that the creature should be restored in order to its eternal and unchangeable perfection' through the Incarnation of the Son, since 'the craftsman by the intelligible form of his art, whereby he fashioned his handiwork, restores it when it has fallen into ruin'. The idea that it was suitable for the Image of God (the Word) to be Incarnate among the image of the Image (human beings) is also found in patristic writing and comes to particularly lyrical expression in Bonaventure.[8]

For Aquinas there is also something particularly fitting that human beings, whose distinguishing perfection is intellect or

---

[7] *ST* III.3.8.

[8] For instance, Athanasius, *On the Incarnation of the Word*, 7; Bonaventure, *Breviloquium*, IV.2.6, V.1.1–2, V.3.2; for a parallel in Aquinas, see the prologue to the *Commentary on the Sentences*, text in Thomas Aquinas, *Selected Writings*, ed. and trans. Ralph McInerny (London: Penguin Classics, 1998), 52–53.

wisdom, should be made perfect by the Incarnation of the *Word*: 'for the consummate perfection of man it was fitting that the very Word of God should be personally united to human nature'. We find an overlap here with another of Aquinas' arguments, that since Adam and Eve were said to have fallen through a desire for knowledge, 'it was fitting that by the Word of true knowledge man might be led back to God, having wandered from God through an inordinate thirst for knowledge'.[9]

Other theologians have taken a different view of the Father and Spirit becoming Incarnate. Anselm, for instance, considered it impossible.[10] His arguments on this score strike me as entirely wrongheaded, based as they are on a univocal equivalence between divine and human generation,[11] or on Incarnation effecting a change in God.[12] However, his arguments for the *fittingness* of the Incarnation of the Son have somewhat greater cogency. Bonaventure was on yet stronger ground when he argued against the Incarnation of the Father, as the Person who sends: '"to become Incarnate" is nothing other than "to be sent in the flesh", as Augustine understands it. But it is impossible for the Father to be sent, since he has no one from whom he is. Therefore it is impossible for the Father to become Incarnate'.[13] In the twentieth century, Karl Rahner also

---

[9] Aquinas covered the same ground in *SCG* IV.42, although with different Biblical references, notably 1 Cor. 11.7 and Col. 1.15.

[10] *On the Incarnation of the Word*, 10, taken up later with a parallel discussion in *Cur Deus Homo*, II.9, translations in *Anselm of Canterbury*, 250–52 and 324–25, respectively.

[11] 'If the Holy Spirit became flesh, as the Son became flesh, surely the Holy Spirit would become the son of a human being. Therefore there would be two sons in the Divine Trinity, namely the Son of God and the son of the human being' (*On the Incarnation of the Word*, 10, p. 250).

[12] 'Therefore, if the Holy Spirit were to have been born of the Virgin, one person would be greater, and the other person lesser, by reason of the dignity of their origin, since the Son of God would have only the more excellent origin from God, and the Holy Spirit only the lesser origin from a human being' (ibid.).

[13] Bonaventure, *In III Sent.*, dist. 1, a. 1, q. 2, *sed contra* 2, translation from Dylan Schrader, *Shortcut to Scholastic Latin* (New York: Paideia Institute, 2019), 32.

argued along these lines, across a number of works, insisting that Incarnation of either Father or Spirit would subvert or reverse the direction of the eternal processions, adding that 'the revelation of the Father without the Logos and his Incarnation would be the same as a wordless utterance'.[14]

Like Rahner, Robert Jenson traced the origin of the proposal that the other Persons could be Incarnate to Augustine, with considerable disapprobation.[15] That approach, he thought, tends to 'sand down' the distinctive characteristics of origin and relation in the Trinity, treating the Persons as so many equivalent instantiations of divine essence. I agree, but I would point out that discussions of possibility have typically been preparatory for, and subordinate to, discussions of suitability, and with suitability, the particularity of the Persons returns.

Other writers do not raise the matter so much as a question, but simply assume that Incarnation pertains to the Son. Keith Ward is an example, for whom it is characteristic of the Son – even determinatively so – to be the 'aspect of the divine being which enters into a specific relation of love with one (or more) created persons. This is God embodied in creation and expressing the divine nature in finite form'. Ward goes on to write that this form 'does not have to be

---

[14] 'Remarks on the Dogmatic Treatise "De Trinitate"', 91. Other texts addressing this question include 'On the Theology of the Incarnation', in *Theological Investigations Volume 4*, trans. Kevin Smyth (London: Darton Longman and Todd, 1966), 105–7, and *Foundations of Christian Faith: An Introduction to the Idea of Christianity*, trans. William V. Dych (London: Darton, Longman and Todd, 1978), 215. These texts are discussed by Stephen T. Davis, Daniel Kendall, and Gerald O'Collins, eds., 'The Incarnation: The Critical Issues', in *The Incarnation* (Oxford: Oxford University Press, 2002), 19–21. This strong isomorphism between the missions and the processions is not surprising, given Rahner's commitment to the idea that the economic Trinity is the immanent Trinity, and vice versa.

[15] Robert Jenson, *Systematic Theology – Volume 1: The Triune God* (New York: Oxford University Press, 1997), 111–12, citing the influence of Lombard, *Sentences*, III.1.3. He lauds John of Damascus for stressing the congruence between Christ as Son of God and as Son of Man (*On the Orthodox Faith*, 77.5–8).

human. It could be any form of being which is capable of expressing more-or-less well the divine nature'.[16]

Applying these discussions to life elsewhere, the general parallels are clear. Arguments in favour of Incarnation of the Second Person are frequently based on the role of the Son in creation. As the Word, and the exemplar of all that is, all creatures come into being and are patterned after him. The same might be said of invocations of reason and wisdom. In as much as the natures that might be taken up by Incarnation are rational natures – a topic to which we will soon turn – the fittingness of assumption, restoration, and elevation by the Word also holds true. With a third set of arguments, to do with sonship, the arguments may be diffused a little, but they are not undone. We have no idea what patterns of generation – of coming to be – might apply elsewhere, but there will surely be something like it for any creature, providing an affinity with the Second Person as the one said to be eternally begotten.

The Nature Assumed

As we have seen, some arguments for the suitability of the Incarnation of the Son, rather than the Father or the Spirit, rest on the specific characteristics of the nature assumed: as knowing and desiring, for instance. We now turn, therefore, to the question of what sort of created nature would be suited for a divine Person to take up.[17] Talk of suitability here, however, calls for care and clarity. Discussion of 'capability', for instance, risks suggesting that there is a capacity for Incarnation *on the side of the nature itself*, as if Incarnation were a native faculty belonging to natures of a certain sort, which might imply not only a possibility, but even an

---

[16] Ward, *Christ and the Cosmos*, 249.

[17] Ward, as we have seen, writes that 'It could be any form of being which is capable of expressing more-or-less well the divine nature' (ibid.).

expectation of Incarnation, perhaps following the Aristotelian principal that nothing that pertains to a nature belongs to it in vain.[18]

Here, again, we can turn to Aquinas for a survey of this territory.[19] He begins by invoking the distinction between 'active' and 'passive' potency. The former belongs to an agent who is not acting in a particular way, but who can do so: it refers to an ability to act, even at a moment when it is not in fact being exercised (as I am capable of multiplying numbers even when I am not actually doing so). In contrast, passive potency is a state that allows something to become other than it is, but only if acted upon in the appropriate way (as a child can be taught to multiply).[20] A potter who is not currently potting is in active potency to the act of throwing a vase, but a lump of clay is in passive potency to becoming one, since no lump of clay becomes a vase by its own powers.

With that distinction in place, we can follow Aquinas in making two points. The first is that human nature has no active potency for Incarnation. Nothing about human nature plays an active role in being assumed (although we should note that Mary plays her part, not least in giving her assent: 'be it unto me according to thy word').[21] Nor is there an inherent capacity in human nature to be assumed that could be called even a 'natural *passive* power [or potency]': we should not suppose that 'being assumed by God' is something that quite normally, or naturally, belongs to human nature.[22] Clay

---

[18] Aristotle applies this broad principal, for instance, in *De anima*, I.12 (434a30–32); *Generation of Animals*,II.6 (744a37–b2); *Progression of Animals* IA (704b11–17). It is ably discussed by James Lennox in 'Nature Does Nothing in Vain ...', in *Aristotle's Philosophy of Biology: Studies in the Origins of Life Science* (Cambridge: Cambridge University Press, 2001), 205–23.

[19] *ST* III.4.1.

[20] 'The power of producing an effect on something else [*potentia activa*] and the power of receiving the effect of another in the form of an action [*potentia passiva*]' (Roy Joseph Deferrari and M. Inviolata Barry, *A Lexicon of St. Thomas Aquinas: Based on The Summa Theologica and Selected Passages of His Other Works* (Washington, DC: Catholic University of America Press, 1948), 855).

[21] Luke 1.38.

[22] *ST* III.4.1.

cannot naturally make itself into a vase, but when used by a potter to make one, it is used naturally. Incarnation goes beyond any such natural capacity.[23] *Præter rerum seriem parit deum hominem*, as the mediaeval hymn begins, to be sung before the Gospel reading at Christmas: 'outside the natural order of things, one is born who is God and human'. That rests on divine initiative – *præter rerum seriem* – and not on some power, active or passive, belonging to human nature as such.

In this, Aquinas addresses what we might think of as a characteristically Barthian concern: the worry that any discussion of the suitability of human nature for divine assumption would render the Incarnation less than a miracle, or create some expectation that it might take place. Nothing about human nature, however, demands or extends to Incarnation of itself, and that would apply equally to any other creaturely nature. The Incarnation is grounded in the nature of God, not in the nature of humanity. If the Incarnation was fitting, then it 'befits God' (*conveniens est Deo*), not humanity.[24] 'To be united to God in unity of person', Aquinas wrote, 'was not fitting to human flesh, according to its natural endowments, since it was above its dignity; nevertheless, it was fitting that God, by reason of His infinite goodness, should unite it to Himself for man's salvation'.[25]

That said, Aquinas did find suitability, as we have seen, in a congruence in the Incarnation between human nature and God, whose image it bears. That raises the question as to what might make a nature more or less suitable for God to take up by grace. For his

---

[23] There are parallels here to discussions about the way in which the beatific vision does or does not relate to the nature and capacities of a human being as a creature, with long-running and fiercely contested arguments about how a supernatural end relates to human nature as such.

[24] *ST* III.1.1.

[25] *ST* III.1.1 *ad* 2. On there being no one most perfect form of creatures, such that God would only most suitably take up that nature, see De Concilio, *Harmony between Science and Revelation*, 227–29.

part, Aquinas set this out in terms of two considerations – dignity and need – and their combination. In the human being we have a nature that both possess suitable dignity and stands in a position of suitable need. Those who subscribe to the position of 'Incarnation anyway', not making it contingent on sin, would deny the relevance of that category of need. In this passage, Aquinas was principally using the idea to exclude Incarnation as an angel.[26]

The category of need makes it clear that 'dignity' does not mean merit or desert, or perfection, even in a creaturely sense. For Aquinas, dignity means a nature that bears God's likeness as 'rational and intellectual', which 'was made for attaining to the Word to some extent by its operation, viz. by knowing and loving Him'.[27] In characteristically Augustinian form, knowing and willing here are not principally the faculties as such, but as they are referred to knowledge and love of God, as their ultimate goal and fulfilment.

The capacities to know and to love are time-honoured criteria for a sense of personhood. They are also closely associated with relationality, and for Aquinas, with receptivity and agency: to be capable of knowing is to be open to receiving the truth or form of things into oneself; to be capable of will or love is to be able to reach out, to orientate oneself towards that which is external to you. As I noted above, in the light of more recent science, we should acknowledge more of a gradation within nature on this front. As we have seen, from one perspective, anything that is alive at all can, to some extent, receive information from its surroundings, and can also make some response: it can, in however limited a fashion, trim the sails of its existence so as to chart a different path through the future than it would otherwise.[28] On the other hand, for all that

---

[26] On non-Incarnation as an irrational animal (on the basis of dignity), see *ST* III.4.1, *ad* 2; on non-Incarnation as an angel (on the basis of need), see *ST* III.4.1, *ad* 3.

[27] *ST* III.4.1.

[28] For a survey, see my 'All Creatures', 181–83.

continuity across the broad field of life, we recognize something fundamentally different in degree between ourselves and a bacterium or a fern, and can say that with humans something *other* has also come to be. Such an outlook, for us seen in more evolutionary terms, is integral to Aquinas' sense of what makes a nature suitable for assumption by the Son.

Just as to know is not simply to receive the imprint of things, but to do so reflexively – not only to know, but to know that you know – so also to will or love is not simply to be oriented towards that which lies beyond you but to do so reflexively – with understanding and freedom, however mysterious the latter category may prove to be. Only with beings of that sort can there be a relation that blossoms into what we call a 'relationship'. Here the doctrine of the *imago dei* is shown to be particularly remarkable: human beings are in a proper sense absolutely distinct from God, yet across the divide of that distinction there flashes a true sense of likeness. That is not the same as equivalence – entirely far from it – but neither does that non-equivalence serve entirely to efface the likeness.[29] Of course, the rock, the earthworm, and the human being are equally not God: they are creatures, not creator. Nothing can be said to dilute that sentence, and yet something marks the human being out: the image above the trace.[30] Most suitably, then, was God Incarnate as a human being, and not as a rock or worm.[31] In his early *Commentary on the Sentences*, Aquinas had held that the assumption of any created nature fell within the absolute power of God,[32] although since God's power is always ordered to God's nature and purpose, certain

---

[29] I have written about this in *Participation in God*, for instance, pp. 146–50.

[30] See Chapter 8.

[31] The Franciscans Richard Middleton, William of Ware, and Duns Scotus all argued for the importance of being able to say that God could have been incarnated as an irrational creature. On these, and several other writers, on this topic see Richard Cross, 'Incarnation, Indwelling, and the Vision of God: Henry of Ghent and Some Franciscans', *Franciscan Studies* 57 (1999): 79–130.

[32] *Commentary on the Sentences*, book 3, dist. 2, q. 1, a. 1, qc. 1, co.

natures could have greater 'congruity [*congruitas*]' if assumed than others. Among other factors, that aligns with the assumption of a rational nature, which bears the divine image, rather than an irrational one, that bears only the vestige. By the time he wrote *ST* III.4.1, however, Aquinas had more or less changed his mind. Although the discussion there is largely set out in terms of suitability, such that it might be thought that an irrational nature could be assumed but less fittingly, he nonetheless ends the *responsio* by writing categorically 'Hence it follows that only human nature was assumable'.[33]

Thomas' restriction of Incarnation here to 'human nature' (as I have already stressed) should not be taken to imply a limitation on an astrobiological stage, since other creatures could fulfil the criteria he sets out. Indeed, as we saw in Chapter 9, his contention that there is only one rational animal is based upon the idea that anything that is both rational and animal would be the same, single kind of thing for broad-brush theological and philosophical purposes.

We do not know how any of these categories, such as intellect or desire, would play out elsewhere in the cosmos, although, as I wrote in Chapter 9, I think that an argument can be made for seeing some of them as basic and therefore universal. (There I added memory, and aligned memory, intellect, and will with living in relation to the past, present, and future, respectively.)[34] The lineaments

---

[33] Perhaps more accurately, Aquinas hovers somewhere between the language of possibility and fittingness here. On the one hand, the seemingly binary category of whether something is 'assumable' is in play, and on the other hand, it is worked out in term of 'fitness' for assumption. That said, animals are not said to be 'less fitting' recipients of Incarnation': they have 'no fitness to be united with Him in personal being' (*ST* III.4.1 *ad* 2).

[34] The concentration by Aquinas here is on a divine likeness in two faculties, intellect and will, since for him the faculty of memory is different, in being shared with other animals (*ST* I.78.4). In contrast, Augustine's emphasis is on a threefold human likeness in memory, intellect, and will (*The Trinity*, X, ch. 3, n. 11; XV, ch. 4, nn. 21–23).

of suitability when it comes to the assumption of a creaturely nature by God might more broadly include intellect and will, openness and agency, self-awareness, freedom, and the forms of relationality that come from them. Spanning all of that, however difficult it is to define, is the category of *personhood*. Nebulous though it may be, it is perhaps our best criterion for the suitability of assumption: for that 'dignity' that Aquinas writes about. Or perhaps not: we do not know what forms life might take elsewhere, and if such life exists or has existed, our categories may not prove up to the task of imagining or describing it.

Before moving on, we should note that Aquinas discusses the question of what nature might be assumed in a strongly eschatological register. The human being is characterized by understanding and love, and more specifically by understanding and loving God, in which the human being, and those faculties, find their fulfilment. At the heart of the discussion is the sense that a nature that might be assumed is one with a capacity for a relationship with another and thus, with God. Rahner provided some insightful, if dense, reflections on these relations when he wrote that in Christ the human orientation towards God (in knowledge and love) is met by God coming, as it were, in the other direction, by the hypostatic embrace of humanity in Christ.[35] Important for Aquinas was the idea that the Incarnation was about establishing friendship between God and humanity.[36] Indeed, that might serve as an unexpectedly simple criterion for considering what sorts of nature might suitably be taken up by Incarnation: if creatures of the nature concerned are capable of being or becoming friends of God.[37]

All of that is to say something about 'dignity'. Alongside this, we can remember that Aquinas adds the criterion of 'need'. He thought

---

[35] The theme animates all of Chapter 6 of Rahner, *Foundations of Christian Faith*; see, for instance, especially 217, 225.

[36] *SCG* I.54.6.

[37] See comments on friendship in Chapter 8.

that the kind of nature God might assume would be one in need of restoration, 'having fallen under original sin'.[38] Again, to talk about the 'need' of creatures is not to imply that God *needed* to do anything in response, just as speaking of their dignity need not imply a capacity for elevation by hypostatic union that makes Incarnation in any way natural, expected, or necessary. Nonetheless, what is given in the Incarnation leads to the further perfection of that nature, not to its violation. Aquinas' perspective here is consistent with the gentle distance he has placed between his own perspective and one of 'Incarnation anyway'. Were one instead to take that 'anyway' perspective, the category of 'need' may be recast in terms of an absence: as suitability for Incarnation not in terms of creatures needing deliverance from sin, but in terms of an as-yet-ungiven gift to raise them to a state of glory and participation in God, beyond that which pertains to nature.

This discussion of Persons assuming and natures assumed concludes our discussion of aspects of what I have called 'Christological detail', related as they are to explorations of the sense that it might or might not make to say that multiple Incarnations are possible. Already hovering around those discussions, however, has been the idea that possibility is not the only register or modality in which these conversations can and do play out. As I commented in Chapter 12, the other dominant register in existing writing is one of necessity and, alongside those, the idea of suitability of fittingness. It is to questions of necessity, and to my preferred category of suitability, that we now turn.

---

[38] *ST* III.4.1.

16 | Multiple Incarnations

Necessity and Suitability

The category of suitability has become increasingly important for me, particularly having spent time thinking about astrobiology. In this chapter, I come to that theme by way of the contrasting category of necessity. Later in the chapter, the notion of suitability will then underpin my warmth towards the idea of multiple Incarnations: not that they would be necessary, but that they seem particularly fitting, for reasons I will set out with a contrast between the openings of Star Wars and Luke's Gospel.

Alongside arguments about possibility, notions of necessity find their way into theological writing about astrobiology in various ways, for instance, in a confident assertion that the Word *would* necessarily have been Incarnate elsewhere, or in discussions about why multiple Incarnations would *not* be necessary. The mood, however, is the same: the matter is settled, and to say that something *definitely would not* need to happen breathes the same air as saying that it definitely would. Although not writing about exobiology, both Leo the Great and Anselm provide confident assertions of necessity concerning the Incarnation and redemption. Consider Leo, in *Sermon 77*:

> For if man, made after the image and likeness of God, had retained
> the dignity of his own nature, and had not been deceived by the dev-
> il's wiles into transgressing through lust the law laid down for him,
> *the Creator of the world would not have become a Creature*, the Eter-
> nal *would not have entered the sphere of time, nor God the Son, Who
> is equal with God the Father, have assumed the form of a slave and*

the likeness of sinful flesh. But because 'by the devil's malice death entered into the world', and *captive humanity could not otherwise be set free without His undertaking our cause,* Who without loss of His majesty should both become true Man, and alone have no taint of sin, the mercy of the Trinity divided for Itself the work of our restoration in such a way that the Father should be reconciled, the Son should reconcile, and the Holy Ghost enkindle.[1]

As the phrases picked out in italic indicate, not only did Gregory write that no other means *could* have saved us than those found in the Christian story, he was also thinking in terms of necessity when he wrote that the Word *would not* have been Incarnate other than as response to sin. A similar approach is found in Anselm's *Cur Deus Homo*: for instance, in his arguments that God could not simply have forgiven us, that God must wish at least some human beings to be saved, that it is necessary for one who atones to belong to the same race as those for whom he is atoning, that atonement must involve God being given more than what is simply due, and, since obedience is due, that the one who dies must be one who could choose not to die.[2]

Ascriptions of necessity to the works of God sit uneasily with me, partly in deference to divine freedom and sovereignty, but also because God's dealings with creatures involve the giving of gifts, which is marked by gratuity. For a significant swathe of theological tradition, necessity marks none of God's dealings with creatures (any work *ad extra*, as the theological phrase has it):

---

[1] Leo, *Sermon* 77.1–2, emphasis added, translation from *A Select Library of Nicene and Post-Nicene Fathers of the Christian Church. Second Series – Volume 12: Leo the Great and Gregory the Great*, ed. Philip Schaff and Henry Wallace, trans. Charles Lett Feltoe (Edinburgh: T&T Clark, 1988), 192. Leo, as we can see, does not take the 'Incarnation anyway' approach that will be discussed in the next chapter.

[2] Anselm, *Cur Deus Homo*, I.9, 15–18, 24, II.5, 11. These passages are discussed in David Brown, '"Necessary" and "Fitting" Reasons in Christian Theology', in *The Rationality of Religious Belief: Essays in Honour of Basil Mitchell*, ed. William J. Abraham and Steven W. Holtzer (Oxford: Clarendon Press, 1987), 212–14.

not how salvation is achieved, or that it is achieved at all, nor the Incarnation – either that it needed to happen, given sin, or that it would or would not have happened without sin – or creation, either that it would come to be in the first place, or that it would be as it is.[3] In disavowing the logic of necessity, I wish to be similarly cautious when it comes to speculation about God's dealings with life elsewhere. We cannot reason out what God would do with probative force.

In this, the tradition of 'voluntarism' – which puts an emphasis on divine will and freedom – has something to teach us (for all I am generally more critical of voluntarist impulses than sympathetic). God is free, and his actions are not necessitated. On the other hand, however, radical voluntarism has deficiencies of its own, especially were it to imply that God acts out of uninformed will or rudderless freedom. The divine work is never shapeless, and is at every point stamped by the character of God's own nature.

Were we to deny both rigid necessity and shapeless freedom, a third category comes into focus, with the now familiar idea of suitability, or fittingness. God's actions are always suitable or fitting. The idea is captured admirably in the Latin notion of *convenientia*, in saying that God's actions are *conveniens*.[4] We find the idea across scholastic writing (and earlier, for instance, in

---

[3] For instance, *ST* I.19.3; I.25.6; III.1.2, 46.2; Bonaventure, *Breviloquium*, IV.1.1.

[4] For discussions of this idea, see David Brown, '"Necessary" and "Fitting" Reasons'; Zachary Hayes, 'The Meaning of "Convenientia" in the Metaphysics of St. Bonaventure', *Franciscan Studies* 34 (1974): 74–100; Anthony D. Baker, 'Convenient Redemption: A Participatory Account of the Atonement', *Modern Theology* 30, no. 1 (2014): 96–113; Frederick Christian Bauerschmidt, *Thomas Aquinas: Faith, Reason, and Following Christ* (Oxford: Oxford University Press, 2013), 160–88; Gilbert Narcisse, 'Les Enjeux Épistémologiques de L'argument de Convenance Selon Saint Thomas d'Aquin', in *Ordo Sapientiae et Amoris: Image et Message de Saint Thomas d'Aquin À Travers Les Récentes Études Historiques, Hérméneutiques et Doctrinales. Hommage Au Professeur Jean-Pierre Torell OP À L'occasion de Son 65e Anniversaire*, ed. Carlos-Josaphat Pinto de Oliveira (Fribourg: Éditions universitaires de Fribourg, 1993), 143–67; *ST* I.32.1 *ad* 2.

Athanasius),[5] not least in the discussions of the person and work of Christ in the third part of the *Summa theologiae*, which is elaborated as 'a torrent of suitabilities', as Gilbert Narcisse has put it.[6]

If necessity would tend to close freedom down, and possibility to leave it open, suitability marries freedom with judgement. I wrote in Chapter 4 that God's actions are neither determined nor random: God is free, but what God does is always consistent with who God is.[7] To this, the retort could be made that fittingness ultimately collapses into necessity. It seems reasonable to say that God will always do that which is 'most fitting', which therefore becomes necessary, after all. Here, Aquinas' reply is that while what God does is always something right and even perfect, such perfection is not constrained to take one form, and that form only. No one way of disposing creation would so exhaust the expression of who God is as to leave every other action impossible, with no fitting alternatives. As Aquinas puts it,

> the divine goodness is an end exceeding created things beyond all proportion. Whence the divine wisdom is not so restricted to any particular order that no other course of events could happen. Wherefore we must simply say that God can do other things than those He has done'.[8]

[5] For instance, in Athanasius, *On the Incarnation of the Word*. For a discussion of the idea, and additional references, see Matthias Joseph Scheeben, *Handbook of Catholic Dogmatics: Book Five Soteriology – Part One: The Person of Christ the Redeemer*, trans. Michael Miller (Steubenville, OH: Emmaus Academic, 2020), §208.

[6] Narcisse, 'Enjeux Épistémologique', 146–47, quoted by Paul Gondreau, 'Anti-Docetism in Aquinas's Super Iohannem', in *Reading John with St. Thomas Aquinas: Theological Exegesis and Speculative Theology*, ed. Michael Dauphinais and Matthew Levering (Washington, DC: Catholic University of America Press, 2005), 272. The principal discussions in Aquinas are to be found in SCG IV.53–5 and ST III.1.1. For equivalent discussions in Bonaventure, see *Sermon II on the Nativity* and *In III Sententiarum* d. 1, a. 2, q. 2, *ad* 5, as cited by Ilia Delio, 'Christ and Extraterrestrial Life', *Theology and Science*, 5, no. 3 (2007): 249–65, 254. *Breviloquium* IV.1.1 could equally be described as such a 'torrent'.

[7] SCG II.23–24; ST I.19.3.

[8] ST I.25.5. The responses to *obj.* 2 and 3 are significant, not least in stressing that although God is bound to himself to do that which is fitting to what God has chosen, that does not bind the divine will to have chosen in that way.

Such is the incommensurability between creatures and creator that no created state of affairs could so compel the divine will that no other could be chosen. Approaching this from the side of creation, we might say that the realisation of different combinations of finite creaturely goods are themselves incommensurable, incomparable, and ungradable, such that the idea of a 'best possible world', which God would have to choose, simply does not make sense. Possible worlds, if we were to speak that way, can be differently good in a way that makes it impossible to rank them absolutely, one over or against another.

It has often been noted that invocations of fittingness have an aesthetic register to them. In the words of Paul Gondreau, 'In Thomas's vocabulary ... *conveniens* signifies not only fittingness but also coherence, or even ordered beauty'.[9] The comparison with artistic creations is useful, since a beautiful human work, whether in music, painting, or architecture, will combine the twin traits of freedom and structure. No note or chord is necessitated in Mozart or Messiaen, yet note follows note, chord follows chord, as an unfolding of extraordinary order, clarity, and logic.[10] The same could be said of painting or architecture, especially at their best. Fritz Bauerschmidt has usefully compared arguments approached in terms of logic and of fittingness in these terms:

> The difference between *scientia* and *convenientia* might be thought of in this way: both have to do with a kind of 'seeing', but in the former case one 'sees' in the way that one might see how a geometry proof 'works' by following its argument, while in the latter case

---

[9] Paul Gondreau, 'Anti-Docetism in Aquinas's Super Iohannem', in *Reading John with St. Thomas Aquinas: Theological Exegesis and Speculative Theology*, ed. Michael Dauphinais and Matthew Levering (Washington, DC: Catholic University of America Press, 2005), 272.

[10] I mention these composers precisely because, to me, they illustrate the coinherence of freedom and rightness particularly well.

one sees in the way one might 'see' how a particular piece of art or architecture 'works'.[11]

A crucial difference, Bauerschmidt points out, is that in the former case one could in principle recreate the reasoning oneself in some analytic manner, while in the second case one sees and appreciates the congruence involved 'without being able to create such art or have an exhaustive knowledge of it'.[12]

Uniting Divine Freedom with Necessity

Before moving on, I should note a counterposition in Christianity, more at ease with notions of divine necessity, and uncomfortable with 'could have been otherwise' counterfactuals as to what God might have made, or done. Alongside various precursors, including Gottfried Wilhelm Leibniz and Baruch Spinoza, Friedrich Schleiermacher offers a particularly clear presentation of this position. For him, the theologian must say that freedom and necessity perfectly overlap in God, and that God's willing of the world, indeed even the world as it is, is entailed in God's 'willing of himself' (a phrase that not all other theologians would embrace).

> We must ... think of nothing in God as necessary without at the same time positing it as free, nor as free unless at the same time it is necessary. Just as little, however, can we think of God's willing Himself, and God's willing the world, as separated one from the other. For if He wills Himself, He wills Himself as Creator and Sustainer, so that in willing Himself, willing the world is already included... the necessary will is included in the free, and the free in the necessary.[13]

---

[11] Frederick Christian Bauerschmidt, *Thomas Aquinas: Faith, Reason, and Following Christ* (Oxford: Oxford University Press, 2013), 161–62.

[12] Ibid., 162.

[13] Friedrich Schleiermacher, *The Christian Faith*, trans. H. R. Mackintosh and J. S. Stewart (London: T&T Clark, 1999), §54.4, 217.

Similar ideas animate a recent discussion by David Bentley Hart of central themes in his own thinking, where he writes that in God 'there is no meaningful modal distinction between freedom and necessity ... neither is [the drama of creation and salvation] something external to the divine identity'.[14] For Hart, any presentation of God as a being able to choose between options would fall foul of anthropomorphism, or confuse creator with a creature.

> God is not a finite being in whom the distinction of freedom from necessity has any meaning. Perfect freedom is the unhindered realization of a nature in its proper end; and God's infinite freedom is the eternal fulfilment of the divine nature in the divine life ... [deliberative liberty] is a condition not of freedom as such, but only of finitude ... [and, consequently, since God's freedom is not finite] creation inevitably follows from who he is.[15]

Hart takes it that the idea that creation 'might not have been' is valid only as a comment about its 'ontological contingency', which is to say that it 'has no necessity intrinsic to itself'.[16] It would not mean that the divine act of creating it is contingent, since there is no contingency in God or in God's works. Since God is 'all in all ... no dimension of the divine fullness can be lacking, even the dimension of that fullness expressing itself "beyond itself"'.[17] This seems to run even to creation being as it is.

I certainly wish to take divine simplicity seriously, and to uphold the idea that God is all act, with no potentiality. I am not yet convinced, however, that this requires us to say that creation had

---

[14] David Bentley Hart, *You Are Gods: On Nature and Supernature* (Notre Dame, IN: University of Notre Dame Press, 2022), §12, 105.

[15] Ibid., §25, 115–16.

[16] Ibid., 116.

[17] Hart, *You Are Gods*, §28, 118. See also, §11, 104, and §10, 112. In the later passage, Hart writes that something like the argument above, for divine freedom on the grounds of incommensurable forms of a good creation – albeit presented starkly as 'a voluntarist subject arbitrarily selecting among an infinity of possible worlds' – is to be 'rejected without remainder'.

to be or, even less, that it had to be as it is. I recognise that there is a tension between saying that and saying that God is simple, and act-without-potential. Nonetheless, I note that the tradition has typically felt compelled to affirm both that and a sense that God could have acted differently, not least on scriptural grounds. How this holds together may lie beyond our capacity to know. I similarly recognise that freedom and determination are not incompatible, even for creatures, as when a dancer might seem most to experience freedom in performing a particularly excellent piece of pre-determined choreography. Nonetheless, I am wary of anything that would seem to make creation co-eternal with God (for all it is still entirely derived), or which begins to undermine the asymmetry that creation is determined by God, while God is not determined by creation.

On account of that, I do not think that suitability need collapse into necessity. If the reader disagrees, then what I write below about suitability may need to be taken as a form of necessity after all. It would still retain a strong sense of openness, but that would be the epistemological openness that comes from not being able to fathom the divine ways (which I also wish to stress), but not any more ontological lack of determination of choice in God.

What Shapes the Divine Work?

If God's dealings with creatures are neither formless nor constrained by necessity, what might shape them? Three suggestions might present themselves. I have already mentioned the first, namely that God's actions flow from the divine nature, and are always consistent with it. Richard Hooker (1554–1600) explored this territory in the *Laws of Ecclesiastical Polity*:

> They err therefore who think that of the will of God to do this or that there is no reason besides his will. Many times no reason is known to us; but that there is no reason thereof I judge it most unreasonable to imagine, in as much as he worketh all things *katà tền boulền*

toû thelêmatos autoû, not only according to his own will, but 'the
Counsel of his "own will"'. And whatsoever is done with the counsel or wise resolution hath of necessity some reason why it should
be done; albeit that reason be to us in some things so secret, that it
forceth the wit of man to stand ... amazed thereat.[18]

The first source of shape to divine action, then, is God's own nature.
The second is the nature of the creatures that God has created. We
need to proceed with some caution here since, in an obvious and
important sense, God is not a debtor to anyone. Discussing this
matter, however, Aquinas points out that, in a certain fashion, God
is constrained by the nature of the things he has made, not primarily so as to be bound by his creatures, but rather by himself. Having
created, God becomes a debtor not to the created thing, but to himself, and to his own purpose. It is worth quoting a passage from
Aquinas at some length here, since it develops this second sense of
a shape to divine dealings (shaped from the side of the creature) in
terms of the former and foundational sense of being shaped by the
divine character itself:

In the divine operations debt may be regarded in two ways, as due
either to God, or to creatures, and in either way God pays what is
due. It is due to God that there should be fulfilled in creatures what
His will and wisdom require, and what manifests His goodness. In
this respect, God's justice regards what befits Him; inasmuch as He
renders to Himself what is due to Himself. It is also due to a created
thing that it should possess what is ordered to it; thus it is due to
man to have hands, and that other animals should serve him. Thus
also God exercises justice, when He gives to each thing what is due
to it by its nature and condition. This debt however is derived from

---

[18] Richard Hooker, *Laws of Ecclesiastical Polity*, I.ii.5 in *The Works of That Learned
and Judicious Divine Richard Hooker: With an Account of His Life and Death by
Isaac Walton*, ed. John Keble, vol. 1 (Oxford: Oxford University Press, 1845), 151,
transliterating the Greek quotation of Eph. 1.11. Hooker's translation follows the AV,
while the NRSV translates this phrase as 'according to his counsel and will'.

the former; since what is due to each thing is due to it as ordered to it according to the divine wisdom. And although God in this way pays each thing its due, yet He Himself is not the debtor, since He is not directed to other things, but rather other things to Him.[19]

On this matter, even the far more voluntarist John Duns Scotus (c. 1266–1308) agreed: 'where creatures are concerned [God] is debtor... to his generosity, in the sense that he gives creatures what their nature demands'.[20]

Aquinas applied these principles to the objection that the Incarnation was inappropriate, since God could have achieved its ends directly by simple exercise of his will, with the advantage that this would achieve its ends 'as quickly as possible', indeed immediately.[21] He responded that while 'God's will suffices for doing all things, nevertheless, the divine wisdom requires that provision be made for the various classes of things in harmony with themselves, for He has suitably established the proper causes of various things'. Consequently, while God was able 'by His will alone to effect in the human race every useful good which we are saying came from God's Incarnation ... nevertheless, it was in harmony with human nature to bring about these useful goods through God made man'.[22]

---

[19] *ST* I.21.1 *ad* 3. Dealing with this in *SCG* II.28–29, Aquinas denied that there is any 'dueness' of justice here 'properly so called' (II.28–29.14). Later, in this response in *ST* I.21, Aquinas made a more acute distinction: God owes nothing to creation by *commutative* justice, but there is a sense in which God owes the *distributive* justice of giving to each creature as is fitting to 'its nature and condition' (*ad* 3). This 'due' does not bind God in any external way, because it is founded on the prior 'due' of God to himself: 'what is due to each thing is due to it as ordered to it according to the divine wisdom'.

[20] John Duns Scotus, *Ordinatio*, IV, dist. 46, translation from *Duns Scotus on the Will and Morality*, trans. Allan Bernard Wolter (Washington, DC: Catholic University of America Press, 1986), 190. Scholars disagree over how strongly voluntarist Scotus was on such matters. See Thomas Williams, 'The Unmitigated Scotus', *Archiv Für Geschichte Der Philosophie* 80, no. 2 (1998).

[21] *SCG* IV.53.3.

[22] *SCG* IV.55.4.

If the reasons for the Incarnation involve 'provision ... for the various classes of things in harmony with themselves', then we can also say (as this second angle of three), quite boldly, that the works of God are also shaped 'at our end', which is to say with the sort of skill of an artist who knows the nature of the material with which she is working. They are shaped at our end, shaped to be suitable or fitting not only in relation to God, the donor, but also in relation to us, the recipient. Of course, we are shaped by the divine wisdom, so, in acting fittingly with respect to us, God is acting fittingly with respect to himself, and his own plans.

So far, we have two of the three aspects that shape the suitability of divine action in all its freedom: fittingness to what God eternally is and fittingness to what God has made us to be. These are both cases of a fittingness *given*: the first fittingness given what God is like, the second given what we are. The former is absolute, the latter derivative. The third angle is also a 'fittingness given', but differently so, since it does not lead from something, but towards it. Here, alongside fittingness given God and given God's creatures, stands fittingness given what God is doing with or for creatures. It is a matter of fitting means, given the end in view. Speaking in Aristotelian terms, God's absolutely free efficient causation is suitably shaped by his own nature as formal cause (our first sense), by the material causation of creatures themselves (our second sense), being the kind of things they are ('out of which' God is achieving his work), and by the final causation that entails God achieving his purpose for creation (our third sense).

As a way into exploring the interweaving of ends and means here, we can note, as David Brown has commented, that the etymology of *convenientia* points to the idea of 'coming together' (he even calls this the 'root meaning').[23] This accords with the definition of suitability (or 'aptness') offered by the young Augustine, at around the age of twenty-six, in a work that was already lost by the time

---

[23] Brown, '"Necessary" and "Fitting" Reasons', 219.

he came to write his *Confessions* (entitled *De Pulchro et Apto*: 'On the Beautiful and the Fitting').[24] According to the definition offered there, beauty can belong to things in themselves, whereas aptness or fittingness pertains to the relation of one thing with another: something is fitting 'because it is well adapted to some other thing' [*quoniam apte accommodaretur alcui*]'.[25] As he went on to write in the *Confessions*, 'I proposed a definition and a distinction between the beautiful as that which is pleasing in itself, and the fitting as that which pleases because it fits well into something else' [*aptum autem, quod ad aliquid accommodatum deceret*]'.[26]

In God's works, the means and the ends are drawn together, as we often find celebrated in patristic and scholastic writing. In this way, the means are not a dispensable way to the ends; they are part of what is to be achieved: not least part of its glory. We can turn back to Leo for examples.

> Humility is assumed by majesty, weakness by power, mortality by eternity, and in order to pay the debt of our condition the inviolable nature was united to a possible nature, so that, as was appropriate for our remedies, one and the same mediator of God and men, the man Christ Jesus, might from the one be able to die and from the other to be unable.[27]

Here, the shape or means of God's dealing with creatures is not simply for the sake of an end; the excellence of the means becomes part of the end itself, part of how the whole thing hangs together, part of its own excellence.

---

[24] *Confessions* 4.13.20, translation from Chadwick, 65. These passages are quoted in Benin, *Footprints of God*, 99–100.

[25] *Confessions*, 4.13.20. We may note the invocation of accommodation here, and in the next quotation.

[26] *Confessions*, 4.15.24, translation from Chadwick, 67.

[27] Leo the Great, *Sermon* 20.2, translation from *Select Homilies for Holy Days and Seasons, Translated from the Writings of the Saints*, vol. 2 (London: James Burns, n.d.), 21, no translator identified.

Aquinas explored these themes in a passage that opens with a quotation from Augustine's *On the Trinity*:

> 'God was able to assume human nature elsewhere than from the stock of Adam, who by his sin had fettered the whole human race; yet God judged it better to assume human nature from the vanquished race, and thus to vanquish the enemy of the human race'. And this for three reasons: First, because it would seem to belong to justice that he who sinned should make amends; and hence that from the nature which he had corrupted should be assumed that whereby satisfaction was to be made for the whole nature. Secondly, it pertains to man's greater dignity that the conqueror of the devil should spring from the stock conquered by the devil. Thirdly, because God's power is thereby made more manifest, since, from a corrupt and weakened nature, He assumed that which was raised to such might and glory.[28]

The means of salvation, through the Incarnation, are integral to the goal.[29] The means are shaped by the end, and in that are part of its good: part of the end itself.

As we have seen in Chapter 15, Thomas' discussion of which divine Person might assume human nature is full of references to *convenientia*, not least in this sense of 'that in which things come together'. The Incarnation of the Son unites relations on Earth to relations in God: the Son of God becomes the Son of Man, such that the Son born eternally of the Father without a mother is born in time of a human mother without a human father.[30] The particular suitability of the Incarnation of the Son is that what is effected in time, among creatures, is particularly congruous with the place of

---

[28] *ST* III.4.6, quoting *De Trinitate* XIII.18(23).

[29] As one aspect of this, the end of salvation is for human beings to be united to God, and in Christ we see human nature perfectly united to God in a personal union Aquinas explores in terms of the intellect in *SCG* IV.54.2. There is a parallel in terms of the will in 54.5.

[30] John of Damascus, *On the Orthodox Faith*, 4.14; *ST* III.3.5, *obj.* 1, 2, and 3.

the Son, as eternally in the Godhead: by 'Him Who is the natural Son', human beings come to 'share this likeness of sonship by adoption'.[31] No fewer than four doctrines are drawn together here: the Son as the Word of the Father, creation as made after the image of the Word, the Incarnation of the Word, and the restoration of the corrupted image through the Incarnation.[32]

It may not be necessary for redemption to be accomplished by one of the same nature as the redeemed, but it has a glory that makes it so appropriate. The question, of course, then still remains as to whether 'nature' here is best understood broadly (God assuming creaturehood for creatures; God in a created rational being for created rational beings) or narrowly (God as human for the sake of humanity, perhaps with other, parallel Incarnations).

Speaking of the topic of other Incarnations in terms of suitability relieves us of any need to say what God would or would not do in concrete detail. We do not know what divine dealings with any other life would look like. That need not involve complete agnosticism, however, and in what has just been discussed I have set out what I take to be three characteristics of divine *convenientia* that we might expect to characterise God's dealings elsewhere, even if we know nothing of the details: that they will be supremely representative of the character of who God is, that they will be artfully accommodated to the created natures involved, and that there will be an equally artful going beyond mere instrumental means, such that the manner by which God deals with things becomes part of the glory of the ends achieved, or indeed part of the end itself.

When, therefore, we find Aquinas writing that the work of Christ is sufficient to redeem many worlds, I find no reason to disagree, as a straightforward theological statement:

---

[31] *ST* III.3.8.

[32] The rest of this article deserves attention, for instance, the discussion of the suitability of the image being restored by the Word as both exemplar and original 'craftsman'.

It is clear that the grace of Christ ... is infinite in its influence ... so that the grace of Christ is sufficient not merely for the salvation of some men, but for all the people of the entire world: 'He is the offering for our sins; and not for ours only, but also for those of the entire world', and even for many worlds, if they existed.[33]

No other Incarnation is necessary. I take this both to be true, but also not to preclude other Incarnations, since there is a largess to the acts of God that goes beyond the minimum necessary to the gloriously fitting.

Multiple Incarnations: The View from Elsewhere

If the Incarnation is simply a means, and redemption is procedural, then it *need* only happen once, in one place, and that could be that: if, for instance, one thought that some blood had to be spilt, or a life be rendered up. I take it, however, that the Incarnation and redemption are more splendid and interwoven than that approach would suggest. It matters that the Incarnation, and all that prepares for it and follows on from it, is a drama into which human life, history, and culture is gradually drawn. In particular, I take it that Incarnation and redemption are about putting things right in and through the very nature that has proven so full of wickedness. Moreover, Incarnation and redemption, as we know them, are about God drawing close, indeed more than close: coming among us as one of us, drawing us into the mode of love known as friendship.

---

[33] *Commentary on the Gospel of John*, ch. 3, lect. 6, n. 544, commenting on John 3.34, and here quotes 1 John 2.2. The passage is discussed by Edward Oakes in *Theology of Grace*, 240, n. 25. Aquinas makes the same point in commenting upon Col. 1.24 in his *Commentary on Colossians* (lect. 6): 'the blood of Christ is sufficient for redemption, even of many worlds' (ed. Daniel A. Keating, trans. Fabian R. Larcher (Naples, FL: Sapientia Press, 2006)).

My openness towards the idea of multiple Incarnations rests on those considerations. It may be possible for God to communicate to another species that he has entered into created life and culture by entering into that of another species of rational animal: human beings. It might be possible for them to identify with us and see that 'flesh hath purged what flesh had stained', even if that involved the flesh of human beings, and not their own.[34] They might delight that God has become the friend of creatures by taking up human nature. All that might be so, but it seems to me significantly different from what it feels like to inhabit the Christian story as a human being. If the shoe were on the other foot, with a single Incarnation elsewhere, and the story of redemption and union with God were presented to us only as a set of facts about a far-off place, that would not have the same texture or appeal as the Word becoming flesh, as a human being, and dwelling among us on Earth. It would be very different to open the Gospel of Luke and to read not 'In the sixth month the angel Gabriel was sent by God to a town in Galilee called Nazareth, to a virgin engaged to a man whose name was Joseph, of the house of David. The virgin's name was Mary', but instead 'A long time ago in a galaxy far, far away ...' (as in the opening credits of the Star Wars films).[35]

Such considerations might apply all the more forcefully if we imagine that rational life elsewhere would have very different bodily forms and ways of life from us, and especially if one accepts that these would ground their cognition and thought, rendering it significantly different from our own. In such a context, it may be that our Gospel story would read to them as 'A long time ago in a galaxy far, far away, something that you cannot conceptualise happened to a sort of creature that you cannot imagine ...' That is so different from what unfolds for us in the Gospels, which are intelligible

[34] *Aeterne Rex altissime*, office hymn for the Ascension, fifth century, often associated with Ambrose, trans. J. M. Neale.
[35] Luke 1.26–27.

because they are human stories, told by human beings for other human beings. This is not to impugn God as the perfect communicator. God could tell the story of Christ to another species as perfectly as that tale could be told to them, but that would not stop it being the tale of God entering our story, not theirs, as a human being among human being, or of this being God taking up specifically human flesh, not theirs. It seems to me that God cannot make the story about one species be a story about another, any more than God can make a square circle. There might be analogies and metaphors for another species that would speak to them of God-in-Christ, but the difference is all important: for them the hypostatic union would be communicated to their minds as an idea; for us it has been communicated as flesh in the Virgin's womb.[36]

I entirely accept that one Incarnation could redeem the whole cosmos, and I see grace as having priority over creaturely decision, and redemption as grounded in the ontology Christ's actions, not the epistemology of creaturely understanding, such that Christ's work would not depend on the enlightenment of creaturely intellects. Any creature, even all creatures, could benefit from Christ's work without having to understand it. I emphasise the impediment to communication that comes from Incarnation in a different species not because I think that the work of the Incarnation can be reduced to communication, but because communication is nonetheless important. As the ancient Eucharistic preface for Christmas has it, in Christ as human being, we human beings see God made visible humanly:

---

[36] The only way around this would be if we could say that human beings and that other species have so much in common that our story is also directly their story: for instance, if one could say that they recognise it as the story of God taking on their nature as rational animals. However, would not much that makes for identification in a story, that makes for real sharing or participation, come down to things that would probably differ significantly: modes of living and dying, forms of sociality, eating and drinking, sickness and health? Nonetheless, if rational, embodied life anywhere else shares the same modes of being as us, perhaps a single Incarnation here could have a direct and intimate communicative sense there too.

for through the mystery of the Incarnation of the Word, the light of your glory has newly shone upon the eyes of our mind, so that, while we know God visibly, by him we are drawn to love of what we cannot see.[37]

Could an intelligent creature of a different species elsewhere in the universe see God 'made visible' in Jesus Christ, through stories retold, be they in words, visions, or even holograms? I can see reasons for doubting how much a human life and story could speak to another species in that way. In contrast, in Jesus, God came to be seen, heard, even handled by human beings.[38] The message to another species, however, would be that in Jesus, the Son had been seen, heard, and touched by us, and not by them, standing at an extreme distance not only of space, and perhaps time, but also of bodily comprehensibility. That seems to me to risk making the Incarnation precisely what it has not been for us: a message from afar.[39]

---

[37] *Quia per incarnati Verbi mysterium, nova mentis nostrae oculis lux tuae claritatis infulsit: ut dum visibiliter Deum cognoscimus, per hunc in invisibilium amorem rapiamur (Missale Romanum et Anglicum: Ordo Missae* (Birmingham: C. Goodliffe Neale, 1966), 14–15, my translation. Aquinas makes this point in *ST* III.1.1, *sed contra*. 'It would seem most fitting that by visible things the invisible things of God should be made known; for to this end was the whole world made, as is clear from the word of the Apostle (Romans 1.20) … But, as Damascene says, by the mystery of Incarnation are made known at once the goodness, the wisdom, the justice, and the power or might of God' (going on to quote John of Damascus, *On the Orthodox Faith*, III.1).

[38] 1 John 1.1–3. We might also point to Acts and ask whether a report at a distance would align with a divine intention that it should be that 'each one heard them speaking in the native language of each' (Acts 2.6). We might also note that God was not simply seen in Jesus, but seen 'face-to-face'. John Robinson entitled his work on Christology *The Human Face of God* (London: SCM, 1973), and John Paul II used this image in his liturgical reflection of 11 January 2004: Jesus is 'the human face of God and the divine face of man' (*Ecclesia in America*, §67).

[39] That was what led Pierre Teilhard de Chardin to write trenchantly that 'the hypothesis of a special revelation, in some millions of centuries to come, teaching the inhabitants of the system of Andromeda that the word was Incarnate on Earth is just ridiculous. All that I can entertain is the possibility of multi-aspect Redemption, which would be realised on all the stars' ('Fall, Redemption, and Geocentrism', 44).

Ted Peters has written that

> Perhaps we should distinguish two types of Christology: a revelatory Christology versus an atoning-work Christology. On the one hand, an astrochristology which emphasizes that Jesus is primarily revelatory would find it logical to affirm multiple incarnations. As revelatory, the cosmic Christ could appear to many rational civilizations with the same message. On the other hand, an astrochristology which emphasizes that Jesus's work of atonement is efficacious for the entire creation would find it logical to affirm a single incarnation. The soteriological work accomplished on Earth would apply to the cosmos regardless of who knows or does not know about it.[40]

His point holds: the more one supposes that the result of Incarnation is communication, the more important it becomes that creatures know about it; the more one places the emphasis on results that are achieved whether one knows about them or not, the less necessary widespread communication becomes. Why should that communication be by means of Incarnation to other species? Because, I have argued here, Incarnation is the form of communication supremely fitting for a particular nature, and therefore multiple Incarnations, into different natures, would seem to be the supremely fitting way to communicate most fittingly to such a range of natures.

Few theologians today are likely to favour an account of Christ's work that runs only to teaching, but even in respect to an approach focussing on redemption as ontological change, knowledge of God's solidarity with us in our nature is not insignificant. Just as it is supremely appropriate for God to have communicated to us as one of us, so it is supremely appropriate that the one redeeming should be of the same nature as the ones being redeemed. Examining Peters' comment about a single Incarnation, the logic seems to be one of necessity: 'Jesus's work of atonement is efficacious for the entire

---

[40] Ted Peters, 'Astrobiology and Astrochristology', *Zygon* 51, no. 2 (June 2016): 484–85.

creation', so no other is needed.[41] On the less parsimonious logic of suitability, however, what is merely sufficient as a means may not be enough for God. In that regard, therefore, while I am willing to say that God will do what God will do, nonetheless, in as much as we might sit on Earth and wonder, I can at least see why multiple Incarnations might be the abundantly fitting way.

In much that I have written so far, I have tried to hold a balance, recognising that writing on the work of Christ, and on multiple Incarnations, has often been set out in terms of redemption for sin, while also pointing out that the work of Christ is more than remedial. A wide range of traditions understand this in terms of theosis: as a participation in God by grace that far outstrips anything that would belong by nature to even a sinless creature.[42] With that in mind, the topic of Incarnation (multiple or singular) is not restricted to situations where a restoration from sin is in view, and I will move to consider the case of a sinless species in the final chapter of this section.

---

[41] Although Peters sets that out in terms of remedy, questions about what would simply suffice, and what might be even more appropriate than that, also apply to such gifts of grace that Incarnation would bring to an unfallen race. That, in turn, reminds us that Incarnation can offer, even to a sinful race, more than only remedy.

[42] For a detailed survey, see Andrew Hofer, Pavel L. Gavriljuk, and Matthew Levering, eds., *Oxford Handbook of Deification* (Oxford: Oxford University Press, 2023).

17 | The Dealings of God with Unfallen Creatures

Having considered the dealings of God with fallen creatures, I conclude this section by returning the other branch of the distinction I made at the beginning of this section of the book, between God's dealings with sinful and sinless species. While the tendency in theological writing about astrobiology has been to assume that the Incarnation enters the picture only in relation to fallen creatures, recognition that this need not be so broadens the discussion significantly. Given the fruit of the Incarnation was not only redemption from sin but also deification, this would have been just as good a place to have started. Among the avenues that could follow from that, I will concentrate on two, each in its way about giving first place to Christ. One asks whether the ecclesial vision of God united to a species as its head makes sense – or adds something – outside a picture of sin and restoration (to which it has been joined in the human case). The other avenue asks what implications follow from taking the Incarnation (or more than one Incarnation) to be the purpose of creation: whether that 'priority of Christ' is augmented, or diminished, by talking about more than one Incarnation.

Little Christian theology today would deny that human beings are not simply restored to some putative pre-fallen state by the work of Christ, but are also raised to a dignity beyond that imagined even at the beginning (in whatever sense we understand that 'beginning' to apply). This contention lies behind the striking idea of the *felix culpa*, mentioned in Chapter 10: that the dignity of the redeemed human being is such – over and above any state of innocence, whether real, or of an imagined or structural significance – that the liturgy can acclaim even the Fall as a 'happy' part of that unfolding story.

Central to this is the remarkable new dignity conferred on human beings by God's assumption of human nature in Christ. Adam and Eve, in the story at the beginning of Genesis, are God's creatures. That is a glorious thing, but it is greater still to share a nature with the Incarnate Son of God, and in that way to be God's child. A distinction will often be made here between human beings in general and those who are brought into relation with God through baptism. To belong to the Church is to belong to the body of Christ. It is to be united to God, through Christ, in a way that exceeds any pre- or unfallen state. Baptism marks the difference between being a creature of God, even a creature made in the image of God, and being God's child.

The Destiny of Non-Fallen Rational Beings

With the idea of unfallen species before us, we can usefully remember that Christian traditions have had things to say about a possible (but forfeit) elevation of a primordial unfallen humanity above its initial state. Augustine, for instance, imagined a confirmation in health and conferral of incorruptibly, had our first parents chosen differently. He distinguished between humans as at first 'ensouled', with the future prospect of being 'enspirited': Adam was 'still to be admitted, if he lived obediently, to the company of the angels, with his body changed from being "ensouled" to being "enspirited"'.[1] Before this transformation, human beings would have been preserved from disease or aging by eating from the Tree of Life. Thus, although in an earlier work Augustine had written that 'only after sin did the human body begin to be fragile and subject to decay

---

[1] Augustine of Hippo, *City of God*, book 13, ch. 1; 'Literal Meaning of Genesis', XI.18.24, 441–42.

and destined to die',[2] by the time he wrote the *Literal Commentary on Genesis* he had reached a position later endorsed by Aquinas: that human beings are naturally mortal, but that a gift from God – by eating from the Tree of Life – would have kept them from death, disease, or aging.[3] Nonetheless, for Augustine, and again for Aquinas, even this augmented state of incorruption was not the ultimate destiny for human beings, which would have involved a transformation perhaps somewhat more akin to the resurrection of the dead.[4] For Aquinas, human beings were created to live in the Earthly Paradise only for 'the whole of their animal life', before translation into the empyrean heaven, which is 'highest of corporeal places, and is outside the region of change'.[5] Significantly, however, for the argument in this chapter, even that elevation would not be the same as the union with God achieved by the joining of human nature to God through hypostatic union.

A first distinction, then, among options in respect to unfallen creatures is to ask whether those creatures would be exalted beyond their natural state, followed by a question as to whether that would look different if achieved by a union of God with the creature through Incarnation.[6] While it is difficult to judge excellence added to excellence, bliss to bliss, in these matters, as we will see in Chapter 18, it seems to me that there is a greater gift

---

[2] *On Genesis: A Refutation of the Manichees*, II.7.8, translation from 'On Genesis: A Refutation of the Manichees', 65.

[3] For Aquinas, human beings are naturally mortal (without the gift of original justice) because 'the human body is composed of contrary elements and, therefore, is corruptible of its very nature' (*Lectures on the Letter to the Romans*, ch. 5, lect. 3, n. 416), with parallels in *Disputed Questions on De Anima*, 8, *Commentary on the Metaphysics*, book 5, lect. 6, no. 833; *De Malo*, 5.5. On why he thinks that human bodies have to be thus, see *ST* I.91.1. I am grateful to Daria Spezzano for these references. In this way, human beings are mortal on the part of their matter, while immortality befits them with respect to the nature of their form (*De Malo*, 5.5, and see *ST* II-II.164.1 *ad* 1).

[4] 'Literal Meaning of Genesis', XI.32.42, 453. Aquinas, *ST* I.102.2.

[5] *ST* I.102.2 *ad* 2 and 102.4.

[6] See also the discussion of a conceived state of 'pure nature' at the end of Chapter 10.

and dignity in attaining to an incorruptible life, and the vision of God, through a means by which God shares one's nature than there is without.

What the Hypostatic Union Adds

Robert Grosseteste deserves to rank highly among writers who have explored the fundamental reason for the Incarnation as lying beyond remedy, and as destined to have been accomplished even if remedy were not needed. Brendan Case has highlighted two particularly appealing examples among his arguments as to why Christ's Incarnation is 'logically prior to the Fall'.[7] One is 'the unsurpassable goodness of a creature which is worthy of worship' which 'makes the ensemble of creatures inestimably more glorious than they would be without the Incarnate One'. Of this, Grosseteste wrote,

> thus, since the flesh of Christ is not at all to be counted as outside the creaturely universe, the creatures of the universe have in the flesh of Christ, which is worthy of worship, a gloriousness inestimably greater than they could have, were the Word of God never incarnate … The creaturely universe is more glorified in the flesh assumed by the Word, I might even say, ignited by the deity of the assuming Word, although the other creatures are not themselves ignited, than it could be glorified without this.[8]

The other argument is that the completeness of creaturely (here, human) beatitude involves not only seeing God immaterially as God, but also in seeing him with our creaturely senses, as having come among us in the flesh: 'This was the whole good of humanity,

[7] Brendan Case, "'More Splendid Than the Sun": Christ's Flesh among the Reasons for the Incarnation', *Modern Theology* 36, no. 4 (October 2020): 758.

[8] *De Cessatione Legalium* 3.1.8, translation from ibid., 764.

that whether they were coming in or going out, they would find pasture in their maker, pasture outwardly in the flesh of the Savior, pasture inwardly in the divinity of the Creator'.[9]

Such discussions as to whether an unfallen race could receive the dignity and benefit of an Incarnation relate (as we have seen) to the perspective of 'Incarnation anyway' (explored recently rather brilliantly from a largely Protestant perspective, by Edwin van Driel).[10] In Grosseteste, as generally in the past, the idea was entertained as a counterfactual: not as an exploration of what happens elsewhere, but as what might have happened for human beings had they not sinned. For our purposes, the idea can effectively be transposed from a realm of alternative Earthy possibilities into one of parallel species, separated by time and space.

One possibility is that an unfallen race would be united to God through Christ on Earth. The language of 'united to' here – participatory language – throws the emphasis on the ontological consequences of God's Incarnation in Christ, parallel to an 'ontological' model of redemption, based on God raising and vivifying our nature by sharing it, except that this would be worked out here in terms of the elevation of a nature, without the accompanying aspect of rescue: this is theosis without the need for remedy. Such exaltation or theosis for non-human creatures through Jesus Christ has not featured prominently in theological discussions of extraterrestrial life, likely because theologians who place a premium on the effect of the Incarnation as more than remedial, and therefore as being of consequence for an unfallen species as well as to a fallen one, have tended to favour *multiple* 'Incarnations anyway', and so have not explored the effect of a single Incarnation to that end. Nonetheless, even a single Incarnation could be seen as elevating other creatures, including unfallen ones. For the reasons

---

[9] *De Cessatione Legalium* 3.1.22, translation from ibid., 765.

[10] Edwin Chr van Driel, *Incarnation Anyway: Arguments for Supralapsarian Christology* (Oxford: Oxford University Press, 2008).

given in the previous chapter, however, my theological instinct comes down on the side of multiple Incarnations, with respect to unfallen species as for fallen ones.

Departing from Aquinas in Linking Headship to Remedy

I contend that there is much to be said for supposing that other creatures, even ones without need of redemption from sin, are open to exaltation by means of an Incarnation. In this way, they receive great dignity, and a solidarity with God that, in our case, we call being a brother or sister. Strikingly, however, this was not part of Aquinas' imagination, and at least twice he wrote that solidarity, or incorporation into Christ – including the language of Christ as head – belongs squarely to a redemptive scenario. His context in each case was ruling out sexual relations and begetting among creatures in the life of the world to come:

> If after the resurrection there is to be human generation, those who are generated will either be once again corrupted or they will be incorruptible and immortal. But, if they are to be incorruptible and immortal, the awkward consequences are many. First, indeed, one will have to hold that those men are born without original sin, since the necessity of dying is a punishment that follows on original sin. This is contrary to the Apostle's word: "By one man came sin to all and by sin death" (Rom. 5.12). Next, it follows that not all would require the redemption which is from Christ, *and so Christ will not be the head of all men*. And this is contrary to the Apostle's teaching: "As in Adam all die so also in Christ all will live again" (1 Cor. 15.22).[11]

---

[11] *SCG* IV.83.7, emphasis added. The parallel, discussing the same topic in directly comparable ways, comes in *Commentary on the Sentences*, book 2, dist. 31, q. 1, a. 2, *sed contra* 2. Marie George cites these passages in 'Aquinas on Intelligent Extra-Terrestrial Life', *Thomist* 65, no. 2 (2001): 252.

Although I think otherwise, perhaps Christ cannot be the head of the human race unless all are sinners and all are redeemed by him. If so, that needs to be established by argument, and that is missing from Aquinas here. To go from 'As in Adam all die so in Christ will all live again' to saying that unless one has died in Adam, and is restored through Christ's death and Resurrection, Christ cannot be head of humanity, strikes me as a *non sequitur*. Nor does that seem to be implied by discussions of Christ as head elsewhere in Aquinas.[12] Whether or not there are sins to atone for, Christ would be head of humanity by means of having taken up our nature by hypostatic union, and being God-as-king in our flesh.

Much would rest on whether being part of the Church as the body of Christ is only conceivable in terms of redemption. For Aquinas, the conditions and degrees of corporate, ecclesial union with Christ run from degrees that show only a potentiality for union, on to union by faith, then by charity, and finally being united to Christ by glory, as the summit and fulfilment of union.[13] It strikes me that all of that could be established by the hypostatic union (and, if relevant, by other Incarnations), without sin or redemption from sin having to be in the picture. In fact, in the article where Aquinas discusses this, we see the root of the fallacy of linking headship with redemption. His *sed contra* reads, '"He is the propitiation for our sins, and not for ours only, but also for those of the whole world" (1 John 2.2). Now to save men and to be a propitiation for their sins belongs to Christ as Head. Therefore Christ is the Head of all men'.[14] To say, however, that Christ redeems as head does not mean

---

[12] Consider the discussion of Christ as Head of the Church, or of Christ as head with respect to human bodies (*ST* III.8.1 and 2), both of which open angles on headship that are not reliant on remedy. The definition of headship in III.8.6 *sed contra* also clearly runs to more than remedy: '"The head" of the Church is that "from which the whole body, by joints and bands being supplied with nourishment and compacted groweth unto the increase of God" (Col. 2.19)'.

[13] *ST* III.8.3.

[14] *ST* III.8.3 *sed contra*. He also quotes 1 Tim. 4.10.

that his role as head involves only redemption, or that it extends only as far as the redeemed. By the law of the logical contrapositive, we cannot go from 'All who are redeemed are redeemed by virtue of Christ's headship' to 'All who come under Christ's headship do so by way of redemption'.

Significantly, in these discussions Aquinas goes out of his way to equate the grace by which Christ is head of the Church with the grace of Christ by virtue of the hypostatic union, saying that the latter has priority, and is the font of the former.[15] In as much as one can imagine that any creature, even without sin, could be elevated by grace to a more-than-natural state (and any Thomist would acknowledge that), I can see no reason why that might not come through Incarnation, and that creatures receiving that gift in that way would also receive the benefit of an incorporation into Christ (or another Incarnation, if that were to be what we are considering).

The Priority of Christ

The principle that the work of Christ is about more than remedy suggests either that the Incarnation in Jesus of Nazareth could be significant for non-fallen species (if there is only one Incarnation), or that thought of additional Incarnations, into unfallen species, is worth having in mind. That latter route considers additional Incarnations as not being contingent upon sin.[16] It is instructive to note a tension here, however, that in placing such emphasis on the Incarnation, the very traditions that have wanted to see it as more than simply a response to sin may also be oriented away from the

---

[15] *ST* III.8.4. Although these two accounts of the grace of Christ are equated, Aquinas adds that they can still properly be distinguished.

[16] Richard Cross attributes the origins of this 'minority tradition' as to the 'motive for the incarnation' to Rupert of Deutz (c. 1075–1229/30), citing *De gloria et honore filii hominis super Matthaeum*, 13 (*Duns Scotus* (Oxford: Oxford University Press, 1999), 127).

idea of there being more than one. The Christocentrism of Barth, for instance, suggests that. It may be possible to interpret that Barthian emphasis mainly in an epistemological sense: that our *concern* is to focus on God revealed to us in Christ, and speculation about God's dealings with other creatures is to be avoided. God could act in other ways elsewhere, but that is not for us to think about. More likely, however, Barth's emphasis on the identification between God and Jesus Christ will be taken to be more absolute, more ontological, defining God's work, even defining God himself, rather than being a matter of epistemological limitation or discipline.

Franciscan writing of the high to late Middle Ages also placed such emphasis on Incarnation as to make all else secondary. John Duns Scotus was a leading exponent, holding that God's becoming human in Jesus was always the highest plan for creation, quite separate from whether human beings had ever sinned or needed redemption:

> so far as priority of the objects intended by God is concerned, the predestination of anyone to glory is prior by nature to the prevision of sin or damnation of anyone … So much the more is this true of the predestination of that soul [Christ's] which was destined beforehand to possess the very highest glory possible.[17]

That language of Christ's soul is useful here, since it allows us to talk about the particularity of Jesus Christ, marked out by his soul, while

---

[17] John Duns Scotus, *Ordinatio*,III, d. 7, q. 3, translation (with facing Latin) from Allan Wolter, 'John Duns Scotus on the Primacy and Personality of Christ', in *Franciscan Christology*, ed. McElrath, 139–82, here p. 149, quoted by Oakes, *Theology of Grace*, 236–37. For an analysis of the argument, see Cross, *Scotus*, 127–29. Bonaventure discusses the supreme fittingness of the Incarnation of the Son in, for instance, *On the Reduction of the Arts to Theology*, nn. 12–20. In the assessment of Ilia Delio, 'Unlike other thinkers of his time, Bonaventure did not ask whether the Word would have become incarnate had Adam not sinned. He did ask, however, what the *ratio praecipua* of the Incarnation might be and in his answer he tried to avoid anything external to God necessitating the divine in any way' (Ilia Delio, 'Revisiting the Franciscan Doctrine of Christ', *Theological Studies* 64, no. 1 (February 2003): 10–11).

remaining within the Christological conviction that his Person, by whose being that soul exists as a particular human soul, is the Person of the Son.

Oakes addressed the priority of Christ in terms of exobiology in *A Theology of Grace in Six Controversies*. He recognised that it is important not to expect direct responses from the first-century text of the New Testament to questions that it was not written to answer.[18] For example, I agree with his caution regarding the Johannine expression 'of the whole world' in 1 John 2:2 – 'Christ is the atoning sacrifice for our sins; and not only for our sins but the sins of the whole world [*holou tou kosmou*]'. As Oakes puts it: 'what does kosmos mean here in this context: our world or the world of extraterrestrial intelligent life? Since the question never arose in the first century, the verse, taken alone, cannot be probative'.[19] In the more doctrinal register of the 'priority of Christ', however, Oakes does think that it is possible to say that the universe was created for the sake of the glory of Jesus Christ – that one divine human being – without any necessary reference to sin or redemption. He traces this back, through Scotus, to Colossians: '"All things were created through him and for him"... which gives a retrospective plausibility to the interpretation that holds that Christ's atoning sacrifice applies to all conceivable worlds'.[20] Working with a Franciscan-influenced view in this respect, Oakes is committed to Jesus Christ being the sole redeemer of the whole universe.

While I am no Scotist, I do follow Scotus in the territory of 'Incarnation anyway'. We can usefully turn to the specificity of his claim that Christ was predestined for the highest possible glory. A discussion of what 'highest possible' means here might mirror the discussion of 'uniqueness' in Chapters 8 and 9: it could mean the highest possible for a human being, but not preclude other

---

[18] Oakes, *Theology of Grace*, 240.

[19] 1 John 2:2, Oakes, 240.

[20] Col. 1.16; Oakes, 240.

Incarnations, or it could mean the highest such that there could be no parallels. As in the earlier discussion, I would follow the less competitive interpretation. Even if there are other Incarnations, it would remain true that Jesus Christ has been granted, from his conception, the highest possible glory that he could have been granted. That glory would not be lessened if the Word also took up other creaturely natures. Other Incarnations do not stop the soul of Christ having been predestined to the highest glory, especially if we take that to mean 'to the highest glory that a creaturely form could possibly enjoy, namely that of hypostatic union'. A counter-argument might be that redeeming the whole cosmos involves a higher glory than redeeming only one's species, or else that standing alone as the redeemer of all is greater than standing alongside others who also redeem all. In as much as these arguments spring from the theology of Scotus, however, it is instructive to note that he specifically defined the highest glory as independent of being a redeemer or not. It is about the hypostatic union, and Christ is no less who he is on that account, if there are other hypostatic unions. I am also wary of an assumption that sharing involves diminishment.

Behind these various questions lies a divide in emphasis between 'Incarnation' and 'the Incarnation': whether *Incarnation* is the central feature of the history and destiny of the cosmos, recurring as a pattern of God coming to dwell with his people wherever they are, hypostatically uniting their nature to himself, or *the* Incarnation – that God became human in Jesus of Nazareth. In one sense, there may be theological merit in choosing a Person (namely Jesus Christ) rather than something more abstract (a potentially vague 'Incarnational principle') as the more elevated emphasis. On the other hand, speaking about the importance of Incarnation (as a principle) turns out to serve the purpose that an emphasis on 'the Incarnation' might be taken to stress: it under-lines that it would be fitting for *all* of God's creatures, and not just humans, to be able to turn to a person, rather than an abstract or foreign idea.[21] Beyond that, given that I think there are other reasons for being open to the idea of many Incarnations, as I discussed in Chapter 16, it may be possible to uphold 'the priority of Christ', but broaden it by saying that the Universe exists for the sake of the full range of Incarnations that God brings about by hypostatic unions, and that the highest good of the Cosmos lies in that.

Conclusion

In teaching, I have found that attention to questions around God's dealings with an imagined sinless species of rational animals opens up some profitable questions, not least in provoking us to think about how the working of grace among humans can involve more than rescue, taking in a destiny and elevation beyond anything that could belong to nature. We might have thought that the current interest in theosis across traditions, which has been building a head of steam for some time now, might have pointed in this direction. As of yet, however, discussions of exobiology and soteriology seem generally not to have caught up, and rescue and remedy alone typically set the running.

The topics we have covered in this chapter also raise useful questions about the priority of Christ. We have considered, in particular, whether we should talk about that in terms of the priority of the God-man Jesus Christ, or in terms of the priority of Incarnation – here entertained as having occurred more than once – as the goal of creation, marking God's ultimate act of friendship with creatures.

I have also suggested that the place of the hypostatic union in deification is worth looking at again, as is the headship of Christ (or of another Incarnation) as a gift to a sinless species. It is perhaps surprising that a theologian as committed to ideas of theosis

---

[21] I am indebted to Austin Stevenson for putting it this way.

as Aquinas seems to have associated that union and that headship rather exclusively with a paradigm of remedy for sin. In contrast, I would stress that, since they bring elevation as well as remedy to human beings, they would apply, and confer a distinctive grace, even outside of a need to address sin.

Those themes have turned out to offer good examples of the difference between a theological approach based in notions of suitability and one worked out more primarily in terms of possibility and necessity. From those latter perspectives, one can say that the goods of human redemption could come without Christ being made the head of humanity by hypostatic union: salvation was possible without; these angles were not necessary. In contrast, an approach based in suitability will be less willing to separate means from ends and, as I have set it out here, will see those means as an important part of the glory of the ends that are achieved.

Having worked through themes of Incarnation from several angles in the past few chapters, we turn in the final section to eschatology. We will find that the position one takes on multiple Incarnations is of considerable consequence, especially in terms of what one might say about when it is that God might call time on history, in relation to the span of time during which there will be human beings on Earth.

Part V | Eschatology

Among the principal topics in Christian theology, eschatology may seem to offer the least complicated integration with the prospect of life elsewhere in the universe. Just as the doctrine of creation already takes in everything that exists, precisely because it deals with existence *per se*, so eschatology also already has everything in view, in relation to God as goal, judge, and fulfilment. How that bears upon irrational creatures is contested. Much traditional Christianity has held that they have no future beyond this world. God stands as their goal in the sense that their natural good, which they intrinsically seek, represents a particular form of participation in God as the source of all good.[1] If exobiology amounts only to other non-rational life, that would not change this picture or, if our theology could expand to include an eschatological future for non-sentient creatures on Earth, it could then also take in non-sentient life elsewhere. When it comes to sentient creatures, Christian theology has typically set out their end in terms of the beatific vision (alongside the possibility of hell). At least in broad outline, none of that should be difficult to explore in relation to other sentient life in the cosmos.

Eschatology, therefore, like creation, seems naturally able to take in astrobiology, since it naturally serves to gather together. Indeed, in one sense eschatology promises an even more perfect integration of creatures than does the doctrine of creation. Creation could contain many different forms of rational being, but spread far apart in time and space, and therefore unaware of each other. The

---

[1] *SCG* I.82. See my *Participation in God*, 58–59.

eschaton, however, would bring them together, allowing sentient creatures – perhaps in their common vision of God – to rise to a new awareness of one another. In the new creation, a previously unknown commonality among creatures would become known and celebrated.

Historically, eschatology has not been considered in relation to astrobiology as widely or as deeply as we might expect.[2] Among those for whom it has been in view, it has stood for one author as the chief glory of what other life has to offer to our theological picture, while for another, it underlies its chief problem. In the former case, I have in mind Alice Meynell, whose theological poem on astrobiological themes, 'Christ in the Universe', we have already encountered. In it, she imagines creatures from across time and space meeting in the life of the world to come. Encountering one another, they compare notes about God's dealings with them. In Meynell's imagination, their wonder centres most of all on news of other Incarnations, and the stories that go along with them: 'His pilgrimage to thread the Milky Way', and the 'myriad forms of God those stars unroll'. The human task in that is to 'show to them a man'. In contrast, such an eschatological meeting lies at the heart of Brian Hebblethwaite's *rejection* of multiple Incarnations, and his conclusion that discovery of intelligent life elsewhere in the universe would be the undoing of Christian theology.[3] As we have seen, in the previous section of this book, for him it would seem absurd for the Word Incarnate in one species to come into the resurrected physical presence of the Word Incarnate in another. In Chapter 16, I discussed why that does not disturb me as it disturbs him.

---

[2] Note, for instance, its near complete absence from the essays surveying doctrinal themes in Peters et al., *Astrotheology: Science and Theology Meet Extraterrestrial Life*, and brief treatment of a few eschatological themes by O'Meara in Thomas O'Meara, *Vast Universe*, 57–61. David Wilkinson devotes two pages to eschatology in *Search for Extraterrestrial Intelligence*, 169–71.

[3] Hebblethwaite, 'Impossibility of Multiple Incarnations'.

Those topics address what we could call the 'nature of the final state', as one principal domain for thinking eschatologically about life elsewhere in the universe. In as much as eschatology has featured in theological discussions of astrobiology, this is what has received attention. Astrobiology also brings another aspect of eschatology into focus, however, and, as far as I can tell, it has received little attention, if any. It asks not so much about the nature of the final state as about the form of its arrival: about how, and especially *when*, it happens. Christian theology has typically taught that the cosmos will not end by virtue of its own natural processes, but with a divine interruption of history. Quite reasonably, up to now, it has taken that to be an irruption within the span of human history. However, if humanity, Earth, and the human story are not unparalleled in the history of the cosmos, that assumption may need to be challenged. Astrobiology therefore forces us to think eschatologically not only about the nature of the final state, to which I will turn first in what follows, but also about the manner of its arrival, and the mode and time of its accomplishment. Taking the prospect of life elsewhere in the universe seriously is likely to be more disruptive of the latter question, at least if we approach it having come to think that God's dealings with life on other planets would not be subservient to God's dealings with our own. I will take up that issue in the final chapter.

18 | The Final State

If we take widespread sentient life in the universe as a serious possibility, at least two broad sets of questions present themselves about the nature of the world to come: how various sorts of creatures relate to God, and how they relate to each other. These will be our themes in this chapter, in which I will address a topic necessarily shrouded in mystery: the state of the life of the world to come. Among the traditional theological topics that I hope will be enriched by that discussion are the nature of our beatifying 'vision' of God, the meaning of the Ascension, and the role of the saints in the human drama of salvation.

Of those two questions – the eschatological relation to God and that to other creatures – the former ultimately poses few problems. Our traditional language would need some expansion, and we will look at that, but it is not likely to be difficult. Responsible theological thinking about eschatology will already be aware of its own limitations when it comes to the descriptions offered. Indeed, it is a central conviction of Christian theology that

> no eye has seen, nor ear heard,
> nor the human heart conceived,
> what God has prepared for those who love him.[1]

Eschatology does not lend itself to precision when it comes to detail. The Congregation of the Doctrine of the Faith of the Roman Catholic Church, which is not a body known for any attachment to

---

[1] 1 Cor. 2.9.

inexactitude, made that point well in 1979. Their 'Letter on Certain Questions Concerning Eschatology' lists 'the fundamental truths of faith' on that topic as rather few in number. These run to 'the resurrection of the dead', as an extension of Christ's Resurrection to others, body as well as soul; the survival of a 'spiritual element' (the soul) between death and general resurrection; an attitude of expectancy towards 'the glorious manifestation of our Lord, Jesus Christ'; and belief in 'the happiness of the just who will one day be with Christ ... [as well as in] eternal punishment for the sinner, who will be deprived of the sight of God, [and in] the possibility of a purification for the elect before they see God, a purification altogether different from the punishment of the damned'.[2] Beyond these basic themes, the Letter cautions humility, since our imagination cannot grasp what lies beyond this life: 'When dealing with man's situation after death, one must especially beware of arbitrary imaginative representations: excess of this kind is a major cause of the difficulties that Christian faith often encounters'. Emphasis is to be placed upon discerning the 'profound meaning' of 'the images employed in the Scriptures', while nonetheless recognising that 'neither Scripture nor theology provides sufficient light for a proper picture of life after death'.

The Congregation addressed two features of Christian eschatology that are likely to receive widespread support across Christian traditions. One is 'the fundamental continuity, thanks to the power of the Holy Spirit, between our present life in Christ and the future life'. This is expressed in terms of the continued primacy of love: 'charity is the law of the Kingdom of God and our charity on earth will be the measure of our sharing in God's glory in heaven'. The other basic feature is awareness of a 'radical break between the present life and the future one, due to the fact that the economy of faith

---

[2] Sacred Congregation for the Doctrine of the Faith, *Letter on Certain Questions Concerning Eschatology* (Boston: Daughters of St Paul, 1979), §7. Issued by Franjo Cardinal Seper, as Prefect.

will be replaced by the economy of fullness of life'. The Letter goes on to say that 'Our imagination may be incapable of reaching these heights, but our heart does so instinctively and completely'.

Among that which we cannot now know fall questions about the relation between continuity and discontinuity in how much the life of the world to come will resemble the present life. That bears directly on the question of how different creatures might relate to one another in the new creation. We do not know, for instance, whether to think of a distribution in space or place that is comparable to our current experience, or of what form. Certainly, in talking about the final state, Christian theology is not concerned with a cohort of disembodied souls but with an ensemble of resurrected bodies. That already suggests both continuity and discontinuity:

> So it is with the resurrection of the dead. What is sown is perishable, what is raised is imperishable. It is sown in dishonour, it is raised in glory. It is sown in weakness, it is raised in power. It is sown a physical body, it is raised a spiritual body. If there is a physical body, there is also a spiritual body.[3]

What is raised is a body, just as what was sown, but it is sown physical and raised spiritual, sown in dishonour but raised in honour. There is continuity, as a body, but difference in mode or manner.

Beatific Vision, Community, and Other Senses

Exponents of an eschatology that stresses discontinuity may feel that they can avoid having to address questions about the future relation of creatures, but those who stress continuity, and wish to set out a vision of that future life in terms of our present experience, would have to grapple with questions of communication and

[3] 1 Cor. 15.42–44.

setting. Among the challenges here is the observation that different forms of life could not necessarily flourish within the same medium or environmental setting. Approaches to eschatology that place the emphasis on the vision of God may wish to account for the knowledge of one creature by another through the mediation of the knowledge of God, as memorably expressed by Gregory the Great, who asked the question 'seeing they do in that place [heaven] with unspeakable brightness (common to all) behold God, what is there that they know not, that know him who knoweth all things?'[4]

While an eschatology focused on the beatific vision is integral to several traditions, the thought of exobiology also serves to remind us of the contingency, or human-specificity, in that language of 'vision' and sight. A range of creatures from across the cosmos would likely embody a range of senses used to apprehend the world around them. Of course, there may be a considerable convergence among them. To use James Gibson's language of 'affordances', wherever light is present, it will afford the possibility of sight; wherever there is air, it will afford the possibility for hearing and smell.[5] Nevertheless, given a wide variety of environments, and the effects of randomness running against convergence, we would also do well to expect the evolution of variety when it comes to the senses. Already, on Earth, we know that sight can be attenuated or absent in species that live in the dark, and that organisms can apprehend the world in ways that go beyond anything that we ourselves possess or can imagine, such as echolocation, deployed by bats and dolphins, and electrolocation, as found in many aquatic animals, including cartilaginous fish (such as sharks and rays), dolphins, and the platypus.

---

[4] Gregory the Great, *Dialogue* IV.33, translation from *The Dialogues of Saint Gregory, Surnamed the Great*, ed. Edmund G. Gardner, trans. Philip Woodward (London: P. L. Warner, 1911). See also Augustine, *De Trinitate*, XV, ch. 4, n. 26, 421. Aquinas endorses these points in *ST* I.12.8 *obj.* 1; *SCG* III.60.5.

[5] On this, see my *Participation in God*, 310–12.

We talk of the beatific vision, but there are modalities of sense beyond sight (as, indeed, there are for human beings) and, as we have noted, if a species evolved in the dark, it would not have sight at all, at least in the narrow sense of viewing the world by detecting photons. That need not upend the core idea of the beatific vision, but it reminds us that the language of 'vision' there is an analogy, metaphor, or synecdoche: the whole being described in terms of a part. Theologians have singled out sight as the most elevated of the senses (Augustine stands as a good example),[6] and yet they have also stressed that whatever we mean by the beatific vision it transcends use of the eye, or any corporeal organ even of the resurrected body. Aquinas quoted Augustine here: 'No one has ever seen God either in this life, as he is, nor in the angelic [future] life, as visible things are seen by corporeal vision'.[7] Indeed, Aquinas thought that 'it is impossible for God to be seen by the sense of sight, or by any other sense, or any faculty belonging to our sensible power [i.e. the human capacity to sense] … God cannot be seen by the sense or imagination, but only by the intellect'.[8] For him, the beatific vision is so much a gift of grace as to involve the direct divine impartation to the knowing mind (by means of the *lumen gloriae*) of that which is to be known or 'seen' – namely God – at a more fundamental level than through any mediation by sight and other senses.[9]

Here then, once again, questions posed by astrobiology help us to clarify what we might think about more specifically human theological questions. In this case, they encourage us to consider how other senses might feed into the beatific 'vision', even for

---

[6] While considering all the senses, and the 'inner sense' as distinct from all of them, Augustine referred to reason as the 'head or eye of the soul' (*On Free Choice of the Will*, II.6, 40); *ST* I.78.3.

[7] *ST* 12.3, *sed contra*, quoting Augustine, *Epistle* 147.11.28. By *in angelorum vita*, I take Augustine and Aquinas to refer to some eschatological state for the human being, not to knowledge of God by angels.

[8] *ST* I.12.3.

[9] *ST* I.12.5, 6.

human beings. Our intellect is informed not only by sight, but by the integrated witness of the senses in combination. As Aquinas put it, human knowledge is grounded in what comes to us as integrated from the senses as a whole (forming the *sensus communis*, or 'common sense').[10] While there may be good reason generally to privilege sight in the ways in which we talk about knowledge and cognition, the intellect works with a synthesis of all the senses. If the beatific vision is imparted directly to the intellect by grace, it informs a faculty constituted by receptivity to the integrated witness of senses, not as one shaped only in terms the reception of sight.[11] We should therefore probably say that God is experienced, in the beatific vision, according to the full symphonic breadth of what the intellect is capable of receiving. In the beatific 'vision', God would be 'heard' and 'touched', 'tasted' and 'smelt', as well as 'seen' or, rather, God will be known in a way that transcends the modality of any one sense. Any different or additional sensory power possessed by another creature with an eternal destiny could readily be taken into this perspective. They, too, would be granted to apprehend God after the fullest, most integrated manner of which their intellects are capable, received into minds shaped by, or for, the particular combination of senses proper to that species.

Accounts of the final state grounded in the beatific vision can easily deal with creaturely variety when it comes to those creatures' relation to God. Their corresponding weakness can be a lack of emphasis on the relation between creatures in the life of the world to come. That already shows itself in the history of Christian

---

[10] *ST* I.77.4.

[11] Of course, not every human being possesses all of the senses, in view of which we have all the more reason to recognise that the intellect is informed by the combined witness of more than one. The question of what theology has to say about the experience of those in the life of the world to come who have not had the exercise of a particular sense in this life is a significant matter, and one in which I defer to those whose expertise lies in that area.

thinking about human eschatological sociality.[12] The principal problem has been how to say that the vision of God fulfils the human being without rendering anything else entirely superfluous, given that the human destiny is a communal destiny, for example, and an embodied one. So, although, for instance, Aquinas held friendship between human beings to be integral to happiness in this life, he nonetheless wrote that 'if we speak of perfect happiness which will be in our heavenly Fatherland, the fellowship of friends is not essential to happiness; since man has the entire fullness of his perfection in God'.[13] The most he could manage to write was that while 'the fellowship of friends is not essential to happiness', since in seeing God the human being has 'the entire fullness of his or her perfection in God', nonetheless 'the fellowship of friends conduces to the well-being of happiness'.[14] Quite what that means goes unaddressed, although it certainly means that there is a fittingness to a social dimension to eternal beatitude, even if it is not thought to be necessary. For my part, I am wary of accounts of the relation of a creature to its creator that are taken to be sufficiently like that between one creature and another to be comparable to the latter. The superlative and transcendent quality of the relation of the creature to the creator, relative to relations between creatures, may allow us to suppose that no comparison or eclipsing contrast should be made between happiness grounded in one and happiness grounded in the other. Attention to long-standing discussions about how the Resurrection of the body can be said to be integral to the happiness of those who enjoy the beatific vision could also offer resources for thinking about the part that sociality might also play.[15]

[12] I have discussed this deficiency in *Participation in God*, 123–26, 131, making reference to Germain Grisez's usefully provocative paper 'The True Ultimate End of Human Beings: The Kingdom, Not God Alone', *Theological Studies* 69, no. 1 (2008): 38–61.

[13] *ST* I-II.4.8.

[14] *ST* I-II.4.5.

[15] This discussion is ably presented in Stephen Yates, *Between Death and Resurrection: A Critical Response to Recent Catholic Debate Concerning the Intermediate State* (London: Bloomsbury Academic, 2017), 215–30.

We may not be able to say a great deal about what a creaturely awareness of other redeemed creatures might look like. Accounts of eschatology that may do a satisfying job when it comes to inter-human contact would not necessarily be able to account for relations across greater creaturely differences, with very different bodily and social lives, and perhaps different forms of intellect. In contrast, although accounts of the future life set out more or less entirely in terms of the vision of God may seem weak in their sense of social relation between creatures, they more easily allow for appreciation of other creatures, despite our differences, on the grounds that those who see God understand all things in the vision of the one who made and knows all things.

A Satirical Parallel from Rupert Brooke

In Chapter 6, we saw Yeats imagine different creatures, with varied perspectives on God, each based on the distinctiveness of what they receive from God as their creator and exemplar. Around thirty years later, Rupert Brooke wrote on similar territory in his poem 'Heaven' (reproduced at the end of this chapter), only in his case undoubtedly with a scepticism, or cynicism, absent from the earlier poem.[16] I turn to Brooke's poem here because it is worked out in explicitly eschatological terms.

Brooke's creatures are fish. As with Yeats, they think of God according to the manner of what they can conceive, namely a piscine one.

> And there (they trust) there swimmeth One
> Who swam ere rivers were begun,
> Immense, of fishy form and mind,

---

[16] Written in 1913, it was first published in the collection *1914 and Other Poems* (London: Sidgwick & Jackson, 1915).

> Squamous, omnipotent and kind;
> And under that Almighty Fin,
> The littlest fish may enter in.

Their vision of a future life is also one suitable for a perfected fishiness:

> But somewhere, beyond Space and Time,
> Is wetter water, slimier slime!

Brooke is gently mocking the idea of a future life as simply an extrapolation of all that is most pleasant in this one: not only 'wetter water' and 'slimier slime' but also 'Fat caterpillars' and 'Paradisal grubs', and various benign absences – 'Oh! never fly conceals a hook,/Fish say, in the Eternal Brook'. His deployment of Biblical images is particularly clever, with the transposition of 'the worm that never dies' from an image of torment in the perpetual consumption of human flesh in Gehenna to one of perpetual foodstuff for fish.[17] But the most damning reference comes in the final couplet: 'And in that Heaven of all their wish,/There shall be no more land, say fish'. This takes up, but inverts, a phrase from the final chapter of Revelation: 'there was no more sea'.[18] In Revelation (as elsewhere in the Bible), the sea stands as a sign of chaos, and is therefore abolished. In the imagined religion of the fish, water is their medium for life, while land represents the element of death, so it is land that is forever set aside. The fun that Brooke is poking hits home because of the absoluteness and incompatibility of the two visions: all land and no water, versus all water and no land.

In his poem, and especially in those final lines, Brooke crystalises a problem for the Christian theologian thinking eschatologically about distinctly different forms of life elsewhere in the universe. In as much as what makes for life in each case is different, and indeed incompatible, how can that be realised simultaneously? The

---

[17] Mark 9.48.
[18] Rev. 21.1 (KJV).

theologian's best response is no doubt one of caution and due to agnosticism as to eschatological detail. It highlights, however, that the more emphasis we place on the distinctive bodiliness of resurrected life, the more questions there are to answer on this front. Perhaps one might simply say that there is varied geography in the new creation.

Insofar as eschatology ought first and foremost to be about union with God, which Brooke's poem is not, rather than the magnification of creaturely delights, his poem falls short in comparison with Yeats'. The fun it pokes is elegantly done, however, and it points to useful themes, not least for our work in this book, even if Brooke is not as theologically acute as Yeats.

Ascension

Also significant for thinking about theology and exobiology is the topic of the Ascension, although not in the rather crude sense of a putatively space-travelling Christ. Whatever is meant by ascending into the heavens, it should be taken as more than a spatial cosmic journey. Rather, if the Ascension opens onto useful material for our discussions here, it is in relation to the closely associated doctrine of the 'session' of Christ: that, as the Apostles' Creed has it, 'He ascended into heaven, and *sitteth* on the right hand of God the Father Almighty'.[19]

Discussion of exobiology encourages us to think about this 'being seated' beyond literal, spatial terms.[20] The notable twentieth-century Thomist Josef Pieper wrote with Heinrich Raskop that sitting at the right hand of God 'must not be taken in a literal, bodily sense. It simply means that the glorified Christ, still Man as well as God, has

---

[19] *Book of Common Prayer*, emphasis added.

[20] In Chapter 7, we saw Thomas Kuhn proposing the presence of other life in the universe would raise questions as to where God's throne is located.

taken permanent possession of His highest kingship and highest kingly authority'.[21] Martin Luther interpreted the phrase in much the same way, as part of his Eucharistic doctrine: the 'right hand' at which Christ sits is not 'an imaginary heaven in which a golden throne stands, and Christ sits beside the Father in a cowl and golden crown, the way artists paint it'.[22] Rather, Luther interpreted the 'right hand of God' according to his notion of the ubiquity of Christ's human body, as discussed in Chapter 14.

> The Scriptures teach us, however, that the right hand of God is not a specific place in which a body must or may be, such as on a golden throne, but is the almighty power of God, which at one and the same time can be nowhere and yet must be everywhere. It cannot be at any one place [and yet] ... it must be essentially present at all places, even in the finest tree leaf ... he himself must be present in every single creature in its innermost and outermost being, on all sides, through and through, below and above, before and behind, so that nothing can be more truly present and within all creatures than God himself in his power.[23]

Even for those rejecting Lutheran notions of ubiquity on Chalcedonian grounds, Luther offers a useful reading of the session, not as a spatial location where only one creature could be present, but as an ascription of honour and power – 'the Scriptures ascribe all miracles and works of God to his right hand'.[24] After all, God the Father does not have a physical right hand.

Keith Ward, for his part, retains a perhaps surprising degree of spatial reference in writing about eschatology, suggesting that Jesus may be king 'of the human sector' of heaven: our 'little corner'.[25]

---

[21] Josef Pieper and Heinz Raskop, *What Catholics Believe*, trans. Christopher Huntington (London: Burns & Oates, 1954), 40.

[22] Luther, 'That These Words', 55.

[23] Ibid., 57–58.

[24] Ibid., 58, citing Acts 5.31; Ps. 118.15f; Acts 17.27f; Rom. 11.36; Jeremiah 23.23f; Isa. 66.1.

[25] Ward, *Christ and the Cosmos*, 140–41.

Perhaps he is not to be taken literally here: perhaps such spatial metaphors are indispensable for human thought, but only intimate what we cannot conceive. Indeed, Ward's eschatology more typically reflects his inclination towards idealism: that after death, for instance, 'biological nature' is 'left behind'.[26]

The Blessed Virgin Mary and Other Saints

Even within the current rather limited eschatological writing on astrobiology, we find occasional comment that the role that has been attributed to some of the saints in the future state, at least within some varieties of Christian theology and piety, may need to be revisited if the cosmos is widely populated with life: Mary as the Queen of Heaven, for instance, or St Peter as its gatekeeper.[27] Of course, these ideas and associations are not universally shared among Christians. Mary's status is not embedded in Protestant thought the same way it is in Catholic and Orthodox doctrine. Moreover, in Orthodoxy, while the Theotokos has an exalted place in piety and doctrine, the image of Mary as Queen is far less prominent than it is in Roman Catholicism. The place of Peter belongs even more to the realm of popular belief – it is a leap to go from the entrustment of the keys to Peter to Peter as the gatekeeper of heaven – although that is not to say that such images should be passed over lightly. There will be Christians for whom the position or role of the saints is a deeply affecting matter, for whom, indeed, a disturbance in these areas may feel more disruptive than in areas in which the systematic theologian might emphasise.

Perhaps the best way to navigate these roles – should we wish to – is to treat them as local or human matters: as part of our story,

---

[26] Ibid., 168.

[27] Kostro, 'Some Philosophical and Theological Implications of Modern Astrobiology', 264; Ward, *Christ and the Cosmos*, 139–41.

as a role in relation to our species. Peter's exceptional status in the Gospels, for instance, is not diminished if we understand the Gospel text to mean that he and his successors have power to bind and loose on Earth, and in heaven *with respect to earthly affairs*.[28] His prerogative to bind and loose (and that of his successors, if they enjoy that right) would apply to the heavenly destiny of Earthly people, but not to the denizens of other parts.

Turning to Mary, we may do well to set the language of queenship aside, since it is a relative latecomer in Mariology, and not shared even by all Christian traditions that accord the Mother of Jesus particularly high honour. If we were to retain it, we could again stress particularity, with Mary as Queen of redeemed humanity. Queenship, or monarchy more generally, is inherently particular: Elizabeth II was my Queen, and no less so because the USA is a Republic, or because someone in the Netherlands or Norway has a monarch of her own. Other Marian roles and honours are squarely grounded in Mary's role in the economy of salvation. To call her *Theotokos*, the God-bearer or Mother of God, is an absolute claim, and again not diminished if God also took a different sort of flesh elsewhere. She remains the one who represented humanity at the Annunciation, the one from whom God took human flesh, the chief human agent, alongside Christ, in the drama of redemption.[29] She would remain *Madonna*: Our Lady. Indeed, that title may be ideally suited for use in a cosmic setting. The shift, if there are other Incarnations, would simply be to say that Mary's response and role belong within the Earthly story, even if there are others.[30]

---

[28] Matt. 16.18–19. Catholic, Orthodox, and Anglican theology will extend that authority, or much of it, to the bishops, and to the priests on whom they confer elements of that authority in turn.

[29] *ST* III.4.6.

[30] The passage from *ST* III.4.6 quoted in Chapter 16 from Aquinas (about a threefold fittingness to redemption having been worked out in Christ as a human being) is cast a little more specifically, in a way that is relevant here. The point there is not simply

Other saints would also retain their place within our particular story, often within the focus of some yet more local or community-specific history. The roles of these saints are already specific, and no less valuable for that. For Benedictines, St Benedict remains their father among the saints, and for Dominicans, St Dominic. Hagiological bonds of affection and association often function that way, and are no less significant just because they are not of equal and universal standing. I am associated with St John of Beverley on account of my place of birth, in a way that I am not associated with St John of Bridlington, a town that lies thirty-five miles to the northeast. Our human communion of saints – our cultures of sanctity, with their variegated patterns of honour and belonging – can happily stand alongside others, even if those involve other species.

Conclusion

I opened this chapter with some comments about circumspection. I am wary of proceeding too far when it comes to speculation about the state of the life of the world to come. That judgement, however, is a subjective one, and some readers may think that I have already pressed too far, while others might wish for those explorations to have gone further.

Our theological traditions do offer some bearings when it comes to the future life, however, for instance, in the Resurrection of the body, God as the fulfilment of rational creatures (here set out explicitly in terms of the beatific vision), and in wanting to do justice to the continuing identity of rational creatures (or at least of human beings) as social beings. Traditions other than those strongly influenced by Protestantism may also have questions about how roles or

the fittingness of God redeeming human beings as human beings, but also that the humanity that God took in Christ should be taken from 'the stock of Adam' (in this case, from Mary) rather than from matter or flesh created independently, even *ex nihilo*.

patterns of affection associated with certain holy figures may feature within the wider eschatological picture suggested by astrobiology. The way in which that perspective may be most provocative, however, is not so much in terms of the nature of the final state, discussed in this chapter, but as to the nature, or timing, of its arrival. We turn to that in the next chapter.

--

Rupert Brooke, 'Heaven'

> Fish (fly-replete, in depth of June,
> Dawdling away their wat'ry noon)
> Ponder deep wisdom, dark or clear,
> Each secret fishy hope or fear.
> Fish say, they have their Stream and Pond;
> But is there anything Beyond?
> This life cannot be All, they swear,
> For how unpleasant if it were!
> One may not doubt that, somehow, Good
> Shall come of Water and of Mud;
> And, sure, the reverent eye must see
> A Purpose in Liquidity.
> We darkly know, by Faith we cry,
> The future is not Wholly Dry.
> Mud unto mud! – Death eddies near –
> Not here the appointed End, not here!
> But somewhere, beyond Space and Time,
> Is wetter water, slimier slime!
> And there (they trust) there swimmeth One
> Who swam ere rivers were begun,
> Immense, of fishy form and mind,
> Squamous, omnipotent and kind;

And under that Almighty Fin,
The littlest fish may enter in.
Oh! Never fly conceals a hook,
Fish say, in the Eternal Brook,
But more than mundane weeds are there,
And mud, celestially fair;
Fat caterpillars drift around,
And Paradisal grubs are found;
Unfading moths, immortal flies,
And the worm that never dies.
And in that Heaven of all their wish,
There shall be no more land, say fish.

19 | The Arrival of the End

The nature of the final state is not the only topic in eschatology provoked to further questions by astrobiology. There is also how the end arrives, and particularly its timing. This, perhaps unexpectedly, turns out to be one of the few areas in Christian theology that may be significantly challenged or disturbed when thought about in astrobiological terms. We may, as we will see, end up thinking not only about the prospect of life on other planets, but also about the prospect of a time in which human life has passed from the Earth, indeed eventually all terrestrial life. That highlights our ecological responsibilities, and raises questions about the connection between the Resurrection of Christ and the restoration of the cosmos.

Jesus said that the Kingdom of God is 'in your midst' or 'among you', rather than deferring its arrival to the future.[1] Not every theological tradition stresses this fact, but few will entirely ignore the sense in which down payment of the future promise has already been given. A scheme where the renewal of all things is deferred completely to the future would be atypical for Christianity. In the words of Jacques Maritain, 'what comes after time is prepared in time': eschatology is at least partly 'realised'.[2] That said, few traditions would hold to a fully realised eschatology either. Historically speaking, Christian theology typically looks to some future moment when the definitive achievement of God's promises will break in. Alongside an at-least-partly 'realised' dimension therefore stands

---

[1] Luke 17.21.
[2] Jacques Maritain, *True Humanism*, trans. M. R. Adamson (London: Centenary Press, 1938), 94. This was published in the United States as *Integral Humanism*.

something more apocalyptic, stressing interruption, calling time on history. This is the eschatology of the last trumpet and the second coming. That matters a great deal, when it comes to astrobiology, since Christian theology has naturally looked upon this interruption of the history and processes of creation as a moment in human history. It has supposed that the end of the whole cosmos will come with the return to Earth of the human Messiah. Across the New Testament, this is expressed in the need for vigilance, because Christ will return unexpected, as a thief in the night.[3] In the words of 2 Peter, with that 'the heavens will pass away with a roar, and the heavenly bodies will be burned up and dissolved'.[4] If, however, there is life across the cosmos, an expected synchrony with human history seems likely to be disrupted, at least if God's dealings with that other life are as remarkable and intimate as they are on Earth.

If we were only talking about the existence of other creatures without sentience, human beings would still stand in a league apart. It would not be difficult, in that case, to suppose that the end would come during human history. The same could be said if there is other rational life, but only one Incarnation. Nothing about an otherwise inanimate or else non-sentient universe, nor one having received only one Incarnation, need challenge the assumption that the irruptive end of all things will come while there is human life on Earth. The picture likely looks quite different, however, if we imagine not only that the universe is full of life, but also that God's dealings with that life are not subordinated to God's dealings with us. Put sharply, if the universe is home to a great many sentient species and cultures, and if God relates to them as intimately and directly as God relates to us, then it becomes arbitrary to place human beings at the centre of the timing of the eschaton. (In this, we should also think about any species and civilisations in the history of our cosmos that have known and loved God but are now perished.) This point strikes me as the most disruptive

[3] Matt. 24.43; 1 Thess. 5. 2, 4; 2 Pet. 3.10; Rev. 16.15.
[4] 2 Pet. 3.10.

352

challenge that astrobiology poses to the articles of Christian belief, indeed perhaps the only challenge that might call for serious revision, rather than simply expansion, on the part of the theological tradition.

Francis Young has noted the prospect of a cosmic history that carries on beyond humanity, not thinking that it deserves much by way of theological comment.[5] Ward noted it, and recognised the consequences for Christian eschatology.

> The destruction of the earth, while it is certain at some point, probably in the far future, will almost be irrelevant to this larger cosmic story. This too is a huge contrast with the Biblical view that the whole universe (that is, basically, the earth) came into existence about six thousand years ago, and may end at any moment.[6]

However, although the difference in perspective here is 'huge', he thinks that Christianity can assimilate it:

> It does not matter that we are on the periphery of the universe and that we will probably die out as a species in the blink of a cosmic eye. We in our small corner of the universe will have been united to Eternity through the actions of the God who has been revealed to us in the form of one who was Son of God and Son of Man as well as the Father and Spirit of that Son.[7]

For my part, I would suggest that the idea of a future for the Earth after humanity represents rather more of a significant provocation for Christian theology than this suggests, adding that the theological work of thinking through the implications of a future for the universe, indeed even for the Earth, that plays out into post-human time, has hardly begun.

---

[5] Frances Margaret Young, *God's Presence: A Contemporary Recapitulation of Early Christianity* (Cambridge: Cambridge University Press, 2013), 63. John Polkinghorne mentions a post-human future for life on Earth in *Science and the Trinity* (London: SPCK, 2004), 178–79.

[6] Ward, *Christ and the Cosmos*, 10.

[7] Ibid., xiii.

This may be the most significant provocation from astrobiological speculations for a wholesale development in Christian theology, but our theological traditions nonetheless contain significant resources for the task. One aspect is the church's thinking about getting used to Christ not having returned. Until recently, it was common to talk about a crisis in early Christianity around the 'delayed Parousia', which would have called for a change of theological perspective. We might turn to the end of the Fourth Gospel, as witness to a community coming to terms with the fact that what Jesus had said had not meant, after all, that John would not die before Jesus returned, simply 'If it is my will that he remain until I come, what is that to you?'[8] More recently, scholarship has questioned whether there was an expectation of a return so soon after the Ascension. Either way – in having found ways to face a crisis, and get beyond it, or in ways in which at least some Christians, even early on, did not in fact feel challenged at all – we have a history of thinking about how the end of all things relates to an extending period of time in which humanity and the church has lived, thrived, struggled, and continued, and more and more people died, and the lengthening passage of time during which Christ has not returned. That is not the same as thinking about a future for the universe after the Earth has perished, but it offers ways in.[9]

Within this picture, if we have multiple Incarnations in mind, we would presumably also have to think about the eventual eschatological irruption – whenever that happens – as involving the return of all the ways in which God has been Incarnate, alongside the gathering of all creatures into the resurrected existence. The end is, in any case, already seen as a great gathering together, a moment when the general resurrection brings together all that is going to endure. We would simply now transpose onto a canvas as large as the ocean of

---

[8] John 21.23.

[9] See the edition of *Early Christianity* (9.1) on this topic, including N. T. Wright, 'Hope Deferred: Against the Dogma of Delay', *Early Christianity* 9, no. 1 (2018): 37–82, and an editorial which provides an orientation to the topic by Simon Gathercole, 'Editorial: The "Delay of the Parousia"', *Early Christianity* 9, no. 1 (2018): 1–7.

stars what is expressed in Earthly terms in the Bible: 'and the sea gave up the dead that were in it, Death and Hades gave up the dead that were in them, and all were judged according to what they had done'.[10]

Christianity contains traditions, which we might refer to as 'Adventist', that have conceived of the return of Christ in strongly immanentized ways – for instance, with a period of a thousand years (Millennialism) – in which the future state has been set out in concrete, Earthly terms. These have only infrequently been the subject matter of mainstream academic systematic theology, but they may have a greater capacity to imagine more local ends, and a return worked out on this planet alone. (These traditions, however, have not tended to be particularly involved in discussions with contemporary natural science.) That would allow, in theory, for a string of local ends, worked out on many worlds. Such traditions, however, alongside others in Christianity, might object that this would represent quite a reduction to the picture of eschatology as *cosmic* renewal, widely embraced by theologians today. Moreover, it leaves the question of the end of the cosmos as a whole unaddressed.

An alternative way to approach these questions might come through a reappropriation of elements of existentialist theology, in which eschatology has exerted its influence mainly as an ever-present demand upon the individual and community to live 'authentically' in light of the prospect of death and the summons issued by the gospel. As the Christian stands before the message of the gospel and, more widely, as the human being stands before the prospect of death, she encounters something apocalyptic, in the sense of an 'unveiling' or making clear, something eschatological, with both threat and promise of resolution.[11] This interpretation stresses that Christ always addresses the present moment. The end might arrive as some climatic cosmic conclusion, or it might come in death. The point is to face its demands upon us *now*.

[10] Rev. 20.13.

[11] John Macquarrie, *An Existentialist Theology* (London: SCM Press, 1955), 193–204.

Writing on Christian existentialism, John MacQuarrie presented a theological vision in which the Biblical texts are less significantly about history, and more centrally about a message (or 'kerygma') that addresses the human being, laying bare their 'inauthenticity' and offering transformation, but only in as much as the person addressed makes a decision.[12] One does not perhaps have to embrace his assessment of scripture in terms of 'myth' to the extent that he does for this approach to be useful: 'Nowadays, for us who no longer look for a supernatural cataclysmic end to the world (even if in some sense we still look for an ultimate consummation of the divine "purpose"), it is the existential significance of the myth that remains – as the element of permanent value in it'.[13] On a cosmic scale, one could still hold to a non-natural rolling up of history. However, within the history of any particular planet, living in preparation for that conclusion would already be held alongside readiness for an ending in death, with every possibility that would come first. Today, we might add that the death of our species, or of our planet, might similarly come first.

Another avenue on this is to point out that a central contention within existentialist eschatology has been that grace can transform *chronos* into *kairos*. *Chronos* is time running its course, known in the ticking of a clock. It is a part of the natural order, and we measure it as duration. In contrast, *kairos* is not general, but particular. Most of all, it is time coming to us as a moment of opportunity. A shift in our apprehension of time, from *chronos* to *kairos*, is integral to the message of the gospel. The present moment is to be apprehended, in the light of the gospel proclamation, as a time of opportunity – for repentance, for encounter with God – but also as a moment that does not remain forever, adding a note of urgency.

The Christian message about time would not ever properly or mainly be about some duration or other, or about timings

---

[12] John Macquarrie, *Studies in Christian Existentialism: Lectures and Essays* (London: SCM Press, 1965), 99–112.

[13] Ibid., 121.

approached according to general scientific or natural processes; it is about the call for repentance, for an encounter with God, or for the charitable deed, *in this moment*. Nothing is changed about that just because the natural, scientific, 'chronos' story of the Earth might be different from how we saw it previously. Whether the end is to come in human history or not, the message is about apprehending the present moment as the time and occasion for grace: 'See, now is the acceptable time; see, now is the day of salvation!'[14]

Such a view represents more than simply a trend in the mid- to late twentieth century. The supplement to the *Summa Theologiae*, for instance, offers a comment on the signs traditionally associated with the coming of Christ, such as war and a time of fear, as being more about a call to timely repentance than items in an eschatological spotter's guide. For one thing, Aquinas noted (here following Augustine) that those signs can presage many things, and are therefore ambiguous. They accompanied the fall of Jerusalem, for instance, and are widespread in human history. They are not to be the stuff of speculative analysis about what I have called matters of *chronos*. Instead, what we might call the existential dimension remains in the forefront: by such signs the human heart is to be provoked to preparedness for Christ as 'the coming judge'.[15]

The existentialist emphasis on a disposition of life – on a life lived in readiness for death and judgement – need not undo belief in a cosmic end, even if it places questions of future timing in the background. One could still believe, just as firmly as before, that the trumpet will sound *at some stage*, and that there will be an irruptive or interruptive end to the universe that is not merely natural. That, however, may or may not happen in any given span of time: for instance, over the course of the existence of humanity, or while the Earth orbits the sun. Christian theology could retain its characteristic perspective that the end of the universe is not, ultimately,

---

[14] 2 Cor. 6.2.
[15] *ST suppl.* 73.1.

going to play out according to natural processes. Whether scientific theories point to an open-ended future of ever-greater entropy and the dissipation of matter and energy into randomness and separation ('heat death'), or a halt to cosmic expansion, followed by contraction to a 'Big Crunch',[16] God would at some stage, in fact, interrupt and call time on the proceedings.

From the perspective of piety or religious practice, we are already familiar with the idea that the end of all things may or may not happen during one's own lifetime. It would not take much to transpose this onto the scale of planets and species: the end may or may not come during our planet's time. In any case, one would seek to live one's life ready to hear the last trumpet and, in that, also nurture a disposition ready to meet death. Even a cosmologically and apocalyptically orientated discussion of eschatology such as 2 Peter 3 turns, in this way, from the dissolution of the elements by fire to its implications for a manner and disposition of life:

> The day of the Lord will come like a thief, and then the heavens will pass away with a loud noise, and the elements will be dissolved with fire, and the earth and everything that is done on it will be disclosed. Since all these things are to be dissolved in this way, what sort of people ought you to be in leading lives of holiness and godliness, waiting for and hastening the coming of the day of God, because of which the heavens will be set ablaze and dissolved, and the elements will melt with fire? But, in accordance with his promise, we wait for new heavens and a new earth, where righteousness is at home.[17]

Preparation for the second coming and preparation for death have long gone alongside each other in Christian theology and piety. As an example, we find them woven together in one of Johann Sebastian Bach's vocal masterpieces, his Cantata 106 (the *Actus*

---

[16] Observation of an accelerating expansion to the cosmos suggests heat death rather than a crunch.
[17] 2 Peter 3.10–13.

Tragicus). In the second movement, the choir meditates on death –
'It is the old covenant: Man, you must die!' while a soprano solo-
ist turns simultaneously to the second coming – 'Yes, come Lord
Jesus, come!'[18]

In one sense, then, Christian theology has the resources it needs
to respond to the idea of a cosmos whose end may not come in
the history of the Earth. Nonetheless, that would call us to think
through something not often considered by theology in its more
traditional forms, namely the prospect of a post-human story for
the Earth, and for the universe more widely. The Earth will not
endure forever, even if time is allowed to roll on. The sun would
eventually fail, and expand, destroying our planet. Indeed, there
is reason to suppose that humanity would eventually pass away
sooner than that, either in outright extinction, or by continuing evolution (or self-adaptation) leading to a species other than
human. Some of those options raise significant theological questions, especially for Christology and soteriology. Although provoked by thinking about theology alongside astrobiology, I leave
them to be pursued elsewhere, since the consequences are not
about astrobiology in themselves, but an Earth, and a Cosmos,
after a time of the humans.

Here, the practical value of the topics explored in this book
may take on a further dimension. It looks likely that part of the
human failure to oppose despoilation of the Earth has come from
religious impulses to think that God will soon destroy it in any
case. A change of perspective by which we recognise that the
Earth could have a long history ahead of it, with or without us,
may help us to see that the future habitability of the planet lies in
our hands. I fear, however, that the traditions of Christianity most
content to treat the rest of nature with contempt on eschatological

---

[18] 'Es ist der alte Bund: Mensch, du mußt sterben!' (Sirach 14.17); 'Ja, komm, Herr Jesu,
komm!' (quoting Rev. 22.20).

grounds will also be those least likely to entertain the idea that the dealings of God with this planet might be only one of many glorious stories.[19]

Many Resurrections and the Transformation of the Cosmos

Across this book, I have stressed my conviction that, should it need to, Christian theology has the resources to adjust to a view of the world in which God's dealings with creatures elsewhere are comparable with those in our own story. Nonetheless, it would seem to be in the realm of eschatology that those adjustments may cause the most disorientation. In addition to what has been covered already in this chapter, the relation of the Resurrection of Christ to the cosmos as a whole would bear further attention.

The disjunction here comes from seeing the Resurrection of Christ as the dawn of a new creation, which naturally – even necessarily – strikes us as bearing upon the cosmos as a whole. Not for nothing is the Resurrection of the dead compared in the scriptures with the radical newness of creation.[20] Easter Day in the Christian tradition is counted as the 'eighth day': the first day of the new creation of the world. Just as the first day in Genesis refers to all of created reality, so too are we accustomed to speaking about the

---

[19] Also of eschatological, or apocalyptic, consequence in relation to guardianship of the Earth is an interpretation of the Fermi Paradox, associated with Enrico Fermi (1901–1954). This contrasts the idea that there might be a good deal of other life, given the size of the universe (and, we now know, the number of stars with planets) with what seems to be the observation that we have been visited neither by that other life nor its technology. One straightforward response is that no life progresses beyond a certain stage in terms of technological capabilities without wiping itself out, or destroying its planet. On interpretations of the paradox, see Stephen Webb, *If the Universe Is Teeming with Aliens. Where Is Everybody? Seventy-Five Solutions to the Fermi Paradox and the Problem of Extraterrestrial Life*, 2nd ed. (Cham: Springer, 2015).

[20] 2 Macc. 7.28; Rom. 4.17. On these passages, see my *Participation in God*, 16, 18 n. 17.

renewal of all creation in relation to the Day of the Resurrection. Within Christian theology, Christ alone may be the first fruits of the new creation for now, although many Christians will add Mary as the second person to have shared already in the Resurrected life, whether that is held as a matter of dogma or of piety. Nonetheless, with Christ's Resurrection, a transformation has begun. We may wonder if that would need reframing if we were to think of Incarnation and Resurrection in more than one place and time.

The only author I know to have addressed that challenge directly is Jacques Arnould.[21] While his account is consistent, it strikes me as rather deflationary as to the significance of the Resurrection of Christ. For him, multiple Resurrections offer no particular difficulties, since he approaches the Resurrection of Christ (and presumably those others) as an indication rather than a cause: as a sign of something more ultimate. For him, the meaning of the Resurrection is that 'as God did not abandon his Messiah … so he will not abandon his creation', and that God renews both.[22] The Resurrection of Christ is a sign, announcement, or confirmation not only of what God will do, but also of what God always does, and is, and has been. It 'reminds, emphasizes, [and] teaches [*rapelle, souligne, enseigne*] that God does not stop creating anew'.[23] In my view, that connection tends to rob the Resurrection of its own radical

---

[21] David Wilkinson has three pages on 'New Creation' in *Search for Extraterrestrial Intelligence*, 169–71, in which he discusses the cosmic consequences of the Resurrection of Jesus, quoting N. T. Wright ('with the resurrection itself, a shock wave has gone through the entire cosmos: the new creation has been born, and must now be implemented' (*The Resurrection of the Son of God* (London: SPCK, 2003), 239). He does not discuss what the implications might be of many Incarnations, that not being his favoured theological trajectory. O'Meara asks whether 'there [are] modes of transformation for each planet, for every knowing and free creature', having talked about the Resurrection of Christ on Earth, but he does not consider any problems in the idea of the inauguration of the end within time on more than one occasion, in more than one place (*Vast Universe*, 58).

[22] Arnould, *Turbulences Dans l'univers*, 238, my translation, here and below.

[23] Ibid., 240.

newness, leaving it as perhaps a new sort of manifestation, but not the manifestation of something new. Moreover, and crucially, there is no sense in Arnould that the Resurrection of Christ is the cause of the remaking of all things.[24] At most, the Resurrection of Christ is part of 'a yet greater divine work', unfolding both now and in the future. Although he thinks that his perspective does not involve 'reducing [*minimiser*]' the rising of Christ (whereas I think it does), he admits that it will tend 'to relativise [*reativiser*]' it, by setting it in the context of 'links and relations' to a wider pattern in the cosmos.[25] We can also note that, just as the eschatological work of new creation is disconnected for Arnould, causally speaking, from the Resurrection of Christ, so is Resurrection (now taken as a more ultimate principle than the Resurrection of Christ) disconnected from the Incarnation. Arnould writes that 'the Resurrection is not a consequence of the Incarnation, nor is the Incarnation a [prior] condition for the Resurrection'.[26] For Arnould, the appearance of Resurrection, as a general principle, may be associated, as it happens, with the Resurrection of the Incarnate Son, at least in our story, but the Incarnation is neither its cause nor even a necessary condition.

There is more here for the theologian to consider, and additional resources to bring to bear. On this territory, we find Aquinas charting the sort of middle way for which he is known. On the one hand, what we might call his reverence for the power and freedom of God cautions him not to draw a link of absolute necessity between the general Resurrection and the Resurrection of Christ, or even with the Incarnation. The Incarnation was not necessary for the 'restoration of human nature [*ad humanae naturae reparationem*]' in any absolute sense, so neither would his Resurrection be

---

[24] Arnould bases what he writes here particularly on the way in which the Resurrection of Christ did not bring about the end of time (ibid., 242).

[25] Ibid., 239.

[26] Ibid., 238.

necessary.[27] We are not operating in the realm of strict necessity. Rather, in a way now familiar, the role of Christ's story is stressed in terms of suitability: that restoration was achieved 'better and more fittingly [*melius et convenientius*]' that way.

Did Aquinas understand the Resurrection to be the cause of the wider restoration, or merely as a sign? As we might expect, he answers 'both/and'. The sense of sign or manifestation, which tells the whole story for Arnould, is strongly present. It lies behind four of the five reasons he gives for the fittingness of the Resurrection in *Summa Theologiae* III.53.1. The fifth, however, goes further, into causal territory: Christ also rose 'in order to complete the work of our salvation, [so that as he died] that He might deliver us from evil, so was He glorified in rising again in order to advance us towards good things'. Here Aquinas quotes Rom. 4.25: 'He was delivered up for our sins, and rose again for our justification'. Later, in a reply to an objection, he adds that Christ's Resurrection is the 'beginning and exemplar of all good things' in human salvation.[28] Not only do the terms 'beginning' and 'exemplar' tend to have causal implications in Aquinas' writing, here they are also presented to amplify a discussion as to how our salvation was wrought (*operata est nostram salutem*). The causal role of Christ's Resurrection – his as the cause of ours – is also underlined in a later question (citing 1 Cor. 15.20–21), where Aquinas wrote that 'the Word of God first bestows immortal life upon that body which is naturally united with Himself, and through it works the resurrection in all other bodies'.[29] Nonetheless, even here, Aquinas added that 'the Divine justice in itself is not tied down to Christ's Resurrection as a means of bringing about our resurrection: because God could deliver us in some other way than through

---

[27] *ST* III.1.2 (the original English translation had 'conveniently').

[28] *ST* III.53.1 *ad* 3.

[29] *ST* III.56.1. He analyses this in terms of the Resurrection as the 'secondary, and … instrumental cause' (*ad* 2); the 'efficient and exemplar cause' (*ad* 3) of our resurrection; and in *Supp.* 76.1, in terms of equivocal causation (as 'Christ as God') and univocal causation ('as God and man rising again').

Christ's Passion and Resurrection ... But having once decreed to deliver us in this way, it is evident that Christ's Resurrection is the cause of ours'.[30] This topic is also addressed in the *Supplement*, which again sets out ways in which Christ's resurrection is the cause of ours, adding that 'God's power is not tied to any particular second causes', so that while 'according to the order appointed to human things by Divine providence, Christ's resurrection is the cause of ours ... yet He could have appointed another order, and then our resurrection would have had another cause ordained by God'.[31]

Here it might be useful to return to the point I made in Chapter 16 about the means being part of the ends in the story of salvation. We should perhaps not define a certain end rather forensically and then separately suppose that it can be achieved in many different ways as if the means did not colour the end or constitute part of its glory. Turning back to the very beginning of the *tertia pars*, Aquinas' final reason for why the Incarnation was particularly fitting as the means of salvation is offered 'with regard to the full participation of the Divinity, which is the true bliss of man and end of human life; and this is bestowed upon us by Christ's humanity'.[32] While a certain participation in deathless life could be granted to human beings (as the tradition has often supposed would have come to humanity without sin) even without the Incarnation or Easter Day, to be elevated to such life through the hypostatic union in Christ, and his Resurrection, is a different, and indeed more glorious, thing than being given that gift without those means. Someone might be granted to see God in the beatific vision without the Incarnation, death, and Resurrection of Christ, but by those means the human being is also made a brother or sister of Christ. In that way, while the Resurrection of Christ may not be necessary for God to restore or elevate creatures, what humanity, at least, has been offered is not only restoration and elevation but

---

[30] ST III.56.1 *ad* 2.
[31] *ST Supp.* 76.1 *ad* 2.
[32] *ST* III.1.2.

restoration-and-elevation-through-Christ-and-by-means-of-his-Resurrection. If the former can be given without Resurrection, the latter cannot. That follows tautologically, but does not rob the distinction or discussion of its cogency.

Returning in this way to the detail of the Christian story may go some way toward resolving the dilemma posed at the beginning of this section. How does the Resurrection of Christ relate to the wider cosmos if the Son, having also taken up another created nature, also dies and rises elsewhere? Well, if there is more than one Incarnation, that points to the importance of the union of God with a species in the specificity of its nature. If that then also involves Resurrection, that would be because it is fitting for a nature to be vivified by the rising of God in that nature, as the arrival in that nature of the new creation. There may, perhaps, seem to be some lack of neatness to more than one definitive breaking in of the coming age by Resurrection, but the counterbalancing principle would be that if the drama of God's dealings is fittingly played out with particularity for each species, then it is proper for the full sweep of that story to run its course in each case. In any case, superfluity may be more appropriate in the works of God than neatness. Any one Incarnation might redeem the whole cosmos, but it may be fitting for there to be more than one. Similarly, even if any one Resurrection of the Son of God – if there is more than one such rising – would be enough to cause and inaugurate the new creation, that does not rule out many. A barren hillside might be restored with the sprouting of a single seed, left to multiply over time, but it would not be unfitting to achieve it by scattering the seed of many species in abundance.

Conclusion

Up to now, the message that might have been taken from this book is that Christian theology will be considerably more robust in meeting any confirmation of exobiology than is often assumed in journalistic writing on the topic, in part because there is the under-appreciated legacy from centuries of existing thought on other life, but also because so much Christian theology bears upon those questions, although largely unexplored at present. With eschatology, however, we reach a topic where Christian theology, at least in its more traditional or conservative forms, is likely to encounter significant challenges, or is likely to benefit most from a broader degree of flexibility. Even here, however, there are parallels with previous discussions, so the theologian is not left without resources. Here again we see that benefits accrue from approaching existing theological topics from new angles, here in particular in terms of the relation between eschatology and environmental responsibilities, and of the relation between the Resurrection of Christ (and, possibly, of other Incarnations) and the future restoration of all things.

Conclusion

Writing with other life in in mind, and an eschatological encounter, Alice Meynell urged herself and her readers to anticipation and readiness: 'O, be prepared, my soul'. Today, a little over a century later, we can hope for a more mundane disclosure of other life first, given away by its effect on the chemical composition of a planet's atmosphere. That prospect also calls for preparedness. We will do well to have thought about the implications of such news beforehand.

As we have seen across this book, theological discussion of the implications of life elsewhere in the universe has a long history, yet much of that historical material is surprisingly shallow. As I have argued, the main benefits of what existing traditions have to offer will not so much come from older texts that are addressed directly to this theme, but from different passages: from texts – vastly more numerous – that address other ideas, other questions, other conundrums, other debates; texts not written with extraterrestrial life in mind, but which bear upon it nonetheless. There is, in other words, a work of retrieval to be done in connecting contemporary questions posed by scientific work on astrobiology to resources from our theological traditions, to help us to take up this particular part of the task of thinking about God and all things in relation to God.[1]

This book is offered as a contribution to that, acknowledging that other topics could be added, and other sources considered, even other resources from Aquinas, prominent though he has already

---

[1] *ST* I.1.7.

been. More could be said, for instance, about the relevance of themes in ecclesiology, or about the extension of ideas of the communion of saints. No claims for comprehensiveness – ultimately rather absurd – are being made.

Already, members of the Christian churches (for whom I have primarily been writing) are asking what the prospect of other life in the universe might mean for their sense of themselves, and of their place in the cosmos, and what impact any such life would have on time-honoured, and time-honed, doctrines and beliefs. The themes covered in this book are of use not only as part of preparation for addressing future needs, however. In addressing them theological attention to astrobiology will already pay off today, and not only tomorrow, in offering fresh angles on familiar topics. It is my hope that this book stands as an illustration that, as a work of research. I hope also that the value of bringing this topic into teaching will have become clear, since that is how it first featured in my work, and first engaged my interest.

Bibliography

Works of Thomas Aquinas: Texts, Translations and Abbreviations

For Latin texts, I have consulted the editions of the Leonine Commission (*Sancti Thomae Aquinatis Doctoris Angelici. Opera Omnia. Iussu Leonis XIII*, Rome: Vatican Polyglot Press, 1882–). For texts currently without a volume in the Leonine edition, I have used the Parma edition (*Opera Omnia*, Parma: Fiaccadori, 1852–73). English translations are generally as follows (sometimes with small emendations), unless I indicate that I have produced my own. Where no reference is given to the part of an article cited from the *Summa Theologiae*, or one of the sets of disputed questions, it is to the main body or response. The Latin titles below are those given by Gille Emery his 'Brief Catalogue'.[1] The following works have been cited with familiar Latin names: *De Malo, De Potentia, De Veritate, Summa Contra Gentiles* (*SCG*), and *Summa Theologiae* (*ST*).

Commentary on the De Anima of Aristotle [Sentencia Libri De anima]. Aristotle's De Anima, in the Version of William of Moerbeke and the Commentary of St. Thomas Aquinas. Trans. Kenelm Foster and Silvester Humphries. London: Routledge and Kegan Paul, 1951.

Commentary on Colossians [Super Epistolam Beati Pauli ad Colossenses lectura]. Ed. Daniel A Keating. Trans. Fabian R Larcher (Naples, FL: Sapientia Press, 2006).

Commentary on the Sentences [Scriptum super libros Sententiarum]. Various translations as given in respective footnote.

Commentary on the Metaphysics of Aristotle [Sententia super Metaphysicam]. Trans. John P. Rowan. Chicago: Regnery, 1961.

---

[1] Emery, 'Brief Catalogue'

Disputed Question on the Union of the Word Incarnate [*Quaestiones disputatae De unione Verbi incarnati*]. Trans. Jason Lewis Andrew West. https://aquinas.cc/la/en/~QDeUni. Accessed 23 January 2022.

Disputed Questions on Evil [*Quaestiones disputatae De malo*] *On Evil*. Edited by Brian Davies. Trans. Richard J. Regan. Oxford: Oxford University Press, 2003.

Disputed Questions on the Power of God [*Quaestiones disputatae De potentia*]. Trans. English Dominican Fathers. Westminster, MD: Newman Press, 1952.

Disputed Questions on De Anima [*Quaestiones disputatae De anima*]. *The Soul: Disputed Questions on De Anima*. Trans. John Patrick Rowan. St Louis: B. Herder, 1949.

Disputed Questions on Truth [*Quaestiones disputatae de veritate*]. Trans. Robert W. Mulligan, James V. McGlynn, and Robert Schmidt. 3 vols. Chicago: Henry Regnery Company, 1952.

Exposition of Aristotle's Treatise On the Heavens [*Sententia super librum De caelo et mundo*] Trans. Fabian R. Larcher and Pierre H. Conway. Columbus, OH: College of St Mary of the Springs, 1963.

'The heavenly Word proceeding forth' [*Verbum Supernum prodiens* in *Officium de festo Corporis Christi*]. Trans. John Mason Neale and the compilers of Hymns Ancient and Modern. In *New English Hymnal*. Norwich: Canterbury Press, 1986.

Commentary on the Gospel of John [*Lectura super Ioannem*]. Ed. Daniel Keating and Matthew Levering. Trans. Fabian Larcher and James A. Weisheipl. 3 volumes. Washington, DC: Catholic University of America Press, 2010–12.

Lectures on the Letter to the Romans [*Super Epistolam ad Romanos lectura*]. Ed. John Mortensen. Trans. Fabian Larcher. Lander: Aquinas Institute, 2012.

Quodlibetal Questions [*Quaestiones de quolibet*]. *Thomas Aquinas's Quodlibetal Questions*. Trans. Turner Nevitt and Brian Davies. New York: Oxford University Press, 2020.

On Kingship [*De regno ad Regem Cypri*]. *On Kingship to the King of Cyprus*. Trans. Gerald B. Phelan and Ignatius Theodore Eschmann. Toronto: Pontifical Institute of Mediaeval Studies, 1982.

On the De Trinitate of Boethius [*Super Boetium De Trinitate*]. In *The Trinity and The Unicity of the Intellect against the Averroists*. Trans. Rose Emmanuella Brennan. St. Louis, MO: B. Herder, 1946.

On Separated Substances [*De substantiis separatis*]. Trans. Francis J. Lescoe. West Hartford, CN: Saint Joseph College, 1959.

Summa contra Gentiles (*SCG*). Trans. Anton C. Pegis, James F. Anderson, Vernon J. Bourke, and Charles J. O'Neil. 5 vols. New York: Hanover House, 1955.

Summa theologiae (*ST*). Trans. Fathers of the English Dominican Province. 2nd ed. 22 vols. London: Burns, Oates & Washbourne, 1912.

General Bibliography

Aarsleff, Hans. 'John Wilkins (1614–1673): Life and Work'. In *John Wilkins and 17th-Century British Linguistics*, edited by Joseph L. Subbiondo, 1–42. Amsterdam: J. Benjamin, 1992.

Adler, Mortimer Jerome. *The Angels and Us*. New York: Touchstone, 1993.

Albertus Magnus. *Opera Omnia*. Edited by Augustus Borgnet. Vol. 9. Paris: Vives, 1890.

Alston, William. 'Substance and the Trinity'. In *The Trinity*, edited by Stephen T. Davis, Daniel Kendall, and Gerald O'Collins, 179–201. Oxford: Oxford University Press, 2002.

Ambrose. *Hexameron, Paradise, and Cain and Abel*. Translated by John J. Savage. New York: Fathers of the Church, 1961.

Anselm. *The Major Works*. Edited by Brian Davies and G. R. Evans. Oxford: Oxford University Press, 2008.

Arendt, Hannah. *The Human Condition*. Chicago: University of Chicago Press, 1958.

Aristotle. *Aristotle's Physics: A Guided Study*. Edited and translated by Joe Sachs. New Brunswick, NJ: Rutgers University Press, 2011.

Aristotle. 'On the Heavens'. In *Complete Works of Aristotle: The Revised Oxford Translation*, edited by J. Barnes, translated by J. L. Stocks, 1: 447–511. Princeton, NJ: Princeton University Press, 1984.

Arnold, Bill T. *Genesis*. Cambridge: Cambridge University Press, 2013.

Arnould, Jacques. *Turbulences Dans l'univers: Dieu, Les Extraterrestres et Nous*. Paris: Albin Michel, 2017.

Arthur, Wallace. *The Biological Universe: Life in the Milky Way and Beyond*. Cambridge: Cambridge University Press, 2020.

Athanasius. 'Contra Gentes'. In *Nicene and post-Nicene Fathers: A Select Library of the Christian Church – Second series, volume 4*, edited by Archibald Robertson, translated by John Henry Newman and Archibald Robertson, 1–30. Grand Rapids, MI: Eerdmans, 1980.

Augustine. *Augustine Catechism: Enchiridion on Faith Hope and Charity*. Edited by Boniface Ramsey. Translated by Bruce Harbert. Hyde Park, NY: New City Press, 2008.

Augustine. *Concerning the City of God against the Pagans*. Edited by G. R. Evans. Translated by Henry Bettenson. London: Penguin, 2003.

Augustine. 'Literal Meaning of Genesis'. In *On Genesis*, translated by Edmund Hill. Hyde Park, NY: New City Press, 2002.

Augustine. *On Free Choice of the Will*. Translated by Thomas Williams. Indianapolis, IN: Hackett, 1993.

Augustine. 'On Genesis: A Refutation of the Manichees'. In *On Genesis*, translated by Edmund Hill, 21–97. Hyde Park, NY: New City Press, 2002.

Augustine. 'Unfinished Literal Commentary on Genesis'. In *On Genesis*, edited by John E. Rotelle, translated by Edmund Hill, 103–51. Hyde Park, NY: New City Press, 2002.

Aulén, Gustaf. *Christus Victor: An Historical Study of the Three Main Types of the Idea of the Atonement*. Translated by A. G. Herbert. London: SPCK, 1931.

Badham, Paul, and Linda Badham. *Immortality or Extinction?* London: SPCK, 1984.

Baker, Anthony D. *Diagonal Advance: Perfection in Christian Theology*. Eugene, OR: Cascade, 2011.

Barker, Sarah, and Maria Nilsson. *Fifty Things to See in the Sky*. London: HarperCollins, 2019.

Barth, Karl. *Church Dogmatics: The Doctrine of Creation (III/1)*. Translated by O. Bussey and H. Knight. Edinburgh: T&T Clark, 1958.

Barth, Karl. *Church Dogmatics: The Doctrine of Creation (III/3)*. Translated by Geoffrey W. Bromiley and J. R. Ehrlich. Edinburgh: T&T Clark, 1961.

Barth, Karl. *Church Dogmatics: The Doctrine of Reconciliation (IV/1)*. Translated by G. W Bromiley. Edinburgh: T&T Clark, 1956.

Barth, Karl. *Church Dogmatics: The Doctrine of the Word of God (I/1)*. Translated by G. W. Bromiley. Second edition. Edinburgh: T&T Clark, 1975.

Barth, Karl. *Church Dogmatics: The Doctrine of the Word of God (I/2)*. Translated by G. T. Thomson and Harold Knight. Edinburgh: T&T Clark, 1956.

Basil. *The Treatise de Spiritu Sancto, the Nine Homilies of the Hexaemeron and the Letters of Saint Basil the Great*. Translated by Blomfield Jackson. Edinburgh: T&T Clark, 1895.

Baxter, Richard. *The Reasons of the Christian Religion*. London: R. White, for Fran. Titon, 1667.

Beeck, Franz Jozef van. *God Encountered: Part III – Finitude and Fall*. Collegeville, MN: Liturgical Press, 1995.

Benin, Stephen D. *The Footprints of God: Divine Accommodation in Jewish and Christian Thought*. Albany, NY: State University of New York Press, 1993.

Benner, Steven A. 'Defining Life'. *Astrobiology* 10, no. 10 (December 2010): 1021–30.

Bentley, Richard. *A Confutation of Atheism from the Origin and Frame of the World*. London: H. Mortlock, 1693.

Berkhof, Hendrikus. *Christian Faith: An Introduction to the Study of the Faith*. Translated by Sierd Woudstra. Grand Rapids, MI: Eerdmans, 1979.

Bertka, Constance M., ed. *Exploring the Origin, Extent, and Future of Life: Philosophical, Ethical, and Theological Perspectives*. Cambridge: Cambridge University Press, 2009.

Blatner, David. *Spectrums: Our Mind-Boggling Universe from Infinitesimal to Infinity*. New York: Bloomsbury, 2014.

Bonaventure. *Breviloquium*. Translated by José de Vinck. Paterson, NJ: St Anthony Guild Press, 1963.

Bonaventure. *Commentary on the Sentences: Philosophy of God*. Translated by R. E. Houser and Timothy B. Noone. Saint Bonaventure, NY: Franciscan Institute, 2013.

Bonaventure. *Itinerarium mentis in Deum*. Translated by Zachary Hayes. St. Bonaventure, NY: Franciscan Institute Publications, 2002.

Bonaventure. *On the Reduction of the Arts to Theology*. Translated by Zachary Hayes. St Bonaventure, NY: Franciscan Institute, 1996.

Book of Common Prayer. Cambridge: Cambridge University Press, 2004.

Bosley, Richard, and Martin M. Tweedale, eds. *Basic Issues in Medieval Philosophy: Selected Readings Presenting the Interactive Discourses among the Major Figures*. Orchard Park, NY: Broadview Press, 1997.

Brake, Mark. *Alien Life Imagined: Communicating the Science and Culture of Astrobiology*. Cambridge: Cambridge University Press, 2012.

Brazier, Paul. H. 'C. S. Lewis: The Question of Multiple Incarnations'. *Heythrop Journal* 55, no. 3 (2014): 391–408.

Brewster, David. *More Worlds Than One: The Creed of the Philosopher and the Hope of the Christian*. Corrected and Enlarged Edition. London: Murray, 1854.

Brooke, John Hedley. *Science and Religion: Some Historical Perspectives*. Cambridge: Cambridge University Press, 1991.

Brooke, Rupert. *1914 and Other Poems*. London: Sidgwick & Jackson, 1915.

Brown, David. '"Necessary" and "Fitting" Reasons in Christian Theology'. In *The Rationality of Religious Belief: Essays in Honour of Basil Mitchell*, edited by William J. Abraham and Steven W. Holtzer, 211–30. Oxford: Clarendon Press, 1987.

Brown, William P. 'Knowing God in Light of Job and Astrobiology'. In *Knowing Creation: Perspectives from Theology, Philosophy, and Science*, edited by Andrew B. Torrance and Thomas H. McCall, 141–54. Grand Rapids, MI: Zondervan, 2018.

Bruno, Giordano. *De l'infinito universo et Mondi: All'illustrissimo Signor di Mauuissiero*. Venetia [London]: Charlewood, 1584.

Bryson, Steve, Michelle Kunimoto, Ravi K. Kopparapu, Jeffrey L. Coughlin, William J. Borucki, David Koch, Victor Silva Aguirre, et al. 'The Occurrence of Rocky Habitable-Zone Planets around Solar-like Stars from Kepler Data'. *Astronomical Journal* 161, no. 1 (22 December 2020): 36.

Buffon, Georges Louis Leclerc. *Histoire Naturelle: Générale et Particulière, Contenant Les Époques de La Nature*. Paris: de l'Imprimerie Royale, 1778.

Bulgakov, Sergius. *Icons, and the Name of God*. Translated by Boris Jakim. Grand Rapids, MI: Eerdmans, 2012.

Bulgakov, Sergius. *Jacob's Ladder: On Angels*. Translated by T. Allan Smith. Grand Rapids, MI: Eerdmans, 2010.

Burgess, Stuart. *He Made the Stars Also: What the Bible Says about the Stars*. Leominster: DayOne, 2008.

Calvin, Jean. *Commentaries on the First Book of Moses, Called Genesis*. Translated by John King. Vol. 1. 2 vols. Edinburgh: Calvin Translation Society, 1847.

Calvin, Jean. *Ioannis Calvini opera quae supersunt omnia*. Edited by Edouard Cunitz, Johann-Wilhelm Baum, and Eduard Wilhelm Eugen Reuss. Vol. 49. New York: Johnson, 1964.

Calvin, John. *Concerning the Eternal Predestination of God*. London: James Clarke, 1961.

Calvin, John. *Institutes of Christian Religion*. Edited by John T McNeill. Translated by Ford Lewis Battles. Philadelphia: Westminster Press, 1960.

Campanella, Tommaso. *A Defense of Galileo, the Mathematician from Florence*. Edited and translated by Richard J. Blackwell. Notre Dame, IN: University of Notre Dame Press, 1994.

Carty, Anthony, and Janne Nijman. *Morality and Responsibility of Rulers: European and Chinese Origins of a Rule of Law as Justice for World Order*. Oxford: Oxford University Press, 2018.

Case, Brendan. '"More Splendid Than the Sun": Christ's Flesh among the Reasons for the Incarnation'. *Modern Theology* 36, no. 4 (October 2020): 758–77.

Catholic Church. *Catechism of the Catholic Church: Revised in Accordance with the Official Latin Text Promulgated by Pope John Paul II*. Second edition. Vatican City: Libreria Editrice Vaticana, 1997.

Catling, David C., and Kevin J. Zahnle. 'The Archean Atmosphere'. *Science Advances* 6, no. 9 (February 2020): eaax1420.

Chase, Steven, ed. *Angelic Spirituality: Medieval Perspectives on the Ways of Angels*. New York: Paulist Press, 2002.

Chatterji, Mohini M., trans. *The Bhagavad Gîtâ or the Lord's Lay*. Boston: Ticknor and Co, 1887.

Chesterton, Gilbert Keith. *Charles Dickens: A Critical Study*. New York: Dodd Mead and Co, 1906.

Chesterton, Gilbert Keith. *The Everlasting Man*. San Francisco: Ignatius Press, 1993.

Cho, Francisca. 'Comparing Stories about the Origin, Extent, and Future of Life: An Asian Religious Perspective'. In *Exploring the Origin, Extent, and Future of Life: Philosophical, Ethical and Theological Perspectives*, edited by Constance M. Bertka, 303–20. Cambridge: Cambridge University Press, 2009.

Clark, Stephen R.L. 'How to Believe in Fairies'. *Inquiry* 30, no. 4 (January 1987): 337–55.

Cleland, Carol E. *The Quest for a Universal Theory of Life: Searching for Life as We Don't Know It*. Cambridge: Cambridge University Press, 2020.

Cleland, Carol E., and Mark A. Bedau, eds. *The Nature of Life: Classical and Contemporary Perspectives from Philosophy and Science*. Cambridge: Cambridge University Press, 2010.

Cleomedes. *Cleomedes' Lectures on Astronomy: A Translation of The Heavens*. Translated by Alan C. Bowen and Robert B. Todd. Berkeley: University of California Press, 2004.

Clough, David L. *On Animals – Volume I: Systematic Theology*. London: Bloomsbury, 2012.

Coakley, Sarah. *God, Sexuality and the Self: An Essay 'On the Trinity'*. Cambridge: Cambridge University Press, 2013.

Coleman, Monica A. 'Invoking Oya'. In *Polydoxy: Theology of Multiplicity and Relation*, edited by Catherine Keller and Laurel C. Schneider, 186–202. London: Routledge, 2011.

Collins, Robin. 'Extraterrestrial Intelligence and the Incarnation'. In *God and the Multiverse: Scientific, Philosophical, and Theological Perspectives*, edited by Klaas J. Kraay, 211–26. London: Routledge, 2014.

Congar, Yves. 'Has God Peopled the Stars?' In *The Wide World My Parish*, translated by Donald Attwater, 184–88. Baltimore: Helicon Press, 1964.

Conselice, Christopher J., Aaron Wilkinson, Kenneth Duncan, and Alice Mortlock. 'The Evolution of Galaxy Number Density at $Z < 8$ and Its Implications'. *The Astrophysical Journal* 830, no. 2 (13 October 2016): 83.

Consolmagno, Guy. 'Would You Baptize an Extraterrestrial?' In *The Impact of Discovering Life beyond Earth*, edited by Steven J. Dick, 233–44. Cambridge: Cambridge University Press, 2015.

Cooper, Adam. 'The Reception of Aquinas in Nouvelle Théologie'. In *The Oxford Handbook of the Reception of Aquinas*, edited by Matthew Levering and Marcus Plested, 424–41. Oxford: Oxford University Press, 2021.

Coward, Harold G. *The Perfectibility of Human Nature in Eastern and Western Thought*. Albany, NY: State University of New York Press, 2008.

Coyne, George V. 'The Evolution of Intelligent Life on the Earth and Possibly Elsewhere: Reflections from a Religious Tradition'. In *Many Worlds: The New Universe, Extraterrestrial Life, and the Theological Implications*, edited by Stephen Dick, 177–88. Philadelphia: Templeton Foundation Press, 2000.

Cressy, David. 'Early Modern Space Travel and the English Man in the Moon'. *American Historical Review* 111, no. 4 (1 October 2006): 961–82.

Crisp, Oliver. *God Incarnate: Explorations in Christology*. London: T & T Clark, 2009.

Cross, Frank Leslie., and Elizabeth Anne Livingstone, eds. *The Oxford Dictionary of the Christian Church*. Third revised edition. Oxford: Oxford University Press, 2005.

Cross, Richard. *Duns Scotus*. Oxford: Oxford University Press, 1999.

Cross, Richard. 'Incarnation, Indwelling, and the Vision of God: Henry of Ghent and Some Franciscans'. *Franciscan Studies* 57 (1999): 79–130.

Cross, Richard. *The Metaphysics of the Incarnation: Thomas Aquinas to Duns Scotus*. Oxford: Oxford University Press, 2002.

Crowe, Michael J. 'A History of the Extraterrestrial Life Debate'. *Zygon* 32, no. 2 (1997): 147–62.

Crowe, Michael J. *The Extraterrestrial Life Debate, 1750–1900*. Mineola, NY: Dover, 1999.

Crowe, Michael J., ed. *The Extraterrestrial Life Debate: Antiquity to 1915 – A Source Book*. Notre Dame, IN: University of Notre Dame Press, 2008.

Crysdale, Cynthia S. W. 'God, Evolution, and Astrobiology'. In *Exploring the Origin, Extent, and Future of Life: Philosophical, Ethical and Theological Perspectives*, edited by Constance M. Bertka, 220–42. Cambridge: Cambridge University Press, 2009.

Cunningham, David S. 'The Way of All Flesh: Rethinking the Imago Dei'. In *Creaturely Theology: On God, Humans and Other Animals*, edited by Celia Deane-Drummond and David Clough, 100–117. London: SCM Press, 2009.

Dabić, Snežana. *W. B. Yeats and Indian Thought*. Newcastle upon Tyne: Cambridge Scholars Publishing, 2015.

Daneau, Lambert. *The Wonderful Workmanship of the World*. London: Andrew Maunsell, 1578.

Daniélou, Jean. *Les Anges et Leur Mission, d'après Les Pères de l'Église*. Second edition. Paris: Éditions de Chevetogne, 1953.

Daniélou, Jean. *The Angels and Their Mission: According to the Fathers of the Church*. Notre Dame, IN: Christian Classics, 2011.

Danielson, Dennis, and Christopher M. Graney. 'The Case against Copernicus'. *Scientific American* 310, no. 1 (January 2014): 72–77.

Däniken, Erich von. *Chariots of the Gods? Unsolved Mysteries of the Past.* Translated by Michael Heron. London: Souvenir, 1969.

Dante, Alighieri. *Paradiso.* Translated by Robin Kirkpatrick. London: Penguin, 2007.

Davis, Stephen T., Daniel Kendall, and Gerald O'Collins, eds. 'The Incarnation: The Critical Issues'. In *The Incarnation*, 1–28. Oxford: Oxford University Press, 2002.

Davison, Andrew. 'All Creatures That on Earth Do Make a Dwelling: Ecological Niche Construction and the Ubiquity of Creaturely Making'. *Philosophy, Theology and the Sciences* 7, no. 2 (2020): 181–204.

Davison, Andrew. 'Biological Mutualism: A Scientific Survey'. *Theology and Science* 18, no. 2 (24 May 2020): 190–210.

Davison, Andrew. 'Christian Doctrine and Biological Mutualism: Some Explorations in Systematic and Philosophical Theology'. *Theology and Science* 18, no. 2 (24 May 2020): 258–78.

Davison, Andrew. 'Christian Systematic Theology and Life Elsewhere in the Universe: A Study in Suitability'. *Theology and Science* 16, no. 4 (2 October 2018): 447–61.

Davison, Andrew. 'Creation and Divine Action'. In *The Oxford Handbook of Creation*, edited by Simon Oliver. Oxford: Oxford University Press, 2023.

Davison, Andrew. '"He Fathers-Forth Whose Beauty Is Past Change", but "Who Knows How?": Evolution and Divine Exemplarity'. *Nova et Vetera* 16, no. 4 (November 2018): 1067–1102.

Davison, Andrew. 'Human Uniqueness: Standing Alone?' *The Expository Times* 127, no. 5 (2016): 217–24.

Davison, Andrew. 'Living Worlds in Christian Theology'. In *Life as a Planetary Phenomenon*, edited by William Storrar and Joshua Mauldin. Forthcoming.

Davison, Andrew. 'Looking Back towards the Origin: Scientific Cosmology as Creation Ex Nihilo Considered "from the Inside"'. In *Creatio Ex Nihilo: Origins and Contemporary Significance*, edited by Markus Bockmuehl and Gary Anderson, 367–89. Notre Dame, IN: University of Notre Dame Press, 2017.

Davison, Andrew. 'Machine Learning and Theological Traditions of Analogy'. *Modern Theology* 37, no. 2 (April 2021): 254–74.

Davison, Andrew. 'More History, More Theology, More Philosophy, More Science: The State of Theological Engagement with Science'. In *New Directions in Theology and Science: Beyond Dialogue*, edited by Peter Harrison and Paul Tyson, 19–35. London: Bloomsbury, 2022.

Davison, Andrew. *Participation in God: A Study in Christian Doctrine and Metaphysics*. Cambridge: Cambridge University Press, 2019.

Davison, Andrew. *The Love of Wisdom: An Introduction to Philosophy for Theologians*. London: SCM Press, 2013.

Davison, Andrew, and Jacob Holsinger Sherman. 'Science and Christian Platonism'. In *Christian Platonism: A History*, edited by Alexander Hampton and John P. Kenney, 355–380. Cambridge: Cambridge University Press, 2020.

Dawkins, Richard. *The Ancestor's Tale: A Pilgrimage to the Dawn of Life*. London: Weidenfeld & Nicolson, 2004.

De Concilio, Januarius. *Harmony between Science and Revelation*. New York: Fr Pustet, 1889.

De Vere, Aubrey. *Poems from the Works of Aubrey De Vere*. Edited by Margaret Domvile. London: Catholic Truth Society, 1904.

Deacon, Terrence W. 'Emergence: The Hole and the Wheel's Hub'. In *The Re-Emergence of Emergence: The Emergentist Hypothesis from Science to Religion*, edited by Philip Clayton and Paul. C. W. Davies, 111–50. Oxford: Oxford University Press, 2006.

Deane-Drummond, Celia. 'The Alpha and the Omega: Reflections on the Origin and Future of Life from the Perspective of Christian Theology and Ethics'. In *Exploring the Origin, Extent, and Future of Life: Philosophical, Ethical and Theological Perspectives*, edited by Constance M. Bertka, 96–112. Cambridge: Cambridge University Press, 2009.

Deferrari, Roy Joseph, and M. Inviolata Barry. *A Lexicon of St. Thomas Aquinas: Based on the Summa Theologica and Selected Passages of His Other Works*. Washington, D. C.: Catholic University of America Press, 1948.

Delano, Kenneth J. *Many Worlds, One God*. Hicksville, NY: Exposition Press, 1977.

Delio, Ilia. 'Revisiting the Franciscan Doctrine of Christ'. *Theological Studies* 64, no. 1 (February 2003): 3–23.

Dick, Steven J. *Astrobiology, Discovery, and Societal Impact*. Cambridge: Cambridge University Press, 2020.

Dick, Steven J, ed. *Many Worlds: The New Universe, Extraterrestrial Life, and the Theological Implications*. Philadelphia: Templeton Foundation Press, 2000.

Dick, Steven J, ed. *The Impact of Discovering Life beyond Earth*. Cambridge: Cambridge University Press, 2015.

Diogenes Laertius. *Lives of Eminent Philosophers*. Translated by Robert Drew Hicks. Vol. 2. Cambridge, MA: Harvard University Press, 2005.

Domagal-Goldman, Shawn D., Katherine E. Wright, Katarzyna Adamala, Leigh Arina de la Rubia, Jade Bond, Lewis R. Dartnell, Aaron D. Goldman, et al. 'The Astrobiology Primer v2.0'. *Astrobiology* 16, no. 8 (August 2016): 561–653.

Doolan, Gregory. *Aquinas on the Divine Ideas as Exemplar Causes*. Washington, D. C.: Catholic University of America Press, 2008.

Dov Baer. *Magid Devarav Le-Yaʿakov*. Edited by Rivka Schatz Uffenheimer. Jerusalem: Magnes Press, Hebrew University, 1976.

Driel, Edwin Chr van. *Incarnation Anyway: Arguments for Supralapsarian Christology*. Oxford: Oxford University Press, 2008.

Duhem, Pierre Maurice Marie. *Medieval Cosmology: Theories of Infinity, Place, Time, Void, and the Plurality of Worlds*. Translated by Roger Ariew. Chicago: University of Chicago Press, 1985.

Duns Scotus, John. *Duns Scotus on the Will and Morality*. Translated by Allan Bernard Wolter. Washington, D. C.: Catholic University of America Press, 1986.

Eliot, Thomas Stearns. *Four Quartets*. London: Faber and Faber, 1974.

Emery, Gilles. 'Brief Catalogue of the Works of Saint Thomas Aquinas'. In *Saint Thomas Aquinas – Volume 1: The Person and His Work*, edited by Jean-Pierre Torrell, translated by Robert Royal, revised edition, 330–361. Washington, D. C.: Catholic University of America Press, 2005.

Fabro, Cornelio. 'The Intensive Hermeneutics of Thomistic Philosophy: The Notion of Participation'. Translated by B. M. Bonansea. *Review of Metaphysics* 27, no. 3 (1974): 449–91.

Fergusson, David. *The Providence of God: A Polyphonic Approach*. Current Issues in Theology. Cambridge: Cambridge University Press, 2018.

Ford, David. 'Barth's Interpretation of the Bible'. In *Karl Barth: Studies of His Theological Method*, edited by Stephen Sykes, 55–87. Oxford: Clarendon Press, 1979.

Freddoso, Alfred J. 'Human Nature, Potency and the Incarnation'. *Faith and Philosophy* 3, no. 1 (1986): 27–53.

Gaine, Simon Francis. 'Did Christ Die for Neanderthals?' *New Blackfriars* 102, no. 1098 (March 2021): 225–38.

Garrigou-Lagrange, Réginald. *Grace: Commentary on the Summa Theologica of St. Thomas, Ia IIae q.109–114.* Translated by Nuns of Corpus Christi monastery. Saint Louis, MO: B. Herder, 1957.

Gassendi, Petri. 'Syntagmatis Philosophici'. In *Opera Omnia*, 4:1–166. Florence: Cajetanum Tartini et Sanctem Franchi, 1727.

Gathercole, Simon. 'Editorial: The "Delay of the Parousia"'. *Early Christianity* 9, no. 1 (2018): 1–7.

Gavriljuk, Pavel L. 'The Retrieval of Deification: How a Once-Despised Archaism Became an Ecumenical Desideratum'. *Modern Theology* 25, no. 4 (2009): 647–59.

Genet, Jacqueline. *William Butler Yeats: Les Fondements et l'évolution de La Création Poétique.* Villeneuve-d'Ascq: Publications de l'Université de Lille, 1976.

George, Marie. 'Aquinas on Intelligent Extra-Terrestrial Life'. *Thomist* 65, no. 2 (2001): 239–58.

George, Marie. *Christianity and Extraterrestrials? A Catholic Perspective.* Bloomington, IN: iUniverse, 2005.

Gess, Wolfgang Friedrich. *Das Dogma von Christi Person und Werk.* Basel: Detloff, 1887.

Gilson, Étienne. *Jean Duns Scot: Introduction à Ses Positions Fondamentales.* Paris: J. Vrin, 1952.

Gilson, Étienne. *The Spirit of Thomism.* New York: Kenedy and Sons, 1964.

Gladden, Lee, and Vivianne Cervantes Gladden. *Heirs of the Gods: A Space Age Interpretation of the Bible.* Beverly Hills, CA: Bel-Air Publishing Corporation, 1982.

Godfrey-Smith, Peter. *Other Minds: The Octopus, the Sea, and the Deep Origins of Consciousness.* New York: Farrar, Straus and Giroux, 2016.

Goldblatt, Colin. 'The Inhabitance Paradox: How Habitability and Inhabitancy Are Inseparable'. In *Conference Proceedings of Comparative Climates of Terrestrial Planets II.* Moffett Field, CA, 2015. https://arxiv.org/abs/1603.00950.

Gondreau, Paul. 'Anti-Docetism in Aquinas's Super Iohannem'. In *Reading John with St. Thomas Aquinas: Theological Exegesis and Speculative Theology*, edited by Michael Dauphinais and Matthew Levering, 254–76. Washington, D.C.: Catholic University of America Press, 2005.

Gould, Stephen Jay. *Wonderful Life: The Burgess Shale and the Nature of History*. London: Norton, 1989.

Graham, Billy (William Neil). *Angels: God's Secret Agents*. Second edition. Nashville: W Publishing, 1994.

Graney, Christopher M. 'Stars as the Armies of God: Lansbergen's Incorporation of Tycho Brahe's Star-Size Argument into the Copernican Theory'. *Journal for the History of Astronomy* 44, no. 2 (May 2013): 165–72.

Graney, Christopher M. 'The Telescope against Copernicus: Star Observations by Riccioli Supporting a Geocentric Universe'. *Journal for the History of Astronomy* 41, no. 4 (November 2010): 453–67.

Grant, Edward. 'The Condemnation of 1277, God's Absolute Power, and Physical Thought in the Late Middle Ages'. *Viator* 10 (1979): 211–44.

Gregersen, Niels Henrik, ed. *Incarnation: On the Scope and Depth of Christology*. Minneapolis, MN: Fortress Press, 2015.

Gregory of Nazianzus. *On God and Christ: The Five Theological Orations and Two Letters to Cledonius*. Translated by Frederick Williams and Lionel R. Wickham. Crestwood, NY: St. Vladimir's Seminary Press, 2002.

Grinspoon, David Harry. *Earth in Human Hands: The Rise of Terra Sapiens and Hope for Our Planet*. New York: Grand Central, 2016.

Grisez, Germain Gabriel. 'The True Ultimate End of Human Beings: The Kingdom, Not God Alone'. *Theological Studies* 69, no. 1 (2008): 38–61.

Guillaume de Vaurouillon. *Quattuor librorum Sententiarum Compendium: venerabilis patris fratris Guillermi Vorrillonis*. Basel: Adam Petri de Landendorf, 1510.

Guillermus Vorrilong [de Vaurouillon]. *Guillermus Vorrillong Super Quattuor Libris Sententiarum Nouiter Correctus [et] Apostillatus*. Per Bonetum Locatellum Bergomensem presbyterum, 1502.

Guitton, Jean. *Jésus*. Paris: B. Grasset, 1956.

Hallacker, Anja. 'On Angelic Bodies: Some Philosophical Discussions in the Seventeenth Century'. In *Angels in Medieval Philosophical Inquiry: Their Function and Significance*, edited by Isabel Iribarren and Martin Lenz, 201–14. London: Routledge, 2016.

Harkins, Franklin T. 'The Early Aquinas on the Question of Universal Salvation, or How a Knight May Choose Not to Ride His Horse'. *New Blackfriars* 95, no. 1056 (2014): 208–17.

Harkins, Franklin T. 'The Embodiment of Angels: A Debate in Mid-Thirteenth Century Theology'. *Recherches de Théologie et Philosophie Médiévales* 78, no. 1 (2011): 25–58.

Harrison, Peter. *The Territories of Science and Religion*. Chicago: University of Chicago Press, 2015.

Hart, David Bentley. *The Experience of God: Being, Consciousness, Bliss*. New Haven: Yale University Press, 2013.

Hart, David Bentley. 'The Secret Commonwealth'. In *A Splendid Wickedness and Other Essays*, 23–27. Grand Rapids, MI: Eerdmans, 2016.

Hart, David Bentley. *You Are Gods: On Nature and Supernature*. Notre Dame, IN: University of Notre Dame Press, 2022.

Hay, William. 'Religio Philosophi'. In *Works of William Hay*, 1:171–300. London: J. Nichols, 1794.

Hebblethwaite, Brian. 'The Impossibility of Multiple Incarnations'. *Theology* 104, no. 821 (1 September 2001): 323–34.

Hebblethwaite, Brian. 'The Resurrection and the Incarnation'. In *The Resurrection of Jesus Christ*, edited by Paul D. L. Avis, 155–70. London: Darton, Longman and Todd, 1993.

Heidelberg Catechism: Text of Tercentenary Edition. Cleveland, OH: Publishing House of the Reformed Church, 1877.

Heppe, Heinrich. *Reformed Dogmatics*. Edited by Ernst Bizer. Translated by G. T. Thompson. London: Allen and Unwin, 1950.

Hesburgh, Theodore. 'Foreword'. In *The Search for Extraterrestrial Intelligence: SETI*, edited by Philip Morrison, John Billingham, and John Wolfe, vii. Washington, D. C.: Government Printing Office, n.d.

Hewlett, Martinez. 'The Copernican Revolution That Never Was'. In *Astrotheology: Science and Theology Meet Extraterrestrial Life*, edited by Martinez Hewlett, Joshua M. Moritz, Robert John Russell, and Ted Peters, 90–105. Eugene, OR: Cascade, 2018.

Hofer, Andrew, Pavel L. Gavriljuk, and Matthew Levering, eds. *Oxford Handbook of Deification*. Oxford: Oxford University Press, 2023.

Horovitz, S., and I. A. Rabin. *Mekhilta De-Rabi Yishmaʻel*. Second edition. Jerusaelm: Sifre Vahrman, 1970.

Houck, Daniel W. *Aquinas, Original Sin, and the Challenge of Evolution.* Cambridge: Cambridge University Press, 2020.

Hunt, Dave. *Cosmos, Creator and Human Destiny: Answering Darwin, Dawkins, and the New Atheists.* Bend, OR: Berean Call, 2010.

Huygens, Christian. *Cosmotheoros.* The Hague: Adriaan Moetjens, 1698.

Huygens, Christian. *The Celestial Worlds Discover'd.* London: Timothy Childe, 1698.

Jain, Sushil Kumar. 'Indian Elements in the Poetry of Yeats: On Chatterji and Tagore'. *Comparative Literature Studies* 7, no. 1 (1970): 82–96.

Jaki, Stanley L. 'Christ, Extraterrestrials and the Devil'. In *A Late Awakening; and Other Essays*, 93–106. Port Huron, MI: Real View Books, 2006.

Jaki, Stanley L. *Maybe Alone in the Universe, After All.* Pinckney, MI: Real View Books, 2000.

Jenson, Robert. *Systematic Theology – Volume 1: The Triune God.* New York: Oxford University Press, 1997.

Jenson, Robert. *Systematic Theology – Volume 2: The Works of God.* New York: Oxford University Press, 1999.

John of St Thomas. *Cursus Theologicus D. Thomae.* Colonia Agrippina: Metternich, 1711.

Johnson, Elizabeth A. 'Deep Christology'. In *From Logos to Christos: Essays on Christology in Honour of Joanne McWilliam*, edited by Kate Leonard and Ellen M. Merriman, 163–79. Waterloo: Wilfrid Laurier University Press, 2009.

Johnson, Elizabeth A. 'Jesus and the Cosmos: Soundings in Deep Christology'. In *Incarnation: On the Scope and Depth of Christology*, edited by Niels Henrik Gregersen, 133–56. Minneapolis, MN: Fortress Press, 2015.

Johnson, Mark Leonard. *The Body in the Mind: The Bodily Basis of Meaning, Imagination, and Reason.* Chicago: University of Chicago Press, 1992.

Julian of Norwich. *Showings.* Translated by Edmund Colledge and James Walsh. Mahwah, NJ: Paulist Press, 1978.

Kane, Stephen R., Margaret C. Turnbull, Benjamin J. Fulton, Lee J. Rosenthal, Andrew W. Howard, Howard Isaacson, Geoffrey W. Marcy, and Lauren M. Weiss. 'Dynamical Packing in the Habitable Zone: The Case of Beta CVn'. *The Astronomical Journal* 160, no. 2 (27 July 2020): 81.

Kant, Immanuel. *Allgemeine Naturgeschichte und Theorie des Himmels.* Königsberg: Johann Friederich Petersen, 1755.

Kant, Immanuel. *Universal Natural History and Theory of the Heavens or an Essay on the Constitution and Mechanical Origin of the Whole Universe Treated According to Newton's Principles*. Translated by W. Hastie. Ann Arbor, MI: University of Michigan Press, 1969.

Kärkkäinen, Veli-Matti. *One with God: Salvation as Deification and Justification*. Collegeville, MN: Liturgical Press, 2004.

Karttunen, Hannu, Pekka Kröger, Heikki Oja, Markku Poutanen, and Karl Johan Donner. *Fundamental Astronomy*. Sixth edition. Berlin: Springer, 2016.

Kauffman, Stuart A. *A World beyond Physics: The Emergence and Evolution of Life*. Oxford: Oxford University Press, 2019.

Kaufmann, Yehezkel. *The Religion of Israel: From Its Beginnings to the Babylonian Exile*. Translated by Moshe Greenberg. New York: Schocken Books, 1972.

Keck, David. *Angels and Angelology in the Middle Ages*. Oxford: Oxford University Press, 1998.

Keck, David. 'Bonaventure's Angelology'. In *A Companion to Bonaventure*, edited by Jay M. Hammond, J. A. Wayne Hellmann, and Jared Goff, 289–332. Leiden; Boston: Brill, 2014.

Kennedy, Daniel Joseph. *St Thomas Aquinas and Medieval Philosophy*. New York: Encyclopedia Press, 1919.

Kepler, Johannes. *The Harmony of the World*. Translated by Eric J. Aiton, Alistair Matheson Duncan, and Judith Veronica Field. Philadelphia: American Philosophical Association, 1997.

Kereszty, Roch A. *Jesus Christ: Fundamentals of Christology*. Second edition. New York: Alba House, 2002.

Kevern, Peter. 'Limping Principles: A Reply to Brian Hebblethwaite on "The Impossibility of Multiple Incarnations"'. *Theology* 105, no. 827 (September 2002): 342–47.

Kimbrough, S. T., Jr. *Partakers of the Life Divine: Participation in the Divine Nature in the Writings of Charles Wesley*. Eugene, OR: Cascade, 2016.

Kirk, Robert. *The Secret Commonwealth of Elves, Fauns, and Fairies*. New York: New York Review Books, 2007.

Klein, Elizabeth. *Augustine's Theology of Angels*. Cambridge: Cambridge University Press, 2018.

Koninck, Charles de. 'The Cosmos'. In *The Writings of Charles de Koninck*, edited and translated by Ralph McInerny, 235–354. Notre Dame, IN: University of Notre Dame Press, 2008.

Kostro, Ludwik. 'Some Philosophical and Theological Implications of Modern Astrobiology'. In *The History and Philosophy of Astrobiology: Perspectives on Extraterrestrial Life and the Human Mind*, edited by David Duner, Joel Parthemore, Erik Persson, and Gustav Holmberg, 245–56. Newcastle upon Tyne: Cambridge Scholars Publishing, 2013.

Koyré, Alexandre. *From the Closed World to the Infinite Universe*. New York: Harper and Brothers, 1958.

Kraay, Klaas J., ed. *God and the Multiverse: Scientific, Philosophical, and Theological Perspectives*. London: Routledge, 2014.

Krissansen-Totton, Joshua, Stephanie Olson, and David C. Catling. 'Disequilibrium Biosignatures over Earth History and Implications for Detecting Exoplanet Life'. *Science Advances* 4, no. 1 (January 2018): eaao5747.

Kuhn, Thomas S. *The Copernican Revolution: Planetary Astronomy in the Development of Western Thought*. Cambridge, MA: Harvard University Press, 1957.

Kuhn, Thomas S. *The Structure of Scientific Revolutions*. Chicago: University of Chicago Press, 1970.

Lai, Tyrone Tai Lun. 'Nicholas of Cusa and the Finite Universe'. *Journal of the History of Philosophy* 11, no. 2 (1973): 161–67.

Lamm, Norman. 'The Religious Implications of Extraterrestrial Life'. *Tradition: A Journal of Orthodox Jewish Thought* 7/8, no. 4/1 (1965): 5–56.

Le Poidevin, Robin. 'Multiple Incarnations and Distributed Persons'. In *The Metaphysics of the Incarnation*, edited by Anna Marmodoro and Jonathan Hill, 228–41. Oxford: Oxford University Press, 2011.

Lee, Hoon J. *The Biblical Accommodation Debate in Germany: Interpretation and the Enlightenment*. Cham: Springer, 2017.

Leo the Great. *A Select Library of Nicene and Post-Nicene Fathers of the Christian Church*. Second Series. Volume 12 – Leo the Great and Gregory the Great. Edited by Philip Schaff and Henry Wallace. Translated by Charles Lett Feltoe. Edinburgh: T&T Clark, 1988.

Lerner, Ralph, and Muhsin Mahdi, eds. *Medieval Political Philosophy: A Sourcebook*. Ithaca, NY: Cornell University Press, 1972.

Levy, David H. *David Levy's Guide to the Night Sky*. Cambridge: Cambridge University Press, 2001.

Lewis, Clive Staples. *Miracles: A Preliminary Study*. London: Geoffrey Bles, 1947.

Lewis, Clive Staples. *Perelandra: A Novel*. London: Bodley Head, 1943.

Lewis, Clive Staples. *The Collected Letters of C. S. Lewis*. Edited by Walter Hooper. Vol. 3. San Francisco: HarperSanFrancisco, 2004.

Lewis, Clive Staples. *The Discarded Image: An Introduction to Medieval and Renaissance Literature*. Cambridge: Cambridge University Press, 1994.

Lovin, Robin W. 'Astrobiology and Theology'. In *The Impact of Discovering Life beyond Earth*, edited by Steven J. Dick, 222–32. Cambridge: Cambridge University Press, 2015.

Lubac, Henri de. *Surnaturel: Études historiques*. Paris: Aubier, 1946.

Lucianus. *Lucian: Volume 1*. Translated by Austin Morris Harmon. Cambridge, MA: Harvard University Press, 2006.

Lucretius. *De Rerum Natura*. Translated by W. H. D. Rouse and Martin F. Smith. Cambridge, MA: Harvard University Press, 1924.

Luther, Martin. 'Confession Concerning Christ's Supper'. In *Luther's Works – Volume 37: Word and Sacrament III*, edited by Helmut T. Lehmann, translated by Robert H. Fischer, 151–372. Philadelphia: Concordia, 1961.

Luther, Martin. *Luther's Works – Volume 33: Career of the Reformer III*. Translated by Philip Saville Watson and Benjamin Drewery. Philadelphia: Fortress Press, 1972.

Luther, Martin. *Luther's Works – Volume 54: Table Talk*. Edited by Theodore Gerhardt Tappert. Translated by Helmut T. Lehmann. Philadelphia: Fortress Press, 1967.

Luther, Martin. 'That These Words of Christ, "This Is My Body" Etc. Still Stand Firm against the Fanatics'. In *Luther's Works – Volume 37: Word and Sacrament III*, edited by Helmut T. Lehmann, translated by Robert H. Fischer, 3–150. Philadelphia: Concordia, 1961.

Lynch, Michael J. *John Davenant's Hypothetical Universalism: A Defense of Catholic and Reformed Orthodoxy*. Oxford: Oxford University Press, 2021.

Macdonald, Paul A. 'In Defense of Aquinas's Adam: Original Justice, the Fall, and Evolution'. *Zygon* 56, no. 2 (2021): 454–66.

Macquarrie, John. *An Existentialist Theology*. London: SCM Press, 1955.

Macquarrie, John. *Principles of Christian Theology*. London: SCM Press, 1966.

MacQuarrie, John. *Studies in Christian Existentialism: Lectures and Essays.* London: SCM Press, 1965.

Maimonides, Moses. *The Guide of the Perplexed.* Translated by Shlomo Pines. Vol. 2. 2 vols. Chicago; London: University of Chicago Press, 1974.

Mandonnet, Pierre. *Siger de Brabant et l'averroisme Latin Au XIIIe Siècle.* Vol. 2. 2 vols. Louvain: Institut Supérieur De Philosophie, 1908.

Mare, Leonard P. 'Psalm 8: God's Glory and Humanity's Reflected Glory'. *Old Testament Essays* 19, no. 3 (2006): 926–38.

Maritain, Jacques. *True Humanism.* Translated by M. R. Adamson. London: Centenary Press, 1938.

Martinez, Alberto A. *Burned Alive: Bruno, Galileo and the Inquisition.* London: Reaktion, 2018.

Mascall, Eric Lionel. *Christian Theology and Natural Science: Some Questions on Their Relations.* London: Longmans, Green and Co., 1956.

Mascall, Eric Lionel. *He Who Is: A Study in Traditional Theism.* London: Longmans, Green and Co., 1943.

Mascall, Eric Lionel. *The Angels of Light and the Powers of Darkness.* London: Faith Press, 1954.

Mascall, Eric Lionel. *Via Media: An Essay in Theological Synthesis.* London: Longmans, Green, 1956.

McCabe, Herbert. *God Matters.* London: Chapman, 1987.

McCabe, Herbert. 'The Myth of God Incarnate'. *New Blackfriars* 58, no. 687 (1977): 350–57.

McColley, Grant, and H. W. Miller. 'Saint Bonaventure, Francis Mayron, William Vorilong, and the Doctrine of a Plurality of Worlds'. *Speculum* 12, no. 3 (1937): 386–89.

McDonald, Peter, ed. *The Poems of W. B. Yeats.* Vol. 1. London: Routledge, 2020.

McGuckin, John A. 'Angels'. In *Encyclopedia of Eastern Orthodox Christianity,* edited by John A. McGuckin, 1:28–30. Chichester: Wiley-Blackwell, 2010.

McInerny, Ralph M. *The Logic of Analogy: An Interpretation of St. Thomas.* The Hague: Nijhoff, 1971.

McIntosh, Mark. *The Divine Ideas Tradition in Christian Mystical Theology.* Oxford: Oxford University Press, 2021.

McMullin, Ernan. 'The Origin of Terrestrial Life: A Christian Perspective'. In *Exploring the Origin, Extent, and Future of Life: Philosophical, Ethical and Theological Perspectives*, edited by Constance M. Bertka, 80–95. Cambridge: Cambridge University Press, 2009.

Melanchthon, Philipp. *Corpus Reformatorum – Series 1: Melanthonis Opera Quae Supersunt Omnia*. Edited by Carolus Gottleib Bretschneider. Vol. 13. 28 vols. Halis Saxonum: C. A. Schwetschke et Filium, 1846.

Melanchthon, Philipp. *Initia Doctrinae Physicae: Dictata In Academia Witebergensi*. Vitebergae: Crato, 1565.

Meynell, Alice. *Collected Poems*. London: Burns & Oates, 1913.

Michael, Scot. *Eximii atque: excellentissimi physicorum motuum cursusque*. Bologna: Justinianum de Ruberia, 1495.

Middleton, J. Richard. *The Liberating Image: The Imago Dei in Genesis 1*. Grand Rapids, MI: Brazos Press, 2005.

Midgley, Mary. *The Solitary Self: Darwin and the Selfish Gene*. Durham: Acumen, 2010.

Milbank, John. 'Fictioning Things: Gift and Narrative'. *Religion & Literature* 37, no. 3 (2005): 1–35.

Milbank, John. 'Stanton Lecture 8: The Surprise of the Imagined'. Faculty of Divinity, University of Cambridge, 8 March 2011.

Miller, Hugh. *The Foot-Prints of the Creator: Or, The Asterolepis of Stromness*. Boston: Gould and Lincoln, 1868.

Milne, Edward Arthur. *Modern Cosmology and the Christian Idea of God*. Oxford: Clarendon Press, 1952.

Missale Romanum et Anglicum: Ordo Missae. Birmingham: C. Goodliffe Neale, 1966.

Mix, Lucas John. *Life Concepts from Aristotle to Darwin: On Vegetable Souls*. Cambridge: Palgrave Macmillan, 2018.

Mix, Lucas John. 'Life-Value Narratives and the Impact of Astrobiology on Christian Ethics'. *Zygon* 51, no. 2 (June 2016): 520–35.

More, Henry. *Democritus Platonissans, or, An Essay upon the Infinity of Worlds*. Cambridge: Roger Daniel, 1646.

Morris, Simon Conway. *Life's Solution: Inevitable Humans in a Lonely Universe*. Cambridge: Cambridge University Press, 2008.

Morris, Thomas V. *The Logic of God Incarnate*. Ithaca, NY: Cornell University Press, 1986.

Newman, John Henry. 'Inspiration in Its Relation to Revelation'. In *Stray Essays on Controversial Points*, 1–36. Birmingham: [Privately Printed], 1890.

Nicholas of Cusa. *Nicholas of Cusa on Learned Ignorance: A Translation and an Appraisal of De Docta Ignorantia*. Translated by Jaspar Hopkins. Minnesota, MN: Arthur J. Banning Press, 1985.

Nicholson, Daniel J. 'The Return of the Organism as a Fundamental Explanatory Concept in Biology'. *Philosophy Compass* 9, no. 5 (May 2014): 347–59.

Nieuwenhove, Rik van. *An Introduction to Medieval Theology*. Cambridge: Cambridge University Press, 2012.

Oakes, Edward T. *A Theology of Grace in Six Controversies*. Grand Rapids, MI: Eerdmans, 2016.

Ockham, William of. *Scriptum in Librum Primum Sententiarum (Ordinatio), Distinctiones 19–48*. Edited by Girard Etzkorn and Franciscus Kelley. St Bonaventure, NY: Franciscan Institute, 1979.

O'Meara, Thomas F. 'Christian Theology and Extraterrestrial Intelligent Life'. *Theological Studies* 60, no. 1 (1 February 1999): 3–30.

Origen. *On First Principles*. Translated by John Behr. Oxford: Oxford University Press, 2019.

O'Rourke, Fran. 'Virtus Essendi: Intensive Being in Pseudo-Dionysius and Aquinas'. *Dionysius* 15 (1990): 31–90.

Paine, Thomas. *The Thomas Paine Reader*. Edited by Michael Foot and Isaac Kramnick. London: Penguin Classics, 1987.

Pannenberg, Wolfhart. *Systematic Theology*. Translated by Geoffrey W. Bromiley. Vol. 2. 3 vols. Edinburgh: T&T Clark, 1994.

Patel, Bhavesh H., Claudia Percivalle, Dougal J. Ritson, Colm D. Duffy, and John D. Sutherland. 'Common Origins of RNA, Protein and Lipid Precursors in a Cyanosulfidic Protometabolism'. *Nature Chemistry* 7, no. 4 (April 2015): 301–7.

Pawl, Timothy. 'Brian Hebblethwaite's Arguments against Multiple Incarnations'. *Religious Studies* 52, no. 01 (March 2016): 117–30.

Pawl, Timothy. 'Thomistic Multiple Incarnations'. *The Heythrop Journal* 57, no. 2 (March 2016): 359–70.

Peacocke, Arthur. 'The Challenge and Stimulus of the Epic of Evolution to Theology'. In *Many Worlds: The New Universe, Extraterrestrial*

Life, and the Theological Implications, edited by Stephen Dick, 88–117. Philadelphia: Templeton Foundation Press, 2000.

Peden, Alison. 'The Medieval Antipodes'. *History Today*, December 1995.

Pendergast, R. J. 'Terrestrial and Cosmic Polygenism'. *Downside Review* 82, no. 268 (July 1964): 189–98.

Perler, Dominik. 'Thought Experiments: The Methodological Function of Angels in Late Medieval Epistemology'. In *Angels in Medieval Philosophical Inquiry: Their Function and Significance*, edited by Isabel Iribarren and Martin Lenz, 143–53. London: Routledge, 2016.

Peters, Ted. 'Astrobiology and Astrochristology'. *Zygon* 51, no. 2 (June 2016): 480–96.

Peters, Ted. 'One Incarnation or Many?' In *Astrotheology: Science and Theology Meet Extraterrestrial Life*, edited by Ted Peters, Martinez Hewlett, Joshua M. Moritz, and Robert John Russell, 271–302. Eugene, OR: Cascade, 2018.

Peters, Ted. *Science, Theology, and Ethics*. Aldershot: Ashgate, 2003.

Peters, Ted. 'The Implications of the Discovery of Extra-Terrestrial Life for Religion'. *Philosophical Transactions of the Royal Society A: Mathematical, Physical and Engineering Sciences* 369, no. 1936 (13 February 2011): 644–55.

Peters, Ted, Martinez Hewlett, Joshua M. Moritz, and Robert John Russell, eds. *Astrotheology: Science and Theology Meet Extraterrestrial Life*. Eugene, OR: Cascade, 2018.

Piatigorsky, Joram. 'A Genetic Perspective on Eye Evolution: Gene Sharing, Convergence and Parallelism'. *Evolution: Education and Outreach* 1, no. 4 (2008): 403–14.

Pieper, Josef, and Heinz Raskop. *What Catholics Believe*. Translated by Christopher Huntington. London: Burns & Oates, 1954.

Pittenger, Norman. *The Word Incarnate*. London: Nisbet, 1959.

Plato. *Plato's Cosmology: The Timaeus of Plato*. Translated by Francis Macdonald Cornford. Indianapolis, IN: Hackett, 1997.

Plato. *Republic*. Translated by Robin Waterfield. Oxford: Oxford University Press, 1994.

Pohle, Josef. *Die Sternenwelten und ihre Bewohner*. Second edition. Köln: Bachem, 1899.

Polkinghorne, John C. *Science and the Trinity*. London: SPCK, 2004.

Polkinghorne, John. *Theology in the Context of Science*. New Haven: Yale University Press, 2010.

Pope Pius XII. *Humani Generis*. Vatican City: Libreria Editrice Vaticana, 1950.

Preus, J. Samuel. 'Zwingli, Calvin and the Origin of Religion'. *Church History* 46, no. 2 (June 1977): 186–202.

Pseudo-Dionysius. *The Complete Works*. Translated by Colm Luibheid and Paul Rorem. Mahwah, NJ: Paulist Press, 1987.

Ptolemaeus, Claudius. *Ptolemy's Almagest*. Edited by Gerald J. Toomer. Princeton, NJ: Princeton University Press, 1998.

Puccetti, Roland. *Persons: A Study of Possible Moral Agents in the Universe*. London: Macmillan, 1968.

Quay, Paul M. 'Angels and Demons: The Teaching of IV Lateran'. *Theological Studies* 42, no. 1 (March 1981): 20–45.

Radde-Gallwitz, Andrew. 'The One and the Trinity'. In *Christian Platonism: A History*, edited by Alexander Hampton and John P. Kenney, 53–78. Cambridge: Cambridge University Press, 2020.

Rahner, Karl. *Foundations of Christian Faith: An Introduction to the Idea of Christianity*. Translated by William V. Dych. London: Darton, Longman and Todd, 1978.

Rahner, Karl. 'On the Theology of the Incarnation'. In *Theological Investigations – Volume 4*, translated by Kevin Smyth, 105–20. London: Darton Longman and Todd, 1966.

Randolph, Richard O. 'God's Preferential Option for Life: A Christian Perspective on Astrobiology'. In *Exploring the Origin, Extent, and Future of Life: Philosophical, Ethical and Theological Perspectives*, edited by Constance M. Bertka, 281–302. Cambridge: Cambridge University Press, 2009.

Ray, John. *The Wisdom of God Manifested in the Works of the Creation*. London: Samuel Smith, 1691.

Rees, Martin J. 'Black Holes, Galactic Evolution and Cosmic Coincidence'. *Interdisciplinary Science Reviews* 14, no. 2 (June 1989): 148–61.

Richard of Middleton. Magistri Ricardi de Mediavilla, Seraphici Ord. Min. Convent. Super Quatvor Libros Sententiarvm, Petri Lombardi Quaestiones Subtilissimae. Vol. 1. Brescia: Vincentium Sabbium, 1591.

Riches, Aaron. *Ecce Homo: On the Divine Unity of Christ*. Grand Rapids, MI: Eerdmans, 2016.

Roberts, Alexander, and James Donaldson, eds. *Ante-Nicene Fathers – Volume VII: Fathers of the Third and Fourth Centuries*. Translated by William Fletcher. Edinburgh: T&T Clark, 1994.

Robinson, J. Armitage. *St Paul's Epistle to the Ephesians: A Revised Text and Translation with Exposition and Notes*. Second edition. London: James Clarke and Co., 1969.

Robinson, John A. T. *The Human Face of God*. London: SCM, 1973.

Rolston, Holmes, III. 'Life, Biological Aspects'. In *Encyclopedia of Science and Religion*, edited by J. Wentzel Van Huyssteen, 2:522–23. New York: Macmillan Reference, 2003.

Rose, Seraphim. *Orthodoxy and the Religion of the Future*. Platina, CA: St. Herman of Alaska Brotherhood, 2004.

Rothery, David A., Iain Gilmour, Mark A. Sephton, Mahesh Anand, and Open University, eds. *An Introduction to Astrobiology*. Third edition. Cambridge: Cambridge University Press, 2018.

Roy, Jean-René, Pierre-Yves Bely, and Carol Christian. *A Question and Answer Guide to Astronomy*. Second edition. Cambridge: Cambridge University Press, 2017.

Ruse, Michael. '"Klaatu Barada Nikto" – or, Do They Really Think like Us?' In *The Impact of Discovering Life Beyond Earth*, edited by Steven J. Dick, 175–88. Cambridge: Cambridge University Press, 2015.

Russell, Robert J. 'Life in the Universe: Philosophical and Theological Issues'. In *First Steps in the Origin of Life in the Universe: Proceedings of the Sixth Trieste Conference on Chemical Evolution*, edited by Julián Chela Flores, Tobias C. Owen, and F. Raulin, 365–74. Dordrecht: Kluwer Academic, 2001.

Rusticus. *Rvstici Diaconi contra Acephalos*. Edited by Sara Petri. 100. Turnhout: Brepols, 2013.

Sacred Congregation for the Doctrine of the Faith. *Letter on Certain Questions Concerning Eschatology*. Boston: Daughters of St Paul, 1979.

Sagan, Carl. *Pale Blue Dot: A Vision of the Human Future in Space*. London: Headline, 1995.

Samuelson, Norbert M. 'Jewish Theology Meets the Alien'. In *Astrotheology: Science and Theology Meet Extraterrestrial Life*, edited by Ted Peters, Martinez Hewlett, Joshua M. Moritz, and Robert John Russell, 208–15. Eugene, OR: Cascade, 2018.

Sanders, John. *No Other Name: Can Only Christians Be Saved?* London: SPCK, 1992.

Sarfati, Jonathan D. 'Bible Leaves No Room for Extraterrestrial Life'. *Science and Theology News* 4, no. 7 (March 2004).

Sartorius, Ernst. *Die Lehre von Der Heiligen Liebe*. Stuttgart: Liesching, 1851.

Sayers, Dorothy L. *The Lost Tools of Learning*. London: Methuen and Co., 1948.

Scarpelli Cory, Therese. 'The Distinctive Unity of the Human Being in Aquinas'. In *The Oxford Handbook of the Reception of Aquinas*, edited by Matthew Levering and Marcus Plested, 581–95. Oxford: Oxford University Press, 2021.

Scheeben, Matthias Joseph. *Handbook of Catholic Dogmatics: Book Five Soteriology, Part One – The Person of Christ the Redeemer*. Translated by Michael Miller. Steubenville, OH: Emmaus Academic, 2020.

Schleiermacher, Friedrich. *The Christian Faith*. Translated by H. R. Mackintosh and J. S. Stewart. London: T&T Clark, 1999.

Schneider, Susan. 'Superintelligent AI and the Postbiological Cosmos Approach'. In *What Is Life? On Earth and Beyond*, edited by Andreas Losch, 178–98. Cambridge: Cambridge University Press, 2017.

Schopenhauer, Arthur. *The World as Will and Representation*. Vol. 2. 2 vols. New York: Dover, 1969.

Schrader, Dylan. *Shortcut to Scholastic Latin*. New York: Paideia Institute, 2019.

Select Homilies for Holy Days and Seasons. Translated from the Writings of the Saints. Vol. 2. London: James Burns, n.d.

Sendy, Jean. *The Moon: Outpost of the Gods*. Translated by Lowell Bair. New York: Berkley, 1975.

Shapley, Harlow. *The View from a Distant Star*. New York: Basic Books, 1963.

Smelik, Willem F. *The Targum of Judges*. Leiden: Brill, 1995.

Smith, Howard. 'Alone in the Universe'. *Zygon* 51, no. 2 (June 2016): 497–519.

Smith, Mark S. *The Origins of Biblical Monotheism: Israel's Polytheistic Background and the Ugaritic Texts*. New York: Oxford University Press, 2001.

Smolin, Lee. *The Life of the Cosmos*. Oxford: Oxford University Press, 1997.

Soergel, Philip M. 'Luther on the Angels'. In *Angels in the Early Modern World*, edited by Peter Marshall and Alexandra Walsham, 64–82. Cambridge: Cambridge University Press, 2006.

Soskice, Janet Martin. *The Kindness of God: Metaphor, Gender, and Religious Language*. Oxford: Oxford University Press, 2008.

Spezzano, Daria. *The Glory of God's Grace: Deification According to St. Thomas Aquinas*. Ave Maria, FL: Sapientia Press of Ave Maria University, 2015.

Stevenson, Austin. 'The Unity of Christ and the Historical Jesus: Aquinas and Locke on Personal Identity'. *Modern Theology* 37, no. 4 (2021): 851–64.

Stimac, Valerie. *Dark Skies: A Practical Guide to Astrotourism*. Carlton, Victoria: Lonely Planet, 2019.

Suárez-Nani, Tiziana. 'Angels, Space and Place: The Location of Separate Substances According to John Duns Scotus'. In *Angels in Medieval Philosophical Inquiry: Their Function and Significance*, edited by Isabel Iribarren and Martin Lenz, 89–111. London: Routledge, 2016.

Sulavik, Andrew. 'Protestant Theological Writings on Angels in Post-Reformation Thought from 1565 to 1739'. *Reformation & Renaissance Review* 8, no. 2 (2006): 210–23.

Sullivan, Francis Aloysius. *Salvation Outside the Church? A History of Christian Thought about Salvation for Those 'Outside'*. London: Geoffrey Chapman, 1992.

Sunshine, Glenn S. 'Accommodation Historically Considered'. In *The Enduring Authority of the Christian Scriptures*, edited by Donald A. Carson, 238–65. Grand Rapids, MI: Eerdmans, 2016.

Sutherland, John D. 'Opinion: Studies on the Origin of Life – the End of the Beginning'. *Nature Reviews Chemistry* 1, no. 2 (February 2017): 12.

Tallis, Raymond. 'You Chemical Scum, You'. In *Reflections of a Metaphysical Flaneur: And Other Essays*, 163–68. London: Routledge, 2014.

Tanner, Kathryn. *Christ the Key*. Cambridge: Cambridge University Press, 2010.

Tanner, Norman P., and Giuseppe Alberigo, eds. *Decrees of the Ecumenical Councils: From Nicaea I to Vatican II*. Vol. 1. 2 vols. Washington, D. C.: Georgetown University Press, 1990.

Tanton, Tobias. *Corporeal Theology*. Oxford: Oxford University Press, 2022.

Tanzella-Nitti, Giuseppe. 'Extraterrestrial Life'. Accessed 1 February 2018. https://inters.org/extraterrestrial-life.

Teilhard de Chardin, Pierre. 'Fall, Redemption, and Geocentrism'. In *Christianity and Evolution*, translated by René Hague, 36–44. New York: Harcourt, 1971.

Thomas, O'Meara. *Vast Universe: Extraterrestrials and Christian Revelation*. Collegeville, MN: Liturgical Press, 2012.

Tillich, Paul. *Systematic Theology*. Vol. 2. 3 vols. Chicago: University of Chicago Press, 1957.

Tolkien, John Ronald Reuel. 'On Fairy-Stories'. In *Essays Presented to Charles Williams*, edited by C. S. Lewis, 38–89. London: Oxford University Press, 1947.

Torrance, Thomas F. *Incarnation: The Person and Life of Christ*. Milton Keynes: Paternoster, 2008.

Totani, Tomonori. 'Emergence of Life in an Inflationary Universe'. *Scientific Reports* 10, no. 1 (December 2020): 1671.

Totschnig, Wolfhart. 'Arendt's Notion of Natality: An Attempt at Clarification'. *Ideas y Valores* 66, no. 165 (2017): 327–46.

Townsend, Luther Tracy. *The Stars Not Inhabited: Scientific and Biblical Points of View*. New York: Eaton and Mains, 1914.

Trifonov, Edward N. 'Vocabulary of Definitions of Life Suggests a Definition'. *Journal of Biomolecular Structure and Dynamics* 29, no. 2 (October 2011): 259–66.

Trollope, Anthony. *Barchester Towers*. Edited by John Bowen. Oxford: Oxford University Press, 2014.

Turner, Denys. '"Sin Is Behovely" in Julian of Norwich's Revelations of Divine Love'. *Modern Theology* 20, no. 3 (2004): 407–22.

Vainio, Olli-Pekka. *Cosmology in Theological Perspective: Understanding Our Place in the Universe*. Grand Rapids, MI: Baker Academic, 2018.

Varela, Francisco J., Evan Thompson, and Eleanor Rosch. *The Embodied Mind: Cognitive Science and Human Experience*. Cambridge, MA: MIT Press, 1991.

Ward, Keith. *Christ and the Cosmos: A Reformulation of Trinitarian Doctrine*. Cambridge: Cambridge University Press, 2015.

Webb, Stephen. *Measuring the Universe: The Cosmological Distance Ladder*. London: Springer, 1999.

Weinandy, Thomas. *Does God Change? The Word's Becoming in the Incarnation*. Still River, MA: St Bede's Publications, 2002.

Weintraub, David A. *Religions and Extraterrestrial Life: How Will We Deal with It?* Cham: Springer International Publishing, 2014.

Weisheipl, James A. 'Albertus Magnus and Universal Hylomorphism: Avicebron. A Note on Thirteenth-Century Augustinianism'. *Southwestern Journal of Philosophy* 10, no. 3 (1979): 239–60.

Wesley, John. *A Plain Account of Christian Perfection*. Bristol: William Pine, 1766.

Westermann, Claus. *Genesis 1–11: A Commentary*. Translated by John J. Scullion. Minneapolis, MN: Augsburg, 1994.

Weston, Frank. *The Revelation of Eternal Love: Christianity Stated in Terms of Love*. London: A. R. Mowbray and Co., 1920.

Whewell, William. *Of the Plurality of Worlds*. London: John W. Parker and Son, 1853.

White, Robert. 'Calvin and Copernicus: The Problem Reconsidered'. *Calvin Theological Journal* 15, no. 2 (1980): 233–43.

Wilkins, John. *The Discovery of a World in the Moone. Or, A Discovrse Tending to Prove, That' tis Probable There May Be Another Habitable World in the Moon*. Fifth edition. London: J. Rawlins for John Gellibrand, 1684.

Wilkinson, David. *Science, Religion, and the Search for Extraterrestrial Intelligence*. Oxford: Oxford University Press, 2013.

William of Auvergne. 'De Universo'. In *Guilielmi Alverni Episcopi Parisiensis, Opera Omnia*, 1:593–1074. Frankfurt am Maine: Minerva, 1963.

Williams, Anna N. *The Ground of Union: Deification in Aquinas and Palamas*. Oxford: Oxford University Press, 1999.

Williams, George Huntston. 'Erasmus and the Reformers on Non-Christian Religions and Salus Extra Ecclesiam'. In *Action and Conviction in Early Modern Europe: Essays in Memory of E. H. Harbison*, edited by Theodore K. Rabb and Jerrold Seigel, 319–70. Princeton: Princeton University Press, 1969.

Williams, Rowan. *Being Human: Bodies, Minds, Persons*. London: SPCK, 2018.

Williams, Rowan. *Christ the Heart of Creation*. London: Bloomsbury Continuum, 2018.

Williams, Rowan. 'Religious Experience in the Era of Reform'. In *Companion Encyclopedia of Theology*, edited by Peter Byrne and Leslie Houlden, 576–93. London: Routledge, 1995.

Williams, Thomas. 'The Unmitigated Scotus'. *Archiv Für Geschichte Der Philosophie* 80, no. 2 (1998).

Willis, Edward David. *Calvin's Catholic Christology: The Function of the So-Called Extra Calvinisticum in Calvin's Theology*. Leiden: E. J. Brill, 1967.

Wippel, John F. 'Metaphysical Composition of Angels in Bonaventure, Aquinas, and Godfrey of Fontaines'. In *A Companion to Angels in Medieval Philosophy*, edited by Tobias Hoffmann, 45–78. Leiden: Brill, 2012.

Wittgenstein, Ludwig. *Culture and Value*. Edited by Georg Henrik. von Wright and Heikki Nyman. Translated by Peter Winch. Amended second edition. Oxford: Basil Blackwell, 1980.

Wittgenstein, Ludwig. *Philosophical Investigations: The German Text, with a Revised English Translation*. Translated by G. E. M. Anscombe. Third edition. Oxford: Blackwell, 2001.

Wittgenstein, Ludwig. *Remarks on the Philosophy of Psychology*. Edited by G. E. M. Anscombe and G. H. von Wright. Translated by H. Nyman and C. G. Luckhardt. Vol. 2. Oxford: Basil Blackwell, 1980.

Worsnop, Abraham. *Entire Sanctification Distinct from Justification, and Attainable before Death*. London: R. Davies, 1859.

Wright, N. T. 'Hope Deferred: Against the Dogma of Delay'. *Early Christianity* 9, no. 1 (2018): 37–82.

Wright, N. T. *The Resurrection of the Son of God*. London: SPCK, 2003.

Wright, Thomas. *An Original Theory or New Hypothesis of the Universe*. London: H. Chapelle, 1750.

Wuellner, Bernard. *A Dictionary of Scholastic Philosophy*. Second edition. Milwaukee, WI: Bruce Publishing Company, 1966.

Yates, Stephen. *Between Death and Resurrection: A Critical Response to Recent Catholic Debate Concerning the Intermediate State*. London: Bloomsbury Academic, 2017.

Yong, Ed. 'Life Found Deep under the Sea'. *Nature*, 14 March 2013, nature.2013.12610.

Young, Frances Margaret. *God's Presence: A Contemporary Recapitulation of Early Christianity*. Cambridge: Cambridge University Press, 2013.

Zeller, Benjamin E., ed. *Handbook of UFO Religions*. Leiden: Brill, 2021.

Author Index

Scripture Index

General Index

accommodation, 97, 102–105, 108, 109,
   114, 184
Adventism, 13, 355
analogy, 61, 71–74, 98, 117, 123, 125, 128,
   133, 155, 165, 313, 339
angels, 43–60, 64, 71, 85, 99, 112, 122, 147,
   166–67, 201–202
   as corporeal, 51, 52
   as immaterial, 51, 53
Anglicanism, 10, 189, 206, 229, 230
antipodes, 39–42
Apollinarianism, 259
Ascension, 335, 344–46, 354
astrobiology, 7–11, 29, 38, 43, 95, 97, 109,
   134, 137, 152, 162, 193, 210, 232, 253,
   284, 297, 317, 331–33, 339, 346, 349,
   351–53, 359, 368, See also exobiology
astronomy, 22, 32, 36, 107, 139, 141, 145, 148
atmosphere, 75, 90, 367
atonement, 214, 223, 298, 315–16
   moral, 214–15
   ontological, 216, 218
   substitutionary, 219

Bhagavad Gîtâ, 132
Bible, 32, 41, 45, 49, 54, 57, 73, 99–101, 109,
   121, 126, 132, 151, 157, 164, 204, 343,
   353, 356, See also biblical index
biochemistry, 70
biology, 62–63, 74, 91, 111, 113, 114, 140, 171,
   185, See also astrobiology, exobiology
Book of Common Prayer, 190, 207,
   264, 344

causation, 83–84, 116–17, 122, 124, 133, 204,
   307, 363

chemical system, 64–66
Christology, 218, 225–26, 231,
   233–43, 245–64, 267, 271, 276,
   278, 281, 315, 326, 359, See also
   incarnation(s)
Christological detail, 245–46, 249,
   263, 296
cognition, 169–75, 312, 340
convenientia. See also fittingness
convergence, 125, 169–77, 185, 338
Council of Chalcedon, 240, 245, 248,
   251–53, 262, 281, 345
Council of Trent, 105
creation, 24, 35, 43–44, 50, 54–55, 57, 76,
   79–86, 88, 91, 95, 98, 106, 118, 122,
   127, 129, 131, 157, 163, 166, 197, 206,
   218, 226, 230, 250, 265, 288, 299, 301,
   303–304, 307, 310, 317, 328, 331, 344,
   352, 362, 365
   ex nihilo, 117, 160, 347

dignity, 79–81, 137–47, 193–96, 292–97,
   309, 317, 321–22

embodiment, 123, 156, 166, 173, 175, 182,
   185, 265, 269, 341
emergence, 5, 81, 94, 179
entelécheia, 69
eschatology, 255–57, 295, 331–65
Eucharist, 272, 275, 280, 313, 345
evolution, 5, 63–65, 77, 88–90, 94, 101, 124,
   194, 201, 220, 359
exclusivist, 163
exemplarism, 21, 74, 83, 116–18, 131, 134,
   160, 163–65, 286, 342, 363
existentialism, 355–57

Printed in the United States
by Baker & Taylor Publisher Services